Adobe® Dreamweaver® CS6
The Professional Portfolio

AGAINST THE CLOCK
mastering graphic technology

Managing Editor: Ellenn Behoriam
Cover & Interior Design: Erika Kendra
Copy Editor: Angelina Kendra
Printer: Prestige Printers

10 9 8 7 6 5 4 3 2 1

Print ISBN: 978-1-936201-17-4
Ebook ISBN: 978-1-936201-18-1

AGAINST THE CLOCK
mastering graphic technology

4710 28th Street North, Saint Petersburg, FL 33714
800-256-4ATC • www.againsttheclock.com

Acknowledgements

ABOUT AGAINST THE CLOCK

Against The Clock, long recognized as one of the nation's leaders in courseware development, has been publishing high-quality educational materials for the graphic and computer arts industries since 1990. The company has developed a solid and widely-respected approach to teaching people how to effectively utilize graphics applications, while maintaining a disciplined approach to real-world problems.

Having developed the *Against The Clock* and the *Essentials for Design* series with Prentice Hall/Pearson Education, ATC drew from years of professional experience and instructor feedback to develop *The Professional Portfolio Series*, focusing on the Adobe Creative Suite. These books feature step-by-step explanations, detailed foundational information, and advice and tips from industry professionals that offer practical solutions to technical issues.

Against The Clock works closely with all major software developers to create learning solutions that fulfill both the requirements of instructors and the needs of students. Thousands of graphic arts professionals — designers, illustrators, imaging specialists, prepress experts, and production managers — began their educations with Against The Clock training books. These professionals studied at Baker College, Nossi College of Art, Virginia Tech, Appalachian State University, Keiser College, University of South Carolina, Gress Graphic Arts Institute, Hagerstown Community College, Kean University, Southern Polytechnic State University, Brenau University, and many other educational institutions.

ABOUT THE AUTHOR

Erika Kendra holds a BA in History and a BA in English Literature from the University of Pittsburgh. She began her career in the graphic communications industry as an editor at Graphic Arts Technical Foundation before moving to Los Angeles in 2000. Erika is the author or co-author of more than twenty books about Adobe graphic design software. She has also written several books about graphic design concepts such as color reproduction and preflighting, and dozens of articles for online and print journals in the graphics industry. Working with Against The Clock for more than ten years, Erika was a key partner in developing the Portfolio Series of software training books.

CONTRIBUTING ARTISTS AND EDITORS

A big thank you to the people whose artwork, comments, and expertise contributed to the success of these books:

- **Kelly McCormack,** Adobe Certified Instructor
- **Richard Schrand,** International Academy of Design & Technology, Nashville, TN
- **Pam Harris,** University of North Texas at Dallas
- **Jay Tarby,** John Carroll University
- **Debbie Davidson,** Against The Clock, Inc.
- **Charlie Essers,** photographer, Lancaster, Calif.
- **Samantha Schmitz,** Double D Cupcakes, Lancaster, Calif.

Finally, thanks to **Angelina Kendra**, editor, for making sure that we all said what we meant to say.

Walk-Through

Project Goals

Each project begins with a clear description of the overall concepts that are explained in the project; these goals closely match the different "stages" of the project workflow.

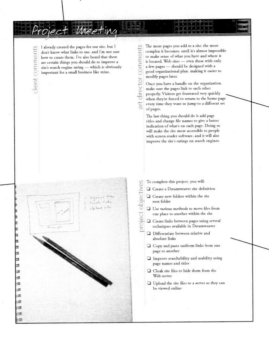

The Project Meeting

Each project includes the client's initial comments, which provide valuable information about the job. The Project Art Director, a vital part of any design workflow, also provides fundamental advice and production requirements.

Project Objectives

Each Project Meeting includes a summary of the specific skills required to complete the project.

Real-World Workflow

Projects are broken into logical lessons or "stages" of the workflow. Brief introductions at the beginning of each stage provide vital foundational material required to complete the task.

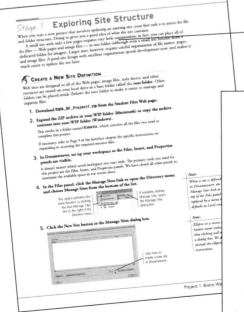

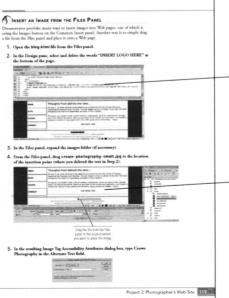

Step-By-Step Exercises

Every stage of the workflow is broken into multiple hands-on, step-by-step exercises.

Visual Explanations

Wherever possible, screen shots are annotated so you can quickly identify important information.

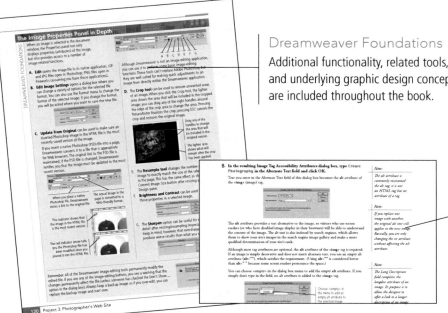

Dreamweaver Foundations

Additional functionality, related tools, and underlying graphic design concepts are included throughout the book.

Advice and Warnings

Where appropriate, sidebars provide shortcuts, warnings, or tips about the topic at hand.

Project Review

After completing each project, you can complete these fill-in-the-blank and short-answer questions to test your understanding of the concepts in the project.

Portfolio Builder Projects

Each step-by-step project is accompanied by a freeform project, allowing you to practice skills and creativity, resulting in an extensive and diverse portfolio of work.

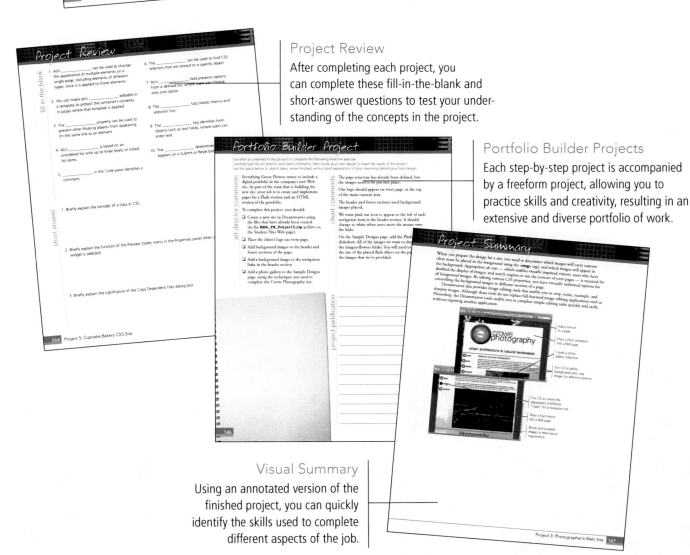

Visual Summary

Using an annotated version of the finished project, you can quickly identify the skills used to complete different aspects of the job.

The Against The Clock *Portfolio Series* teaches graphic design software tools and techniques entirely within the framework of real-world projects; we introduce and explain skills where they would naturally fall into a real project workflow. For example, rather than including an entire chapter about site management, we teach site management where you naturally need to do so — when you begin building a new site in each project.

The project-based approach in the *Portfolio Series* allows you to get in depth with the software beginning in Project 1 — you don't have to read several chapters of introductory material before you can start creating finished artwork.

The *Portfolio Series* project-based approach also prevents "topic tedium" — in other words, we don't require you to read pages and pages of information about marking up text (for example); instead, we explain text-related mark-up as part of a larger project (in this case, as part of a digital book chapter).

Clear, easy-to-read, step-by-step instructions walk you through every phase of each job, from creating a new file to saving the finished piece. Wherever logical, we also offer practical advice and tips about underlying concepts and graphic design practices that will be important as you enter the job market.

The projects in this book reflect a range of different types of Dreamweaver jobs, from organizing a client's site and links to developing a functional site template to building a dynamic site. When you finish the eight projects in this book (and the accompanying Portfolio Builder exercises), you will have a substantial body of work that should impress any potential employer.

The eight Dreamweaver CS6 projects are described briefly here; more detail is provided in the full table of contents (beginning on Page viii).

project 1

Bistro Site Organization

- ❏ Exploring Site Structure
- ❏ Organizing the Site Navigation
- ❏ Naming and Titling Documents
- ❏ Making Files Public

project 2

Digital Book Chapter

- ❏ Preparing the Workspace
- ❏ Working with Semantic Markup
- ❏ Working with Special Characters
- ❏ Creating Lists
- ❏ Attaching an External CSS File

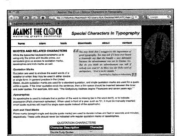

project 3

Photographer's Web Site

- ❏ Working with Static Images
- ❏ Controlling Backgrounds with CSS
- ❏ Working with Other Image Types

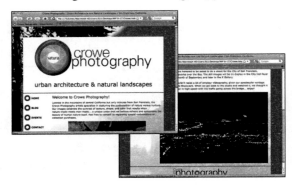

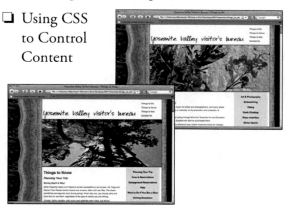
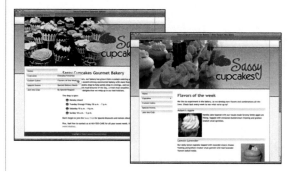
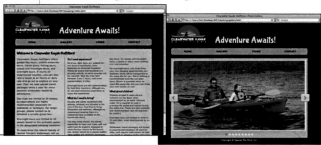

Our goal in this book is to familiarize you with the Dreamweaver tool set so you can be more productive and more marketable in your career as a graphic designer.

It is important to keep in mind that Dreamweaver is an extremely versatile and powerful application. The sheer volume of available panels, options, and features can seem intimidating when you first look at the software interface. Most of these tools, however, are fairly simple to use with a bit of background information and a little practice.

Wherever necessary, we explain the underlying concepts and terms that are required for understanding the software. We're confident that these projects provide the practice you need to be able to create sophisticated artwork by the end of the very first project.

Contents

Contents

Contents

PREREQUISITES

The entire Portfolio Series is based on the assumption that you have a basic understanding of how to use your computer. You should know how to use your mouse to point, click, and drag items around the screen. You should be able to resize and arrange windows on your desktop to maximize your available space. You should know how to access drop-down menus, and understand how check boxes and radio buttons work. It also doesn't hurt to have a good understanding of how your operating system organizes files and folders, and how to navigate your way around them. If you're familiar with these fundamental skills, then you know all that's necessary to use the Portfolio Series.

RESOURCE FILES

All of the files you need to complete the projects in this book — except, of course, the Dreamweaver application files — are on the Student Files Web page at www.againsttheclock.com. See the inside back cover of this book for access information.

Each archive (ZIP) file is named according to the related project (e.g., **DW6_RF_Project1.zip**). At the beginning of each project, you must download the archive file for that project and expand that archive to access the resource files that you need to complete the exercises. Detailed instructions for this process are included in the Interface chapter.

Files required for the related Portfolio Builder exercises at the end of each project are also available on the Student Files page; these archives are also named by project (e.g., **DW6_PB_Project1.zip**).

WEB HOSTING

To make Web files accessible to the browsing public, you need to have access to some type of server. On the inside back cover of this book, you have a code that you need to gain access to the required resource files. The same code also provides access to a six-month, free trial Web hosting account at Pair Networks (www.pair.com).

If you don't already have access to an online server, go to **www.pair.com/atc/** to sign up for your hosting account. You must enter your contact information, and the code from the inside back cover of your book. You should then define a user name in the last field; this will become part of the server name for your hosting account.

After clicking Continue in this screen, the resulting message warns that the setup process can take up to one business day (although it is usually about an hour). When the setup process is complete, you will receive an acknowledgement that your request is being processed. You will receive a confirmation email (sent to the email you defined in the Signup Form) with your username and password information.

SYSTEM REQUIREMENTS

As software technology continues to mature, the differences in functionality from one platform to another continue to diminish. The Portfolio Series was designed to work on both Macintosh or Windows computers; where differences exist from one platform to another, we include specific instructions relative to each platform.

One issue that remains different from Macintosh to Windows is the use of different modifier keys (Control, Shift, etc.) to accomplish the same task. When we present key commands or other system-specific instructions, we always follow the same Macintosh/Windows format — Macintosh commands are listed first, then a slash, followed by the Windows command.

Minimum System Requirements for Adobe Dreamweaver CS6:

Windows

- Intel® Pentium® 4 or AMD Athlon® 64 processor
- Microsoft® Windows® XP with Service Pack 2 (Service Pack 3 recommended); Windows Vista® Home Premium, Business, Ultimate, or Enterprise with Service Pack 1; or Windows 7
- 512MB of RAM
- 1GB of available hard-disk space for installation; additional free space required during installation
- 1280×800 display with 16-bit video card
- Java™ Runtime Environment 1.6 (included)
- DVD-ROM drive
- QuickTime 7.6.6 software required for HTML5 media playback

Mac OS

- Multicore Intel processor
- Mac OS X v10.6 or v10.7
- 512MB of RAM
- 1.8GB of available hard-disk space for installation; additional free space required during installation
- 1280×800 display with 16-bit video card
- Java Runtime Environment 1.6
- DVD-ROM drive
- QuickTime 7.6.6 software required for HTML5 media playback

The Dreamweaver User Interface

Adobe Dreamweaver is an industry-standard application for building Web sites. Typical Dreamweaver work ranges from static HTML pages with hyperlinks to complex, dynamic, database-driven sites, where pages are generated on-the-fly based on individual user requests. Mastering the tools and techniques of the application can significantly improve your potential career options. Our goal in this book is to teach you how to use the available tools to create different types of work that you might encounter in your professional career.

The basic exercises in this introduction are designed to let you explore the Dreamweaver user interface. Whether you are new to the application or upgrading from a previous version, we recommend you follow these steps to click around and become familiar with the basic workspace.

EXPLORE THE DREAMWEAVER INTERFACE

The user interface (UI) is what you see when you launch Dreamweaver. The specific elements you see — including which panels are open and where they appear on the screen — depend on what was done the last time the application was open.

The first time you launch Dreamweaver, you will see the default workspace settings defined by Adobe. When you relaunch the application after you or another user has quit, the workspace defaults to the last-used settings — including specific open panels and the position of those panels on your screen.

As you gain experience and familiarity with the software, you will develop personal working styles and preferences. You will also find that different types of jobs often require different but specific sets of tools. In recognition of this wide range of needs, Dreamweaver includes many options for customizing the arrangement of the application's many panels. We designed the following exercise so you can explore various ways of controlling Dreamweaver's panels.

Note:

Because workspace preferences are largely a matter of personal taste, the projects in this book direct you to use specific panels, but you can choose where to place those elements within the interface.

1. **With nothing open in Dreamweaver, open the Window menu and choose Workspace Layout>Designer.**

   Saved **workspaces** (accessed in the Window>Workspace Layout menu, or in the Workspace switcher) provide one-click access to a defined group of panels.

2. **Open the Window menu again and choose Workspace Layout>Reset 'Designer'.**

   Steps 1 and 2 might not have any obvious effect, depending on what was done before you started this project. If you or someone else changes the interface and quits the application, those changes are remembered when Dreamweaver is relaunched. Because we can't be sure what your application shows, by completing this step you reset the user interface to one of the built-in default workspaces so your screen shots match ours.

3. Macintosh users: Open the Window menu and choose Application Frame to toggle that option on.

Many menu commands and options in Dreamweaver are **toggles**, which means they are either on or off; when an option is already checked, that option is toggled on (visible or active). You can toggle an active option off by choosing the checked menu command, or toggle an inactive option on by choosing the unchecked menu command.

This option should be checked.

Note:

On Windows, the Application Frame menu command is not available; you can't turn off the Application Frame on the Windows OS.

The default workspace includes the Properties panel at the bottom of the screen, and a set of panels attached to the right side of the screen in the **panel dock**.

If the Welcome Screen is not visible, you can open the General pane of the Preferences dialog box (in the Dreamweaver menu on Macintosh or the Edit menu on Windows). Check the Show Welcome Screen box and click OK. After you quit and then relaunch the application, the Welcome Screen will be visible.

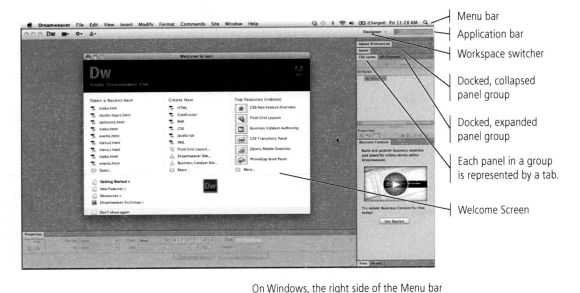

Menu bar
Application bar
Workspace switcher
Docked, collapsed panel group
Docked, expanded panel group
Each panel in a group is represented by a tab.
Welcome Screen

On Windows, the right side of the Menu bar provides access to the same options that are available in the Macintosh Application bar.

The general Macintosh and Windows workspaces are virtually identical, with a few primary exceptions:

- On Macintosh, the Application bar appears below the Menu bar; the Close, Minimize, and Restore buttons appear on the left side of the Application bar, and the Menu bar is not part of the Application frame.
- On Windows, the Close, Minimize, and Restore buttons appear at the right end of the Menu bar, which is part of the overall Application frame.

Note:

When the Application frame is not active on Macintosh, you can toggle the Application bar on and off in the Window menu.

On Macintosh systems, the Application bar at the top of the workspace includes a number of buttons for accessing different view options. On Windows systems, those same options are available on the right side of the Menu bar.

Macintosh users also have two extra menus (consistent with the Macintosh operating system structure). The Apple menu provides access to system-specific commands. The Dreamweaver menu follows the Macintosh system-standard format for all applications; this menu controls basic application operations such as About, Hide, Preferences, and Quit.

On Windows, each running application is contained within its own frame; all elements of the application — including the Menu bar, panels, tools, and open documents — are contained within the Application frame.

Adobe also offers the Application frame to Macintosh users as an option for controlling your workspace. When the Application frame is active, the entire workspace exists in a self-contained area that can be moved around the screen. All elements of the workspace (excluding the Menu bar) move when you move the Application frame.

The Application frame is inactive by default; you can toggle it on by choosing Window>Application Frame. If the menu option is checked, the Application frame is active; if the menu option is not checked, it is inactive.

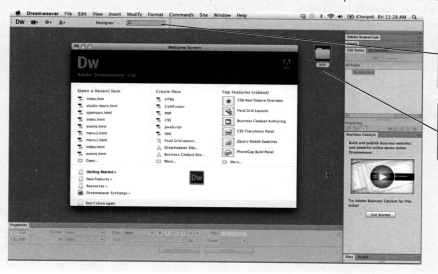

When the Application frame is not active, the Application bar appears below the Menu bar; in this case, the Application bar can be moved or turned off.

When the Application frame is not active, the desktop is visible behind the workspace elements.

4. Click the Files tab in the docked panel group and drag left, away from the dock.

When we provide an instruction to "click and drag" you should hold down the mouse button while you drag.

The area where the panels are stored is called the **panel dock**. Most panels are docked by default, but you can move any panel (or panel group) away from the dock so it appears as a separate panel (called a **floating panel**).

Click the panel tab and drag to move a specific panel.

Click this area (called the panel drop zone) to move an entire panel group.

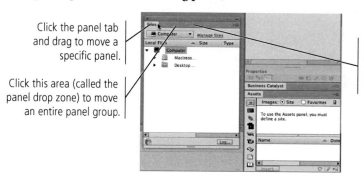

When you release the mouse button, the dragged panel "floats" separate from the panel dock.

5. Click the Files panel tab again and drag back to the dock until a blue line appears to the right of the existing dock column.

Any panel (or panel group) can be dragged to a different location (including into different groups) by dragging the panel's tab; the target location — where the panel will be located when you release the mouse button — is identified by the blue highlight. (If a blue line appears around the existing panel group, keep dragging until the line is only on the right edge.)

You can create multiple columns of panels in the dock. Each column, technically considered a separate dock, can be expanded or iconized independently of other columns.

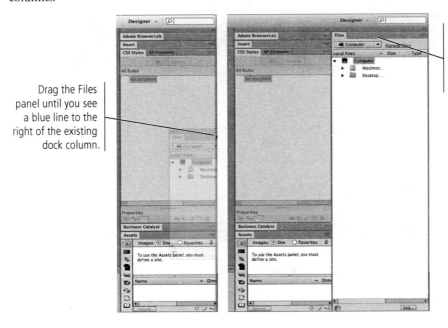

Drag the Files panel until you see a blue line to the right of the existing dock column.

When you release the mouse button, the dragged panel appears to the right of the existing dock column.

Note:

You don't need to move a panel out of the dock before placing it in a different position within the dock. We included Step 4 to show you how to float panels and panel groups.

Note:

Drag a panel into a group's drop zone to add a panel to an existing panel group.

6. In the left column of the panel dock, double-click the Assets panel tab to collapse that panel group.

Although the Assets panel is the only panel tab, it is still referred to as a panel group.

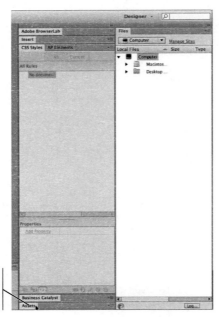

Double-click a panel tab to collapse that group in the dock.

7. Click the Insert panel tab to expand that panel group.

When a docked panel is already collapsed, clicking a panel tab once expands that group.

The Insert panel contains buttons for adding a number of common elements to a Web page. Various commands are categorized into groups, which can be accessed using the menu at the top of the panel.

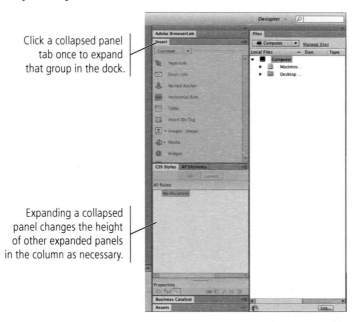

Click a collapsed panel tab once to expand that group in the dock.

Expanding a collapsed panel changes the height of other expanded panels in the column as necessary.

8. Click the line at the bottom of the Insert panel (the line that separates the panel from the CSS Styles panel group). Drag down until all the Insert panel buttons are visible, or until the panel won't expand any further.

When you drag the bottom edge of a docked group, other panels in the same column expand or contract to fit the available space.

Some panels, such as the CSS Styles panel, have a smallest-possible size; depending on your monitor size, you might not be able to fully expand the Insert panel if the CSS Styles panel would be smaller than the required minimum height.

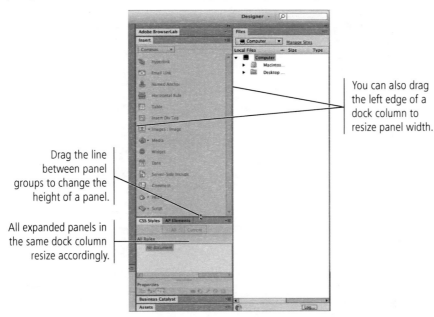

You can also drag the left edge of a dock column to resize panel width.

Drag the line between panel groups to change the height of a panel.

All expanded panels in the same dock column resize accordingly.

9. **Click the Insert panel tab, then drag up and left until a blue line appears immediately below the Application/Menu bar.**

The Insert panel can be displayed as a tabbed row at the top or bottom of the workspace, which can be especially useful if you have a small monitor. When the Insert panel appears in the tabbed format, you can click the tabs in the top row to access the different categories of options.

Dock the Insert panel at the top of the workspace to display it as a series of tabs.

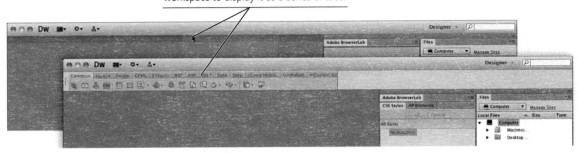

10. **Double-click the dock title bar above the left dock column panel.**

Panels, whether docked or floating, can be collapsed to icons (called **iconic** or **iconized panels**) to save space in the document window. By default, iconized panels appear with the panel name to the right of the icon.

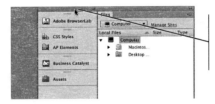

Double-click the title bar over a dock column to toggle between expanded and iconized modes.

Customizing Dreamweaver Behavior

In addition to customizing the workspace, you can customize the way many of the program's options function. The left side of the Preferences dialog box (Dreamweaver>Preferences on Macintosh or Edit>Preferences on Windows) allows you to display the various sets of preferences available in Dreamweaver. As you work your way through the projects in this book, you will learn not only what you can do with these collections of Preferences, but also *why* and *when* you might want to use them.

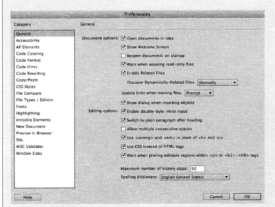

You can also customize the various keyboard shortcuts used to access Dreamweaver commands (Dreamweaver>Keyboard Shortcuts on Macintosh or Edit>Keyboard Shortcuts on Windows). Once you have defined custom shortcuts, you can save your choices as a set so you can access the same custom choices again without having to redo the work.

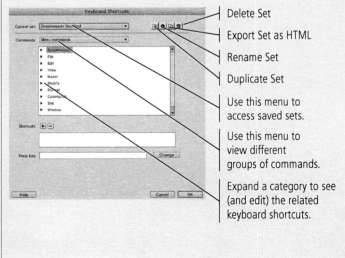

Delete Set

Export Set as HTML

Rename Set

Duplicate Set

Use this menu to access saved sets.

Use this menu to view different groups of commands.

Expand a category to see (and edit) the related keyboard shortcuts.

11. Click the left edge of the iconized panels and drag right.

When panels are iconized, you can reduce the panel buttons to the icons only. This can be particularly useful once you are more familiar with the application and the icons used to symbolize the various panels.

Click the left edge and drag right to reduce the iconized panel buttons to icons only.

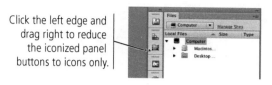

Note:

Floating panel groups can be iconized just like columns in the panel dock. Simply click the title bar of the floating panel group to toggle between expanded and iconized modes.

12. Control/right-click the title bar above the iconized dock column. If the Auto-Collapse Iconic Panels option is not checked, choose that item to toggle on that option.

As we explained in the Getting Started section, when commands are different for the Macintosh and Windows operating systems, we include the different commands in the Macintosh/Windows format. In this case, Macintosh users who do not have right-click mouse capability can press the Control key and click to access the contextual menu. You do not have to press Control *and* right-click to access the menus.

(If you're using a Macintosh and don't have a mouse with right-click capability, we highly recommend that you purchase one. They're inexpensive, they're available at almost any retail store, and they save significant amounts of time accessing contextual options.)

Control/right-clicking a dock title bar opens the dock contextual menu, where you can change the default panel behavior. When the Auto-Collapse Iconic Panels option is toggled on, panels collapse as soon as you click away from them. If you uncheck this option, panels will remain open until you intentionally collapse them.

This option should be checked (active).

Note:

All panels can be accessed in the Window menu.

If you choose a panel that's open but iconized, the panel expands to the left of its icon.

If you choose a panel that's part of an expanded group, that panel comes to the front of the group.

If you choose a panel in a collapsed group, the panel group expands and the selected panel comes to the front of the group.

If you choose a panel that isn't open, it appears in the same position as when it was last closed.

13. In the left column of docked panels, click the bottom button (Assets).

Clicking a docked panel button opens the panel to the left of the panel dock.

Click here to manually collapse an expanded panel group.

Click here to open the panel Options menu.

Hovering your mouse over an iconized panel button shows the name of the panel.

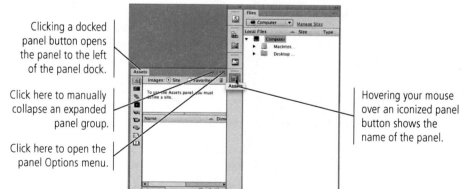

14. Click the third button in the left column to expand the AP Elements panel (and the group containing it).

When panels are grouped, the button you click is the active panel in the expanded group.

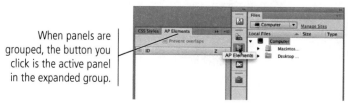

15. Control/right-click the AP Elements panel tab and choose Close in the contextual menu.

When panels are docked, the contextual menu options are the only way to close a panel or panel group. You can also close individual panels by dragging them away from the dock or group, and then clicking the Close button on the floating panel (group).

Control/right-click a panel tab to open the contextual menu.

Closing one panel from a panel group does not affect the other panels in the same group.

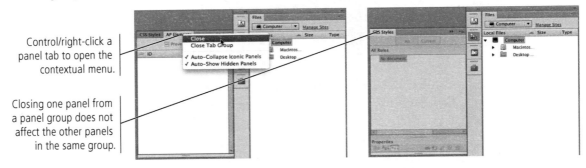

16. Continue to the next exercise.

 CREATE A SAVED WORKSPACE

By now you should understand that you have extensive control over the exact appearance of your Dreamweaver workspace — what panels are visible, where and how they appear, and even the size of individual panels or panel groups. Over time you will develop personal preferences — the Files panel always appears at the top, etc. — based on your work habits and project needs. Rather than re-establishing every workspace element each time you return to Dreamweaver, you can save your custom workspace settings so they can be recalled with a single click.

Note:

The Manage Workspaces option in the Workspace switcher opens a dialog box where you can choose a specific user-defined workspace to rename or delete. You can't rename or delete the default workspaces that come with the application.

1. Click the Workspace switcher in the Application/Menu bar and choose New Workspace.

Again, keep in mind that we list differing commands in the Macintosh/Windows format. On Macintosh, the Workspace switcher is in the Application bar; on Windows, it's in the Menu bar.

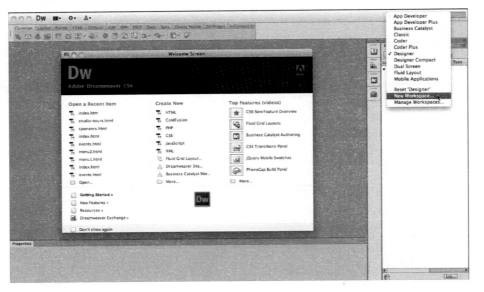

2. In the Save Workspace dialog box, type `Portfolio` and click OK.

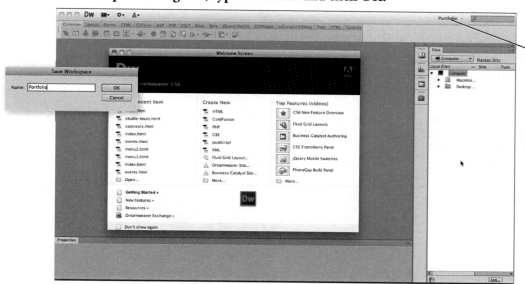

The Workspace switcher shows the name of the active workspace.

3. Control/right-click the Files panel tab and choose Close in the menu.

4. Open the Workspace switcher and choose Designer.

Calling a saved workspace restores the last-used state of the workspace.

On Macintosh, the Files panel is restored to the right dock column because the last-used state of the Designer workspace is the same as the step immediately before you saved the custom Portfolio workspace.

On Windows, the original Designer workspace is restored because you saved a different workspace after making changes.

Note:

This discrepancy between operating systems seems to be an issue with the application — what some might call a bug.

User-defined workspaces are listed at the top of the menu.

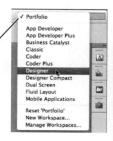

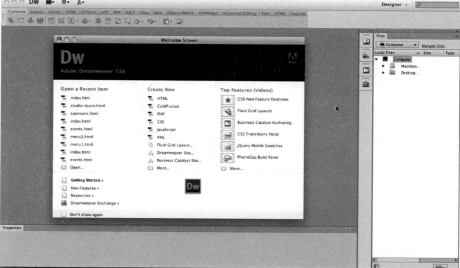

5. Open the Workspace switcher again and choose Portfolio to restore your custom workspace.

Because you closed the Files panel after saving the workspace, Dreamweaver reverts to the last-used version of the custom workspace — without the Files panel.

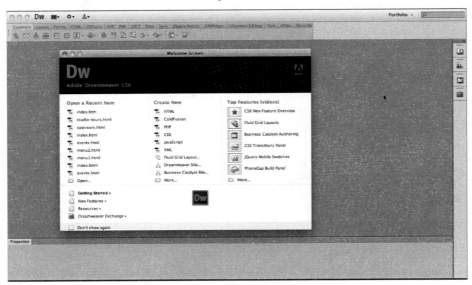

6. In the Workspace switcher menu, choose Reset 'Portfolio'.

The Reset command reverts the workspace back to the original saved state (before you closed the Files panel).

7. Continue to the next exercise.

EXPLORE THE DREAMWEAVER DOCUMENT WINDOW

There is far more to using Dreamweaver than arranging panels in the workspace. What you do with those panels — and even which panels you need — depends on the type of work you are doing in a particular file. In this exercise, you import an existing site into Dreamweaver and explore some of the options for looking at files.

1. **Create a new empty folder named WIP (Work In Progress) on any writable disk (where you plan to save your work).**

2. **Download the DW6_RF_Interface.zip archive from the Student Files Web page.**

3. **Macintosh users: Place the ZIP archive in your WIP folder, then double-click the file icon to expand it.**

Double-click the archive file icon to expand it.

Note:

For the sake of this exercise, it doesn't matter what workspace you use. Our screen shots show a slightly modified version of the Portfolio workspace that we saved in the previous exercise.

Windows users: Double-click the ZIP archive file to open it. Click the folder inside the archive and drag it into your primary WIP folder.

Open the archive file...

...then drag the Interface folder from the archive to your WIP folder.

The resulting **Interface** folder contains all the files you need to complete this introduction.

4. **In Dreamweaver, click the Manage Sites link in the Files panel.**
If you don't see the Manage Sites link, open the Directory menu and choose Manage Sites from the bottom of the list.

If no sites are currently open in Dreamweaver, you can click the hot-text link to open the Manage Sites dialog box.

When sites are already open, the Manage Sites link is not available.

You have to open the Directory menu and choose Manage Sites from the bottom of the list.

Although Dreamweaver can be used to build individual HTML pages with no links to external files, the application is more commonly used to build entire sites. The Manage Sites dialog box is used to create new sites or import existing ones into Dreamweaver.

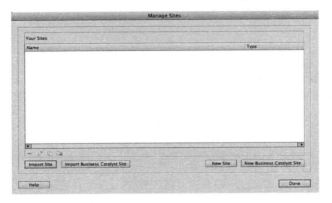

Note:

You can also open the Manage Sites dialog box by choosing Site>Manage Sites.

5. **Click the Import Site button in the Manage Sites dialog box. Navigate to your WIP>Interface folder, select sf-arts.ste in the list of available files, and click Open.**

The ".ste" extension identifies a Dreamweaver site file, which stores information about the site such as URL, FTP login information, etc. By importing this file into Dreamweaver, you can work with an existing site.

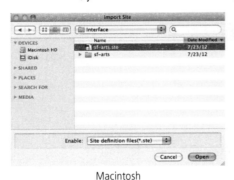

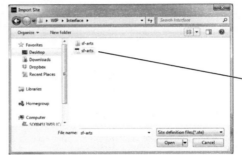

Depending on your system settings, the extension might not appear in your file list.

Macintosh   Windows

6. **When asked to select the local root folder of the site:**

Macintosh users: Select the sf-arts folder (in your WIP>Interface folder) and click Open.

Windows users: Navigate to and open the sf-arts folder (in your WIP>Interface folder), then click Select.

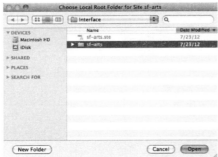

Macintosh   Windows

Note:

*The **root folder** is simply the base folder that contains the files of your site. This is referred to as the "local" root folder because it is the folder on your computer system. When you upload site files to a Web server, you place the files in the remote root folder.*

7. **When asked to select the local images folder for the imported site:**

Macintosh users: Select the images folder in the `sf-arts` folder and click Open.

Windows users: Navigate to and open the `sf-arts`>`images` folder, then click Select.

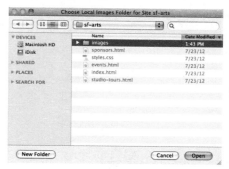

Macintosh

Windows

After you identify the local images folder, files in the site are processed and then the site is listed in the Manage Sites dialog box. The name of the site (in this case, "sf-arts") is used for internal purposes only; it has no relation to the file names in the live HTML files.

After importing the sf-arts.ste file, the site appears in the list.

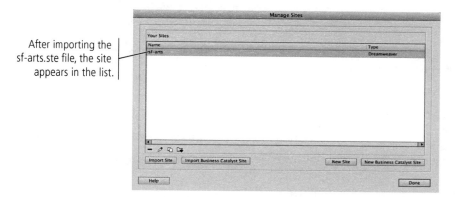

8. **Click Done to close the Manage Sites dialog box.**

A Dreamweaver site typically includes links — from HTML pages to images, from one HTML page to another, and so on — which are the heart of interactive Web sites. When you import a site into Dreamweaver, the application processes the files in the site to identify links and other information required to maintain the integrity of the overall site.

When the import process is complete, the site appears in the Files panel.

Note:

Depending on the number of files in a site, you might see a progress bar indicating that Dreamweaver is processing the files and creating a site cache, which helps the application manage the links between various files in the site.

9. **In the Files panel, click the arrow/plus sign (+) to expand the imported site folder.**

The Files panel provides access to all the elements that make up a Web site, including page files (whether HTML, PHP, or some other format), images, downloadable PDFs, and anything else required for the site to display properly.

On Macintosh, expanded folders show a down-facing arrow; clicking that arrow collapses the folder and changes the arrow to face to the right. You can click a right-facing arrow to expand a folder and show its contents.

On Windows, expanded folders show a "−" symbol; clicking that symbol collapses the folder and changes the "−" to a "+" symbol. You can click a "+" symbol to expand a folder and show its contents.

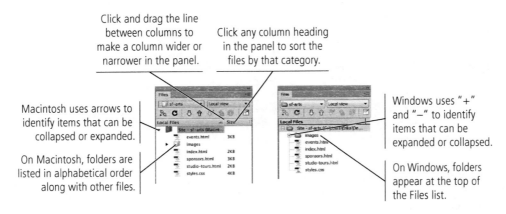

Click and drag the line between columns to make a column wider or narrower in the panel.

Click any column heading in the panel to sort the files by that category.

Macintosh uses arrows to identify items that can be collapsed or expanded.

On Macintosh, folders are listed in alphabetical order along with other files.

Windows uses "+" and "−" to identify items that can be expanded or collapsed.

On Windows, folders appear at the top of the Files list.

10. **In the Files panel, double-click the index.html file.**

Double-clicking a file in the Files panel opens that file in the document window.

For Dreamweaver to effectively monitor and manage the various links to required supporting files (images, scripts, etc.), you should only open and change site files from within the Files panel. If you open and change a file outside the context of the Files panel, Dreamweaver can't keep track of those changes, which can result in broken links.

All open files are represented by document tabs.

Related Files bar

Document toolbar

The Files panel provides access to all the files that make up the site.

The Properties panel presents different options depending on what is selected in the document.

11. If you don't see the Code, Split, and Design buttons above the document window, choose View>Toolbars>Document to toggle on the Document toolbar.

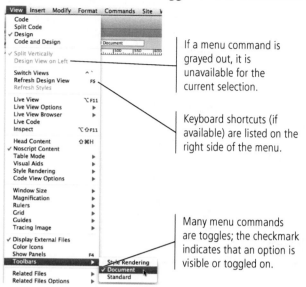

If a menu command is grayed out, it is unavailable for the current selection.

Keyboard shortcuts (if available) are listed on the right side of the menu.

Many menu commands are toggles; the checkmark indicates that an option is visible or toggled on.

Note:

If the Application frame is not active on Macintosh, the first open file will not have a document tab. Instead, a title bar appears at the top of the one open document. When you open more than one file at a time, each open document is represented by a tab at the top of the document window.

12. If you see more than one pane in the document window, click the Design button in the Document toolbar.

Design view is useful for visually-oriented site design, providing a visual preview of the file similar to the way it will appear in a browser window.

13. If necessary, scroll down to show the bottom of the page. Click the "Art&Architechture" logo to select it, then review the Properties panel.

At this point, it isn't necessary to understand what the various properties do; you learn about all these options in later projects. For now, you should simply understand that the Properties panel is context sensitive, which means the available options depend on what is currently selected.

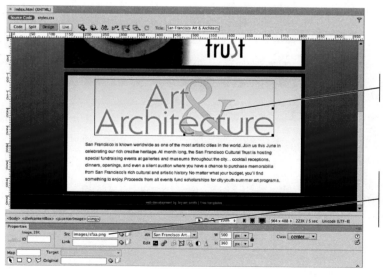

The selected object is an image.

The Properties panel shows options and information specific to the active selection.

14. Double-click the word "Francisco" (in the first line of text below the logo) to select the entire word, and then review the Properties panel.

Unlike many design applications, in Dreamweaver you don't have to choose a specific tool to select objects in a document.

The selected word is editable text.

The Properties panel shows options and information related to the selected text.

15. With the text still selected, click the Split button in the Document toolbar.

Split view shows both the Code and Design view windows. When working in Split view, selecting an object in the Design view highlights the related code in the Code view.

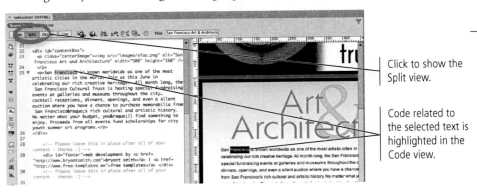

Click to show the Split view.

Code related to the selected text is highlighted in the Code view.

Note:

You can also choose Split Code view in the View menu, which shows the page code in two windows at the same time. This view can be useful if you need to write code in one area that specifically relates or refers to code at another point in the page.

16. Choose View>Design View on Left.

The Split Vertically option is toggled on by default to take advantage of the available space on widescreen monitors. By default, the Split view shows the Code view on the left and the Design view on the right; you can reverse this orientation to suit your personal work preferences.

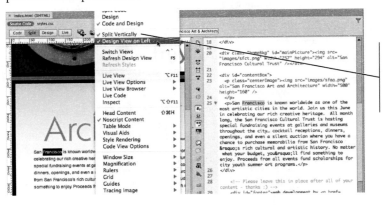

When Split Vertically is active, you can toggle the Design View on Left command to reverse the views in the document window.

17. Choose View>Split Vertically to toggle this option off.

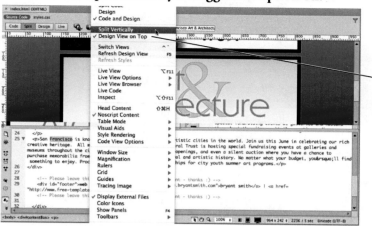

When Split Vertically is not active, you can toggle the Design View on Top command to reverse the views in the document window.

18. Click the Code button in the Document toolbar.

The Code view is useful for people who are familiar with writing code; this mode allows you to (temporarily) ignore the visual design and work solely on the code.

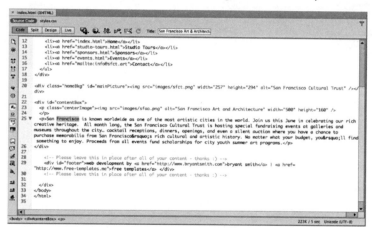

Note:

The design for this site is based on the "Barren Savannah" template by Bryant Smith. The original template was found at www.free-templates.me, one of many online sources for Web design templates that are free to use and modify to meet your specific needs.

19. Click the Design button in the Document toolbar to return to Design view.

20. Continue to the next exercise.

 PREVIEW FILES IN DREAMWEAVER LIVE VIEW

Dreamweaver's Design view does a reasonably good job of allowing you to design Web pages visually, but some common design elements, such as rollovers and multimedia files, are not enabled in the Design view. The Live view provides an internal method for checking many of these elements without leaving the Dreamweaver environment.

You can't edit pages directly in Live view. However, if you are working in Split view, you can make changes to the code and then refresh the Live view to see the effect of those changes.

1. With the sf-arts site open in the Files panel, make sure index.html is open.

2. In the Files panel, double-click studio-tours.html to open that page.

Each open file is represented by a tab at the top of the document window. You can click any tab to make the associated file active in the document window.

Each open file is represented by a document tab.

Various lines indicate the boundaries of specific objects, such as each link in the menu.

3. Click the Visual Aids button in the document toolbar (above the document window) and choose Hide All Visual Aids.

Click to open the Visual Aids menu.

Visual aids make it easier to identify the various elements (such as page divisions) used to create structure but which do not necessarily have a tangible physical appearance. While certainly useful, these visual aids interfere with the physical layout of the site so what you see in the document window is *not* what you get in the browser window.

Turning off visual aids is a good first step in previewing the page as it will actually appear to users.

Note:

*The **Live Code** button splits the document window to show the live design view and a non-editable view of the page code.*

4. Click the Live button in the document toolbar, and then move your mouse cursor over the Sponsors link at the top of the page.

Rollover elements do not function properly in Dreamweaver's Design view. The Live view provides a way to test interactive elements (such as rollovers) within the Dreamweaver environment.

In Live view, the rollover button displays as it would in a browser.

5. Press Command/Control and click the Studio Tours link.

One final reminder: throughout this book, we list differing commands in the Macintosh/Windows format. On Macintosh, you need to press the Command key; on Windows, press the Control key. (We will not repeat this explanation every time different commands are required for the different operating systems.)

In Live view, pressing the Command/Control key lets you preview linked files in the local site folder directly in the Dreamweaver document window. If you click a link to an external file, you will see a "File Not Found" error message.

When working in Live view, the Browser Navigation buttons in the Document toolbar function in the same way that standard browser navigation buttons work: Back, Forward, Stop/Refresh (reload), and Home (the site's index file).

Use these buttons to navigate back and forward, just as you would in a browser.

6. Command/Control-click the Contact link.

This button is set to open a new message in an email client. The Live view does not support non-HTML links, so an error message appears at the top of the document window.

The error message shows that Live view does not support non-HTML links.

This rollover is a link that opens a new email message.

7. In the Document toolbar, click the Live button to return to the normal Design view.

Navigating in the Live view does not technically open the linked pages. When you return to the regular Design view, the previously active page — in this case, studio-tours.html — is still the active one.

8. Click the Close button on the studio-tours.html tab to close that file.

Each document has its own Close button.

9. Click the Close button on the index.html document tab to close that file.

10. Continue to the next exercise.

Note:

On Macintosh systems, clicking the Close button on the document window closes all open files, but does not quit the application.

On Windows systems, clicking the Close (X) button on the Application frame closes all open files and quits the application.

PREVIEW A FILE IN A BROWSER

As you saw in the previous exercise, the Live view can be used to verify the appearance of many common Web design objects. Of course, site users will not be using Dreamweaver to view your pages, so it is always a good idea to test pages using the same method that will actually be used to display your pages — namely, the various browsers that are in common use.

Although there are some standards that govern the way browsers display Web page code, the various browsers do have some different capabilities. Different operating systems also introduce display variables, so what you see in Mozilla Firefox on a Macintosh might appear different than what you see in Firefox on Windows. As a general rule, you should test your pages on as many browsers as possible — on both Macintosh and Windows operating systems.

Note:

It's a good idea to test files at regular intervals throughout the design process, rather than waiting until the end to check your work.

1. **Macintosh: Choose Dreamweaver>Preferences.**
   Windows: Choose Edit>Preferences.

   On the left side of the Preferences dialog box, click Preview in Browser to display the related options.

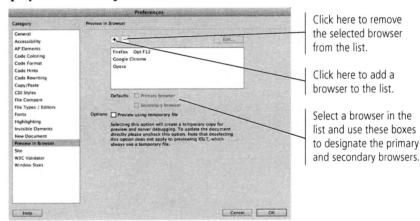

Click here to remove the selected browser from the list.

Click here to add a browser to the list.

Select a browser in the list and use these boxes to designate the primary and secondary browsers.

Note:

Choosing File>Preview in Browser>Edit Browser List opens this pane directly.

2. **Review the list of browsers that are identified by Dreamweaver.**

   When installed, Dreamweaver scans your computer for available browser applications. You likely have at least one browser in this list, and probably even more than one.

3. **If a browser is available on your system but not in Dreamweaver, click the "+" button above the list of browsers.**

4. **In the resulting Add Browser dialog box, click the Browse button and identify the location of the browser you want to add.**

5. **Click OK to return to the Preferences dialog box.**

The list of browsers shows the defined primary and secondary browsers, which you can invoke using the associated keyboard shortcuts. To change the defaults, you can simply select a browser in the list and check the related Defaults options.

6. **Repeat Steps 3–5 as necessary to add all available browsers to Dreamweaver, then click OK to close the Preferences dialog box.**

7. **In the Files panel, double-click the index.html file to open it.**

8. **Click the Preview/Debug in Browser button in the Document toolbar and choose one of the listed browsers.**

9. **In the resulting browser window, click the Contact link on the right side of the menu.**

Because you are previewing the page in an actual browser, you can now test non-html links such as this one, which opens a new mail message in an email application.

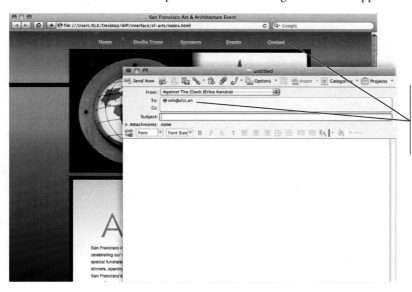

Clicking the link in a browser window correctly opens a new email message in your default email application.

10. **Close the mail message without sending.**

11. **Close the browser window and return to Dreamweaver.**

12. **Close index.html, then continue to the next exercise.**

Note:

Press Option-F12/F12 to preview a page in your primary browser. Press Command/Control-F12 to preview the page in your secondary browser.

If you are using a Macintosh laptop, you also have to press the Function (FN) key to use the F key shortcuts.

Note:

Choosing Edit Browser List in this menu opens the Preview in Browser pane of the Preferences dialog box.

Note:

A mailto: link opens a new mail message in the user's default email application. If a user does not have an email client, or has not specified one as the default option, clicking a mailto: link might open a message asking which application to use to send the email.

REMOVE A SITE FROM DREAMWEAVER

As you gain experience designing and developing Web sites, your site definition list will continue to grow. To keep your list under control, you can export site definitions and remove certain sites from the list. When you remove a site from Dreamweaver, you are not deleting the actual files and folders from your computer; you are simply removing them from Dreamweaver's view.

1. **In the Files panel, open the Directory menu and choose Manage Sites at the bottom of the list.**

2. **In the resulting Manage Sites dialog box, select the sf-arts site in the list and click the "–" button below the list of available sites.**

   In this case, you made no changes to the site definitions or files. Because you already have an STE file with the correct information, it is not necessary to re-export the site definition.

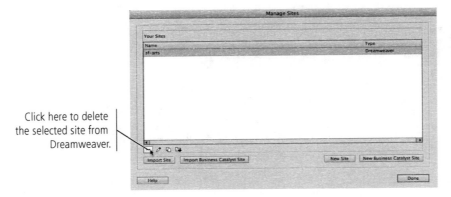

Click here to delete the selected site from Dreamweaver.

3. **Click Yes in the Warning dialog box, and then click Done to close the Manage Sites dialog box.**

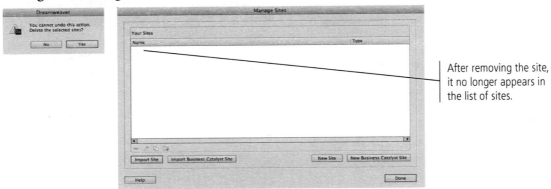

After removing the site, it no longer appears in the list of sites.

Bistro Site Organization

Your client has opened a new restaurant in a fast-growing community in Southern California. He has already designed the pages for his site, but has hired you to make sure everything works properly and then make the site available to the browsing public.

This project incorporates the following skills:

❏ Creating, exporting, and removing site definitions in Dreamweaver

❏ Moving files around in a site root folder

❏ Creating relative links between pages in a site

❏ Defining absolute links to external sites and email addresses

❏ Improving search engine optimization (SEO) with file names and titles

❏ Cloaking site files from a Web server

❏ Uploading files to a Web server

client comments

I already created the pages for our site, but I don't know what links to use, and I'm not sure how to create them. I've also heard that there are certain things you should do to improve a site's search engine rating — which is obviously important for a small business like mine.

art director comments

The more pages you add to a site, the more complex it becomes, until it's almost impossible to make sense of what you have and where it is located. Web sites — even those with only a few pages — should be designed with a good organizational plan, making it easier to modify pages later.

Once you have a handle on the organization, make sure the pages link to each other properly. Visitors get frustrated very quickly when they're forced to return to the home page every time they want to jump to a different set of pages.

The last thing you should do is add page titles and change file names to give a better indication of what's on each page. Doing so will make the site more accessible to people with screen-reader software, and it will also improve the site's ratings on search engines.

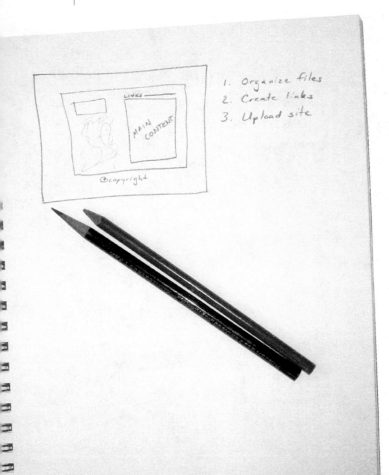

1. Organize files
2. Create links
3. Upload site

project objectives

To complete this project, you will:

❑ Create a Dreamweaver site definition

❑ Create new folders within the site root folder

❑ Use various methods to move files from one place to another within the site

❑ Create links between pages using several techniques available in Dreamweaver

❑ Differentiate between relative and absolute links

❑ Copy and paste links from one page to another

❑ Improve searchability and usability using page names and titles

❑ Cloak site files to hide them from the Web server

❑ Upload the site files to a server so they can be viewed online

Stage 1 Exploring Site Structure

When you start a new project that involves updating an existing site, your first task is to assess the file and folder structure. Doing so gives you a good idea of what the site contains.

A small site with only a few pages requires very little organization; in fact, you *can* place all of the files — Web pages and image files — in one folder (although even a small site benefits from a dedicated folder for images). Larger sites, however, require careful organization of file names, pages, and image files. A good site design with excellent organization speeds development now, and makes it much easier to update the site later.

 ## CREATE A NEW SITE DEFINITION

Web sites are designed so all of the Web pages, image files, style sheets, and other resources are stored on your local drive in a base folder called the **root folder**. Other folders can be placed inside (below) the root folder to make it easier to manage and organize files.

1. **Download DW6_RF_Project1.zip from the Student Files Web page.**

2. **Expand the ZIP archive in your WIP folder (Macintosh) or copy the archive contents into your WIP folder (Windows).**

   This results in a folder named **Kinetic**, which contains all the files you need to complete this project.

   If necessary, refer to Page 11 of the Interface chapter for specific instructions on expanding or accessing the required resource files.

3. **In Dreamweaver, set up your workspace so the Files, Insert, and Properties panels are visible.**

   It doesn't matter which saved workspace you start with. The primary tools you need for this project are the Files, Insert, and Properties panels. We have closed all other panels to maximize the available space in our screen shots.

4. **In the Files panel, click the Manage Sites link or open the Directory menu and choose Manage Sites from the bottom of the list.**

   This option performs the same function as clicking the blue Manage Sites link to the right of the Directory menu.

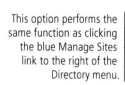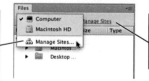

   If available, clicking Manage Sites opens the Manage Sites dialog box.

Note:

When a site is defined in Dreamweaver, the Manage Sites link at the top of the Files panel is replaced by a menu that defaults to Local view.

5. **Click the New Site button in the Manage Sites dialog box.**

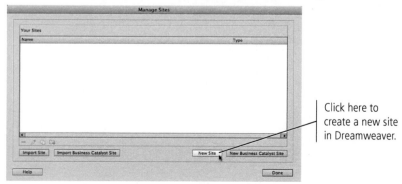

   Click here to create a new site in Dreamweaver.

Note:

Ellipses in a menu or button name indicate that clicking will open a dialog box. We do not include the ellipses in our instructions.

6. **In the Site Setup dialog box, make sure Site is selected in the category list.**

7. **Type Kinetic Site in the Site Name field.**

   The site name can be anything that will allow you to easily recognize the project; it is only for identification within Dreamweaver. For example, you could use "Eve's site" as the site name within Dreamweaver to describe the Web site (www.evelynsmith.biz) that you are creating for your friend.

8. **Click the Browse for Folder button to the right of the Local Site Folder field. Navigate to the WIP>Kinetic folder and click Choose/Select to return to the Site Setup dialog box.**

   Part of the process of defining a site within Dreamweaver is to specify a particular folder as the site root folder of the Web site. Clicking the Local Site Folder button opens a navigation dialog box where you can find the folder you want to use.

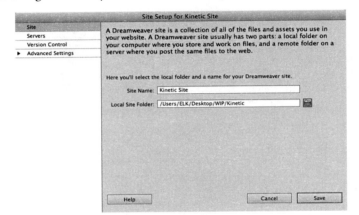

Note:

You will learn about other options in the Site Setup dialog box later in this book.

9. **Click Save to close the Site Setup dialog box.**

10. **In the Manage Sites dialog box, make sure the Kinetic Site item appears in the list of sites, and then click Done.**

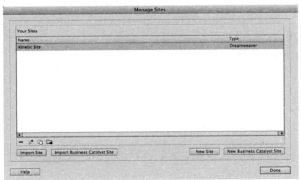

11. **Continue to the next exercise.**

EXAMINE THE SITE FILES

There are many files in the Kinetic Site folder. The first step in organizing the files is to examine the Web page files and understand what they contain.

1. **With Kinetic Site showing in the Directory menu of the Files panel, expand the site folder (if necessary) and examine the files in the site.**

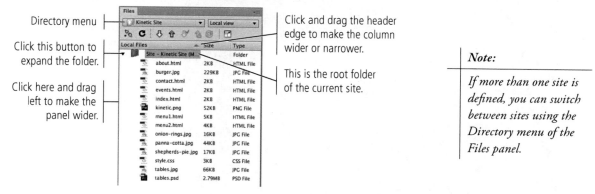

Directory menu

Click this button to expand the folder.

Click here and drag left to make the panel wider.

Click and drag the header edge to make the column wider or narrower.

This is the root folder of the current site.

2. **Double-click index.html in the Files panel to open the file in Dreamweaver.**

   If you see code in addition to the page design, click the Design button in the Document toolbar (above the document window).

   All of the pages in this site use the same basic design. The links at the top of each page need to navigate between the pages. The copyright information at the bottom (in the footer area) needs to navigate to the copyright owner's Web site, which is external to your client's site.

These words will be links, which will appear on every page in the site.

This should be a link to the copyright holder's Web site.

3. **Close index.html, then open `contact.html`.**

As you can see, this page uses the same basic design as the index page. The specific page content also includes an email link, which you need to define so that users can click the link to send your client an email message.

These links should be the same on every page in the site.

This should be an email link to your client's email address.

Note:

The layout for this site is based on the free "Creation" template from www.templatemo.com. Photos are by Charlie Essers.

4. **Close contact.html, then open `menu1.html`.**

Again, the page uses the same basic layout as the other pages in the site. The top area of this page's primary content indicates that there are actually two menus — Dinner and Lunch. As you can see in the Files panel, two separate menu files exist. You will use the two headings at the top of the page to create links to each menu.

Each of these words should link to the relevant menu page.

5. **Close menu1.html, then continue to the next exercise.**

PLAN FOLDER ORGANIZATION

When all files are dumped into the main site folder, it can be challenging to manage your work. A well-organized site is an easy-to-manage site. Ideally, organization occurs before the site is constructed, but Dreamweaver makes it easy to reorganize files and folders at any point in the process.

There are no absolute rules to follow for organizing files and folders — other than the general principle of keeping related components together so you know where to find certain files when you need them.

1. **With Kinetic Site open in the Files panel, scroll to the top of the Files panel (if necessary) and click to select the site name at the top of the list.**

   The basic pages (home, about, contact, etc.) form the root of the site, and they should therefore appear within the root folder of the site. Other pages are better kept in folders that are named based on what they contain.

2. **Control/right-click the site name and choose New Folder from the contextual menu.**

   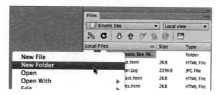

3. **Type `resources` and press Return/Enter to apply the new folder name.**

   When folders are first created, they appear at the bottom of their containing folders.

   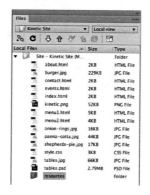

Note:

If after pressing Return/Enter, the folder name remains untitled, Control/right-click the untitled folder, choose Edit>Rename (or press F2), and correct the name.

4. **In the Files panel, click the Refresh button.**

   After refreshing the file list, folders on Macintosh are alphabetized along with all other files and folders; on Windows, folders are moved to and alphabetized at the top of the list, above individual files.

Note:

Press F5 to refresh the file list in the Files panel.

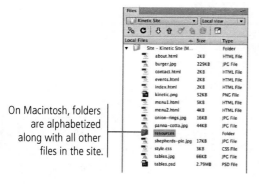

On Macintosh, folders are alphabetized along with all other files in the site.

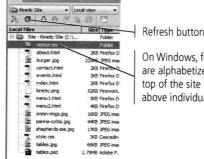

Refresh button

On Windows, folders are alphabetized at the top of the site list, above individual files.

5. **Click to again select the site folder at the top of the Files panel. Control/ right-click the site folder and choose New Folder from the contextual menu.**

If you don't select the site folder first, the new folder would be created inside of the resources folder that you just created. You want another folder at the same level as the resources folder — in the main level of the site root folder — so you first have to select the site folder as the target location for the second new folder.

6. **Type images and press Return/Enter to apply the new folder name.**

Web design convention dictates image files be placed in a folder named "images" for easier organization. If you have many photos in various categories, you might want to create additional nested folders inside the main images folder.

7. **Repeat Steps 5–6 to create another new folder named menus in the site root folder.**

8. **Refresh the list in the Files panel.**

Note:

You can create a new folder inside an existing folder (called nesting) by Control/right-clicking the existing folder — instead of the root folder — and choosing New Folder from the contextual menu.

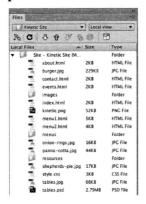

9. **Continue to the next exercise.**

The Files Panel in Depth

DREAMWEAVER FOUNDATIONS

By default, the Files panel displays the files on your local computer. You can also view the files on the remote or testing servers by choosing the appropriate option from the View menu.

The top of the Files panel also includes buttons that allow you to manage the files in your site:

Directory menu
Connect to Remote Host
Refresh
Get Files
Put Files

View menu
Expand to Show Local and Remote Sites
Synchronize
Check In Files
Check Out Files

- **Connect to Remote Host** establishes a connection with the remote server (if you defined one). Otherwise, clicking this button opens the Site Definition dialog box.
- **Refresh** refreshes the file list that displays in the panel.
- **Get Files** copies the selected files from a remote server to the local folder. If the Enable File Check In and Check Out option is active, the copied files are available on the local site in read-only mode, which means you can't modify them. You must click the Check Out Files button to edit the files.
- **Put Files** copies the selected files from the local folder to the remote server. If a new file is added to the server, and if the Enable File Check In and Check Out option is active, the file's status is Checked Out.

- **Check Out Files** copies the selected files from the remote server to the local folder and locks the files so only the user who checked out those files can edit them.
- **Check In Files** copies the selected files from the local folder to the remote server and makes the copied files read-only in the local folder. To edit these files, you need to select them and click the Check Out Files button.
- **Synchronize** synchronizes the files between the local folder and the remote server so the same version of the files appears in both places.
- **Expand** shows both local files and the remote site (if one has been defined). The expanded Files panel has two panes; one displays the files on the remote or test server and one displays the local site files.

SORT AND MOVE IMAGE FILES

When you define a site in Dreamweaver, the application reads all of the pages in the site (a process that can take a few minutes in a large site), notes the links between pages, and identifies which images are used in which pages. These associations between files are stored in a cache that Dreamweaver creates when a new site is defined.

When files are moved or renamed within the site, Dreamweaver recognizes that other files are related to the moved or renamed files, and prompts you to update the links in all of the affected files.

1. **With Kinetic Site open in the Files panel, click and drag burger.jpg into the images folder.**

   Make sure you drag the file directly over the name of the folder or folder icon; if you drag the file too far to the left or right, Dreamweaver will not move the file.

2. **When prompted, click Update to update the affected pages with the new location for the burger.jpg image file.**

When a browser downloads a Web page, it reads the page code, requests the image files from the defined locations, and displays the images within the page. You should understand that images in Web pages are not embedded into Web pages; they are merged into the page by the browser.

Files being updated do not need to be open for Dreamweaver to change the required link information. If pages *are* open, links in those pages are updated, but the changes are not automatically saved; you have to manually save each open file to make the updates permanent.

If you choose Don't Update in the Update Links dialog box, the image will not appear in the page that calls for that file. If you had moved the image file using Windows Explorer or the Macintosh Finder, Dreamweaver would not have been aware of the movement, and you would not have had the opportunity to adjust the path to the image file in pages that link to that image.

The burger.jpg file is now stored in the main images folder. When you move files into a folder, that folder automatically expands in the Files panel.

Note:

To avoid potential problems if you accidentally close a file without saving, you might want to close open files before moving or renaming files in the Files panel.

3. **In the Files panel, click the Type column heading to sort the site files by type.**

    By default, site files are sorted by name. You can sort by another criteria by clicking the column headings in the Files panel. Sorting by type allows you to easily find all of the images that are used in this site.

4. **Click the first JPG file in the list (onion-rings.jpg) to select that file. Press Shift and click kinetic.png to select all consecutive files between the first and the last ones you selected.**

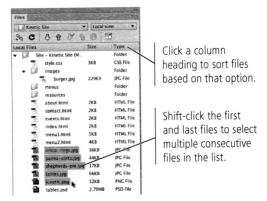

Click a column heading to sort files based on that option.

Shift-click the first and last files to select multiple consecutive files in the list.

5. **Click the icon of any of the selected files, and drag the selected files into the images folder. When asked, click Update to update all links to all of the moved files.**

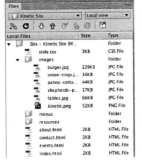

6. **Click the down-facing arrow (Macintosh) or the "–" symbol (Windows) to the left of the images folder name to collapse the folder.**

7. **Click the Local Files column header to re-sort the files by name.**

8. **Select menu1.html and menu2.html, and move them into the menus folder. Update the links when asked.**

    This is a relatively small site, so nesting files into subfolders isn't strictly necessary. However, when you work with larger files, clearly organized subfolders can be extremely helpful in maintaining a site that is easy to update as often as necessary.

Note:

You can change the columns that appear in the Files panel — and the order of those columns — in the File View Columns pane of the Site Setup dialog box.

Note:

Press Shift to select multiple consecutive files in the panel.

Press Command/Control and click to select multiple, nonconsecutive files.

You can also Command/ Control-click to deselect a selected file. For example, if you select a file by accident, you can deselect it by Command/ Control-clicking the file name again.

Note:

Images in Web sites typically have a GIF, JPG, or PNG extension.

9. **Collapse the menus folder.**

10. **Select and move the file `tables.psd` into the `resources` folder.**

   In this case, you are not asked to update links. This is a layered Photoshop file that was used to create the background image behind the page content. It is not part of the actual Web site, but it's a good idea to keep this type of file in the site folder in case you need to make changes later. Later in this project, you will learn how to prevent this file from being uploaded as part of the site.

Note:

You can also copy and paste files into a folder using the Edit options in the contextual menus, or using the standard keyboard shortcuts:

Cut:
Command/Control-X

Copy:
Command/Control-C

Paste:
Command/Control-V

11. **Collapse the `resources` folder.**

   From the folder structure alone, the Web site appears to be better organized. You now know what to expect when you open each folder.

12. **Continue to the next stage of the project.**

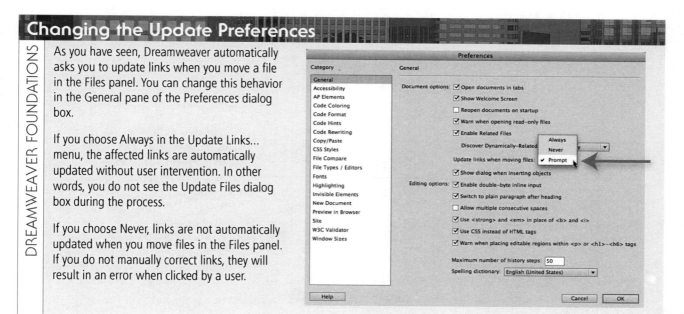

Changing the Update Preferences

DREAMWEAVER FOUNDATIONS

As you have seen, Dreamweaver automatically asks you to update links when you move a file in the Files panel. You can change this behavior in the General pane of the Preferences dialog box.

If you choose Always in the Update Links... menu, the affected links are automatically updated without user intervention. In other words, you do not see the Update Files dialog box during the process.

If you choose Never, links are not automatically updated when you move files in the Files panel. If you do not manually correct links, they will result in an error when clicked by a user.

Stage 2 Organizing the Site Navigation

Hyperlinks (the official term for links) can be created to link pages on a site to other pages within the same site, or to pages on other sites. A well-designed site includes links that make it easy to get to any part of a site from any other part of a site. You should carefully plan the flow of links and connections between pages — always keeping the reader's usability in mind.

Organizing links is a simple application of a science called **information architecture**, which is the organization of a Web site to support both usability and "findability." As you organize site links, remember that your goal is to enable visitors to see a pattern in your links, which will assist them in navigating through your site. Keep the following points in mind when you plan a site's link structure:

- You can't know how visitors will enter your site. The primary site pages (home, about us, etc.) should be accessible from every page on the site.

- When linking secondary pages such as different menus for different mealtimes, don't make users constantly click the browser's Back button. Links should allow users to navigate all sibling pages (at the same level) as easily as navigating the primary structure. For example, users should be able to access the dinner menu or lunch menu in the restaurant's site without first going back to a main "Menu" page.

Using the terms "parent," "child," and "sibling" is simply a way of describing relationships between pages. A large Web site cannot provide links to all of the pages from its home page. By grouping pages, grouping groups of pages, and so on, you create relationships of equality between pages that are grouped together, as well as between groups that are grouped together.

When you plan a new site, you should create this type of flowchart to make sure you create all the necessary links that make the site as user-friendly as possible. A flowchart of the required Kinetic Site link structure is shown below.

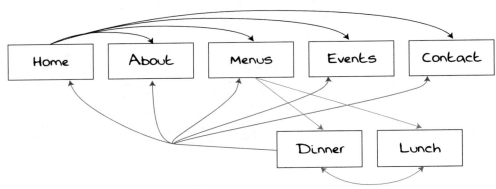

Kinetic Bistro Site Navigation

In this stage of the project, you will learn various techniques to create the necessary links on the Kinetic Site pages.

CREATE HYPERLINKS WITHIN THE SITE

Dreamweaver offers a number of options for creating the necessary links for any Web site structure.

- **Hyperlink Button in the Common Insert Panel.** Clicking the Hyperlink button in the Common Insert panel opens the Hyperlink dialog box, where you define the specific parameters of the link.

- **Insert>Hyperlink menu.** This menu command opens the same dialog box that you see when you click the Hyperlink button in the Insert panel.

- **Properties Panel Fields.** You can also simply define the specifics of a hyperlink in the Properties panel. This method offers the same options as those in the Hyperlink dialog box, but does not require the dialog box interface.

- **Point to File button in the Properties panel.** To create a link using this method, simply click the Point to File button, hold down the mouse button, and drag to a file in the Files panel; Dreamweaver automatically creates a link.

- **Browse for File button in the Properties panel.** The Browse for File button opens a navigation dialog box, where you can select the file that will open when a user clicks on the link.

- **Shift-Drag Method.** You can create a link directly from the document window by pressing Shift and then clicking and dragging from the link source to the destination page in the Files panel. (This method only works for text; you can't Shift-drag to create a link for an image.)

Note:

Dreamweaver often includes several different ways to achieve the same result. You should use the method that is most efficient at the time.

1. **With Kinetic Site open in the Files panel, open index.html.**

2. **At the top of the page, double-click the word "HOME" to select it.**

3. **If your Insert panel is docked above the document window, click the Common tab at the top of the panel.**

    If your Insert panel is docked on the right side of the screen, or if it is floating as a separate panel, choose Common in the menu at the top of the panel.

If docked in standard mode, use the menu at the top of the panel to access different categories of options.

If docked in tabbed mode, use the tabs at the top of the panel to access different categories of options.

DREAMWEAVER FOUNDATIONS

The Common Insert panel contains buttons for frequently used items. For example, to insert a hyperlink, simply click the corresponding button. (Some of the terms and functions in the following descriptions will make more sense as you use those tools to complete later projects.)

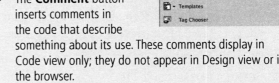

- The **Hyperlink** button opens a dialog box where you can create text or image links to another file, either in the same Web site or in an external Web site.

- The **Email Link** button opens a dialog box where you can create links to email addresses. When a user clicks an email link, it opens the user's default email application with the email address in the To line.

- The **Named Anchor** button marks locations within a page. Links can be provided to these locations from within the same page or from other pages of the same Web site or other Web sites.

- The **Horizontal Rule** button inserts a solid line across the width of the page. This can be useful for visually separating sections of text.

- The **Table** button inserts a table into the page.

- The **Insert Div Tag** button inserts new sections (divisions) in a page. Each division in a page is marked by a dotted line in Dreamweaver; these dotted lines do not appear when the page is viewed in a browser. Divisions are useful for inserting blocks of content you want to format independently from other blocks.

- The **Images** button inserts various types of graphics. If you click the arrow on the button icon, a menu shows the available types of objects (basic images, rollover images, etc.). You can also insert an image placeholder, which reserves a portion of the page for inserting an object later.

- The **Media** button inserts audio-visual files. These files could be in any format, but Dreamweaver also has functionality specific to inserting Flash, QuickTime, and Shockwave files; Java applets; and ActiveX controls.

- The **Widget** is used to insert Spry widgets. Dreamweaver ships with a number of built-in Spry widgets, which you will use in Project 5: Cupcake Bakery CSS Site. You can download other widgets through the online Widget Browser, which is a separate free download. To access this functionality, you can open the Extend Dreamweaver menu in the Application/Menu bar and choose Widget Browser. (If the Widget Browser extension is not yet installed on your system, you will be prompted to download and install the application.)

- The **Date** button inserts the date and time. An option is provided for updating the date and time whenever the file is saved.

- The **Server-Side Include** button inserts a file within a page by creating a link to the external file.

- The **Comment** button inserts comments in the code that describe something about its use. These comments display in Code view only; they do not appear in Design view or in the browser.

- The **Head** button adds information about the page that will be used by browsers. This information is included in the properties of the page. Click the arrow to select the type of information you want to add.

- The **Script** button enables you to add code that will be used by the browser to perform an action when the page is accessed. Click the arrow and click Script from the menu to add the code. Some older versions of browsers might have the script-reading feature disabled; to display alternate content when browsers fail to read the script, click No Script from the menu. You need to know programming languages to use this feature properly.

- The **Templates** button creates a template based on the current document, which is useful when you need to create multiple documents from the same layout.

- The **Tag Chooser** button inserts tags in the code. Tags are elements in the code that define the kind of content that is included. Tags are included automatically when you edit pages in Design view.

4. Click the Hyperlink button in the Common Insert panel.

The Common Insert panel contains many of the common functions you use to create Web pages. If a different Insert panel is showing, you can return to the Common Insert panel by choosing Common in the panel menu.

Note:

From this point on, we will leave our Insert panel docked on the right side of the workspace, immediately below the Files panel. Feel free to organize your workspace however you prefer.

If docked in standard mode, buttons in the panel are identified by icon and name.

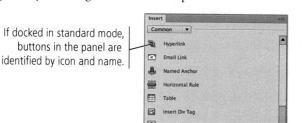

If docked in tabbed mode, hover your mouse over a button to find its name.

This word is selected.

5. In the Hyperlink dialog box, click the Browse button to the right of the Link field.

The text selected in the document appears in the Text field by default. (If an image is selected, this field defaults to be blank.)

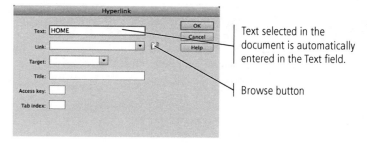

Text selected in the document is automatically entered in the Text field.

Browse button

6. Navigate to your WIP>Kinetic folder, select index.html, and click Open/OK.

In the Link field, you can either type the URL of a location outside the site you're building, or you can click the Browse button to select a file within the current site.

7. **Open the Target menu and choose _self.**

   This option determines where the linked file will open:

   - **_blank** opens every linked file in a new, unnamed browser window.
   - **new** creates a new browser window with the name "_new". Every link assigned the _new target will open in that same _new browser window.
   - **_parent** is relevant if a page includes nested frames; this option opens the link in the frame or window that contains the frame with the link.
   - **_self** opens the link in the same frame or browser window as the link. This is the default behavior if you do not choose an option in the Target menu.
   - **_top** opens the link in the same browser window, regardless of frames.

8. **In the Title field, type `Kinetic Bistro home page`.**

   The Title field defines text that appears when the cursor is placed over the link text. Defining a descriptive title for links can help a page achieve better search engine results.

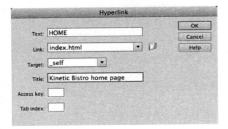

9. **Click OK in the Hyperlink dialog box to create the link.**

10. **Click the Split button in the Document toolbar to review both the design and code views at one time.**

    A Web page is basically a page full of code. A browser reads the code to determine how to treat various elements of the page. HTML code largely revolves around tags, which tell a browser how to interpret specific objects on the page.

    A hyperlink is identified by the **a** element, which starts with the opening **<a>** tag; the link destination and target are defined as attributes of that tag (**href="index.html" target="_self"**). After the actual link text, the closing tag (**</a>**) identifies the end of the link.

Note:

You can change the destination of a link by selecting the linked text or object in the document and choosing Modify>Change Link. This menu command opens the same dialog box as the Browse for File button, where you can navigate to and select the new link destination.

Note:

You can use the Access Key field to define a keyboard shortcut for the link, and use the Tab Index field to specify the number of times a user needs to press the Tab key to select the link.

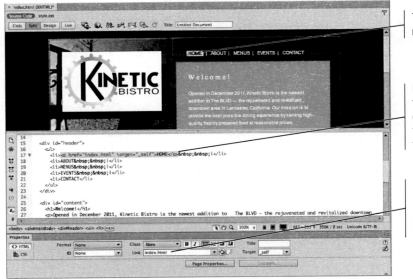

The selected text is now a link.

In the code view, the link text is surrounded by opening and closing <a> tags, which identify the text as a link.

The link destination now appears in the Link field of the Properties panel.

11. **Click the Design button in the Document toolbar to close the Code pane.**

12. **Select the word "ABOUT" at the top of the page.**

13. **Click the Browse for File button to the right of the Link field in the Properties panel.**

    If you don't see the Properties panel, choose Window>Properties. The Properties panel's primary purpose is to review and change the properties of the selected HTML element (such as a heading, paragraph, or table cell).

The word ABOUT is selected.

Browse for File button

Note:

When a link to another page in the site is selected in the document, you can open the related page in Dreamweaver by choosing Modify>Open Linked Page.

14. **In the resulting dialog box, select about.html, and then click Open/OK.**

The link destination now appears in the Link field of the Properties panel.

15. **Select the word "MENUS" at the top of the page.**

16. **Expand the menus folder in the Files panel.**

    You should expand and collapse Files panel folders as necessary, depending on your available screen space. We will not repeat instructions to collapse or expand folders unless it is necessary to perform a specific function.

Note:

You can remove a link by selecting the linked text or object in the document and choosing Modify>Remove Link, or by simply deleting the text from the Link field in the Properties panel.

17. **Click the Point to File button in the Properties panel, hold down the mouse button, and drag to menus/menu1.html in the Files panel.**

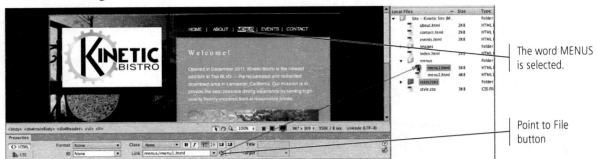

The word MENUS is selected.

Point to File button

18. **Select the word "EVENTS" at the top of the page.**

19. **Press the Shift key, then click the selected text and drag to events.html in the Files panel.**

You have to press the Shift key, and then click and drag to the link destination. If you try to click and drag before pressing the Shift key, this technique will fail.

20. **Use any method you just learned to create a link from the word "CONTACT" to the contact.html file.**

21. **Select the words "Against The Clock, Inc." at the bottom of the page.**

22. **In the Link field of the Properties panel, type http://www. againsttheclock.com and press Return/Enter.**

Dreamweaver can't help you create an external URL link because it's outside the site definition. You have to simply type or paste the address into the Link field.

An external **URL link** must begin with the "http://" protocol, followed by the domain name and, if relevant, the folder path and file name of the page to which you are linking.

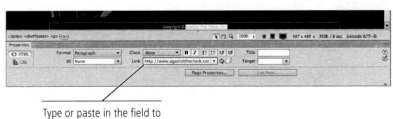

Type or paste in the field to define an external URL link.

Note:

To minimize the repetitive work required, we already defined this link for you on the other pages in the site. In a professional environment, you would need to add this link to every page in the site.

23. **Choose File>Save to save your changes in the file, then continue to the next exercise.**

COPY AND PASTE LINKS

Rather than manually creating the same links on every page, you can now simply copy and paste them from one page to another.

1. **With index.html open (from the Kinetic Site), click in any of the text links to place the insertion point.**

2. **Review the Tag Selector below the document window.**

   The Tag Selector, located in the status bar of the document window, shows the nesting order of HTML tags (the "path of tags") based on the current selection or the current location of the insertion point.

Insertion point

Active tag

Tag Selector

3. **Click the <ul> tag in the Tag Selector.**

   The **<ul>** tag identifies an unordered list, which is how this navigation structure was created; each link is a separate list item (using the **<li>** tag).

   Clicking a tag in the Tag Selector selects that HTML element and all of its content. In the document window, the associated content is highlighted.

   Note:

   You will work more extensively with tags beginning in Project 2: Digital Book Chapter.

Selected tag

The entire unordered list (all of the links) is selected.

4. **Choose Edit>Copy (or press Command/Control-C) to copy the selected content to the Clipboard.**

5. **Close index.html and open about.html.**

6. **Click to place the insertion point anywhere in the list of links at the top of the page, and then click the <ul> tag in the Tag Selector to select the entire unlinked list.**

The selected list does not yet include links.

7. **Choose Edit>Paste (or press Command/Control-V) to paste the copied content from the Clipboard.**

8. **Place the insertion point in any of the links and review the Tag Selector.**

The Tag Selector now shows the **<a>** tag for the current insertion point (in our example, the CONTACT link). The Properties panel also shows the destination of the active link.

The pasted content includes the links.

9. **Save the changes to about.html and close the file.**

10. **Repeat Steps 6–9 to paste the copied content (the links) into all HTML pages in the site root level, as well as the two HTML pages in the menus folder.**

11. **Save and close any open files, and then continue to the next exercise.**

ADJUST RELATIVE LINK PATHS

A **path** is the route taken through the folder structure to link one page to another. By default, Dreamweaver uses **relative paths** when creating links (the application refers to this as "relative to the document"). The alternative is to create **absolute paths** ("relative to the site"); but unless your site is running on a Web server, you can't test links that use absolute paths.

As an example, consider creating a link from index.html to about.html, both of which reside in the root folder (as shown in the figure to the right). In this case, the source and destination pages are in the same folder; the relative-path link simply states the file name of the destination page:

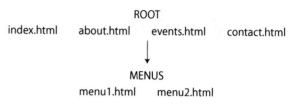

<a href="menu2.html">Link Text</a>

When you drill down into nested levels of folders, the source folder is not identified in the path; the link automatically works starting from the location of the link. To link from index.html to menu1.html, for example, you have to include the nested menus folder in the path:

<a href="menus/menu1.html">Link Text</a>

When the link is in an upward direction, the ../ notation says "go up one folder." To link from menu1.html to index.html in the site root folder means that the link needs to take the visitor up one folder level:

<a href="../index.html">Link Text</a>

Each step up in the folder structure requires another command to "go one step up" in the folder structure. If you had another level of nesting inside the menus folder, for example, a link would have to take the visitor up two folder levels to return to the main index page:

<a href="../../index.html">Link Text</a>

In the next exercise, you are going to adjust the menu links in the menu files so they work properly.

1. **With the Kinetic Site open in the Files panel, open menu1.html.**

2. **Double-click the word HOME at the top of the page to select it.**

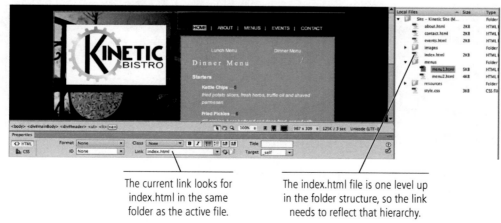

The current link looks for index.html in the same folder as the active file.

The index.html file is one level up in the folder structure, so the link needs to reflect that hierarchy.

3. In the Properties panel, place the insertion point at the beginning of the Link field and type ../ before the existing link.

4. Press Return/Enter to finalize the change.

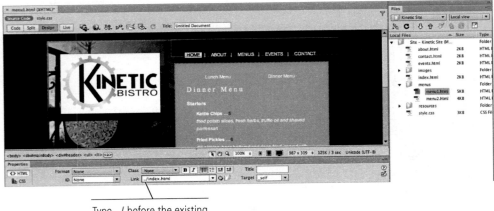

Type ../ before the existing link to move up one folder from the active file.

5. Repeat Steps 2–4 for the ABOUT, EVENTS, and CONTACT links.

6. Select the word MENUS at the top of the page.

In this case, the link is still a problem because it directs the browser to look for a folder named "menus" inside the same folder as the active page. You need to remove the folder part of the path to prevent an error if a user clicks this link from the menu1.html page.

The active file is in the menus folder.

This link would cause a browser to look for a menus folder at the same level as the active file — i.e., another menus folder inside the existing menus folder.

7. In the Properties panel, delete menus/ (including the forward slash) from the existing link.

Delete the folder path from the existing link.

8. **Using any method you already have learned, link "Lunch Menu" to menu2.html and link "Dinner Menu" to menu1.html.**

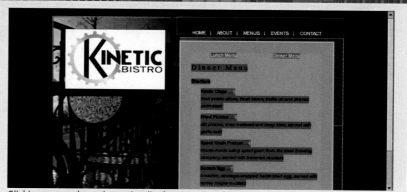

Link this to menu2.html.   Link this to menu1.html.

9. **Repeat the process from Steps 1–8 to adjust the top links and add the necessary secondary links in the menu2.html file.**

10. **Save and close any open files, then continue to the next exercise.**

Accessing Page Content in the Menu Pages

The files for this project were created using divs (using the opening and closing <div> tags), which are simply a way to identify and format parts or sections of a page.

(You will begin working with the idea of divs in Project 2: Digital Book Chapter, and then extensively throughout the rest of the book.) Although you don't need to worry about the underlying page structure for now, you might see some unusual behavior when you first try to select content in the main section of each menu page.

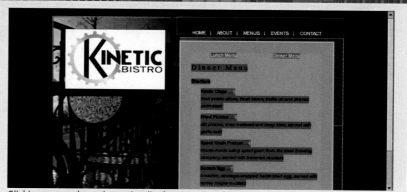

Clicking once selects the entire div that contains the menu content.

The area that holds the actual menu content has a fixed height, but both menus have more content than will fit into the defined size. When the page is viewed in a browser, the area includes a scroll bar for users to access the content that doesn't fit.

In Dreamweaver's Design view, however, this scrollbar doesn't appear. Instead, the first time you click, the entire div is selected and all of the contained text is highlighted.

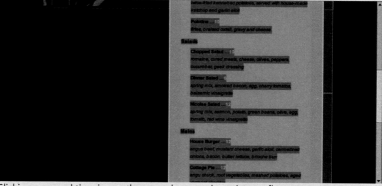

Clicking a second time jumps the page down to show the overflow content.

Clicking inside the area again causes the page to jump down, showing some of the overflow content.

If you click a third time, you can place the insertion point inside the actual text, scroll up as necessary, and then select the link text at the top of the area.

Clicking a third time places the insertion point so you can select specific text in the menu.

CREATE AN EMAIL LINK

Most Web sites include one or more external links (including email links), which require the appropriate protocol to tell the browser what type of link is present.

An **email link** requires the "mailto:" protocol, followed by the appropriate email address. This instructs the browser to open a new mail message with the defined address already in the To line.

1. **With Kinetic Site open in the Files panel, open contact.html.**

2. **Select the words "info@kineticbistro.atc" in the main content area.**

3. **In the Common Insert panel, click the Email Link button.**

Selected text

4. **Review the resulting dialog box, then click OK.**

   If you select text before clicking the Email Link icon, the Text field is completed for you. Dreamweaver also recognizes that the selected text is an email address, so the Email field is filled in for you.

   If the selected text is not recognized as an email address, the Email field defaults to the last address that was defined in the field.

Note:

You can access the same Email Link dialog box by choosing Insert>Email Link.

5. **Click OK to create the email link.**

6. **Review the link field in the Properties panel.**

   An email link must begin with "mailto:" followed by the address. When you use the Email Link dialog box, Dreamweaver automatically inserts the mailto: protocol.

Note:

In many cases throughout this book, we use "[company].atc" as the domain of a site.

Although at the time of writing, none of the domain names we use are real, new domains are registered every day. We use the fictitious ".atc" domain to avoid inadvertently using the domain name of a real company.

7. **Save the file and close it, then continue to the next stage of the project.**

When you upload files to a server, you should use the accurate domain (.com, .gov, .edu, etc.) for the site you are building.

Stage 3 Naming and Titling Documents

When a **Web server** (special computers that store and deliver Web pages) receives a request for a folder but not a specific page, the Web server delivers the default page for that folder — usually named index.html or index.htm. There is no practical difference between the two extensions; most Web servers can serve files with either extension.

To create links to the default page in a specific folder, you do not need to include the file name if you use the index naming convention. Both **www.kineticbistro.com/** and **www.kineticbistro.com/index.html** refer to the same page.

RENAME PAGES FOR SEARCH ENGINE OPTIMIZATION

SEO (search engine optimization) is the process of improving the ranking of a Web site and its pages within **SERPs** (search engine results pages, or the pages that list the results of a search). Search engines certainly use the content of a page for ranking purposes, but the names of folders and files also affect search engine rankings. Descriptive folder and file names also improve usability; you can use **m/menu1.html** for the path to the dinner menu page, for example, but **/menus/dinner-menu.html** is much easier for human visitors to understand — and will also improve your search engine ranking.

In this exercise, you rename the menu pages to more accurately describe what is contained in the files. As with moving files, the application recognizes when a file name has been changed and knows that links to the page must be adjusted.

1. **With Kinetic Site open, click menus/menu1.html in the Files panel to select that file.**

2. **Click the selected filename again to highlight it.**

   This highlights the existing filename, exluding the extension.

3. **Type dinner-menu, then press Return/Enter. In the resulting dialog box, click Update to update all pages that link to this page.**

   Typing when the filename is highlighted replaces the previous file name. Pressing Return/Enter finalizes the change.

   As with moving files, Dreamweaver recognizes that all links to the renamed page need to point to the new file name.

   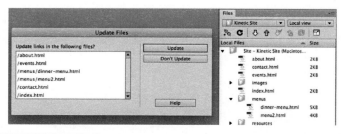

> **Note:**
>
> *If a link does not specify a specific file in a nested folder, the Web server will look for a file named index.html or index.htm inside the defined folder. If you do not have an index file in that folder, the link will result in an error.*

> **Note:**
>
> *You can also Control/ right-click a file in the Files panel and choose Edit>Rename to rename a specific file.*

4. Repeat Steps 1–3 to rename menu2.html as lunch-menu.html.

5. Continue to the next exercise.

Understanding Web File Naming Conventions

The file names of pages should make the content or purpose of each page clear.

Because different servers run on different operating systems, the safest way to name pages is to use only characters that are guaranteed to work perfectly:

- a through z (use only lowercase letters)
- 0 through 9
- Hyphen (great-site.html)
- Underscore (great_site.html)

Consider everything else to be "illegal," including:

- Spaces
- Brackets of all kinds, including ( ), [ ], { }, and < >
- Symbols, including #, @, %, ~, |, *, and &
- Quotation marks, both double (" ") and single (' ')
- Slashes, both back slashes (\) and forward slashes (/)
- Commas, periods, question marks, and exclamation points
- Uppercase characters

Some designers use **CamelCase** — uppercase letters at the beginning of each word within a file name, such as UniversalStudios.html — file names instead of using hyphen or underscore characters to separate words. The problem with mixing the lettercase is that some Web server software is case-sensitive and some is not.

Most Windows-based Web server software is not case-sensitive; but UNIX- and Linux-based Web server software is case-sensitive. Considering that many Web servers run on UNIX- or Linux-based computers, it's best to use only lowercase file and folder names.

CREATE DOCUMENT TITLES FOR INDIVIDUAL PAGES

Appropriate document titles are an important concern for both search engines and site visitors. While the document title does not appear within the body of a Web page, it does appear in the title bar of the browser, as the default name of the page in the Bookmarks or Favorites list, and as the page name in search-engine results pages.

Page titles should be relatively short, around 70 characters or so to avoid their being truncated in various locations (such as a user's Bookmarks/Favorites list). You should separate the components of the title with some type of divider, such as a colon (:) or pipe (|) character.

In this exercise, you add document titles to the new pages to increase the pages' search engine rankings and improve usability for visitors who find the pages in search engines and bookmarks. You also learn to use the Find and Replace function, which can greatly reduce the amount of effort required to create all of the document titles.

1. **With Kinetic Site open in the Files panel, open index.html.**

2. **Make sure the Document toolbar is showing (View>Toolbars>Document).**

3. **Click the Split button in the Document toolbar to show both the Code and Design views at one time.**

4. **Examine the Title field above the document window.**

   When you create a new page in Dreamweaver, the default title is "Untitled Document". That text appears in the Title field of the Document toolbar, and in the title element in the Code pane (wrapped in the opening and closing **<title>** tags).

Document title

5. **Choose Edit>Find and Replace.**

6. **Change the Find In menu to Folder, then click the Browse button to the right of the attached field. In the resulting dialog box, navigate to your WIP>Kinetic folder and click Open/Select.**

   You want to affect all files in the site, so you are selecting the defined site root folder in this dialog box.

7. **Choose Source Code in the Search menu.**

   The document title does not appear in the body of the page, so when you use Find and Replace, you must apply the change to the source code rather than the document text.

Click this button to browse to the proper folder.

8. **In the Find field, type** `Untitled Document`.

9. **In the Replace field, type** `Kinetic Bistro | Lancaster, California | `. **(Include a space after the final pipe character.)**

    All pages in the site will include this block of text at the beginning of the document title. Further detail about individual pages will be added to the right of this information.

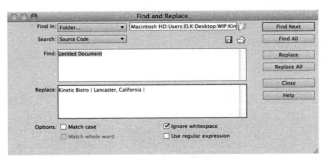

Note:

Some experts disagree whether the company name should come before or after the specific page information in a title. However, putting the company name at the beginning of the page title can help with search engine results because the company name is an important keyword.

10. **Click Replace All. When prompted to confirm whether you want to proceed with this function, click Yes.**

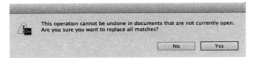

    Like most applications, Dreamweaver has an Undo function that allows you to undo the most recently completed actions; however, this function only works if the document is open. Since you are using the Find and Replace function on the entire folder and not only on an open page, you are making changes in closed documents — which means you cannot use the Undo command.

    After completing the Find and Replace function, Dreamweaver displays the results in the Search panel.

11. **Examine the title in the Document toolbar and the Code pane again for the open file (index.html).**

    As a result of the Find and Replace function, the document title has been changed. The same change has been made in all pages in the site.

12. **Close the Search panel group.**

13. Click in the Code pane to make it active.

14. Click at the end of the existing page title to place the insertion point immediately before the closing </title> tag.

Note:

Making a specific pane active is called "bringing it into focus".

15. Type Gourmet Casual Dining.

You can edit the page title in the Document toolbar or in the Code pane. Changes in either place are automatically applied to the other.

Type the new information immediately before the closing </title> tag.

16. Save index.html and close it.

17. Open about.html. Using either the Title field in the Document toolbar or the Code pane, add Hours of Operation to the end of the existing page title.

18. Save about.html and close it.

19. Repeat this process (Steps 14–18) to change the page titles of the remaining pages as follows:

File	Title
contact.html	Address and Contact Information
events.html	Special Event Facilities
menus/dinner-menu.html	Dinner Menu
menus/lunch-menu.html	Lunch Menu

Note:

Unlike file names, document titles can use mixed lettercase and include spaces and other characters. However, you should avoid both single and double quotation marks.

20. Continue to the final stage of the project.

Stage 4 Making Files Public

To complete the final stage of this project — making your files accessible to the browsing public — you need to have access to some type of server.

On the inside back cover of this book, you have a code that you need to gain access to the required resource files. The same code also provides access to a six-month, free trial Web hosting account at Pair Networks (www.pair.com).

If you don't already have access to an online server, go to **www.pair.com/atc/** to sign up for your hosting account before you complete the final stage of this project. You must enter your contact information, and the code from the inside back cover of your book. You should then define a user name in the last field; this will become part of the server name for your hosting account.

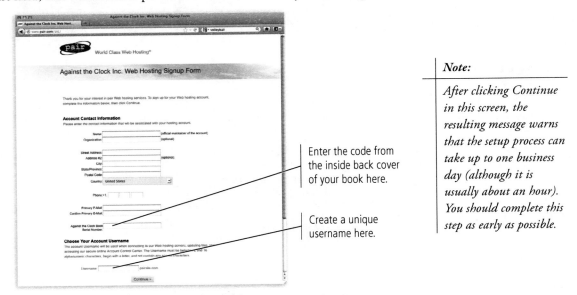

Enter the code from the inside back cover of your book here.

Create a unique username here.

Note:

After clicking Continue in this screen, the resulting message warns that the setup process can take up to one business day (although it is usually about an hour). You should complete this step as early as possible.

After you click Continue, you will receive an acknowledgement that your request is being processsed. You will receive a confirmation email (sent to the email you defined in the Signup Form) with your username and password information. Once you receive the confirmation email, you are ready to complete the final stage of this project.

HIDE FILES FROM THE WEB SERVER

As you saw when you created the folders for the new site, not all of the new files are meant to be uploaded to the Web server — specifically, the Photoshop file in the resources folder. (You should, however, store such files locally as source files or documentation for the work you completed.)

Dreamweaver provides a very useful function — called **cloaking** — that allows you to prevent certain files from uploading. You can cloak an individual file; cloak all files with the same extension (for example, all native Photoshop files with the PSD extension); or cloak a folder, which also cloaks all files in that folder.

1. **With Kinetic Site open in the Files panel, double-click the Kinetic Site name in the Directory menu.**

   This opens the Site Setup dialog box for the selected site. You do not need to go through the Manage Sites dialog box to edit the settings for the active site.

   Double-click the existing site name to open the Site Setup dialog box for that site.

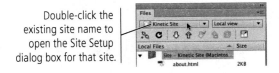

2. **In the Site Setup dialog box, expand the Advanced Settings menu on the left side and click Cloaking to show the related options.**

3. **Make sure the Enable Cloaking check box is active.**

   When Enable Cloaking is checked, you can hide selected files and folders from a Web server. You can also use the Cloak Files Ending With option to hide all files with the extensions that are listed in the field.

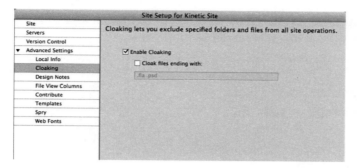

4. **Click Save to close the Site Setup dialog box.**

5. **In the Files panel, collapse all open folders and expand only the resources folder.**

6. **Control/right-click the resources folder and choose Cloaking>Cloak.**

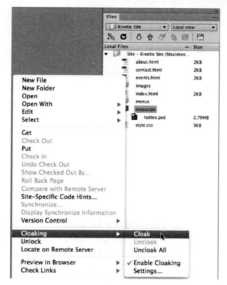

Note:

You can also cloak a specific file by Control/right clicking that file in the Files panel and choosing Cloaking>Cloak.

Notice the red slash through the resources folder icon and the icon for the file in the resources folder. The red slash refers to the cloaking function only; it does not prevent you from working with the files, adding more files, or deleting any of the existing files.

7. **Continue to the next exercise.**

DEFINE REMOTE CONNECTION INFO FOR THE SITE

For Dreamweaver to manage file uploading, you first have to define the hosting server connection settings as part of the site setup information.

1. **With Kinetic Site open in the Dreamweaver Files panel, double-click the site name in the Directory menu to open the Site Setup dialog box.**

2. **In the Site Setup dialog box, click Servers in the list of categories, then click the + button near the bottom of the dialog box to define a new server.**

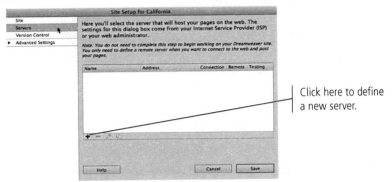

Click here to define a new server.

3. **In the Basic options, type a name for the server you are using.**

   This name is simply for you to identify it in Dreamweaver.

4. **Assuming you are working with a remote server, choose FTP in the Connect Using menu.**

   If you are using a local server, consult your network administrator for the settings to use.

5. **In the FTP Address field, type the hostname for your server.**

   Using our example hosting account at Pair Networks, the FTP host is the same as the server name. (If you signed up for this service, your server name was in the confirmation email that you received after signing up.) Check your hosting account documentation for your FTP hostname and account information.

6. **Type your FTP login (username) and password in the related fields.**

   These are the username and password for your hosting account. Again, this information was probably sent to you via email when you first set up the hosting account; consult your server documentation for the correct information to use.

7. **In the Root Directory field, type the location of the folder where you want the files to be placed.**

   Some hosting providers require you to place public files inside a specific folder, such as public_html or www. When users navigate to your URL, they see the index page located in the designated folder.

   Using a hosting account at Pair Networks, as in our example, public files must be placed in the public_html folder.

8. In the Web URL field, type the URL at which users will access the site.

Dreamweaver automatically defines this URL based on your other choices in this dialog box; the default value will be "http://" plus the FTP Address plus the Root Directory. In our example, the default was http://ekendra.pairserver.com/public_html/

You need to change the URL to the path a user would type in a browser to access your site. In our example, the address is http://ekendra.pairserver.com/.

Note that we removed the public_html/ folder path from the URL; it is only required when you upload files for viewing over the Internet.

Make sure you enter the correct information for your domain name.

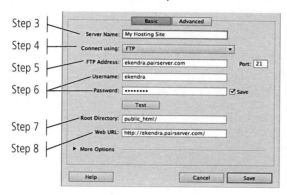

9. Make sure the Save check box (next to the Password field) is checked, and then click Test.

You must receive a message stating that Dreamweaver successfully connected to the Web server. If a connection with the Web server cannot be established, check your entries to make sure your Internet connection is active, and then try again.

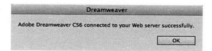

(If you are working on a shared computer, you might want to uncheck the Save option. However, you will have to retype your username and password every time you upload files to your hosting account.)

10. Click Save to return to the Site Setup dialog box.

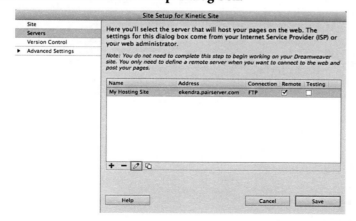

11. Click Save to close the Site Setup dialog box, then continue to the next exercise.

UPLOAD FILES TO A REMOTE SITE

Dreamweaver's FTP functionality makes it easy to put files into the remote site folder (defined in the Site Setup dialog box). You can even synchronize all files on the remote and local sites — which is useful when you are ready to publish the site for public Internet access.

1. **With Kinetic Site open in the Files panel, click the Expand button in the Files panel to show both the local and remote sites.**

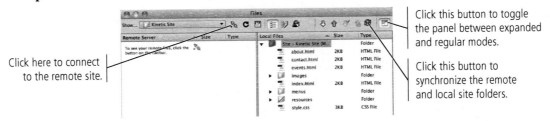

Click here to connect to the remote site.

Click this button to toggle the panel between expanded and regular modes.

Click this button to synchronize the remote and local site folders.

2. **Above the Remote Server pane, click the Connection button to link to and show the remote site.**

After the connection has been made, the remote site appears in the left pane.

Your host account might include a number of default files.

3. **Click the Synchronize button at the top of the expanded Files panel.**

4. **In the Synchronize Files dialog box, choose Entire 'Kinetic Site' Site in the Synchronize menu, and choose Put Newer Files to Remote in the Direction menu.**

   This utility enables you to synchronize an entire site or only selected files. You can also determine which version (local or remote) to synchronize from. For example, if you accidentally delete files from your local site folder, you can choose to synchronize files from the remote site to the local site to restore the missing files.

5. **Click the Preview button.**

   After a few seconds, the Synchronize dialog box shows a list of all files that will be affected by the process. In this case, this is the first time you are uploading to the remote site, so all site files need to be put onto the remote site.

Click these buttons to change the options for selected files in the list.

6. **Click OK to put the files onto the remote site.**

7. **In the Background File Activity dialog box, click the arrow button to the left of the word "Details."**

   When you upload files to the remote server, Dreamweaver keeps a log of affected files. The Background File Activity dialog box shows a list of each file, including any potential problems encountered during the transfer process. Clicking the Details button expands the dialog box and shows the progression of the synchronization.

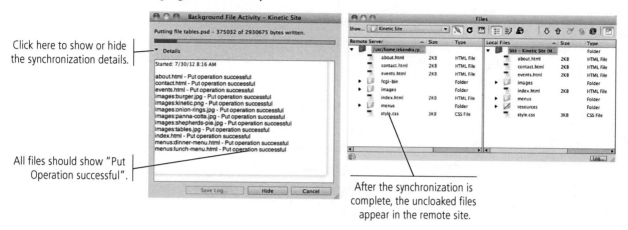

Click here to show or hide the synchronization details.

All files should show "Put Operation successful".

After the synchronization is complete, the uncloaked files appear in the remote site.

8. **Open a browser window. In the navigation bar, type the URL of the Kinetic home page at your domain name.**

   Type the same Web URL you defined in the Servers section of the Site Setup dialog box (see Page 55, Step 8). In our example, the complete URL is http://ekendra.pairserver.com/.

9. **Test the various links in the site.**

10. **Close the browser and return to Dreamweaver, then continue to the next exercise.**

To reduce the potential for confusion, it's a good idea to remove the defined sites of completed projects, leaving only the defined sites of current projects.

As stated in the Interface chapter, removing a site from Dreamweaver does not delete the actual files and folders from your computer; it simply removes them from Dreamweaver. Rather than removing a site, however, you can export a site definition file — which you can later import to restore the same settings and options you already defined (as you did in the Interface chapter when you imported the sf-arts site).

As you work through the projects in this book, you will export and remove site definitions for completed projects so your site list remains manageable. You should get into this habit so you can quickly reinstate site definitions if necessary.

1. **With Kinetic Site open in the Files panel, choose Manage Sites at the bottom of the Directory menu.**

   You can access this menu even when the Files panel is in expanded mode.

2. **In the Manage Sites dialog box, choose the Kinetic Site name, and then click the Export button.**

   This function creates a ".ste" file that stores the Dreamweaver site definition settings.

   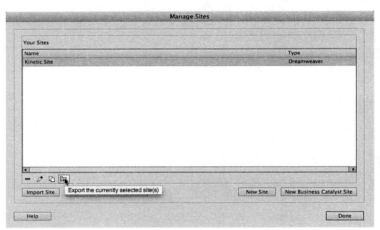

3. **Read the resulting warning. Choose the option you prefer, then click OK.**

   If you are sharing site files with other users, you might want to exclude login and password information in the site setup. Each user should have his or her own password and login information.

   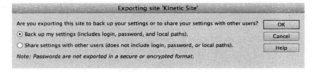

4. **Navigate to WIP>Kinetic and click Save.**

The Export Site dialog box defaults to the current site's root folder. You can restore the site settings by importing the site definition file from this location.

5. **In the Manage Sites dialog box, make sure Kinetic Site is selected and click the "–" button to remove the site from the list.**

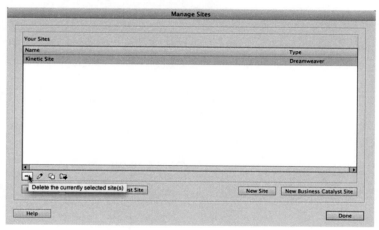

6. **Click Yes to the warning to confirm the removal of the Kinetic Site definition.**

Remember, you are not deleting the files from the site; you are simply removing the site definition from Dreamweaver.

7. **At the bottom of the Manage Sites dialog box, click Done.**

Project Review

1. The _____ extension identifies a Dreamweaver site definition file.

2. The _____ is the primary folder that contains all files and subfolders of a Web site.

3. The _____ is used to view and manage files that make up a site in Dreamweaver.

4. _____ is the process of improving a page's ranking in search engine results pages.

5. A(n) _____ is a path from one file to another, beginning from the current location and moving up or down through folder paths to the target image.

6. The notation _____ tells Dreamweaver to move up one folder from the current location.

7. The _____ shows the nested order of HTML tags to the currently selected object.

8. The _____ protocol is used to define an email link.

9. _____ is the process of hiding certain files in the site so they are not uploaded to the Web server.

10. The _____ pane of the Site Setup dialog box defines the settings you need to upload site files through Dreamweaver's Files panel.

1. Briefly explain why it is important to define a Dreamweaver site file.

2. Briefly explain the importance of creating a site flowchart.

3. Explain three different methods for creating a link to a page in the current site.

Portfolio Builder Project

Use what you learned in this project to complete the following freeform exercise.
Carefully read the art director and client comments, then create your own design to meet the needs of the project.
Use the space below to sketch ideas; when finished, write a brief explanation of your reasoning behind your final design.

Romana Place Town Homes is adding a photo tour to its Web site. The owner is fairly competent at building Web pages, but is having trouble finalizing the new site. Your job is to finish what he started in a professional, organized manner.

To complete this project, you should:

❑ Import the site files into Dreamweaver (from the **DW6_PB_Project1.zip** archive on the Student Files Web page).

❑ Analyze the content of the different pages. Create a flowchart to map the direction of links from one page to another in the site.

❑ Organize the site folder into a clear, understandable structure.

❑ Create the links from one page to another throughout the entire site.

When I started working with our site files I noticed that none of the links exist anymore. I might have worked from an earlier version of the site files, but I'm not sure. Can you fix this for me? Other than the navigation in the middle of the pages, there are a number of other places where links are necessary:

- Users should be able to navigate between the different property pages without going back to the main Properties page.

- There should be a link to our main information email address (info@romanaplace.atc) on every page.

- The original design company's name in the footer should link to its Web site.

Project Summary

This project focused on two of the foundational elements of Web site design — organizing files and creating links. A well-organized site structure includes links that make it easy for users to navigate throughout the entire site. Dreamweaver makes it easy to manage the files in a site — renaming and moving them while maintaining the links between pages within the site. You also learned a number of ways to create links, whether to other pages in the site, to an external URL, or to an email address. The skills you used in this project will be required to complete virtually any site you create in Dreamweaver.

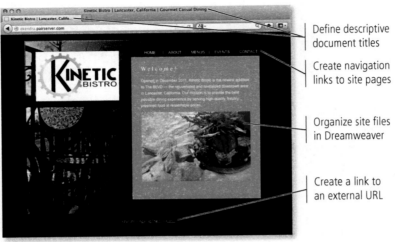

Define descriptive
document titles

Create navigation
links to site pages

Organize site files
in Dreamweaver

Create a link to
an external URL

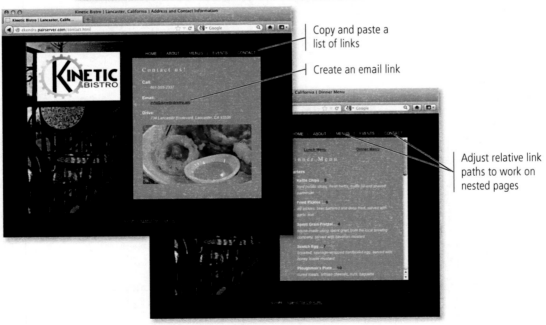

Copy and paste a
list of links

Create an email link

Adjust relative link
paths to work on
nested pages

Digital Book Chapter

Against The Clock Inc. (ATC) publishes textbooks for the graphic communications education market. In addition to application-specific books, the company also has a series of "companion" titles that discuss the concepts underlying the use of digital software — basic design principles, type, color, and so on. You were hired to build an "excerpt" booklet of the companion titles, which ATC will use on its corporate Web site. Visitors will be able to download and read the booklet free of charge. ATC believes this offering will increase sales of the full line of ATC titles. Your task is to structure the content appropriately using HTML code.

This project incorporates the following skills:

❏ Adding text from external sources

❏ Working in both Design view and Code view to add appropriate HTML tags semantically

❏ Organizing content with appropriate heading tags

❏ Properly formatting block quotes and citations

❏ Adding special characters that work in HTML code

❏ Creating lists and tables within text-based content

❏ Attaching a CSS file to new pages

client comments

We publish a series of books, designed as companion titles to our application-specific training books (which is why it's called *The Companion Series*). The companion titles cover general topics that are important to graphic designers — basic design principles, color, writing, typography, and Web design concepts — but don't quite fit into an application-specific book.

These books have been available for several years, but we haven't done any serious marketing of the titles. When we talk to people about *The Companion Series*, they ask, "Why haven't I heard about these books before?" We're hoping the sample chapters will help get the word out about these books and dramatically improve sales.

We want to be sure of two things: first, this Web page needs to be instantly recognizable as part of our existing site, with the same layout and formatting. Second, the page must include searchable text.

art director comments

The publisher sent the text she wants to offer on the site. When you have this much text on a Web page — which isn't uncommon — it's very important to format it with the proper structural tags. If you use Heading 2 because you think Heading 1 is too big, for example, you're causing problems for search engines and anyone with screen-reader software.

As you know, the client already has a corporate Web site. To create the new page, you can use the existing CSS file that defines the appearance of the various structural elements. Once you apply the correct structural tags to the text in the new pages, you can attach the existing CSS file. This will ensure that the existing format maps to the structural tags in your new page.

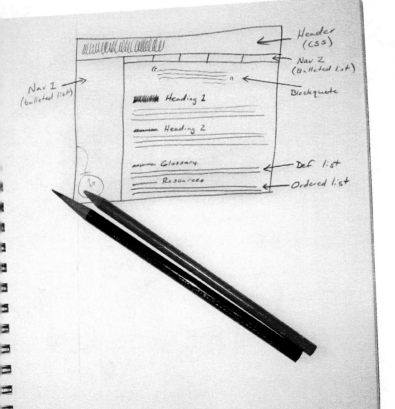

project objectives

To complete this project, you will:

- ❏ Paste text content from a text-only email
- ❏ Apply the appropriate heading and paragraph tags throughout the text
- ❏ Create block quotes and define quote citations
- ❏ Mark up abbreviations for improved usability and accessibility
- ❏ Use the correct HTML tags to show emphasis
- ❏ Add special HTML characters throughout the text
- ❏ Use a table to present well organized content
- ❏ Create ordered, unordered, and definition lists
- ❏ Attach an existing CSS file to the new page

Stage 1 Preparing the Workspace

In many Web design jobs, you need to create new HTML files in addition to working with existing files. The first step in any new project, however, is to define the Dreamweaver site so the application can accurately manage the various files and folders that make up the site. Once the site is defined, it's relatively easy to create as many new files as necessary to complete the job.

DEFINE THE ATC SITE

The procedure for defining the ATC site is essentially the same as it was for the Kinetic Site in Project 1: Bistro Site Organization.

1. Download **DW6_RF_Project2.zip** from the Student Files Web page.

2. **Expand the ZIP archive in your WIP folder (Macintosh) or copy the archive contents into your WIP folder (Windows).**

   This results in a folder named **ATC**, which contains the files you need for this project.

3. **In Dreamweaver, revert the workspace to the default Designer option.**

4. **From the Files panel, choose Manage Sites at the bottom of the Directory menu (or click the link if it is available).**

5. **In the Manage Sites dialog box, click the New Site button.**

6. **In the resulting Site Setup dialog box, type ATC in the Site Name field.**

7. **Click the Browse icon to the right of the Local Site Folder field, navigate to your WIP>ATC folder, and click Choose/Select.**

Note:

You can also choose Site>New Site to open the Site Setup dialog box.

8. **Click Save to accept the Site Setup definition.**

9. **In the Manage Sites dialog box, make sure the ATC site appears in the list of sites, and then click Done.**

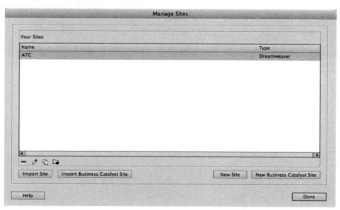

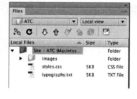

10. **Continue to the next exercise.**

CREATE A NEW HTML DOCUMENT

The content for the excerpt page was sent to you by the client in an email. You need to create a new HTML page and then move the supplied text into the page so you can apply the necessary HTML structure.

HTML was created as a coding language used to apply structure (paragraphs, headings, and lists) to online documents. By 1996, the modern methods of document markup had outgrown the inflexible HTML, so the extensibility concept from XML (eXtensible Markup Language, a language similar to HTML but primarily used for data instead of documents) was added to HTML 4.01, making it better suited to the evolving needs of Web designers.

Extensibility means that the language can incorporate structures that don't exist in HTML. For example, HTML supports six heading levels, from 1 to 6; the extensibility principle in XHTML allows designers to create heading level 7 if necessary.

1. **With the ATC site open in the Files panel, choose File>New.**

2. **In the New Document dialog box, choose Blank Page in the left pane. Choose HTML in the Page Type list, and choose <none> in the Layout list.**

   You can use this dialog box to create new files based on existing templates, or use the <none> option to create a new blank page.

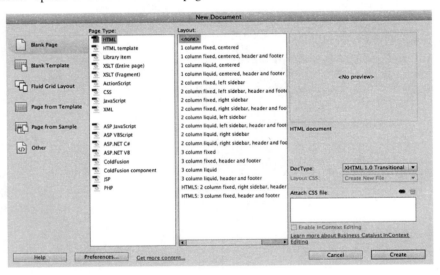

3. **Click Create to create the new blank file.**

4. **If only the Design pane is visible, click the Split button in the Document toolbar.**

   Even though the document appears to be blank in Design view, it contains some XHTML code in the background, which you can see in Code view.

Note:

HTML5 is the newest revision of the HTML standard. Although it is already in use by many developers and is supported (to varying degrees) by most current browsers, HTML 5 is still under development by the World Wide Web Consortium (W3C) and the Web Hypertext Application Technology Working Group (WHATWG). It is expected to become the working standard by 2014.

You will work with HTML 5 features in Project 6: Kayaking HTML5 Site.

Note:

We use the vertical split in our screen shots. Feel free to use whichever Split mode you prefer in your workspace.

5. Examine the code in the document window.

Content within the **head** element — between the opening **<head>** and closing **</head>** tags — is not visible to the user (except for the content enclosed in the **<title>** tags, which appears in the title bar of a browser, as the title of a bookmark, and as the text in search engine results). Visible Web page content is created within the body section, between the opening **<html><body>** and closing **</body></html>** tags.

Note:

The DTD (document type definition) tells the browser what version of HTML is being used.

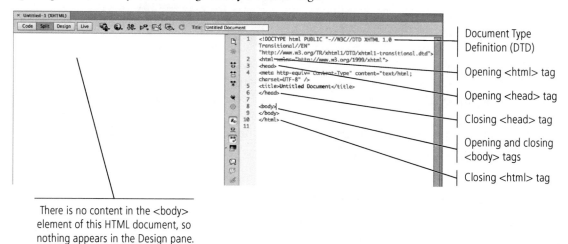

Document Type Definition (DTD)

Opening <html> tag

Opening <head> tag

Closing <head> tag

Opening and closing <body> tags

Closing <html> tag

There is no content in the <body> element of this HTML document, so nothing appears in the Design pane.

6. Select the words "Untitled Document" between the opening and closing <title> tags, then type `Against The Clock | Special Characters in Typography`.

7. Click the Refresh Design View button in the Document toolbar.

Any time you make changes in the Code pane, you have to refresh the Design view to reflect those changes.

Note:

You can also refresh the Design view by clicking the Refresh button in the Properties panel, or by pressing F5.

Refresh Design View button

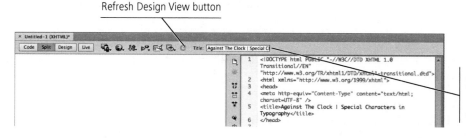

After refreshing the Design view, the new document title appears in the Title field of the Document toolbar.

8. Choose File>Save As. Navigate to your WIP>ATC folder (the root of the ATC site) as the target location and save the document as an HTML file named `typography.html`.

After the file is saved, it automatically appears in the Files panel.

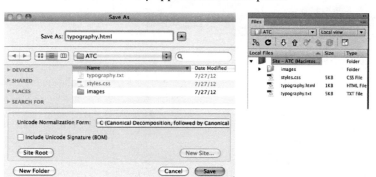

9. Continue to the next stage of the project.

Stage 2 Working with Semantic Markup

Many people have difficulty structuring documents — including word-processing files such as those created in Microsoft Word. Consider creating a heading; the user enters text, and then applies bold styling, increases the font size, and changes the text color. While this **local formatting** makes the text appear to be a heading, it is actually just a styled paragraph. Whether it is a Web page, a PDF file, or a word-processing document, a digital document should make use of available structures to enhance the document's usability. This is where HTML comes into play.

Properly structured HTML documents use tags semantically, to reinforce the meaning of the content, and provide a wide range of benefits to users: they are more accessible, they load quickly in a browser, they reduce bandwidth costs for high-traffic Web sites, they achieve high search-engine rankings, and they are easy to style. As a Web designer, you should take full advantage of these benefits by converting the unstructured or poorly structured documents you receive from clients into properly structured HTML documents. Dreamweaver makes it easy to do this, even if you don't understand a great deal of coding and code syntax.

PASTE TEXT CONTENT IN DESIGN VIEW

HTML is a coding language that defines the structure of the elements in a page; without HTML, the content between the opening and closing **<body>** tags would be completely unstructured. Web browsers depend on the structural markup of HTML to properly display a Web page, so headings stand out from regular text and paragraphs are separated from one another. Without structure, all text on a page would appear as a single, large block of text.

Clients often supply content as plain text without structural markup (paragraph returns do not qualify as structure). When humans read text that doesn't have structural markup, they are able to make logical inferences about the intended structure — for example, they can assume that a short block of text is a heading and a long block is a paragraph. Browsers, however, can't make assumptions; they require structure to correctly display content.

Although not all lines in a text document are paragraphs (some are headings and some are list items), marking each line as a paragraph provides a starting point that you can modify later.

> **Note:**
>
> *Web browsers (and Dreamweaver) ignore extra spaces between words and paragraph returns between lines of text. Properly displaying Web page text requires structural markup.*

1. **With typography.html (from the ATC site) open in Split view, click in the Design pane to place the insertion point.**

2. **Double-click typography.txt in the Files panel to open that file.**

   Text (.txt) files only appear in Code view because there is no "design".

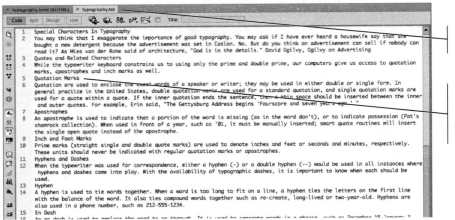

Each open file is accessible in a separate tab.

Although there are smaller and larger blocks of text, there are no codes or styles to separate headings from paragraphs.

3. Choose Edit>Select All, and then copy the selected content to the Clipboard.

Choose Edit>Copy or press Command/Control-C to copy the selected text.

4. Close typography.txt.

5. In typography.html, paste the copied text into the Design pane.

If you pasted the text into the Code pane, the line-break characters would not be included. You will use those bits of codes in the next few steps to apply the proper structure to the paragraphs of text.

Note:

Press Command/Control-A to select all content in an open file or document.

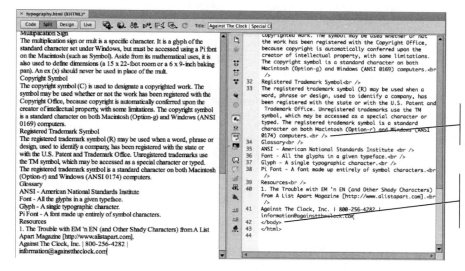

Each paragraph in the pasted text ends with the code for a line break (<br />).

Text pasted into the Design pane automatically appears between the opening and closing <body> tags in the Code pane.

6. Press Command/Control-A to select all the text in the Design pane, then choose Paragraph in the Format menu of the Properties panel.

An HTML paragraph is surrounded by opening **<p>** and closing **</p>** paragraph tags. Because the paragraphs of pasted text are separated by the code for a forced line break (**
**), the entire block of copy is treated as a single paragraph.

When you apply the paragraph structure to the selected text, the entire block is surrounded by a single set of paragraph tags in the Code pane.

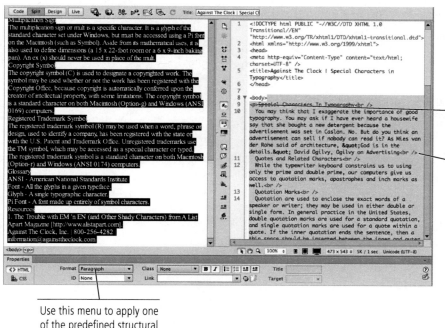

The entire selection is surrounded by a single paragraph tag.

The <br /> tags are not removed or replaced.

Use this menu to apply one of the predefined structural tags to the selected text.

7. **Choose Edit>Find and Replace.**

As you just saw, the line-break code only appears in the Code pane, so you want to search only the source code of the open document.

8. **Choose Open Documents in the Find In menu and choose Source Code in the Search menu.**

9. **In the Find field, type** `<br />`**. In the Replace field, type** `</p><p>`**.**

Do not press Return/Enter when typing in the Replace field, because the dialog box will prematurely run the Find and Replace operation.

Each line in the text currently ends with the line-break code (**
) when it should end with a closing paragraph tag (</p>**). Each line should also begin with the opening paragraph tag (**<p>**), where nothing currently exists.

Using the search and replace function, you can remove all of the line-break codes and place the necessary closing and opening paragraph tags in a single click.

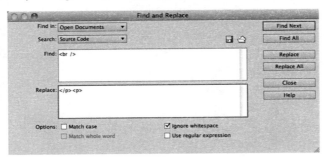

Note:

You cannot undo a Find and Replace in documents that are not open. When doing a Find and Replace that includes files that aren't currently open, you might want to back up the site's root folder outside of Dreamweaver before continuing.

10. **Click Replace All.**

Element Names, Tags, and Attributes

DREAMWEAVER FOUNDATIONS

The **element name** is the text that identifies the tag, such as meta, title, head, or body.

A **tag** consists of the element name surrounded by angle brackets, such as <html>, <head>, or <body>.

An **element** is the tag plus its containing content, such as the title element <title>Untitled Document</title>.

Container tags consist of an opening tag (<title>) and a closing tag (</title>). The closing tag is the same as the opening tag, with the addition of the initial forward slash. For example:

<title>"Weather Forecast"</title>

Empty tags (<meta />) do not have a separate closing tag. In an empty tag, the closing forward slash appears with the closing angle bracket of the tag. For example:

<img src="sun.gif" alt="sunny day" />

Attributes add properties to HTML elements. For example, the cite attribute of the <blockquote> tag allows you to identify the URL of a quotation. Attributes appear in the opening tag only; they consist of the attribute name and the attribute value (for example, attribute="attribute value").

When marking up a short quotation, you would type:

<q cite="http://www.useit.com/alertbox/9710a.html">
People rarely read Web pages word by word.</q>

In this example, the attribute name is cite and the attribute value is http://www.useit.com/alertbox/9710a.html.

Most attributes are optional, such as the cite attribute of the <blockquote> tag. Some attributes are required, such as the alt attribute of the <img> tag, which describes an image for visually impaired visitors. Some attributes are unique to certain elements, such as the src attribute of the <img> tag, which identifies the location (source) of the image.

In HTML, some attributes do not require an attribute value, such as the checked attribute that allows you to preselect a check box option. In XHTML, however, each attribute must have an attribute value (e.g., checked="checked").

Finally, attribute values in XHTML and HTML must be placed within quotes (e.g., width="130").

11. Review the Search panel, and then close the panel group.

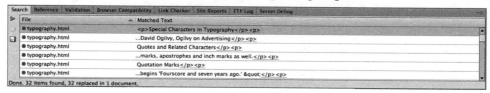

12. Refresh the Design view, then review the results in both panes of the document window.

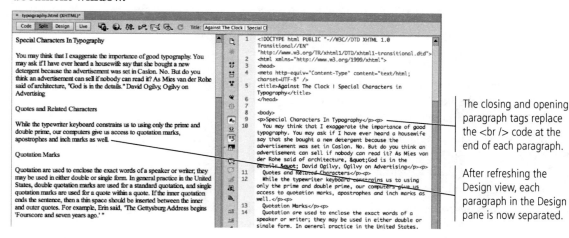

The closing and opening paragraph tags replace the <br /> code at the end of each paragraph.

After refreshing the Design view, each paragraph in the Design pane is now separated.

13. Click the Format Source Code button to the left of the Code pane and choose Apply Source Formatting from the menu.

If you split your screen horizontally, you might not be able to see all of the Code pane buttons (depending on the size of your screen). In that case, you have to click the Show More button to access the Format Source Code button.

This command cleans up the code, moving the opening **<p>** tags to the beginning of each line of copy. Nothing changes in the Design pane when the tags are moved to the appropriate lines.

Format Source Code button

Show More button

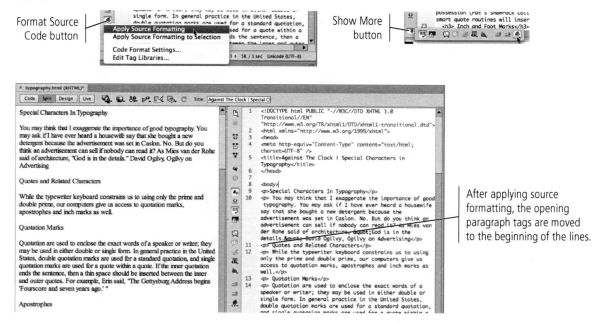

After applying source formatting, the opening paragraph tags are moved to the beginning of the lines.

14. Save the file and continue to the next exercise.

Headings help readers find the information they need. For visual users, a heading is effective as long as it looks like a heading. This is not the case for visually impaired users who use screen-reading software; screen-reading software and some browsers enable users to skip forward and backward through headings. Also, when reviewing the content of a page and its relevance to a particular topic, search engine software uses headings and heading levels (among other criteria) to make evaluations. For these reasons, it is important to use properly structured headings rather than styled paragraphs.

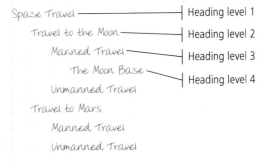

There are six predefined heading levels, **<h1>**, **<h2>**, **<h3>**, and so on to **<h6>**. Heading level 1 is the largest and most important; it should be used only once per page to describe the purpose or title of the Web page. The rest of the headings can be used multiple times, but they should be used in a branch-like pattern or hierarchy.

Many new Web designers complain that heading level 1 appears too large, so they apply heading level 2 or 3 instead. This is a mistake. In a later project, you will learn to use cascading style sheets (CSS) to define the appearance of different elements on a Web page — including different levels of headings.

The special characters described in the text in this project are divided into related groups and subgroups. Your task is to determine which heading level is appropriate for each section. In professional situations, some client-supplied copy will be well-written and well-structured, enabling you to quickly determine appropriate heading levels (called **editorial hierarchy** or **editorial priority**). Other copy will be poorly structured and difficult to decipher; in such a case, you will need to contact the author for clarification or make a best-guess assessment yourself.

Note:

While you should always use properly structured headings, don't overuse them. Some Web pages mark all content as heading level 1, but the various elements are styled differently using CSS. Known as "spamdexing," this method attempts to fool a search engine into ranking the page higher than others with similar content — a technique that generally results in the page being banned from search engines.

1. **With typography.html (from your ATC site) open in Split view, click in the Design pane to place the insertion point in the first paragraph.**

   You should be working with the paragraph "Special Characters In Typography".

2. **In the Properties panel, open the Format menu and choose Heading 1.**

   In the Code pane, the opening and closing **<p>** tags automatically change to the **<h1>** tags that identify the paragraph as heading level 1.

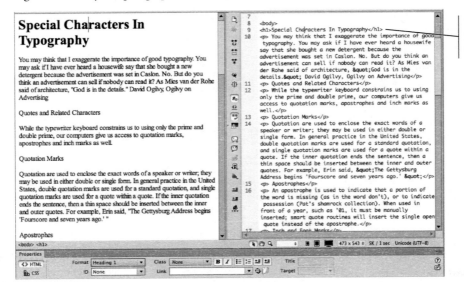

The <p> tags are replaced by the appropriate heading tags (<h1> and </h1>).

Note:

If you use a mouse with a scroll wheel, move the mouse cursor away from the Format menu before you try to scroll through the document window. If the cursor is over the Formatting menu, scrolling with the mouse wheel changes the menu selection.

3. **Move the insertion point to the "Quotes and Related Characters" paragraph and use the Properties panel Format menu to apply the Heading 2 tag.**

After choosing a format in the Properties panel, the Code pane shows that the **<p>** and **</p>** tags have been replaced with **<h2>** and **</h2>** tags, respectively.

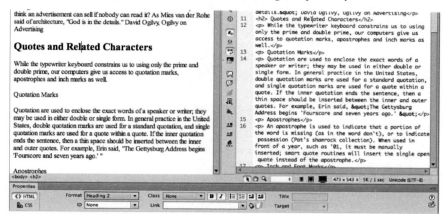

Note:

When you're working in Design view, you can apply paragraph structure and heading levels by choosing from the Format>Paragraph Format menu.

4. **Using the same technique from Step 3, format "Quotation Marks", "Apostrophes", and "Inch and Foot Marks" as Heading 3.**

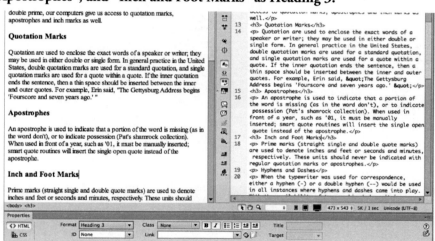

Note:

You can also use keyboard shortcuts to apply common tags:

Paragraph
Command/Control-Shift-p

Heading 1
Command/Control-1

Heading 2
Command/Control-2

Heading 3
Command/Control-3

Heading 4
Command/Control-4

Heading 5
Command/Control-5

Heading 6
Command/Control-6

5. **Apply heading levels to the rest of the document as follows:**

Line Number in the Code pane	Content	Heading Level
19	Hyphens and Dashes	2
21	Hyphen	3
23	En Dash	3
25	Em Dash	3
27	Special Characters	2
28	Multiplication Sign	3
30	Copyright Symbol	3
32	Registered Trademark Symbol	3
34	Glossary	2
39	Resources	2

Note:

The organized content is easier to understand and would enable users (sighted or otherwise) to scan headings and determine whether the page content meets their needs.

6. **Save the file and continue to the next exercise.**

FORMAT A BLOCK QUOTE AND CITATION

The blockquote element formats a quotation as a block of text that is indented from the left and right margins, with extra white space above and below it. The blockquote element requires at least one paragraph element to be nested within it, such as **<blockquote><p>quotation goes here</p></blockquote>**.

The blockquote element has an optional cite attribute designed to identify the URL of the quote source. The URL is not clickable or visible (although in Firefox, you can view the cite URL via the properties of a blockquote or q element).

1. With **typography.html** open in Split view, click in the paragraph immediately below the heading 1 text (at the top of the page).

2. Click the **Blockquote button** in the Properties panel to apply the blockquote element to the selected paragraph.

   In the Design pane, the blockquote has been indented from the left and right margins. In the Tag Selector, the **<p>** tag appears to the right of the **<blockquote>** tag, indicating that the **<p>** tag has been nested within a **<blockquote>** tag. In the Code pane, you can see the opening and closing blockquote tags before and after the paragraph tags.

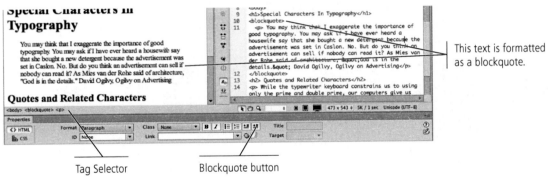

This text is formatted as a blockquote.

Tag Selector   Blockquote button

3. **Select "David Ogilvy, Ogilvy on Advertising" at the end of the block quote.**

4. **Control/right-click the selected text and choose Wrap Tag from the contextual menu.**

   The Wrap Tag command opens the Quick Tag Editor, which allows you to temporarily work with code, while still working in Design view.

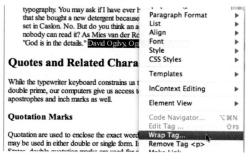

Note:

You can also open the Quick Tag Editor by choosing Modify>Quick Tag Editor or pressing Command/Control-T.

5. **Type ci.**

   As you type the code in the Quick Tag Editor, Dreamweaver provides Code Hints (a list of HTML tags) to assist you. As you type, the Code Hint list scrolls to the first HTML tag beginning with the letter "ci" — cite, which is the tag you want.

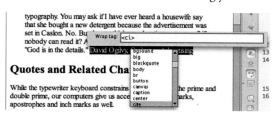

Note:

If the source of a quotation is a URL, you can add the URL as the cite attribute of either the blockquote or q element.

6. **Press Return/Enter to choose cite from the list of tags.**

   When a Code Hint menu is visible, pressing Return/Enter applies the item that is highlighted in the list.

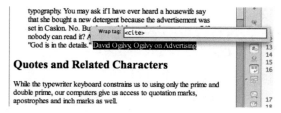

7. **Press Return/Enter again to apply the cite tag to the selected text.**

   The default appearance of the cite element text is italic. As you can see in the Code pane, using the Quick Tag Editor automatically adds the appropriate opening and closing tags.

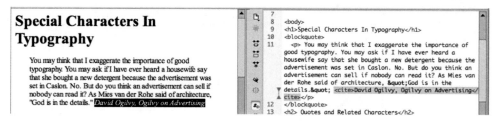

8. **Save your changes and continue to the next exercise.**

Controlling Code Hints

Code hints display by default when you type code in Dreamweaver. You can use the Code Hints pane of the Preferences dialog box to control which code hints display and how.

The Close Tags options can be used to close tags automatically:

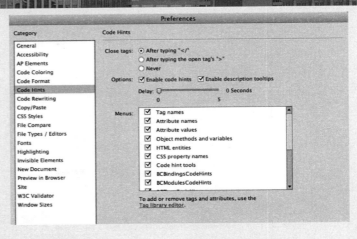

- If you select After Typing "</", the nearest open tag closes when you type the forward slash after the opening carat. This option is selected by default.

- If you select After Typing the Open Tag's ">", Dreamweaver automatically closes a tag as soon as it opens.

- Select Never if you don't want tags to close automatically.

You can disable code hints by deselecting the Enable Code Hints check box. The Delay bar determines how soon code hints display when you open a tag. The Menus options list code categories for which hints can display.

FORMAT AN INLINE QUOTE

The q element is used for marking quotations that are part of a sentence or paragraph, rather than separate paragraphs. (Like the blockquote element, you can also define an optional cite attribute for q element text.)

The current versions of Firefox, Safari, Opera, Chrome, and Internet Explorer automatically place quotation marks around q element text, eliminating the need to insert them as characters in the page content.

In this exercise you will use the Tag Chooser to insert the **<q>** tag. The Tag Chooser provides access for all elements — including the less common ones, for which there are no one-click buttons in the Properties panel or Insert panel.

1. **With typography.html open in Split view, in the Design pane, select the words "God is in the details." (including the period and the quotation marks) at the end of the block quote.**

2. **With the Insert panel in Common mode, click the Tag Chooser button.**

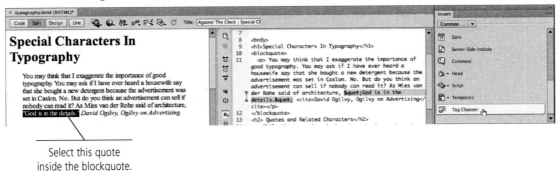

Select this quote inside the blockquote.

3. **In the resulting Tag Chooser dialog box, expand the HTML Tags folder and choose the Formatting and Layout set.**

In the Tag Chooser dialog box, you can select a specific category of tags in the left pane, and then choose a specific tag from the selected category in the right pane.

4. In the right side of the dialog box, scroll to find the q element and select it in the list of available tags.

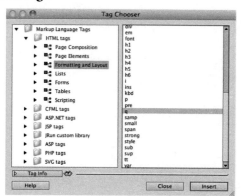

Note:

You can also open the Tag Chooser by choosing Insert>Tag.

5. Click Insert. In the resulting Tag Editor dialog box, click the arrow to the left of Tag Info to expand the dialog box.

The Tag Editor automatically presents additional options related to the selected tag. For the q tag, you can define the cite attribute (other options are also available by clicking a different category in the left pane). The browse button to the right of the Cite field allows you to define a page from your current site as the source of the quotation. If the source of your quotation is a page from another site, you must type the URL into the Cite field. (If the source of your quotation is not a URL, enter nothing in the Cite field.)

In the Tag Editor dialog box, you can click the Tag Info arrow to show usage information about the selected tag.

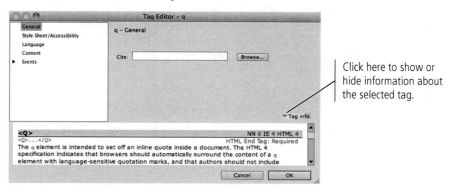

Click here to show or hide information about the selected tag.

6. Click OK to add the tag to the selected text, and then click Close to close the Tag Chooser dialog box.

Clicking OK in the Tag Editor dialog box returns you to the Tag Chooser. Clicking Close in the Tag Chooser dialog box returns you to the document window; the q tag is added to the selected text, which you can see in the Code view:

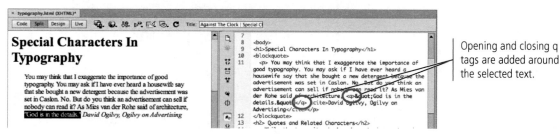

Opening and closing q tags are added around the selected text.

7. **Save the file, then preview the page in one or more browsers, saving when prompted.**

   Safari, Opera, and Chrome apply straight quotes to the q element, while Firefox and Internet Explorer apply curly quotes.

Note:

Older versions of Internet Explorer (7 or earlier) do not add the quotation marks to the tagged text.

8. **Close the browser window and return to Dreamweaver.**

9. **In the Design pane, delete the quote characters from around the "God is in the details." text.**

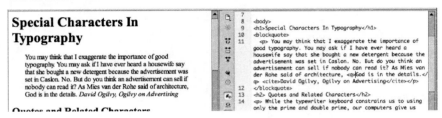

10. **Repeat this process to add the q element tags around the quote in the paragraph after the "Quotation Marks" level 3 heading.**

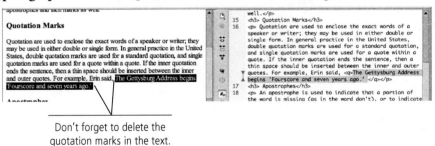

Don't forget to delete the quotation marks in the text.

11. **Save the file and continue to the next exercise.**

MARK UP ABBREVIATIONS IN CODE VIEW

Both abbreviations and acronyms are shortened forms of words or phrases. If you spell out the short form (such as HTML), it is an abbreviation. If you pronounce it like a word (such as NATO), it is an acronym. Some abbreviations are read both ways; SQL, for example, is sometimes spelled out and sometimes spoken as "sequel."

HTML 4 includes two separate elements for these words — the **abbr** element identifies an abbreviation, and the **acronym** element identifies an acronym — but the acronym element has been deprecated (removed) in HTML5, so you should get into the habit of using the abbr element for both types of words.

The title attribute plays a useful role in the **abbr** element. Any text you insert into the title attribute — for example, the full text of the abbreviation or acronym — appears as a tool tip when you hover the mouse over the titled element. People who use screen-reader software also benefit from the title attribute because the software can be set up to read the title text in place of the abbreviation.

In this exercise, you will type directly in the Code pane, using Dreamweaver's code hints to add the necessary tags and attributes.

Note:

Except for the specific tag being used, the basic process for marking up acronyms is the same as for marking up abbreviations. In both cases, the title attribute is used for the long form of the word or phrase.

1. **With typography.html open in Split view, select "ANSI" (in the Design pane) in the paragraph following the Copyright Symbol heading.**

   The text selected in the Design pane is also selected in the Code pane. This is a useful way to locate specific text in code (or vice versa).

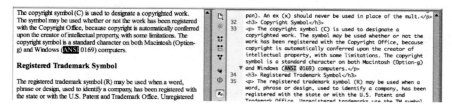

2. **Click in the Code pane to make it the active pane.**

   When working in either pane of Split view, you have to click a pane to bring it into focus (make it active) before you can make changes there.

   When you click the Code pane to bring it into focus, the highlighted text is no longer highlighted.

3. **Place the insertion point before the previously highlighted text, and then type <ab.**

   The abbr tag is selected in the code hint list.

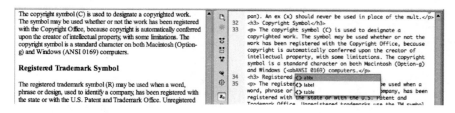

4. **Press Return/Enter to accept abbr.**

   By pressing Return/Enter, you select the **<abbr>** tag. Once you add the tag, the insertion point flashes after the tag, where you can enter attributes of the new tag.

Code View Options

Code View options, which can be toggled on or off in the View menu, determine how code displays.

- Word Wrap ensures that code does not extend beyond the available width of the window. This option only affects the appearance of code in the Code pane; it does not insert actual line breaks in the code or content.

- Line Numbers shows numbers to the left of each line.

- Hidden Characters displays characters such as line-break markers, which would not otherwise display.

- Highlight Invalid Code displays incorrect code (such as a tag that has not been closed) in yellow.

- Syntax Coloring displays the code in defined colors.

- Auto Indent indents every new line of code to the same position as the previous line. A new line is inserted each time you press Return/Enter.

- Syntax Error Alerts in Info Bar displays a yellow message bar at the top of the document window if there is a problem in your code.

Code Coloring Preferences

By default, HTML tags appear in blue. You can use the Code Coloring pane of the Preferences dialog box to change the color of specific tags (or other pieces of code).

The Document Type window lists the various types of code that Dreamweaver supports. (The code type in the active document is selected by default.) If you click the Edit Coloring Scheme button, a secondary dialog box displays a list of all possible parts of the selected code type; you can change the text and background color of any individual part.

Code Format Preferences

Code Format preferences allow you to specify rules that determine how the code is structured; the sole purpose of these rules is to make it easier for you to read code.

- **Indent With** indents the text within each tag so you can easily identify each block of code. You can indent by character spaces or by tabs.

- **Tab Size** specifies the number of spaces that each tab character contains. For example, if you type "4" in this box, each time you press the Tab key, four space characters are inserted.

- **Line Break Type** ensures the line breaks inserted by Dreamweaver are compatible with the operating system of the remote server on which your site will be hosted.

- **Default Tag Case** changes the case of tags, and **Default Attribute Case** changes the case of attributes. We highly recommend lowercase tags and attributes because XHTML does not support uppercase tags. (HTML supports both cases.)

- **Override Case of Tags** and **Override Case of Attributes** change the case of tags and attributes to the options selected in this pane, even if a different case is defined in Tag Libraries.

- The **TD Tag** option prevents a line break or white space from being inserted directly after a <td> (table cell) tag or directly before a </td> tag. Line breaks and white spaces within the tag cause problems in older browsers.

- The **CSS** button allows you to change code formatting definitions in a cascading style sheet file.

- The **Tag Libraries** button opens a dialog box where you can define formatting options such as line breaks and indents for each tag and its associated attributes.

5. Press the Spacebar, and then type t.

Inserting a space after the abbr element name within the tag prompts Dreamweaver to open code hints and present a list of valid attributes for the current tag.

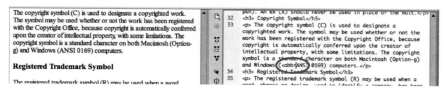

6. Press Return/Enter to accept the title attribute.

When you select the attribute in the code hint list, Dreamweaver follows the attribute with =" " and places the insertion point between the two quotation marks, so you can immediately type a value for the attribute.

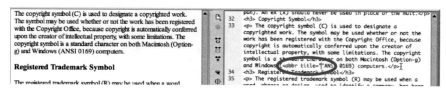

7. Type American National Standards Institute between the quotation marks.

Attribute values must always be surrounded by quotation marks.

8. Move the insertion point to the right of the closing quotation mark and type > to close the tag.

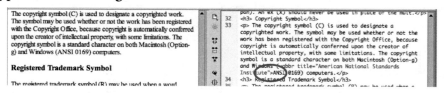

9. Move the insertion point to the right of the text "ANSI," then type </.

In opening tags, the HTML element name is specified between opening and closing angle brackets. In closing tags, the forward slash precedes the element name.

This step shows you another of Dreamweaver's code assistance functions, which is to automatically close the nearest unclosed tag when you type "</". In this case, Dreamweaver closes the abbr tag for you.

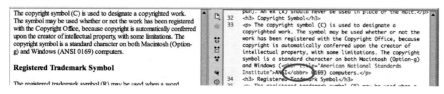

10. **Select all of the code related to the ANSI abbreviation, then choose Edit>Copy to copy the highlighted code to the Clipboard.**

11. **Highlight the instance of "ANSI" near the end of line 35, and choose Edit>Paste to replace the highlighted text with the copied code (including the abbr tags and title attribute).**

Note:

You can also add an abbreviation tag — and a number of other options — using the Insert>HTML>Text Objects submenu.

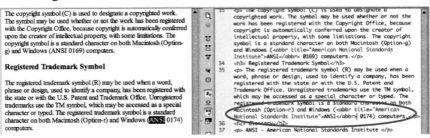

12. **Save the file and then preview the page in one or more browsers. Look for any differences in appearance between abbr elements and regular paragraph text.**

    The Firefox and Opera browsers display a dotted line under elements with a defined title attribute. In Internet Explorer, Chrome, and Safari, you will see no obvious difference in the tagged abbreviation. All browsers display title text as a tool tip when the mouse hovers over the element text.

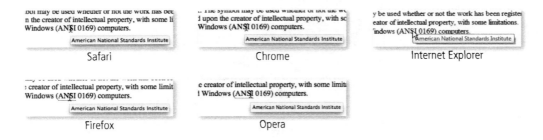

Safari   Chrome   Internet Explorer

Firefox   Opera

13. **Close the browser window(s) and return to Dreamweaver. Continue to the next exercise.**

 FORMAT WITH STRONG AND EM ELEMENTS

Two HTML elements can be used to show emphasis — em and strong. The em element is used when light emphasis is needed, such as "you should go to your brother's game to support him." For stronger emphasis, use the strong element, such as "Don't touch the stove top, it is hot!"

Text marked up with the em element appears in italics; text marked up with the strong element appears in bold. Visually, it is the same as using the **<i>** and **<b>** tags (italic and bold, respectively), but the i and b elements are presentational — not structural — HTML. Screen-reader software changes the tone of voice when it finds em and strong element text, but not when it finds i and b element text.

By default, Dreamweaver inserts a strong or em element when you apply bold or italic styling (respectively) through format menus or other means. Don't assume, however, that there is a direct relationship between b and strong elements and i and em elements. Remember: b and i elements are for presentational purposes only, and strong and em elements are for structural purposes.

1. With **typography.html** open, open the Preferences dialog box (Dreamweaver menu on Macintosh or Edit menu on Windows) and show the General category.

2. In the Editing Options group, make sure the "Use <strong> and <em>" option is checked.

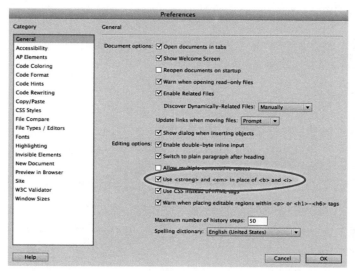

Note:

As you work through this book, remember that preferences are accessed in the Dreamweaver menu on Macintosh and the Edit menu on Windows.

3. Click OK to close the Preferences dialog box.

4. In the Design pane, scroll to the paragraph following the En Dash heading and select "not" in the fourth sentence.

5. Click the Bold button in the Properties panel.

There are no special attributes for the strong and em elements, so you can insert these elements with a single click.

6. With the text still selected, examine the Tag Selector.

The selected text is formatted with the **<strong>** tag, not the **<b>** tag.

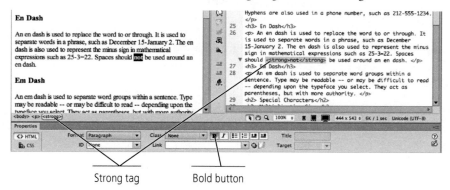

Strong tag   Bold button

7. In the paragraph after the Em Dash heading, select "more authority" in the third sentence and click the Italic button in the Properties panel.

The selected text is now formatted with the **<em>** tag.

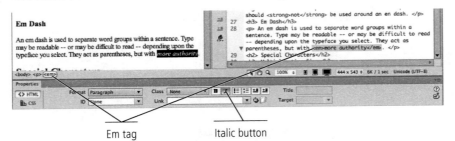

Em tag   Italic button

Note:

You can also click the Bold or Strong buttons in the Text Insert panel to apply the strong tags to selected text.

Click the Emphasis or Italic buttons in the Text Insert panel to apply the em tags to selected text.

8. Save your changes and continue to the next stage of the project.

Stage 3   Working with Special Characters

HTML character entities are characters not directly available from your keyboard. HTML character entities can be specified in code either by name or by number. Using either method, the code begins with an ampersand (&) and ends with a semicolon (;).

- A named character entity uses a specific name for that character such as "©" for the © symbol and "™" for the ™ symbol. Some character names (such as "™") are not supported by all browsers; visitors using these browsers would see "™" in their browser window instead of the ™ symbol.

- Alternatively, you can specify a character using its numeric code, such as "¢" for ¢. (When using the numeric code, be sure to insert a "#" between the ampersand and the number.) All browsers support the numeric codes.

INSERT SPECIAL CHARACTERS

In most cases, you don't need to worry about inserting the codes (named or numbered) for HTML character entities because you can select some of the most common characters from a list in the Text Insert panel; Dreamweaver inserts the code for you.

1. **With typography.html open in Split view, make the Design pane active. Select the hyphen between "December 15" and "January 2" in the paragraph below the En Dash heading.**

2. **With the Insert panel in Text mode, click the arrow button to the right of the Characters button icon.**

   Your button icon might appear different than the one shown in our screen shot because the button reflects the last character inserted from this list. Simply clicking the button (label or icon) — not the arrow — inserts whatever character appears on the button.

Use the menu to show Text options in the Insert panel.

Click the arrow to open the Characters menu.

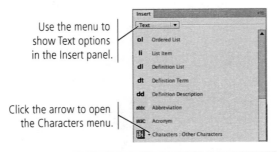

3. Choose En Dash from the pop-up menu.

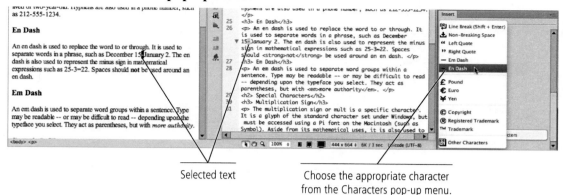

Selected text

Choose the appropriate character
from the Characters pop-up menu.

4. Select the hyphen between "25" and "3" in the same paragraph.

En dashes are as wide as half an em dash. As you might have read in the text of this project page, en dashes are used to replace the word "to" or "through" or in mathematical expressions of subtraction.

Note:

These same characters can be inserted using the Insert>HTML>Special Characters menu.

5. In the Text Insert panel, click the Characters:En Dash button.

Because the button defaults to the last-used character, you can simply click the button to apply another en dash.

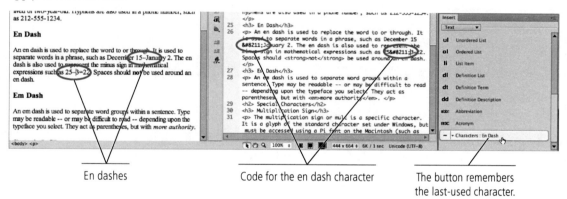

En dashes

Code for the en dash character

The button remembers the last-used character.

6. Use the same techniques from Steps 2–5 to replace both sets of double hyphens with em dashes in the paragraph after the Em Dash heading.

The em dash is as wide as the defined type size. This dash can be used to separate part of a sentence — an aside — from the rest of a sentence. Many authors do not know how to insert an em dash; instead, they use a regular hyphen or a pair of hyphens. As there are strict grammatical rules about when to use a hyphen, an en dash, and an em dash, you should consult a professional copy editor for the proper application of these characters.

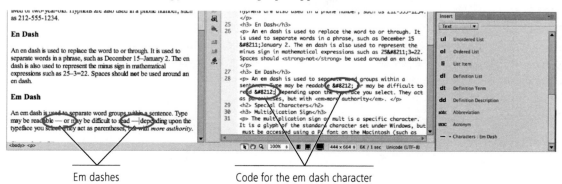

Em dashes

Code for the em dash character

7. **Select the capital C in the first line after the Copyright Symbol heading. Use the Characters menu in the Text Insert panel to replace the letter with the Copyright character.**

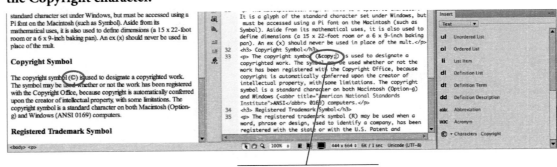

Code for the copyright character

8. **Select the capital R in the first line after the Registered Trademark Symbol heading. Use the Characters menu to replace the selected letter with the Registered Trademark character.**

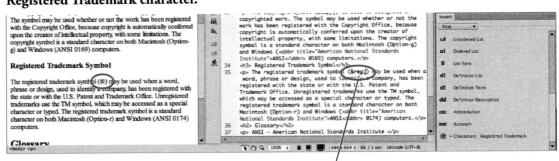

Code for the registered trademark character

9. **Select the capital TM in the same paragraph and use the Characters menu to replace the selected letters with the Trademark character.**

In the Code pane, you can see that Dreamweaver creates this character using the numeric code because some browsers do not support the name for this character.

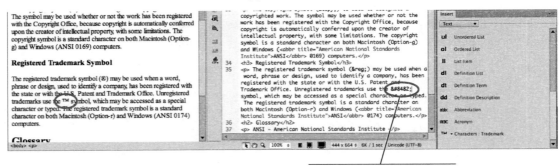

Code for the trademark character

10. **Save the changes to typography.html and continue to the next exercise.**

CREATE A TABLE OF QUOTE CHARACTERS

Common HTML tables that are used to present data or text information consist of only three components: a caption, table header cells, and table data cells.

A caption can be used to briefly describe the contents or purpose of a table. It generally appears at the top of the table. (You can use CSS to move the caption to another position, but many browsers offer poor support for these properties.)

Table data cells make up the majority of the cells in a table. The **<td>** tag is used to mark up the table data cells.

Table header cells, using the **<th>** tag, appear at the top or left (or both) of the table; they label the contents in the regular table cells. Think about a table of the days of the week across the top and the hours of the day down the left side. If the cell at the intersection of the second row and second column contained the text "Staff Meeting," you would know that the staff meeting was scheduled for Tuesday at 10:00 a.m.

The information in table header cells is very important for people using screen-reader software. For example, when they reach the Staff Meeting cell, they can prompt the software to read the headers associated with the cell. The screen-reader would report "Tuesday" and "10:00 a.m." Without proper cell markup, the software would not be able to report the day and time of the meeting.

Note:

When tables are used for layout components of a Web page, they can become very complicated in structure, with tables within table cells (nested tables) and cells that have been merged with other cells. Tables should only be used to present tabular data.

1. With **typography.html** open in Design view, switch the Insert panel to show the Layout options.

2. Place the insertion point at the end of the paragraph after the Inch and Foot Marks heading. Press Return/Enter to create a new empty paragraph.

3. Click the Table button in the Layout Insert panel.

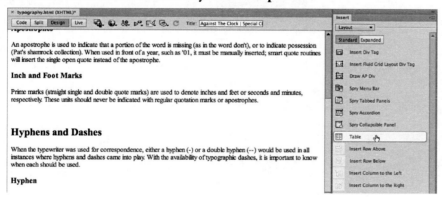

4. In the Table dialog box:

   • Set both the number of rows and number of columns to **2**.

   • Delete any values in the Table Width, Border Thickness, Cell Padding, and Cell Spacing fields.

   • Choose the Top Header option.

   • Type **Quotation Characters** in the Caption field.

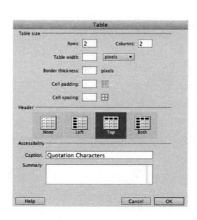

   Many Dreamweaver dialog boxes remember the last-used settings. If you or someone else used the Table dialog box before now, some of these fields might default to other values.

5. **Click OK to create the table.**

6. **Click the Expanded button in the Layout Insert panel.**

   When empty, the four table cells are small and difficult to work with. The Expanded Tables mode enlarges the cells, making them much easier to work with. This is a temporary change that Dreamweaver provides to help designers work with empty table cells; the expanded appearance does not appear in the Web page.

7. **Read the warning message and click OK.**

   This message only appears the first time you choose Expanded Tables mode after launching the application; if you quit and restart Dreamweaver, this message will appear again the first time you choose Expanded Tables mode. If you are sharing your computer with other users, someone might have checked the Don't Show Me This Message Again option; in that case, you might not see the warning shown here.

Note:

Expanded Tables mode is really only necessary when a table is completely empty; once content has been entered in at least one cell per column, you can exit Expanded Tables mode.

8. **Examine the page while Expanded Tables mode is active.**

   Notice the enlarged cells in the table and the blue Exit link at the top of the document window. You can click that link to exit or disable Expanded Tables mode.

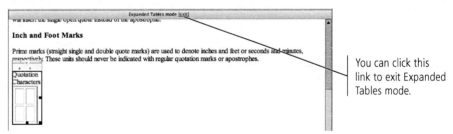

   You can click this link to exit Expanded Tables mode.

9. **Click in the top-left table cell to place the insertion point, and then type Character Description. Press Tab to move the insertion point into the top-right cell, and type Character.**

   As you type the first heading (Character Description), it will wrap to two lines. When you move the insertion point to the top-right cell, the table adjusts to fit the entire first heading on a single line.

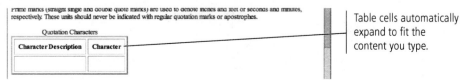

   Table cells automatically expand to fit the content you type.

10. Switch to the Split view and review the code for the table you just created.

- All content that makes up the table is enclosed in opening and closing **<table>** tags.

- The caption that you defined when you created the table is enclosed in opening and closing **<caption>** tags.

- Each row in the table is enclosed in opening and closing **<tr>** tags.

- Each header cell is identified with opening and closing **<th>** tags. The **scope="col"** attribute identifies that column as information with the heading defined in the related cell.

- Each regular cell in the table is enclosed in opening and closing **<td>** tags. As you can see, each table row includes two <td> tags — one for each column in the row.

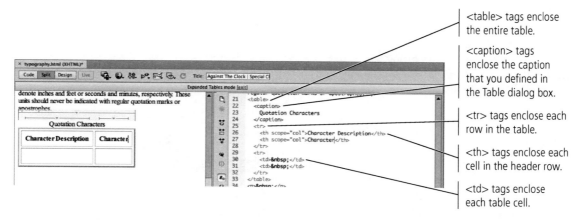

<table> tags enclose the entire table.

<caption> tags enclose the caption that you defined in the Table dialog box.

<tr> tags enclose each row in the table.

<th> tags enclose each cell in the header row.

<td> tags enclose each table cell.

11. Save the file and continue to the next exercise.

Use the Insert Other Character Dialog Box

Although a few special characters are available directly in the Characters menu of the Text Insert panel, there are many more characters available than those in the list. A number of common special characters are available in the Insert Other Character dialog box, which is accessed at the bottom of the Characters menu. Still others (many, in fact) are only available by typing the necessary code in the Code pane.

1. With typography.html open, click in the lower-left empty cell of the table that you created in the previous exercise. Type Double Curly Quotes.

2. Press Tab to move to the right cell, and then choose Left Quote from the Characters menu in the Text Insert panel.

3. Press Space, and then choose Right Quote from the Text Insert panel Characters menu.

4. **Press Tab to insert a new table row.**

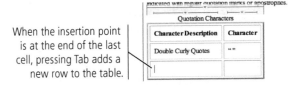

When the insertion point is at the end of the last cell, pressing Tab adds a new row to the table.

5. **In the left cell, type Single Curly Quotes, then press Tab to move the insertion point into the right cell.**

6. **Using the Text Insert panel, open the Characters menu and choose Other Characters from the bottom of the list.**

You can use the Other Characters option to find special characters that aren't included in the default list. This option opens the Insert Other Character dialog box, where you can select a specific character, or type the appropriate code in the field at the top of the dialog box.

7. **In the resulting dialog box, click the Single Left Curly Quote character and then click OK to insert that character into the active table cell.**

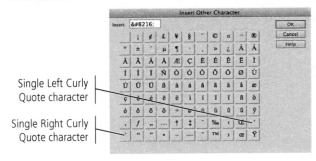

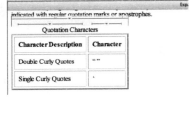

Single Left Curly Quote character

Single Right Curly Quote character

8. **With the insertion point after the quote, press Space and then click the Characters:Other Characters button to reopen the dialog box.**

In this case, the button remembers the last-used option — opening the dialog box — but not the last-used character. Clicking the button opens the Insert Other Character dialog box.

9. **Click the Single Right Curly Quote character and then click OK to insert that character into the table cell.**

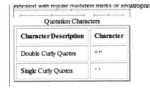

10. **Press Tab to insert another table row. Type** Double Prime (Inches or Seconds) **in the left cell of the new row.**

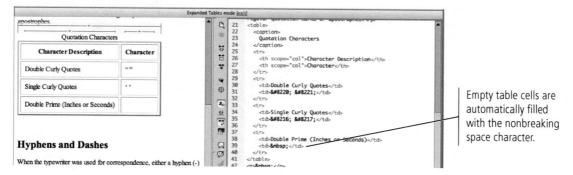

Empty table cells are automatically filled with the nonbreaking space character.

11. **Move the insertion point to the right cell of the new row. Click the Code pane to make it active and type** ″ **(with a capital P) and then refresh the Design view.**

12. **Click in the Design pane to bring it into focus. Place the insertion point after the prime character, then press Tab to insert another table row.**

13. **Type** Single Prime (Feet or Minutes) **in the left column, then move the insertion point to the right cell.**

14. **Click the Code pane to make it active and type** ′ **(with a lowercase p) and then refresh the Design view.**

   The single- and double-prime codes are almost the same; capitalization makes the difference between the two characters.

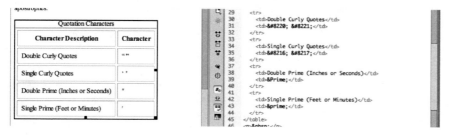

15. **Click the link at the top of the document window to exit Expanded Tables mode.**

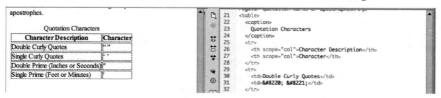

16. **Save the file and continue to the next exercise.**

When HTML tables were first conceived, they were intended to allow Web content developers to more clearly present tabular text — primarily charts of data — in a Web page. It wasn't long, however, before visually oriented designers figured out how to use HTML tables to combine graphic elements on a Web page just as they assemble graphics on the printed page. As a result, a significant number of Web pages were (and still are) designed with tables.

HTML tables were never intended as a graphic design tool. The overall page code that results from this method is extremely long and complex, which results in longer download times (still a significant problem for many users). The complexity of table-based page code also makes it more time consuming to make changes.

Another problem with table-based design is that the resulting code mixes content with purely presentational elements. This makes it very difficult (if not impossible) for accessibility software and search engines to separate the content from the structure, which means that table-based pages might not rank as high as a similar page designed without tables.

To solve the problems with table-based design, cascading style sheets (CSS) provide a way to separate content from presentation. CSS-based layout, which you will see in action at the end of this project, is the recommended method of standards organizations such as the World Wide Web Consortium (www.w3c.org). HTML tables should only be used to present tables of data.

Tables in Design View

When you do work with HTML tables, you have a number of options in the Properties panel, depending on whether the entire table or only specific cells are selected. Keep in mind that all table properties are better defined using CSS, which is why we are not explaining all of these options here.

(Beginning in Project 4: Yosemite CSS Layout, you will work extensively with CSS to control the appearance of individual page elements, as well as the entire page.)

If a table or column has a defined width, the number appears to the left of the column or table menu.

Use these menus to access column-specific options.

Use this menu to access table-specific options.

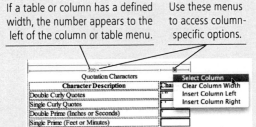

When specific cells are selected, you can change properties of the selected cells.

When the entire table is selected, you can change properties of the overall table.

The Modify>Table Menu

- **Merge Cells** combines selected adjacent cells so they are treated as a single cell.
- **Split Cell** creates multiple cells in a single cell, without affecting other cells in the same row or column.
- **Insert Row** adds a row above the current selection.
- **Insert Column** adds a column left of the selection.
- **Insert Rows or Columns** opens a dialog box where you can add a specific number of rows or columns. You can also choose where to add the new cells relative to the current selection.
- **Delete Row** removes the row of the active cell.
- **Delete Column** removes the column of the active cell.
- **Increase Row Span** merges the current cell with the cell below it.
- **Increase Column Span** merges the current cell with the cell next to it on the right side.

- **Decrease Row Span** splits two or more previously merged or spanned cells into two cells from the bottom.
- **Decrease Column Span** splits previously merged or spanned cells into two cells from the right.
- **Clear Cell Heights** removes all defined numeric row height values from the selected table.
- **Clear Cell Widths** removes all defined numeric column width values from the selected table.
- **Convert Widths to Pixels** and **Convert Widths to Percent** allow you to change defined widths from a percentage of the available space to a specific number of pixels, and vice versa.
- **Convert Heights to Pixels** and **Convert Heights to Percent** allow you to change defined heights from a percentage of the available browser space to a specific number of pixels, and vice versa.

INSERT SPECIAL CHARACTERS IN CODE

The multiplication sign is a seldom-used character; it doesn't even appear in the Insert Other Character dialog box. To insert this character, you can type code directly in the Code pane, or you can use the Insert field in the Insert Other Character dialog box.

There are many lists of HTML character entities on the Internet. Use your favorite search engine to search for "HTML characters." Some Web pages have more characters than others; for very unusual characters, you might need to check a few sites until you find the code you need. Also, make note of both the name and the numeric code because some browsers support one but not the other (test both in your browser).

Note:

To find the necessary code for special characters, look for online sources such as http://www.w3schools.com/html/html_entities.asp.

1. **With `typography.html` open in Split view, use the Design pane to scroll to the paragraph following the Multiplication Sign heading.**

2. **Select the letter "x" between 15 and 22.**

3. **Click the Code pane to bring it into focus, and then delete the selected letter "x".**

4. **Type `&tim` and press Return/Enter to choose `&times;` from the code hint list.**

   The code hints help you insert named character entities, but not numeric character codes.

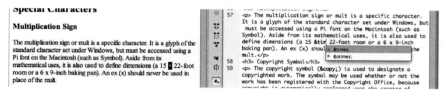

5. **Click the Refresh Design View button in the Document toolbar.**

6. **In the Design pane, compare the appearance of the mult (multiply) character and the letter "x".**

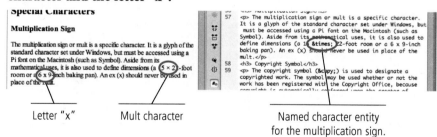

Letter "x"   Mult character   Named character entity for the multiplication sign.

7. **Select the letter "x" between 6 and 9 in the same sentence.**

8. **In the Code pane, replace the selected character with `&#215;` and then refresh the Design view.**

   This is the numeric code for the mult character. Dreamweaver's code hints for character entities in Code view do not support numeric codes for characters.

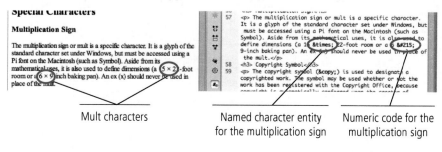

Mult characters   Named character entity for the multiplication sign   Numeric code for the multiplication sign

9. **Preview the page in your browser.**

   The current versions of Firefox, Safari, Opera, Chrome, and Internet Explorer all support both the named and numeric character codes. Older versions, however, might show the characters "**×**" instead of the actual mult character.

10. **Close your browser and return to Dreamweaver.**

11. **Continue to the next stage of the project.**

Stage 4 Creating Lists

There are three common types of lists: definition lists, ordered lists, and unordered lists. Ordered and unordered lists (numbered and bulleted, respectively) are very similar. Definition lists, which include a term and a definition, have a different type of structure.

In this stage of the project, you will create a definition list, an ordered list of references, and an unordered list that becomes navigation links in the final Web page.

CREATE A DEFINITION LIST

Definition lists are designed to match a term with its definition or description. The definition or description doesn't necessarily need to come from a dictionary or thesaurus; it might simply be an explanation of the term.

Three tags are part of a definition list. The **<dl>** tag defines the beginning and end of the entire list of terms and definitions. The **<dt>** and **<dd>** tags within the dl element wrap the definition terms and definition descriptions (respectively).

1. **With typography.html open, scroll to the Glossary heading near the bottom of the page.**

2. **Drag to select the four lines of terms and descriptions in the Glossary section.**

3. **In the Text Insert panel, click the Definition List button to wrap the selected text in a <dl> tag.**

   The entire selection is enclosed in **<dl>** tags, identifying it as a definition list. A definition list automatically tags every other paragraph in the selection with **<dt>** tags to identify a definition term, and alternating lines with **<dd>** tags to identify definition descriptions (in other words, the meaning of the preceding term).

Note:

By default, content in the <dd> tags is indented. This is a presentation property, and can be changed using CSS.

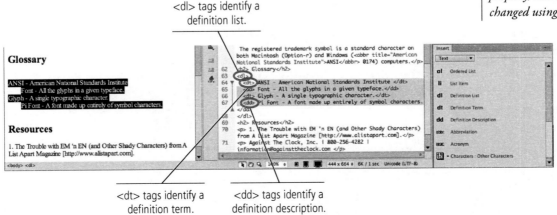

<dl> tags identify a definition list.

<dt> tags identify a definition term.

<dd> tags identify a definition description.

4. **In the Design pane, click to place the insertion point to the left of "American" in the first line.**

5. **Press Delete/Backspace until the spaces and hyphen have been deleted, and then press Return/Enter.**

   The description is now formatted as a definition description. However, the "Font" term is indented at the same level as the ANSI definition, which is incorrect.

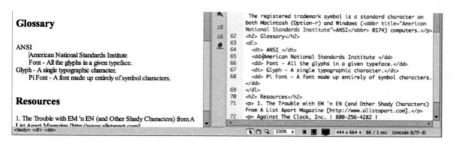

6. **Move the insertion point to the left of "Font," press Backspace, and then press Return/Enter.**

   The line beginning with Font is now formatted as a definition term.

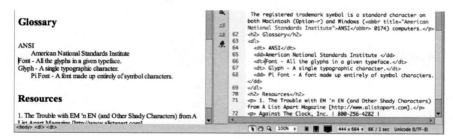

7. **Repeat Steps 5–6 for the rest of the terms and descriptions.**

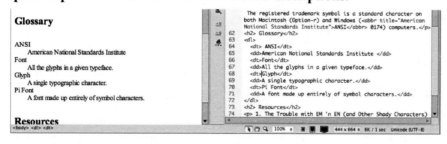

8. **Save the file and continue to the next exercise.**

CREATE AN ORDERED LIST OF WEB RESOURCES

Ordered lists are commonly called numbered lists, although they are not always numbered. You can use Roman numerals (i, ii, iii or I, II, III) or letters (a, b, c or A, B, C).

The purpose of ordered lists is to show a sequence of steps or hierarchical order. If these purposes do not apply to the content of a list, you should use an unordered (bulleted) list instead.

1. **With typography.html open, select the numbered paragraph at the bottom of the page.**

2. **Click the Ordered List button in the Properties panel.**

   The **<ol>** tags surround the entire ordered list, identifying where the list starts and ends. Each list item within the list is surrounded by **<li>** tags.

   In the Design pane, the list as a whole is indented from the left edge of the page, and the space between list items is reduced. These presentation properties clearly identify that the text is part of a list, and not part of a regular paragraph.

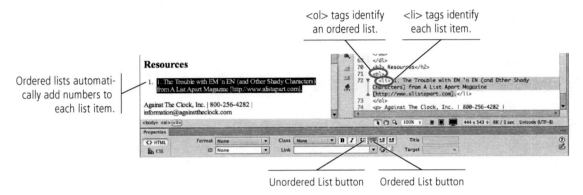

   One of the presentation properties of an ordered list is that each list item is automatically numbered. If you receive content from an outside source, the number might already be typed at the beginning of each list item (as is the case in this project); you should remove the original number from the text of each list item.

3. **In the Design pane, delete the redundant number from the beginning of the list item.**

4. **Click at the end of the text in the numbered list item and press Return/Enter.**

   When you press Return/Enter at the end of a list item in the Design pane, Dreamweaver automatically creates a new numbered list item for you.

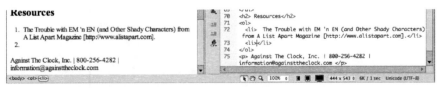

Note:

You have to work in the Design pane to automatically add the new list item. Pressing Return/Enter in the Code pane simply adds white space in the code.

5. **Type HTML entities and other resources at W3schools.com. as the new list item, but do not press Return/Enter.**

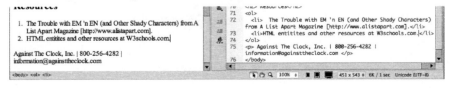

6. **In the first list item, select the URL in the square brackets and cut it to the Clipboard (Edit>Cut or Command/Control-X).**

7. **Delete the two square brackets and the space before them.**

8. **Select "A List Apart Magazine", click in the Link field of the Properties panel, paste the copied URL, and press Return/Enter.**

   As you learned in Project 1: Bistro Site Organization, a link is identified by **<a>** tags. The **href** attribute defines the link destination, or the page that will open when a user clicks the link text.

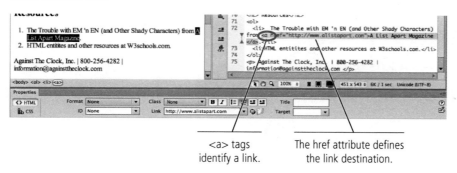

<a> tags
identify a link.

The href attribute defines
the link destination.

9. **Click to place the insertion point in the link.**

   Placing the insertion point removes the highlighting that was applied to the text in the previous step. You can now see the default presentational properties of the <a> tag — blue, underlined text.

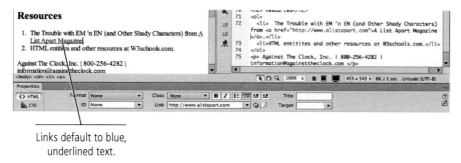

Links default to blue,
underlined text.

10. **In the second list item, make "W3schools.com" a link to http://www.w3schools.com.**

11. **Save the file and continue to the next exercise.**

CREATE AN UNORDERED LIST OF NAVIGATION LINKS

A navigation bar is simply a list of links. It is common practice among Web design professionals to mark up a navigation bar as a list of links; after CSS has been applied, however, the list takes on an all-new appearance. In this exercise, you use the unordered list format to create a navigation bar.

1. **With typography.html open, place the insertion point at the end of the last list item in the Resources section in the Design pane.**

2. **Press Return/Enter twice.**

    Pressing Return/Enter once creates the next list item — in this case, #3.

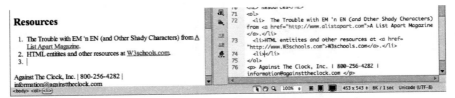

If you press Return/Enter again (before typing anything else), Dreamweaver recognizes that you want to escape from the ordered list, deletes the last empty list item, and moves the insertion point into an empty paragraph below the ordered list.

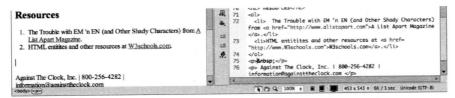

3. **Click the Unordered List button in the Properties panel.**

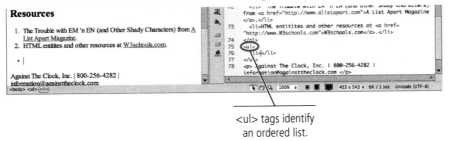

<ul> tags identify
an ordered list.

4. **Add six list items: Home, Store, Tools, Downloads, About, and Contact. Press Return/Enter after each item, but not after the final list item.**

Note:

You will work in depth with CSS in Project 4: Yosemite CSS Layout, including defining your own selectors for both object and layout formatting.

5. **Highlight the word "Home" in the Design pane. In the Properties panel, type # in the Link field, the press Return/Enter to finalize the new link.**

Using the # character in the Link field turns the selected text into a link without defining a specific destination. For the purposes of this project, the important thing is that the text of each list item be tagged as a link.

6. **Repeat Step 5 for each item in the list.**

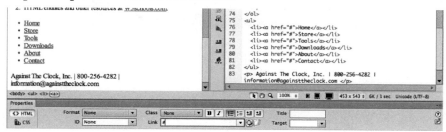

7. **Save the changes and continue to the next stage of the project.**

Stage 5 Attaching an External CSS File

As you might have noticed, we paid particular attention to the tags that were applied to various structural elements through this project. Rather than simply accepting the default presentational properties, you can use cascading style sheets (CSS), which contain instructions that tell a browser how to format those various elements.

As you complete the rest of the projects in this book, you will work extensively with CSS to format both pages and specific page content. In this project, you are going to attach the client's existing CSS file to your page, so the appearance of your page matches the rest of the client's Web site.

Although we will not discuss the finer details of CSS at this point, the following exercises will make more sense if you understand several key issues:

- A CSS file includes **selectors** (rules) that define the appearance of different tags.

- A **<div>** tag identifies a section, or division, of a page.

- An **ID** attribute is a name that uniquely identifies a specific element.

ADD DIV TAGS AND ELEMENT IDs

A div element (using opening and closing **<div>** tags) has no structural meaning; it simply separates one block of content from another on a page. Each div element on a page must have a unique ID to clearly distinguish it from other divs. The ID has no effect on the structure of content, but simply identifies it for the purposes of CSS styling. This allows you to define different appearances for the same elements in different sections. For example, **<p>** tags in a div named "content" can have a different appearance than **<p>** tags in a div named "sidebar".

You can also assign IDs to other tags, such as individual paragraphs, so those identified objects can be controlled separately. In short, if it's named, it can be visually separated using CSS.

1. **With typography.html open in Split view, click in the level 1 heading in the Design pane to place the insertion point.**

2. **In the Design pane, click the <h1> tag in the Tag Selector to select the entire level 1 heading (including the related tags).**

3. **With the Insert panel in Layout mode, click the Insert Div Tag button.**

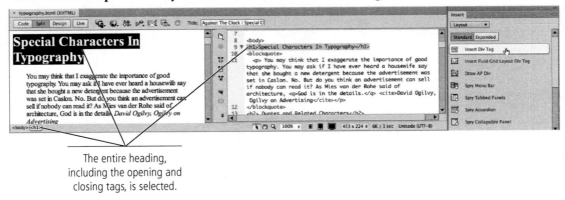

The entire heading, including the opening and closing tags, is selected.

4. **In the resulting dialog box, choose Wrap Around Selection in the Insert menu.**

   You want the div to include the heading tags, so you are wrapping the div tag *around* the current selection.

5. **Type header in the ID field and click OK.**

   The ID you are assigning (header) has defined formatting in the CSS for this site. When you later attach the CSS file to this page, the appropriate header formats will be applied to page content identified (through the ID attribute) as a header.

6. **Click once in the level 1 heading to place the insertion point but deselect the paragraph.**

   The ID attribute sets this heading apart from the rest of the text. The boundaries of the div tag (section) are marked by a gray or dotted line in the Design pane. (If you don't see this border, you can turn on CSS Layout Outlines in the Visual Aids menu in the Document toolbar.)

The gray border identifies the div boundaries.

Use this menu to turn on CSS Layout Outlines.

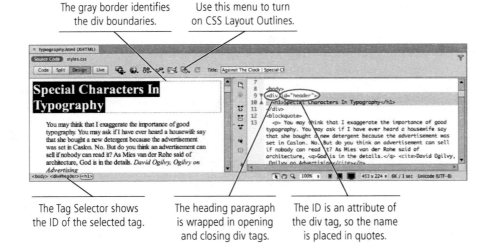

The Tag Selector shows the ID of the selected tag.

The heading paragraph is wrapped in opening and closing div tags.

The ID is an attribute of the div tag, so the name is placed in quotes.

7. **In the Design pane, select "information@againsttheclock.com" in the last paragraph on the page. In the Link field of the Properties panel, type `mailto:information@againsttheclock.com` and press Return/Enter.**

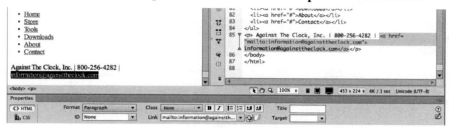

8. **Click the <p> tag in the Tag Selector to select the entire last paragraph.**

9. **Type `footer` in the ID field of the Properties panel, and press Return/Enter to apply the ID to the active paragraph.**

   In this case, no border surrounds the paragraph because you didn't add a new div tag around the selection. Rather, you defined the ID of the active paragraph tag, as you can see in the Tag Selector.

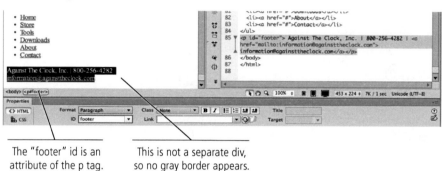

The "footer" id is an attribute of the p tag.

This is not a separate div, so no gray border appears.

Note:

The most important issue is to use the exact same ID for an element as the ID defined in the CSS file that will format the appearance of the different elements. In this case, we are telling you what IDs to use based on the IDs that exist in the CSS file that you will attach to the HTML file; in a professional environment, you would have to examine the CSS styles yourself to determine which IDs are available.

10. **Switch to Design view and select all the text from the blockquote (at the top of the page) to the last numbered list item under the "Resources" heading.**

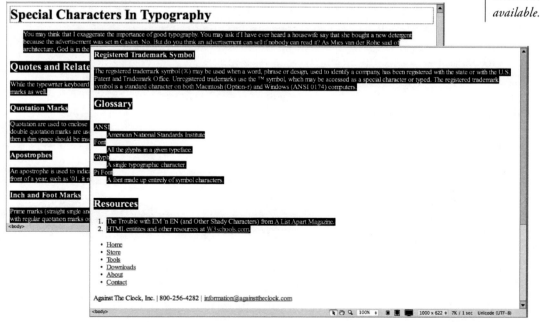

11. **Use the process from Steps 3–5 to wrap the active selection with a new div tag with an ID of content.**

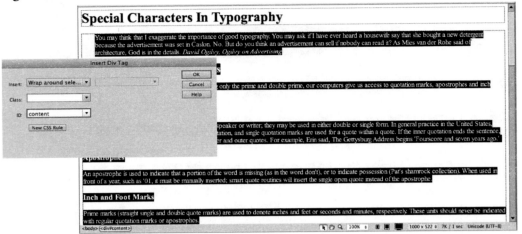

12. **Save the file and continue to the next exercise.**

 ## ATTACH THE CSS FILE

To make this page more visually pleasing to ATC site visitors — and to be consistent with the rest of the ATC site — you need to attach the CSS file already used for other pages in the client's site.

The CSS file, which is a set of instructions on how to display the Web page, is separate from the HTML document. When a browser downloads an HTML file, it examines the code for external files required to display it, such as images and CSS files. The browser then downloads the external files and merges them into the display of the Web page. In the case of a CSS file, the browser reads the instructions, and then applies the styles to the page.

After attaching the style sheet to the page, and depending on what the CSS file defines, you might see a dramatic difference in the appearance of the page. Not only will text styling change, but the layout will change too — even to the point of moving some page components to new locations.

1. **With typography.html open in Design view, open the CSS Styles panel.**

   Remember, all panels can be opened from the Window menu. If a panel is already available in the dock, you can click the relevant panel tab or button to show that panel.

   Attach Style Sheet button

2. **Click the Attach Style Sheet button at the bottom of the panel.**

3. **In the Attach External Style Sheet dialog box, click the Browse button.**

4. **In the resulting Select Style Sheet File dialog box, navigate to styles.css in the root folder of the ATC site (WIP>ATC). Click Open/OK to return to the Attach External Style Sheet dialog box.**

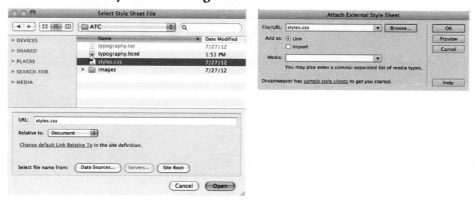

5. **Click OK in the Attach External Style Sheet dialog box to apply the CSS file.**

   The navigation unordered list now appears at the top of the page instead of below the header. It is not formatted properly because you did not yet define an ID for the unordered list. (It is difficult to see because it overlaps the black background.)

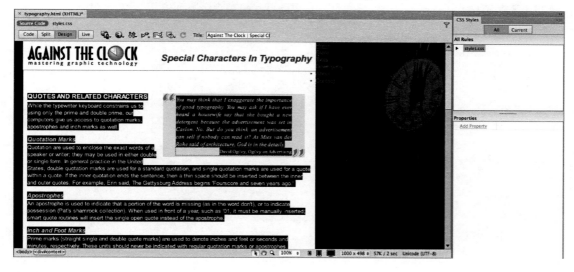

6. **Save the file and continue to the next exercise.**

IDENTIFY THE LIST AS A NAVIGATION BAR

Note:

An ID can only be assigned once in a particular page or section; you have already used header, footer, and content, so those are not included in this menu.

As you can see in Design view, the unordered list is clearly not formatted properly within the context of the rest of the formatted page. We intentionally omitted this element ID in the earlier exercise to show that you don't need to identify every section before attaching the external style sheet. In fact, it can be easier to wait until the CSS file is attached, because the application can help apply the correct IDs.

1. **With typography.html open in Design view, click in any element of the navigation unordered list to place the insertion point.**

2. **Using the Tag Selector, click the <ul> tag to select the entire unordered list.**

3. **In the Properties panel, open the ID menu and choose topnav.**

   This menu shows all available IDs that are defined in the attached CSS file. This method is an easy way to make sure that the ID you apply already exists in the attached CSS file.

   You will work extensively with CSS in later projects. For now, you should simply understand that the attached CSS file includes an ID selector named "topnav", which defines the appearance of the unordered list items as a horizontal navigation bar.

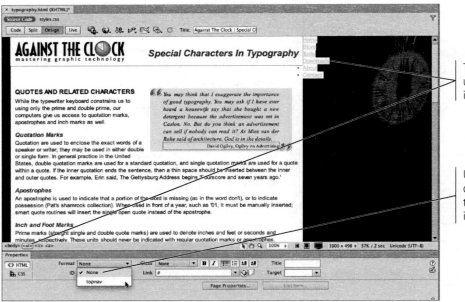

The entire unordered list is selected.

Use this menu to choose an ID from those that are available in the attached CSS file.

Even without the CSS, the text content in this page was very readable. By attaching a CSS file that defines the appearance of various tags and IDs, the page is now visually attractive in addition to being properly structured.

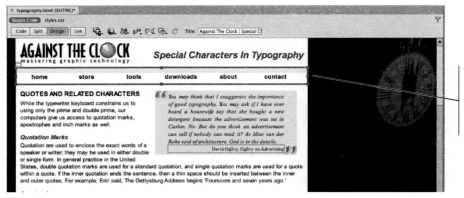

The definition of topnav in the attached CSS file converts the unordered list into a horizontal navigation bar below the header div.

4. Switch to the Live view and review the page.

The Live view is a very good tool for reviewing most design elements. However, you should remember that Dreamweaver is not a browser; site visitors will not use the Dreamweaver Live view to view your pages, so you should also review your work in at least one actual browser application.

Note:

Don't depend solely on Dreamweaver Design view or even Live view when you design pages, and don't depend on a single browser to test your pages. Every browser has its own bugs and weaknesses; to be sure of your design, test your pages in multiple browsers.

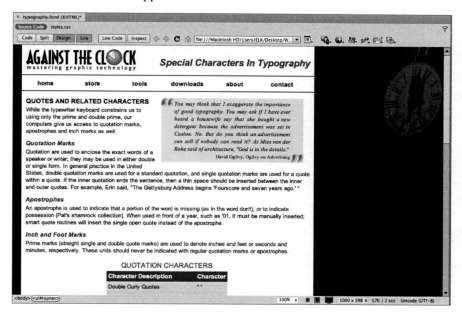

5. Turn off the Live view and then preview the page in at least one browser.

Scroll through the document and review the appearance of different elements (including special characters). If possible, review the document in multiple browsers and on different operating systems.

6. Close any open browsers and return to Dreamweaver.

7. Close typography.html.

8. Choose Manage Sites from the bottom of the Directory menu in the Files panel.

9. In the Manage Sites dialog box, choose the ATC site name, and then click the Export button. Navigate to your WIP>ATC folder and click Save to create the ATC.ste file.

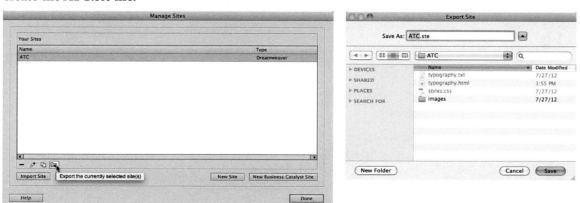

10. In the Manage Sites dialog box, remove the ATC site from the list.

1. The _____ tag marks up individual paragraphs in a story.

2. Each HTML page should have only one _____ element.

3. All visible content of a Web page is contained within the opening and closing _____ tags.

4. _____ appear when you begin typing in the Code pane, showing a list of tags or elements that can be added at the current insertion point.

5. A(n) _____ tag includes both opening and closing tags, such as <title>text</title>.

6. A(n) _____ adds properties to HTML elements, such as the citation of a quote.

7. The _____ element is used to mark up text that is indented on the right and left, with extra white space above and below the affected text.

8. The _____ element is best used to mark up the short form of a phrase that is spoken as letters, such as HTML.

9. The _____ element identifies an individual item in an ordered or unordered list.

10. The _____ allows you to work temporarily with code, while still working in Design view.

1. Briefly explain the importance of properly structuring an HTML document.

2. Briefly explain the difference between an ordered list and an unordered list.

3. Briefly explain the importance of div tags for formatting an HTML page.

Portfolio Builder Project

Use what you learned in this project to complete the following freeform exercise.
Carefully read the art director and client comments, then create your own design to meet the needs of the project.
Use the space below to sketch ideas; when finished, write a brief explanation of your reasoning behind your final design.

art director comments

The owner of Against The Clock has received a number of positive comments — and new sales — because of the *Typography Companion* sample chapter that you created for her to post on her Web site. She would like to add another page with a sample from the *Color Companion* from the same series.

To complete this project, you should:

❏ Use the ATC site folder that you already created for the new page.

❏ Create a new HTML page and copy the text from **ColorCh3.txt** into the file. (The file is in the **DW6_PB_Project2.zip** archive on the Student Files Web page.)

❏ Mark up the page text with proper structural tags.

❏ Create header and footer elements, and attach the same CSS file that you used in the type chapter.

client comments

We've had such a positive response from the type chapter that we also want to include a sample from the *Color Companion*. If we get the same increase in sales leads from this chapter, we'll probably go ahead and do online samples for all of our books.

In addition to the text file for the *Color Companion* chapter, we've sent you a PDF file of the printed chapter so you can more easily see the different text elements — headings, lists, italics, special characters, and so on. You can just ignore the images and sidebars in the printed chapter; we don't need those in the online sample. There is, however, a table near the end of the file that we would like you to include in the online version.

At the end of the text file, we added in the glossary terms that we think are important for this chapter. There aren't any resources, so you can leave out that section.

project justification

No matter how you receive content for a Web page, you will likely need to correct the formatting with the appropriate HTML tags. In this project, you learned how to use HTML tags and elements to semantically structure and mark up a document so all visitors can successfully access and use a Web page. You also learned that by applying ID attributes, <div> tags, and using CSS, you can turn a plain HTML document into a visually pleasing and highly structured Web page.

The Web pages that you create for clients will seldom be as text-intensive as this page, but now that you have a solid understanding of how to work with HTML structures, from both Design view and Code view, you are ready to format any content you receive from a client — regardless of its condition.

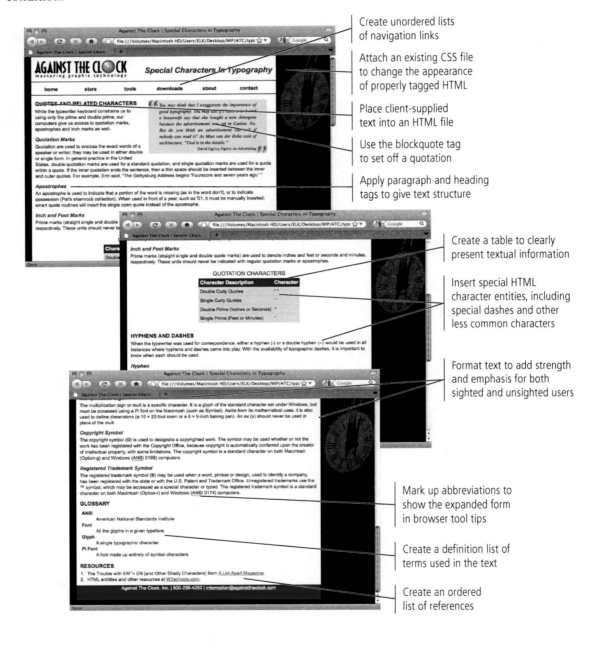

Create unordered lists of navigation links

Attach an existing CSS file to change the appearance of properly tagged HTML

Place client-supplied text into an HTML file

Use the blockquote tag to set off a quotation

Apply paragraph and heading tags to give text structure

Create a table to clearly present textual information

Insert special HTML character entities, including special dashes and other less common characters

Format text to add strength and emphasis for both sighted and unsighted users

Mark up abbreviations to show the expanded form in browser tool tips

Create a definition list of terms used in the text

Create an ordered list of references

Photographer's Web Site

Your client is the owner of Crowe Photography, an art studio in central California near San Francisco. You have been hired to add a number of visual elements to her Web site, including static images, animation, and video.

This project incorporates the following skills:

❑ Using various methods to add static images into a Web page

❑ Assigning alt tags to images for improved usability

❑ Manipulating images in a Web page

❑ Defining background colors and images

❑ Working with multimedia files

❑ Defining a page favicon

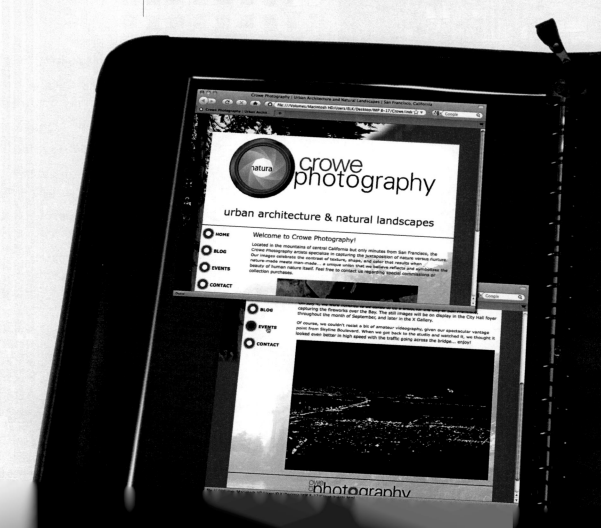

Project Meeting

client comments

Our site is very basic — only three pages. We don't need to be complicated, we just need to get the information out there.

At the same time, we're a photography studio, so we want to include images!

I just created a new logo that I also want to incorporate; there's a regular version and an animated one that I'd like to place on every page.

We're probably going to add a gallery page down the road, but I'm not organized enough to get all the files together. A rotating slideshow on the home page with a few samples should be fine for now.

I just updated the blog page, and I'd like you to place the video that we mention.

art director comments

Dreamweaver makes it very easy to incorporate visual elements into a Web page. You can work directly in the Design view to place the basic images and multimedia objects.

For the background images, CSS makes it relatively easy to define different backgrounds as long as you understand the concepts of HTML elements and selectors.

I chose two of the images the client provided and manipulated them in Photoshop to work well as background images in different sections of the page.

I also think the aperture part of the logo will be a good "hover" image for the navigation links. Again, you can use CSS to make this happen rather than inserting actual rollover images.

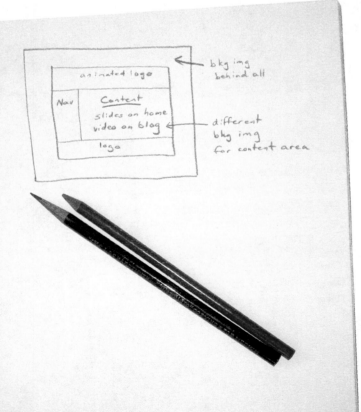

project objectives

To complete this project, you will:

❏ Use multiple techniques to add images to Web pages

❏ Resize images to fit page areas

❏ Resample images to reduce download time

❏ Use CSS to control background colors and images for specific page elements

❏ Insert a Flash animation file, a slideshow, and a video file

❏ Add a page favicon

Stage 1   Working with Static Images

Images serve two primary purposes in Web pages: informing and decorating. Examples of informative images include an illustration of how to fasten a seat belt, or a graphic that serves as a link in a navigation bar. Decorative images are supporting images that could be removed from the site without affecting its content or message, such as the background behind the content of a page.

DEFINE THE CROWE PHOTOGRAPHY SITE

As in the previous project, the first step to working in Dreamweaver is to prepare the site definition. To ensure that links between documents and paths to images are created properly, the site must be defined in Dreamweaver.

1. **Download DW6_RF_Project3.zip from the Student Files Web page.**

2. **Expand the ZIP archive in your WIP folder (Macintosh) or copy the archive contents into your WIP folder (Windows).**

   This results in a folder named **Crowe**, which contains the files you need for this project.

3. **Create a new site named Photography, using the WIP>Crowe folder as the site root folder.**

   The procedure for defining this site is the same as for the sites you created in previous projects (except for the path, which is unique for every project). If necessary, refer to the first exercises in Project 1: Bistro Site Organization for more detailed instructions.

4. **Continue to the next exercise.**

INSERT AN IMAGE ONTO A PAGE

In this exercise, you will learn how to place an image in a Web page — a fairly basic process once you understand what types of images you should use. Four primary formats are used for images and graphics on the Web:

- **JPEG** (Joint Photographic Experts Group), which supports 24-bit color, is used primarily for continuous-tone images with subtle changes in color, such as photographs or other images that are created in Adobe Photoshop.

- **GIF** (Graphics Interchange Format), which supports only 8-bit color or 256 possible values, is best used for graphics with areas of solid color, such as logos or other illustrations created in an application such as Adobe Illustrator. This format also supports simple frame-by-frame animation.

- **PNG** (Portable Network Graphics), which supports both 8- and 24-bit color, as well as a special 32-bit format allowing for partial transparency, can be used for both illustrations and continuous-tone images.

- **SVG** (Scalable Vector Graphics) images are made up of mathematically defined lines called **vectors** (unlike **raster images**, which are made up entirely of pixels). Vector graphics are completely **scalable** without affecting their quality.

Note:

Although current browsers support all four file formats, support in older browsers' versions can be problematic or nonexistent (especially for PNG and SVG formats).

Image Bit Depth

Bit depth refers to how many bits define the color value of a particular pixel. A **bit** is a unit of information that is either on or off (represented as 1 and 0, respectively). One bit has 2 states or colors, 8 bits have 256 possible colors ($2\times2\times2\times2\times2\times2\times2\times2=256$), and 24 bits have 16,777,216 (2^{24}) possible colors.

In an RGB photograph, three color channels define how much of each primary color (red, green, and blue) makes up each pixel. Each channel requires 8 bits, resulting in a total of 24 bits for each pixel (called "true color").

Image Compression

The JPEG format incorporates **lossy compression**, which means that pixels are thrown away in order to reduce file size. When areas of flat color are highly compressed, speckles of other colors (called artifacts) often appear, which negatively impacts the quality of the design.

Both GIF and PNG formats employ **lossless compression** to reduce file size and download time, while ensuring that no information is lost during the compression. The lossless compression routine in the PNG format is generally better than that used in GIF images, so you might achieve a slightly smaller file size if you use 8-bit PNG.

Although 24-bit PNG is capable of displaying as many colors as the JPEG format, PNG uses a lossless compression routine. As a result, PNG doesn't compress 24-bit images as small as the JPEG format.

1. **With the Photography site open in the Files panel, double-click index.html to open the file.**

2. **Review the page contents in the Design view.**

    This is a fairly simple site, with several places marked to add various content. As you complete this project, you will use a number of techniques to place and manage images and other media to add visual interest.

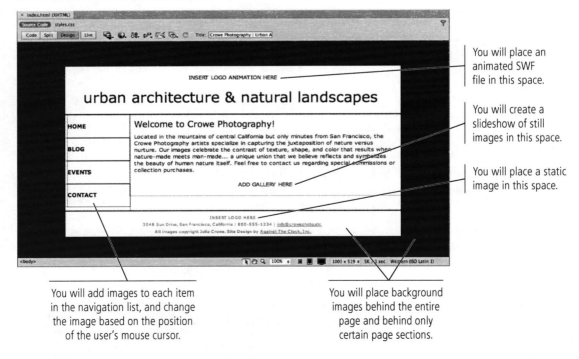

You will place an animated SWF file in this space.

You will create a slideshow of still images in this space.

You will place a static image in this space.

You will add images to each item in the navigation list, and change the image based on the position of the user's mouse cursor.

You will place background images behind the entire page and behind only certain page sections.

3. **Click the Split button in the Document toolbar to show both the Design and Code views.**

In this project we use the horizontal split view to maximize the line length that is visible in both panes. Feel free to use whichever method you prefer.

4. **In the Design pane, select the words "Insert Logo Here" near the bottom of the page.**

5. **Delete the selected text from the Design pane.**

When you delete the footer text, the code for a nonbreaking space (** **) is automatically added as a placeholder inside the **<p>** tags within the footer div.

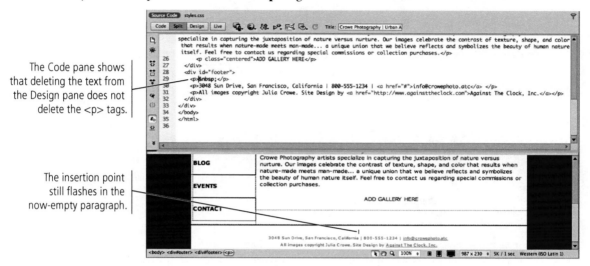

The Code pane shows that deleting the text from the Design pane does not delete the <p> tags.

The insertion point still flashes in the now-empty paragraph.

6. **With the insertion point flashing in the empty paragraph (in the Design pane), click the arrow on the Images button icon of the Common Insert panel and choose Image from the pop-up menu.**

The Images button defaults to the last-used option. If you (or someone else) already used the Images button on the Insert panel, it might say Images: Image or some other type. To be sure you are inserting the correct type of image in this step, click the button icon to open the menu and choose Image from the menu.

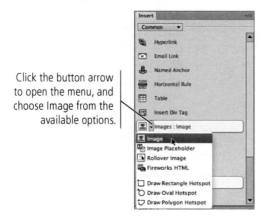

Click the button arrow to open the menu, and choose Image from the available options.

Note:

You can also choose Insert>Image.

7. **In the Select Image Source dialog box, open the site images folder, select the crowe-photography.png file, and click Open/OK.**

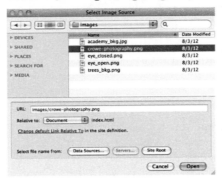 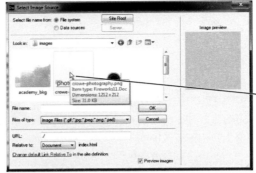

If file extensions are hidden on Windows, move your cursor over a file and wait a second to see the file name and extension in a pop-up window.

8. **In the resulting Image Tag Accessibility Attributes dialog box, type Crowe Photography in the Alternate Text field and click OK.**

Text you enter in the Alternate Text field of this dialog box becomes the **alt** attribute of the **<img>** (image) tag.

The **alt** attribute provides a text alternative to the image, so visitors who use screen readers (or who have disabled image display in their browsers) will be able to understand the content of the image. The alt text is also indexed by search engines, which allows them to show your site's images in the search engine image gallery and make a more qualified determination of your site's rank.

Although most tag attributes are optional, the **alt** attribute of the **<img>** tag is required. If an image is simply decorative and does not merit alternate text, you use an empty alt attribute (**alt=""**), which satisfies the requirement. (Using **alt=""** is considered better than **alt=" "** because some screen readers pronounce the space.)

You can choose <empty> in the dialog box menu to add the empty **alt** attribute. If you simply don't type in the field, no alt attribute is added to the **<img>** tag.

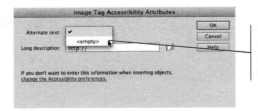

Choose <empty> in the menu to add an empty alt attribute to the selected image.

Note:

The alt attribute is commonly misnamed the alt tag; it is not an HTML tag but an attribute of a tag.

Note:

If you replace one image with another, the original alt text still applies to the new image. Basically, you are only changing the src attribute without affecting the alt attribute.

Note:

The Long Description field completes the longdesc attribute of an image. Its purpose is to allow the designer to offer a link to a longer description of an image on a separate Web page.

9. **With the image selected in the Design pane, examine the Tag Selector and the Code pane.**

The **<img>** tag appears inside the opening and closing **<p>** tags.

Some attributes of the **<img>** tag are automatically populated based on information saved in the image file:

- The **src** attribute defines the file name and location of the image.
- The **width** and **height** attributes are automatically populated based on the file's physical dimensions.
- The **alt** attribute is the alternate text, which you defined in the Image Tag Accessibility Attributes dialog box.

Note:

You can simply type in the Alt field of the Properties panel to assign or change the alt text for a specific image.

Code related to the selected image is selected in the Code pane.

Handles (on the right and bottom sides and the bottom-right corner) indicate that the image is selected.

The <img> tag represents the selected image.

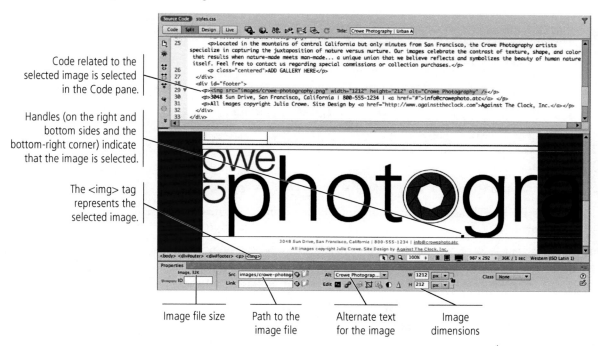

Image file size

Path to the image file

Alternate text for the image

Image dimensions

10. **Save the file (File>Save) and then continue to the next exercise.**

RESIZE AND RESAMPLE AN IMAGE

As you can see in the Design pane, the placed logo is much too large to fit in the footer area of the page. In this exercise, you will adjust the image to better fit the space.

As with most tasks, there is more than one way to resize an image. You can enter new dimensions in the Properties panel, or simply drag the handles of the selected image in the Design view.

1. **With index.html open, click the placed logo to select the image (if necessary).**

The bottom center of the image shows a control handle, which you can drag to resize the height of the placed image. Because this image is so large, you might not be able to see the right edge of the image (depending on the size and arrangement of your workspace).

Since you might not be able to see all of the handles, it is better to use the Properties panel to change the image's dimensions.

Note:

WebAIM (Web Accessibility In Mind, www.webaim.org/) is an organization that promotes Web accessibility and offers instructions and tutorials on how to meet accessibility guidelines.

2. **In the Properties panel, make sure the lock icon to the right of the W and H fields is locked. If the icon is unlocked, click it to make it locked.**

When the icon is locked, changing one dimension applies a proportional change to the other dimension; in other words, changes to the image dimensions maintain the original width-to-height aspect ratio.

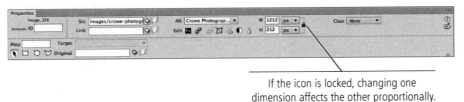

If the icon is locked, changing one dimension affects the other proportionally.

If the icon is unlocked, changing one dimension has no effect on the other dimension.

3. **Highlight the current value in the W field. Type 400, then press Return/Enter to finalize the change.**

After the image has been resized, you should be able to see all three resizing handles.

In the Properties panel, the image dimensions appear in bold, indicating that the image has been resized.

Two additional buttons are now available to the right of the W and H fields. Clicking the **Reset to Original Size button** restores the original image dimensions, regardless of how many times you have changed the image size in the page or in the Properties panel.

Clicking the **Commit Image Size button** changes the placed image file to match the current image dimensions on the page.

Note:

You can usually reduce an image without losing quality, but enlarging an image beyond its original size can result in a significant loss of image quality.

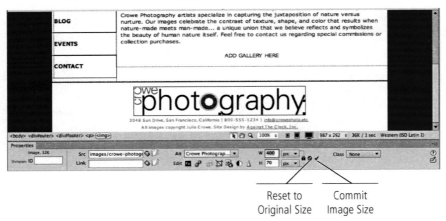

Reset to Original Size   Commit Image Size

4. Click the bottom-right image handle, press Shift, and drag up and left. When the W field shows the width of 300, release the mouse button.

You can drag any of the handles to resize the image in only one direction (by dragging the side handles) or in both directions at once (by dragging the corner handle).

Keep in mind that manually resizing the image using these handles does not honor the Lock icon in the Properties panel. If you drag either of the side handles, or the corner handle without pressing Shift, the lock icon in the Properties panel is automatically unlocked. By pressing Shift while dragging the corner handle, you constrain the resizing process and maintain the image's original aspect ratio.

Note:

Pressing Shift while dragging a side handle does not maintain the image's aspect ratio. You have to Shift-drag the corner handle to resize the image proportionally.

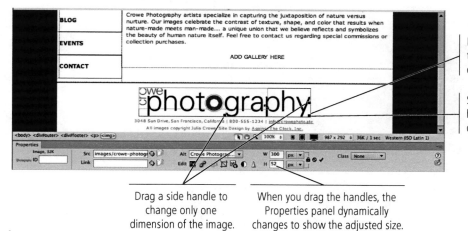

Drag the corner handle to change both dimensions at one time.

Shift-drag the corner handle to change both dimensions proportionally.

Drag a side handle to change only one dimension of the image.

When you drag the handles, the Properties panel dynamically changes to show the adjusted size.

5. In the Files panel, expand the images folder.

6. Control/right-click the crowe-photography.png file, and choose Edit>Duplicate from the contextual menu.

It's a common mistake to insert a large image into a Web page, and then simply resize the image to take up less space on the page. The problem with resizing is that, while the image will *appear* smaller, the file size ("weight") remains the same. Users might need to wait a considerable length of time to download the large image file.

Instead of simply resizing, you should also resample any resized images to include only the necessary data. **Resampling** discards pixels (while downsizing) so the specified dimensions of the image are the actual dimensions of the image. This reduces the weight of the image, which reduces the download time for your visitors.

In the next few steps, you are going to resample the image that you placed into the index.html page. However, you should understand that resampling in Dreamweaver permanently changes the image file. Before you make this type of change permanent, it is a good idea to create a copy of the image file so you can still access the original file if necessary.

7. In the Files panel, click the original crowe-photography.png file once to highlight the file name.

Make sure you don't rename the one that has "Copy" in the file name; that file is the original-size logo. You want to rename the image file that you placed into the footer and decreased to a smaller physical size.

8. **At the end of the current file name, type** `-small`, **then press Return/Enter to finalize the new file name.**

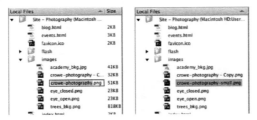

9. **In the resulting dialog box, click Update to update the link in index.html to the new file name.**

10. **With the image selected on the page, click the Commit Image Size button to the right of the W and H fields.**

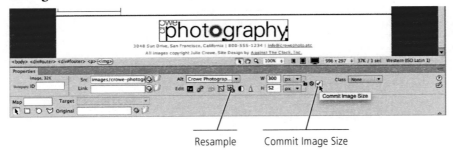

Resample   Commit Image Size

Note:

You could also click the Resample button to accomplish the same effect.

11. **Click OK to acknowledge the warning.**

As we explained earlier, resampling in Dreamweaver permanently changes the image file; the resized dimensions become its (new) actual size. After resampling, the Reset Size button is no longer visible, and the Resample button is grayed out (not available).

Also note the file size of the resampled image; it was originally 32 KB, and now (after resizing and resampling) it's around 10 KB.

Note:

If another user clicked the "Don't show me this message again" option, you won't see this warning.

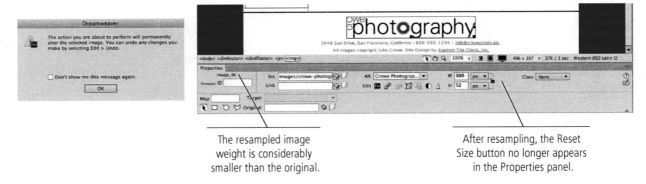

The resampled image weight is considerably smaller than the original.

After resampling, the Reset Size button no longer appears in the Properties panel.

12. **Save the file and continue to the next exercise.**

INSERT AN IMAGE FROM THE FILES PANEL

Dreamweaver provides many ways to insert images into Web pages, one of which is using the Images button on the Common Insert panel. Another way is to simply drag a file from the Files panel and place it onto a Web page.

1. **Open the blog.html file from the Files panel.**

2. **In the Design pane, select and delete the words "INSERT LOGO HERE" at the bottom of the page.**

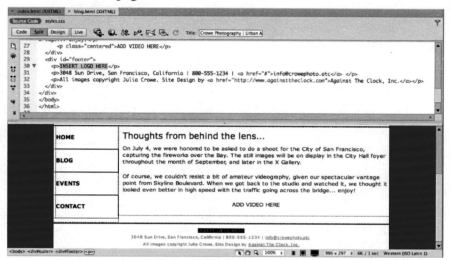

3. **In the Files panel, expand the images folder (if necessary).**

4. **From the Files panel, drag crowe-photography-small.png to the location of the insertion point (where you deleted the text in Step 2).**

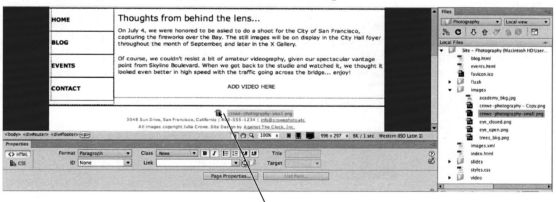

Drag the file from the Files panel to the location where you want to place the image.

5. **In the resulting Image Tag Accessibility Attributes dialog box, type Crowe Photography in the Alternate Text field.**

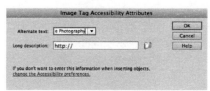

Note:

Do not double-click the image in the Files panel to insert it. Double-clicking an image in the Files panel prompts Dreamweaver to open the file in an image-editing application.

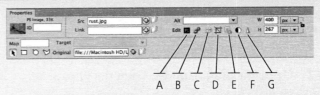

When an image is selected in the document window, the Properties panel not only displays properties (attributes) of the image, but also provides access to a number of image-related functions.

A. **Edit** opens the image file in its native application. GIF and JPG files open in Photoshop; PNG files open in Fireworks (assuming you have those applications).

B. **Edit Image Settings** opens a dialog box where you can change a variety of options for the selected file format. You can also use the Format menu to change the format of the selected image; if you change the format, you will be asked where you want to save the new file.

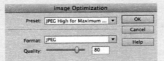

C. **Update From Original** can be used to make sure an inserted Photoshop image in the HTML file is the most recently saved version of the image.

If you insert a native Photoshop (PSD) file into a page, Dreamweaver converts it to a file that is appropriate for Web browsers. The original link to the PSD file is maintained; if the PSD file is changed, Dreamweaver notifies you that the image must be updated to the most recent version.

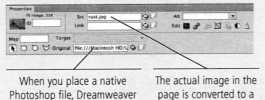

When you place a native Photoshop file, Dreamweaver stores a link to the original file.

The actual image in the page is converted to a Web-friendly format.

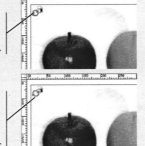

This indicator shows that the image in the HTML file is the most recent version.

The red indicator arrow tells you the Photoshop file has been modified since you placed it into the HTML file.

Although Dreamweaver is not an image-editing application, you can use it to perform some basic image-editing functions. These tools can't replace Adobe Photoshop, but they are well suited for making quick adjustments to an image from directly within the Dreamweaver application.

D. The **Crop tool** can be used to remove unwanted areas of an image. When you click the Crop tool, the lighter area shows the area that will be included in the cropped image; you can drag any of the eight handles around the edge of the crop area to change the area. Pressing Return/Enter finalizes the crop; pressing ESC cancels the crop and restores the original image.

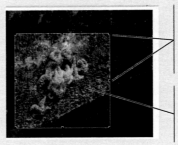

Drag any of the handles to change the area that will be included in the cropped version.

The lighter area shows what will remain after the crop has been applied.

E. The **Resample tool** changes the number of pixels in an image to exactly match the size of the selected instance in the page. This has the same effect as clicking the Commit Image Size button after resizing an image in the Design pane.

F. **Brightness and Contrast** can be used to change those properties in a selected image.

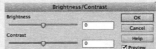

G. The **Sharpen** option can be useful for restoring some detail after resizing/resampling (especially upsizing). Keep in mind, however, that oversharpening can often produce worse results than what you start with.

Remember: All of the Dreamweaver image-editing tools permanently modify the edited file. If you use any of the image-editing buttons, you see a warning that the changes permanently affect the file (unless someone has checked the Don't Show ... option in the dialog box). Always keep a backup image so if you over-edit, you can replace the backup image and start over.

6. **Click OK to return to the document.**

   Dragging an image from the Files panel has the same result as clicking the Images:Image button in the Common Insert panel.

   Because you resampled this image in the previous exercise, it is already the appropriate smaller size.

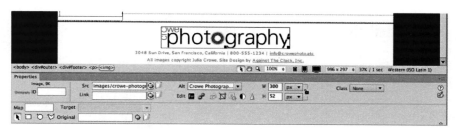

7. **Save the file and close it, then continue to the next exercise.**

INSERT AN IMAGE FROM THE ASSETS PANEL

The Assets panel, which is part of the Files panel group, offers another way to insert images. The Assets panel allows you to sort the various assets in a site by type rather than by their location within the site.

1. **Open the events.html file from the Files panel.**

2. **In the Design pane, select and delete the words "INSERT LOGO HERE" at the bottom of the page.**

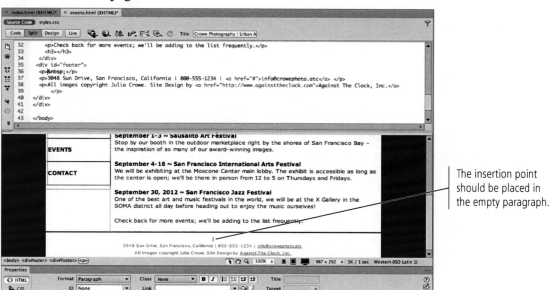

The insertion point should be placed in the empty paragraph.

3. **Open the Assets panel (Window>Assets).**

4. **On the left side of the Assets panel, click the Images button to show all images in the site.**

   The Assets panel displays a thumbnail of the selected image at the top of the panel.

5. **Click the Refresh Site List button to make sure all images are visible.**

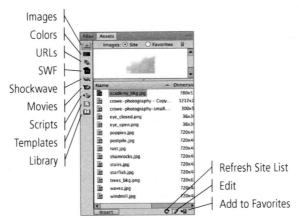

Images
Colors
URLs
SWF
Shockwave
Movies
Scripts
Templates
Library

Refresh Site List
Edit
Add to Favorites

Note:

You can also simply drag images from the Assets panel to place them on a page.

6. **Select crowe-photography-small.png in the panel. With the insertion point flashing where you deleted the text in Step 2, click the Insert button at the bottom of the Assets panel.**

7. **Define Crowe Photography as the alternate text and click OK.**

8. **Save your changes and close the file, then continue to the next stage of the project.**

Creating an Image Map

Although not as common as they once were, you can still use Dreamweaver to create an **image map**, which is an image with certain areas identified as **hotspots** that link to different pages.

When an image is selected on the page, you can use the tools in the bottom-left corner of the Properties panel to define hotspot areas for that image.

In the Design view, Dreamweaver applies a semi-transparent colored shape to represent the location, shape, and size of each hotspot area.

When the page is opened in a browser, there is no immediate visual cue to identify the defined hotspots. The cursor changes to the pointing-hand (link) cursor when the mouse enters the hotspot area. If you want the link to be identified in a tool tip, you should add the title attribute to the <area> tag (in the Code pane).

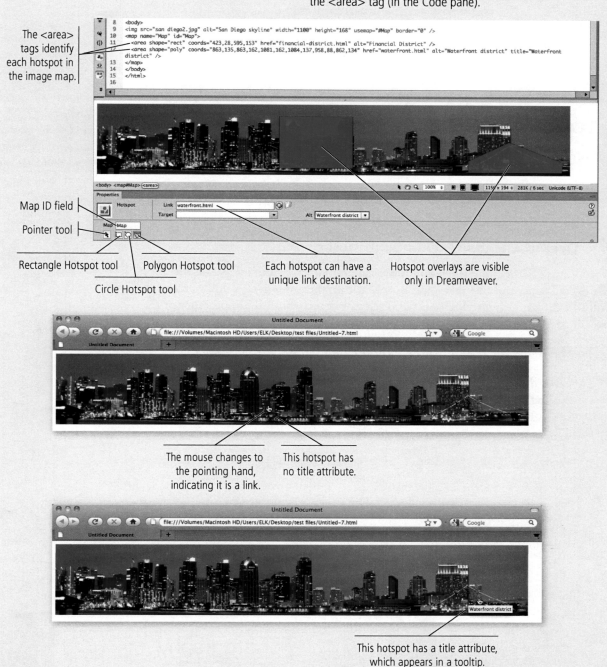

The <area> tags identify each hotspot in the image map.

```
8   <body>
9   <img src="san diego2.jpg" alt="San Diego skyline" width="1100" height="168" usemap="#Map" border="0" />
10  <map name="Map" id="Map">
11  <area shape="rect" coords="423,28,595,153" href="financial-district.html" alt="Financial District" />
12  <area shape="poly" coords="863,135,863,162,1081,162,1084,137,958,88,862,134" href="waterfront.html" alt="Waterfront district" title="Waterfront
    district" />
13  </map>
14  </body>
15  </html>
16
```

Map ID field

Pointer tool

Rectangle Hotspot tool

Circle Hotspot tool

Polygon Hotspot tool

Each hotspot can have a unique link destination.

Hotspot overlays are visible only in Dreamweaver.

The mouse changes to the pointing hand, indicating it is a link.

This hotspot has no title attribute.

This hotspot has a title attribute, which appears in a tooltip.

Stage 2 Controlling Backgrounds with CSS

Knowing how to use and apply CSS is especially helpful when you need to work with background images. Without CSS, a background image can only be placed behind the whole page. With CSS, a background image can be placed behind any HTML element, it can repeat, it can scroll with the element or remain locked in position, and it can be positioned anywhere within the element.

The files in the Crowe Photography site were created with a number of sections or divisions. Each division has been assigned a unique **ID** or name (using the **<div>** tag) so different CSS styles can be applied to different sections of the page, thus applying different backgrounds and formatting options for elements within each division.

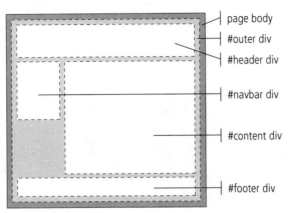

page body
#outer div
#header div
#navbar div
#content div
#footer div

Note:

Background images are properties of CSS styles and do not have the alt attribute option, so you should not put an informative image in the background.

DEFINE A PAGE BACKGROUND IMAGE

The Crowe Photography site requires two different background images — one for the overall page, and one that appears only within the outer div. In this exercise, you will edit the cascading style sheet (CSS) selector that controls the appearance of the overall page.

1. **Make sure the index.html file (in the Photography site) is open.**

2. **Click the Crowe Photography logo near the bottom of the page, then review the Tag Selector.**

   As we explained in Project 2: Digital Book Chapter, the Tag Selector shows the "path of tags", or the nested order of tags to the active selection.

   <body>   This tag identifies the basic page, where all visible content is contained.

   <div#outer>   identifies a div that is used to center the overall page content inside the document window. "#outer" is the ID or name of the div.

   <div#footer>   identifies the specific div that contains footer information for the page. "#footer" is the ID of the div.

   <p>   identifies the specific paragraph that contains the image.

   <img>   identifies the placed image.

Note:

In the Design pane, divisions are identified by dotted lines.

The Tag Selector shows that this element is in the footer div, which is itself inside the outer div.

CONTACT

photography

3048 Sun Drive, San Francisco, California | 800-555-1234 | info@crowephoto.atc
All images copyright Julia Crowe. Site Design by Against The Clock, Inc.

<body> <div#outer> <div#footer> <p> <img>   100%   996 x 500   37K / 1 sec   Western (ISO Latin 1)

3. **Open the CSS Styles panel, and click the All button.**

Remember, you can open all panels from the Window menu, or by clicking the relevant tab if the panel is open in the panel dock.

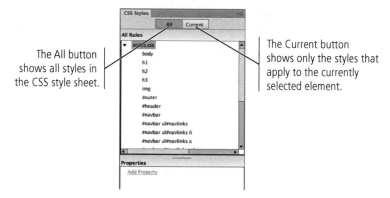

The All button shows all styles in the CSS style sheet.

The Current button shows only the styles that apply to the currently selected element.

4. **Click body at the top of the list to select it. At the bottom of the panel, click the Show Only Set Properties button.**

In the context of the CSS panel, items that define properties of a specific element (such as "body" in this example) are called **selectors** or **rules**.

Using CSS, **tag selectors** assign properties to specific HTML tags. The body selector defines the appearance of the <body> tag — or the overall visible page area.

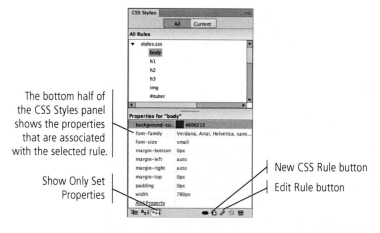

The bottom half of the CSS Styles panel shows the properties that are associated with the selected rule.

Show Only Set Properties

New CSS Rule button

Edit Rule button

Note:

You might need to expand the panel to see the Properties section.

5. **Click the Edit Rule button at the bottom of the panel to open the CSS Rule Definition dialog box.**

6. **In the resulting CSS Rule Definition dialog box, click Background in the Category list (on the left side of the dialog box).**

Note:

You can also Control/right-click a selector name in the panel and choose Edit from the contextual menu.

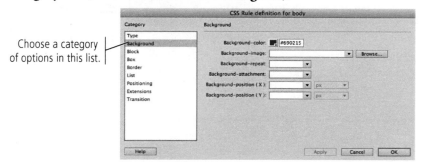

Choose a category of options in this list.

7. **To the right of the Background-image field, click the Browse button. Navigate to the Photography site images folder, select trees-bkg.png, and click Open/OK.**

8. **Choose no-repeat in the Background-repeat menu.**

   Unless you specify otherwise, a background image will repeat (tile) across and down until the background of the element is completely filled with the background image.

   The CSS **background-repeat** property has four options: repeat (the default), repeat-x (horizontally only), repeat-y (vertically only), and no-repeat (the background image appears only once in the top-left corner of the element).

9. **Choose fixed in the Background-attachment menu.**

   By choosing fixed, the image stays attached to the top-left corner of the body element; when a user scrolls the page, the image remains in place while the page scrolls on top of the background image.

   If you choose Scroll in this menu, the image will scroll along with the rest of the page.

10. **Choose left in the Background-position (X) menu, and choose top in the Background-position (Y) menu.**

    The CSS **background-position** property requires two values: horizontal positioning (left, right, or center) and vertical positioning (top, bottom, or center). You can also use measurements such as "5 pixels" to position a background image.

Note:

These fields define the horizontal (X) and vertical (Y) positions of the background image relative to the containing element.

11. **Click OK to close the CSS Rule Definition dialog box and apply the background image to the body element.**

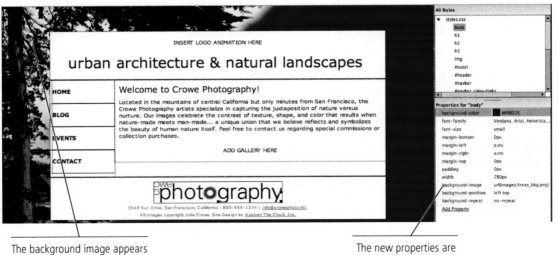

The background image appears once, attached to the top-left corner of the body element.

The new properties are added to the selector in the CSS Styles panel.

12. In the CSS Styles panel, click the color swatch for the background-color property to open the color picker.

After placing the background image, you can see that the dark red background color is not appropriate for the overall site content. You can use CSS to edit the background color of any element in the page.

13. Move the mouse cursor over the blue area in the placed logo image, then click to sample the logo color as the body element background color.

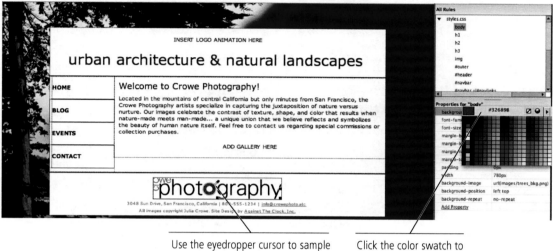

Use the eyedropper cursor to sample the color from the placed logo image.

Click the color swatch to open the color picker.

14. Look at the document bar at the top of the document window.

Although you made changes that affect the appearance of the index.html file, the document tab does not show an asterisk — in other words, the HTML document has not been changed. You do not need to save it before continuing.

All changes in this exercise were made to the CSS file that is linked to the open HTML file. The Related Files bar below the document tab shows an asterisk next to styles.css, indicating that the CSS file has been changed and so should be saved.

The index.html file has not been changed in this exercise.

The styles.css file has been changed in this exercise.

15. Click styles.css in the Related Files bar, then choose File>Save.

When you click one of the related files in the bar, the document window automatically switches to Split view and the file you clicked is displayed in the Code pane.

Clicking one of the related files opens the relevant code in the Code pane of the document window.

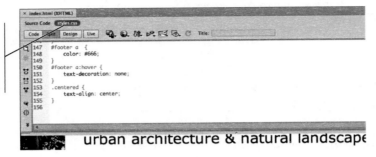

Note:

Although Dreamweaver offers Undo and Redo functions, they don't apply to changes to CSS unless you are working directly on the code of the CSS file (in Code view). If you want to undo a change in the CSS file, you must switch to the CSS file (in the Code pane) and use the Undo command.

16. Click Source Code in the Related Files bar to return to the main HTML file, and then click the Design button to return to Design view.

Clicking the Source Code button restores the active page's HTML code to the Code pane.

Clicking Source Code reverts the Code pane to the HTML file's code.

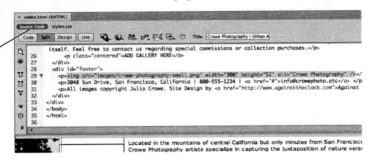

17. Continue to the next exercise.

Hexadecimal Color Codes

The RGB color model describes colors using values for red, green, and blue respectively. Each color can be assigned a value from 0 (none of that color) to 255 (full strength of that color), for a range of 256 values.

Black has zero values for all three colors, so it is represented as 0, 0, 0. White has full values for all three colors, so it is represented as 255, 255, 255. The hexadecimal system is a numeric system that uses 16 numerals from 0–9 plus A–F (11 is represented by A, 12 by B, up to 15 by F). Since 256 = 16 × 16, in hexadecimal code, 256 = F × F.

The range of 256 values for each color is from 0 to FF (by convention, the first 16 values from 0 to F are given a leading zero: 00 to 0F). Since RGB requires a value for each of the three colors, you will see hexadecimal color values such as #EE04F3, #40896C, and #E843A0.

When both digits for a particular color value are the same, you can abbreviate the code to only three digits. For example, the full code for black is #000000, but it can be abbreviated to #000.

In Web design, the hexadecimal color code must be preceded by the "#" sign (called the hash, pound, or octothorpe character). By convention, the letters should be uppercase, but neither Dreamweaver nor browsers differentiate between #EE04F3, #ee04f3, or #eE04f3.

DEFINE A BACKGROUND IMAGE FOR THE OUTER DIV

Many Web pages use different background properties — colors and/or images — to separate different areas of the page. In this exercise, you are going to define a separate background image that appears behind all of the main content (**div#outer**).

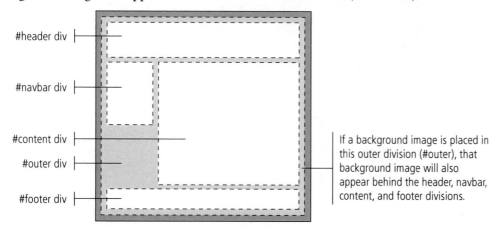

If a background image is placed in this outer division (#outer), that background image will also appear behind the header, navbar, content, and footer divisions.

1. **With index.html open, locate and select #outer in the CSS Styles panel.**

   ID selectors, which begin with the # symbol, assign specific properties to the element that is named with that ID.

2. **In the CSS Styles panel, click the Edit Rule button.**

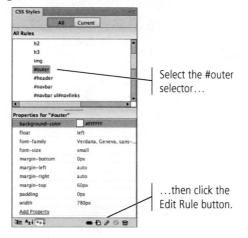

Select the #outer selector...

...then click the Edit Rule button.

3. **In the CSS Rule Definition dialog box, select the Background category.**

4. **Click the Browse button for the Background-image property. Select academy-bkg.jpg (in the site images folder), then click Open/OK.**

5. **Choose no-repeat in the Background-repeat menu.**

6. **Choose right in the Background-position (X) menu, and choose bottom in the Background-position (Y) menu.**

   Remember, these properties define the horizontal (X) and vertical (Y) positions of the background image *relative to the containing element*.

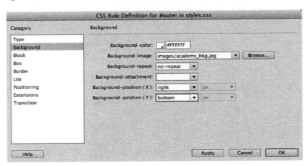

7. **Click OK to apply the change and return to the document window.**

   The new background image appears inside the #outer div — behind all of the actual page content area. (If any of the nested divs had a defined background color or image, the background image in the #outer div would be obscured in those areas.)

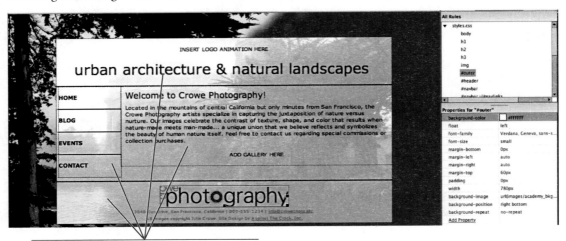

   The background image in the #outer div appears behind the header, navbar, content, and footer divs.

8. **Preview the page in your browser. Read the resulting warning message.**

   When you make changes to CSS rules that are stored in an external CSS file (as they are in this project), Dreamweaver makes the necessary changes in the related CSS file. The styles.css file is tagged with an asterisk in the bar at the top of the document window, indicating that it has been changed but not yet saved.

   The styles.css file has been changed and not yet saved.

9. **Click Yes to save the styles.css file and open the page in your browser.**

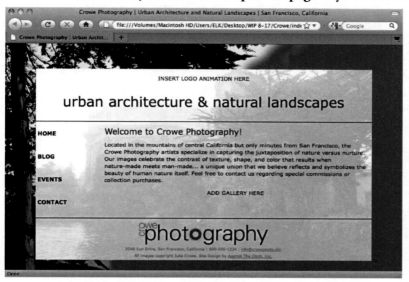

10. **Close the browser window.**

11. **Return to Dreamweaver and continue to the next exercise.**

DEFINE BACKGROUND IMAGES FOR NAVIGATION LINK STATES

One advantage of CSS is that you can define different background properties for every identified element. In this exercise, you will use those capabilities to create a custom background behind every list item in the left navigation bar.

1. **In the open index.html file, place the insertion point in any of the links in the navigation bar.**

2. **Review the Tag Selector below the Design pane.**

   Each navigation link is actually an item in an unordered list, which you can see from the **<ul>** and **<li>** tags in the Tag Selector. The list has been named with the **#navlinks** ID. Because each item is also a link, the final tag in the list is the **<a>** tag.

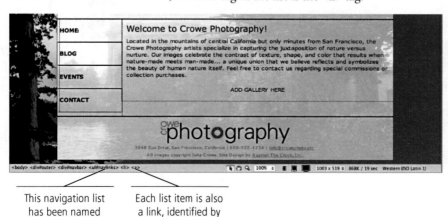

This navigation list has been named with the #navlinks ID.

Each list item is also a link, identified by the <a> tag.

3. **In the CSS Styles panel, locate and select #navbar ul#navlinks a, and then click the Edit Rule button at the bottom of the panel.**

Note:

For the sake of readability, we identify compound selector names in red.

This type of rule is called a **compound** or **descendant selector**, which defines a very specific element that will be affected. The name of this selector tells you where it will apply.

In this case, the "a" at the end of the selector name means that this rule will apply to all links within the unordered list named "navlinks" (ul#navlinks), which is in turn inside the division named "navbar" (#navbar).

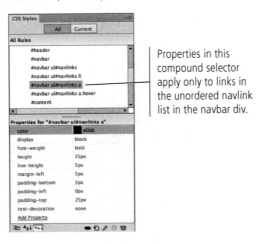

Properties in this compound selector apply only to links in the unordered navlink list in the navbar div.

4. **In the Background category, define eye-open.png (from the main site images folder) as the background image.**

5. **Choose no-repeat in the Background-repeat menu.**

6. **Choose left in the Background-position (X) menu, and choose center in the Background-position (Y) menu.**

7. **Click Apply (don't click OK).**

The Apply button allows you to view the changes without exiting the dialog box.

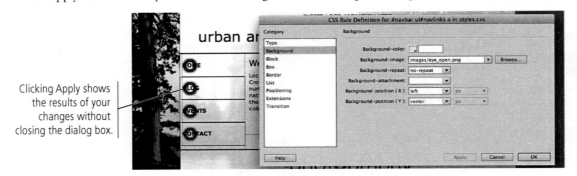

Clicking Apply shows the results of your changes without closing the dialog box.

8. **Switch to the Box category on the left. Type 40 in the Left Padding field and click Apply.**

   Padding is the extra space between the element content and the element border. Background colors and images extend into the padding.

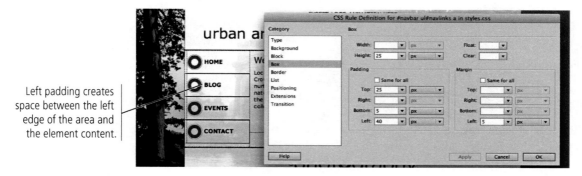

Left padding creates space between the left edge of the area and the element content.

9. **Click OK to close the CSS Rule Definition dialog box.**

10. **Select the #navbar ul#navlinks a:hover selector in the CSS Styles panel and click the Edit Rule button.**

    The "hover" selector defines the **mouseover state** for a particular link, which determines what happens when the user moves the mouse cursor over the link.

11. **In the Background category, browse to select eye-closed.png from the main site images folder. Set the Background-repeat property to no-repeat, choose left in the in the Background-position (X) field, and choose center from the Background-position (Y) menu. Click OK.**

    The **:hover** pseudo-class only applies when the mouse cursor hovers over a link; it does not apply when the mouse cursor is away from the link.

12. **Click the Live button in the Document toolbar and move your mouse cursor over the navigation links to test the hover effect.**

    The **:hover** pseudo-class is a dynamic effect that Dreamweaver's Design pane cannot display. To see the effect, you must view the page in a browser or switch to Live view.

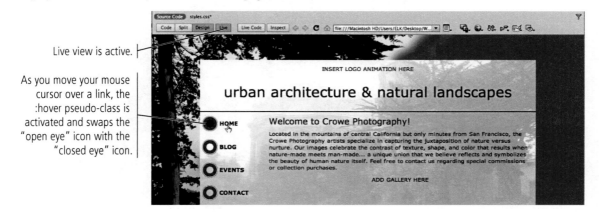

Live view is active.

As you move your mouse cursor over a link, the :hover pseudo-class is activated and swaps the "open eye" icon with the "closed eye" icon.

13. **Click the styles.css button in the Related Files bar. Save the changes in the CSS file.**

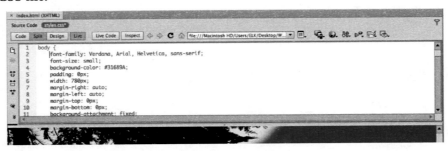

14. **Click the Design button to close the Code pane, then click the Live button to toggle that feature off and return to the regular Design view.**

15. **Continue to the next stage of the project.**

Creating a Rollover Image

In the last exercise you used CSS to create an element that changes based on the position of the user's mouse cursor.

You can also use Dreamweaver to insert a rollover image directly into an HTML page.

To create a rollover image, open the Image menu in the Insert panel and choose Rollover image (or choose Insert>Image Objects>Rollover Image).

In the resulting dialog box, you can define the two images to use — the original or default image, and the rollover image that appears when a user's mouse enters the image area.

If the Preload Rollover Image option is checked, the Web server will automatically download the rollover image when the page is first opened. This prevents a delay when a user triggers the rollover.

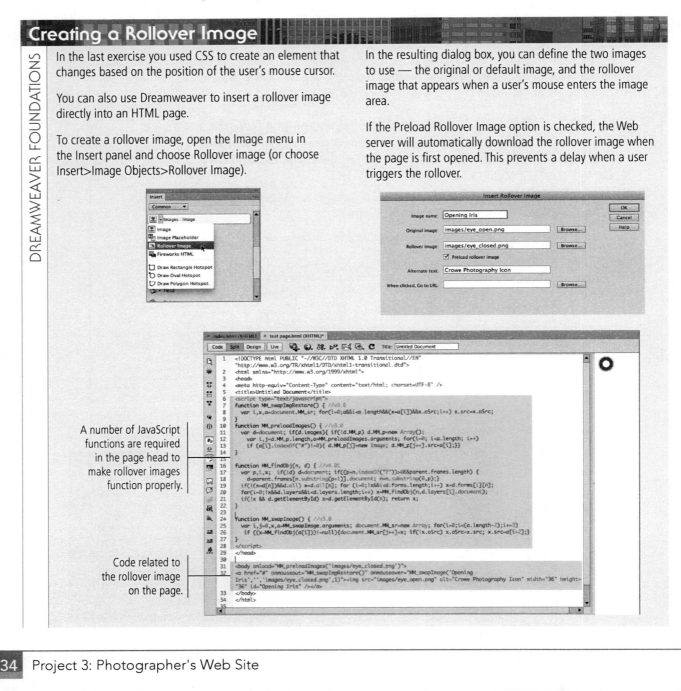

A number of JavaScript functions are required in the page head to make rollover images function properly.

Code related to the rollover image on the page.

Stage 3 Working with Other Image Types

In addition to static images such as photos, logos, and graphic text, two other forms of images are commonly incorporated into Web designs — Flash animations and video files, collectively known as **multimedia**.

Depending on the configuration of a Web page, video and audio files might need to completely download to your computer before playing, or they might be embedded within a Web page so they can play as they download — known as **streaming**. The purpose of streaming is to allow the video or audio to play before the entire file has been downloaded; streaming can also provide some protection because the video and audio files aren't stored on the user's computer.

Adobe Flash can be used to create simple animations such as moving text, as well as more complex animations such as online games. Flash can also be used to display and control video. Although most desktop computers have the required Flash Player plug-in installed, many mobile devices — specifically, those running the iOS operating system — do not support Flash-based animations or video. (You will learn how to add multiple-device support for video in Project 6: Kayaking HTML5 Site.)

Note:

To view Flash objects in your browser, the Flash plug-in must be installed on your computer. In the past, you had to manually download and install the plug-in; today, however, most browsers have the Flash plug-in installed (or it is automatically installed the first time you need the plug-in to view a Flash movie).

 ## INSERT A FLASH ANIMATION

Inserting Flash objects into a Web page requires a complicated mix of HTML tags, including the **<object>** and **<param>** tags. Furthermore, to comply with an ongoing patent dispute regarding embedding plug-ins within a Web page, Flash objects (among others) must be loaded into a browser using JavaScript. Fortunately, Dreamweaver embeds Flash objects within Web pages and properly writes the **<object>** and **<param>** tags for you, surrounding them with the appropriate JavaScript code to comply with the patent.

1. **Make sure index.html in the Photography site is open.**

2. **In Design view, select and delete the words "INSERT LOGO ANIMATION HERE" at the top of the page. Leave the insertion point in the now-empty paragraph.**

3. **With the Insert panel in Common mode, click the arrow on the Media button and choose SWF from the menu.**

    Like the Images button, the Media button remembers the last-used option. To be sure you are inserting the correct type of object in this step, open the menu and choose SWF.

Note:

You can also choose Insert>Media>SWF.

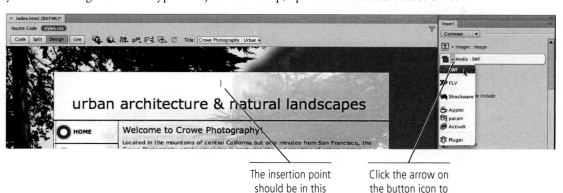

The insertion point should be in this empty paragraph.

Click the arrow on the button icon to open the menu.

4. **Open the flash folder in the Photography site root folder, select
   logo-animated.swf, and click Open/OK.**

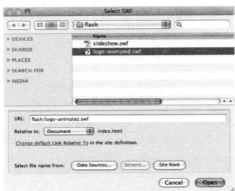

Note:

*SWF is the final,
compressed, uneditable
format of an Adobe
Flash file.*

5. **Type Crowe Photography in the Title field of the Object Tag Accessibility
   Attributes dialog box, and then click OK.**

   The title attribute provides some measure of accessibility to SWF files. This animation
   is simple, containing the text "Crowe Photography," as well as an animated camera
   aperture. In this case, the text of the animation is sufficient for accessibility purposes.

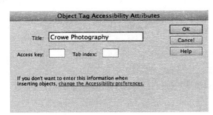

Note:

*Interactive files that
change with user
interaction and include
a large amount of text
require accessibility to
be built into the Flash
object.*

6. **With the placed SWF object selected in the Design pane, examine the
   Properties panel.**

   When a placed SWF file is selected on the page, a blue tag (above the placeholder) displays
   the type and ID of the asset. You can click the eye icon to toggle between the SWF file and
   the information users see if they don't have the correct version of Flash Player.

When the mouse cursor
is over the SWF object,
this tag identifies the
type and ID of the asset.

The Flash object
appears as a gray box
in the Design view.

These options
control the
animation playback.

7. **Click the Live view button in the document toolbar and watch the animation.**

You have to use the Live view to preview a SWF animation in Dreamweaver.

Note:

If you preview the page in Live view, the SWF file plays just as if it were in a browser window.

The background of the Flash object window obscures the underlying background image.

8. **Turn off the Live view, then select the Flash object on the page.**

Remember, you can't select and modify page content when the Live view is active.

9. **In the Properties panel, choose Transparent in the WMode menu.**

The WMode property defines the background color of the window in which the Flash object is placed. By choosing Transparent in the menu, you allow the background image to be visible behind the animation.

Choose Transparent in this menu.

10. **Turn the Live view back on and review the animation.**

The now-transparent window allows the background image to show behind the animation.

11. **Turn off the Live view, then save the file (File>Save). Read the message in the resulting dialog box.**

Some placed assets — including SWF files — require specific scripts to work properly in the final page. When you save a page after placing one of these objects, Dreamweaver identifies the necessary files and alerts you that they will be copied into your site folder. For the SWF file to work properly in the live Web site, these files should be uploaded along with the rest of your site files.

Copy Dependent Files

This page uses an object or behavior that requires supporting files. The following files have been copied to your local site. You must upload them to your server in order for the object or behavior to function correctly.

Scripts/expressinstall.swf
Scripts/swfobject_modified.js

OK

12. **Click OK in the Copy Dependent Files dialog box.**

13. **Repeat this process to insert the animated logo at the top of the `blog.html` and `events.html` files.**

    Don't forget to change the WMode property for the SWF object in each file.

14. **Continue to the next exercise.**

 ## INSERT AND CONFIGURE A FLASH SLIDESHOW

Todd Dominey (www.todddominey.org) created a Flash-based slideshow object that you can easily configure to include your own photos. The slideshow reads the content of an XML file called images.xml, which contains the file names (and paths if necessary) of the photos to be shown in the slideshow. By changing the file names, you can use the same Flash object to show different photos. You must save the images in JPEG format, and you must resize the images to fit within the dimensions of the Flash object. Once those tasks are done, you have access to an easily customizable slideshow animation — without using the full Flash application.

1. **With `index.html` open (from the Photography site), select and delete the words "ADD GALLERY HERE" from the content div.**

2. **In the Common Insert panel, click the Media:SWF button.**

    If you did not continue directly from the previous exercise, and your button does not say "Media:SWF", click the arrow on the button and choose SWF from the top of the list.

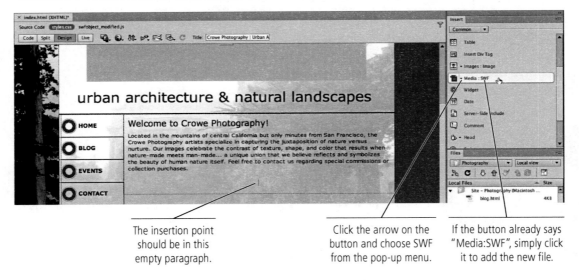

The insertion point should be in this empty paragraph.

Click the arrow on the button and choose SWF from the pop-up menu.

If the button already says "Media:SWF", simply click it to add the new file.

3. **Navigate to the flash folder in the Photography site (if necessary), select slideshow.swf, and click Open/OK.**

4. **In the Title field of the Object Tag Accessibility Attributes dialog box, type `Photos from the Crowe collection`, and then click OK.**

5. Turn on the Live view and review the placed object.

The slideshow is black because the images identified in the XML file don't exist in this site. You need to edit the images.xml file and replace the image file names with those found on this site.

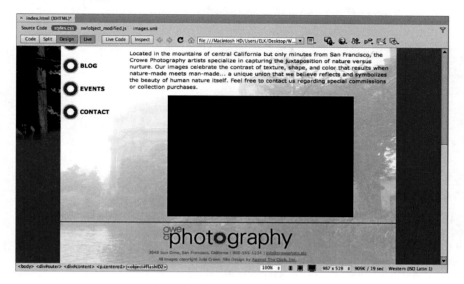

Note:

The slideshow used in this exercise is available at no cost. You can purchase the full SlideShowPro (www.slideshowpro.net), which contains a wide range of options and features.

6. Using the Files panel, double-click **images.xml** (in the site root folder) to open the XML file.

Some options for the slideshow are described in the comments at the top of the XML file; they are inserted as attributes of the opening <gallery> tag.

Use as many images as you like by listing them here.

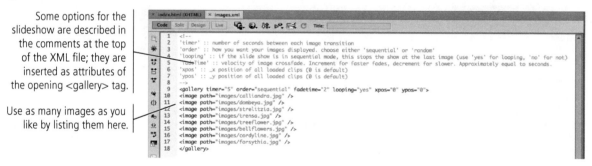

7. In the Files panel, expand the slides folder.

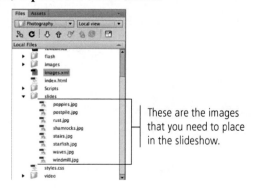

These are the images that you need to place in the slideshow.

8. **Select the first image path in the XML file code (images/calliandra.jpg) and replace it with** `slides/poppies.jpg`.

Leave the quotes from the original image path in place, and simply type the new path name.

Change the first image path to match the path of the image you want to show.

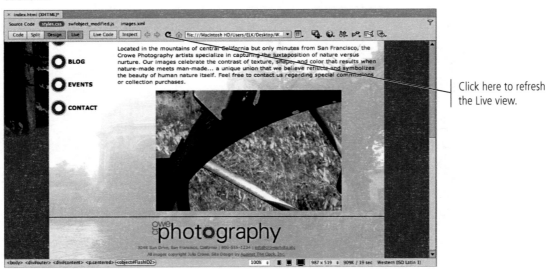

```
1    <!--
2    'timer' :: number of seconds between each image transition
3    'order' :: how you want your images displayed. choose either 'sequential' or 'random'
4    'looping' :: if the slide show is in sequential mode, this stops the show at the last image (use 'yes' for looping, 'no' for not)
5    'fadeTime' :: velocity of image crossfade. Increment for faster fades, decrement for slower. Approximately equal to seconds.
6    'xpos' :: _x position of all loaded clips (0 is default)
7    'ypos' :: _y position of all loaded clips (0 is default)
8    -->
9    <gallery timer="5" order="sequential" fadetime="2" looping="yes" xpos="0" ypos="0">
10   <image path="slides/poppies.jpg" />
11   <image path="images/dombeya.jpg" />
12   <image path="images/strelitzia.jpg" />
13   <image path="images/trensa.jpg" />
14   <image path="images/treeflower.jpg" />
15   <image path="images/bellflowers.jpg" />
16   <image path="images/cordyline.jpg" />
17   <image path="images/forsythia.jpg" />
18   </gallery>
```

9. **Replace the image paths for the remaining images in the code, using the correct names from the site's slides folder.**

For this slideshow to work properly, the file slideshow.swf can be placed in any folder within your site, but images.xml must be placed in the same folder as the page calling the file. Because of code in the slideshow.swf file, images.xml cannot be renamed; if you want to use it for two different slideshows in the same folder, you must move one of the slideshows to another folder. Finally, the paths to the images must be relative to the location of the images.xml file. (You can also use absolute paths, but you won't be able to preview the slideshow from your local computer.)

```
5    'fadeTime' :: velocity of image crossfade. Increment for faster fades, decrement for slower. Approximately equal to seconds.
6    'xpos' :: _x position of all loaded clips (0 is default)
7    'ypos' :: _y position of all loaded clips (0 is default)
8    -->
9    <gallery timer="5" order="sequential" fadetime="2" looping="yes" xpos="0" ypos="0">
10   <image path="slides/poppies.jpg" />
11   <image path="slides/postpile.jpg" />
12   <image path="slides/rust.jpg" />
13   <image path="slides/shamrocks.jpg" />
14   <image path="slides/stairs.jpg" />
15   <image path="slides/starfish.jpg" />
16   <image path="slides/waves.jpg" />
17   <image path="slides/windmill.jpg" />
18   </gallery>
```

10. **Save the changes to images.xml and close the file.**

11. **With the Live view active, click the Refresh button in the Document toolbar.**

Click here to refresh the Live view.

12. **Turn off the Live view, save the file and close it, and then continue to the next exercise.**

The FLV format is the native Flash video format. Using Adobe Media Encoder (a separate application that is included with Flash), you can import videos in a variety of formats and save them in the Flash video format (.flv or .f4v). You can wrap video inside a Flash video player, and then use Dreamweaver to embed the video in a Web page. This way, your visitors can view the video from directly within the Web page.

As with the SWF format, support for the FLV format is not available on some mobile devices. You will learn different options for working with video files in Project 6: Kayaking HTML5 Site.

1. **Open blog.html from the Photography site root folder.**

2. **Select and delete the text "ADD VIDEO HERE" from the bottom of the content div.**

3. **In the Common Insert panel, click the arrow on the Media button and choose FLV from the menu.**

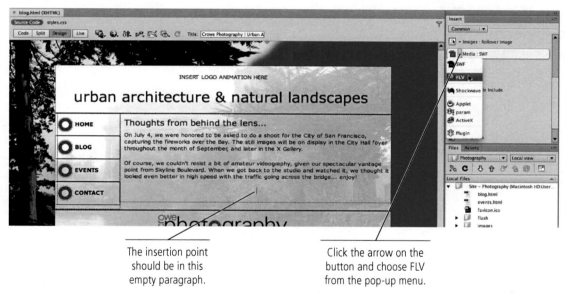

The insertion point should be in this empty paragraph.

Click the arrow on the button and choose FLV from the pop-up menu.

4. **In the resulting Insert FLV dialog box, make sure the Video Type menu is set to Progressive Download Video.**

The other option, Streaming Video, is used when the video is very large, the copyright owner doesn't want visitors to have a copy of the video on their systems, or there is a continuous feed from the source.

5. **Click the Browse button to the right of the URL field. In the resulting navigation dialog box, choose fireworks.flv from the Photography site's video folder and click Open/OK.**

6. **Click the Detect Size button.**

The width and height of the video are detected and the fields are filled. The dimensions of the video affect the skin options (which we explain in the next step).

7. **Open the Skin menu and choose Clear Skin 3.**

   The **skin** is the appearance of the video controls that are added to the video object. There are three basic skin appearances — Clear, Corona, and Halo. Each skin appearance has three Width options. The Width options affect the number and appearance of video controls. Video controls include play, pause, stop, skip to anywhere within the video, mute the sound, and increase/decrease the volume. A narrow-width video has less room for video controls. This video is wider than any of the minimum widths, so any Skin option will work.

   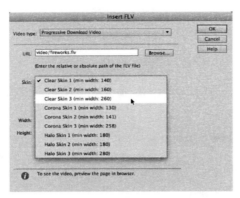

8. **Uncheck the Auto Play option below the Height field.**

   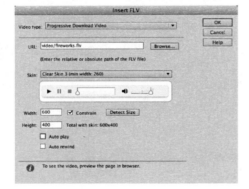

9. **Click OK to insert the video into the open HTML file.**

   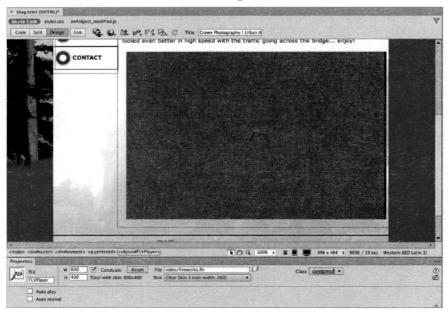

10. Turn on the Live view and watch the video.

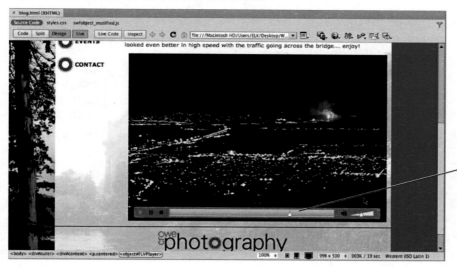

After the video starts playing, the controls fade out. If you move your mouse over the video, the controls reappear.

11. Save the file and close it, then continue to the final exercise.

 ## ADD A PAGE FAVICON

Favicon is a word created by combining "favorite" and "icon." It refers to the icon that represents a site in your Favorites or Bookmarks list (beside the site name). A favicon is not randomly generated; it is downloaded from the bookmarked site. In addition to the Favorites or Bookmarks list, the favicon also appears at the left end of the browser's address bar or tab (if your browser supports tabs).

A favicon is an image in the icon format, which supports a limited number of colors and is generally restricted to 16×16 and 32×32 pixels. (The format supports both resolutions within the same file, which is one reason why it is unique.)

Although some desktop graphics applications can create icons, some graphic and Web design applications (such as Adobe Photoshop and Fireworks) do not support the icon format. There are a number of free online applications for converting GIF, PNG, JPEG, or BMP images to the icon format; we used the converter at www.favicon.cc to create the icon file for this project.

Because the icon is commonly used as a representation of an entire Web site, the favicon.ico file is commonly stored in the root folder of the Web site. The file must be named "favicon.ico".

The following code block is supported by most browsers:

```
<link rel="shortcut icon" type="image/x-icon" href="favicon.ico" />
```

Dreamweaver does not provide code hints for most of the attribute values of the **<link />** tag, so it is easiest to simply type the code in the appropriate location.

1. **Open index.html from the root folder of the Photography site.**

2. **Click the Code button to switch to Code view.**

3. **Click to the left of the closing </head> tag on line 8, press Return/Enter three times, and move the insertion point into the middle empty line.**

   In general, the **<link />** tag should be used to insert the favicon as the last tag in the head section of the document.

4. **Type the code required to insert the favicon:**

   ```
   <link rel="shortcut icon" type="image/x-icon" href="favicon.ico" />
   ```

Note:

In an actual site, you would likely use an absolute path to the favicon file, so the browser will always look for the favicon.ico file in the root folder of the Web site. Since you can't use absolute paths when previewing pages on your local computer, however, you must use a relative path.

   As you type, code hints appear when Dreamweaver recognizes a specific tag. In this case, it is easier to simply ignore these hints and type the required code.

5. **Save the file, and then preview the page in your browser.**

   If possible, preview in a browser other than Safari or Internet Explorer; these browsers require the site to be online, not local.

There's the favicon in Firefox.

6. **Return to Dreamweaver and close index.html.**

7. **Export a site definition named Photography.ste into your WIP>Crowe folder, and then remove the Photography site from Dreamweaver.**

   If necessary, refer back to Project 1: Bistro Site Organization for complete instructions on exporting a site definition or removing a site from Dreamweaver.

Project Review

fill in the blank

1. The _____ attribute of the <img> tag is required to make images accessible for all Web users.

2. The _____ attribute defines the specific file that will appear in the <img> tag location.

3. The _____ property of CSS can be used to tile a single background image horizontally, vertically, or both throughout the entire document window.

4. _____ is the process of cutting out/off portions of an image.

5. The _____ format supports continuous-tone color but not transparency; it is best used for photographs.

6. The _____ format supports transparency but not a large gamut of color; it is best used for graphics and artwork.

7. A(n) _____ replaces one image with another when the mouse cursor enters the image area.

8. The _____ extension identifies an animation file that was exported from Adobe Flash.

9. The _____ extension identifies a Flash video file.

10. A _____ is a graphic that appears to the left of the site URL in the browser's navigation bar.

short answer

1. Briefly describe three image file formats that might be used on the Web, including advantages and disadvantages of each.

2. Briefly explain the importance of resampling, relative to resizing images in Dreamweaver.

3. Briefly explain the advantages to using CSS to define background colors and images.

Portfolio Builder Project

Use what you learned in this project to complete the following freeform exercise.
Carefully read the art director and client comments, then create your own design to meet the needs of the project.
Use the space below to sketch ideas; when finished, write a brief explanation of your reasoning behind your final design.

art director comments

Everything Green Flowers wants to include a digital portfolio in the company's new Web site. As part of the team that is building the new site, your job is to create and implement pages for a Flash version and an HTML version of the portfolio.

To complete this project, you should:

❏ Create a new site in Dreamweaver using the files that have already been created (in the **DW6_PB_Project3.zip** archive on the Student Files Web page).

❏ Place the client's logo on every page.

❏ Add background images to the header and footer sections of the page.

❏ Add a background image to the navigation links in the header section.

❏ Add a photo gallery to the Sample Designs page, using the techniques you used to complete the Crowe Photography site.

client comments

The page structure has already been defined, but the images need to be put into place.

Our logo should appear on every page, at the top of the main content area.

The header and footer sections need background images placed.

We want our pink icon to appear to the left of each navigation item in the header section. It should change to white when users move the mouse over the links.

On the Sample Designs page, add the Flash-based slideshow. All of the images we want to show are in the images>flowers folder. You will need to modify the size of the placed Flash object on the page to fit the images that we've provided.

project justification

_____
_____
_____
_____
_____
_____
_____
_____
_____
_____
_____
_____
_____
_____
_____

Project Summary

When you prepare the design for a site, you need to determine which images will carry content (they must be placed in the foreground using the **<img>** tag), and which images will appear in the background. Appropriate alt text — which enables visually impaired visitors, users who have disabled the display of images, and search engines to use the content of your pages — is required for all foreground images. By editing various CSS properties, you have virtually unlimited options for controlling the background images in different sections of a page.

Dreamweaver also provides image-editing tools that enable you to crop, resize, resample, and sharpen images. Although these tools do not replace full-featured image-editing applications such as Photoshop, the Dreamweaver tools enable you to complete simple editing tasks quickly and easily, without requiring another application.

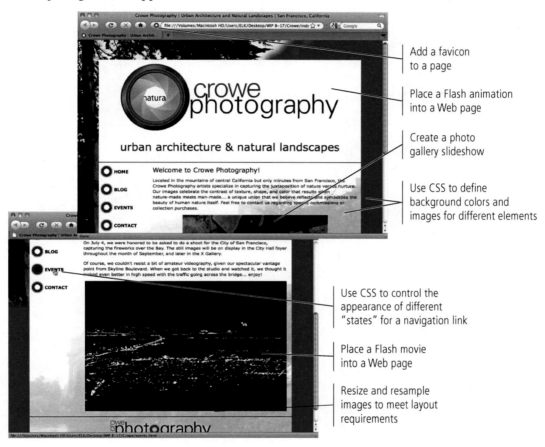

Add a favicon to a page

Place a Flash animation into a Web page

Create a photo gallery slideshow

Use CSS to define background colors and images for different elements

Use CSS to control the appearance of different "states" for a navigation link

Place a Flash movie into a Web page

Resize and resample images to meet layout requirements

4

Yosemite CSS Layout

The Yosemite Valley Visitor's Bureau hired you to build a new Web site to provide area visitors with as much information as possible about the activities and opportunities that are available in and around the national park. The client wants a Web site that can be quickly and easily updated and modified. In addition, the site should project a consistent look and style across all pages. To fulfill these requirements, you will create and apply a cascading style sheet for the Web site.

This project incorporates the following skills:

❑ Working with tracing images to replicate a site designed in an image-editing application

❑ Creating and linking an external CSS file

❑ Understanding the CSS box model

❑ Creating a layout with div elements

❑ Editing CSS rules to adjust the layout

❑ Defining HTML tag selectors and compound tag selectors

❑ Creating pseudo-class selectors

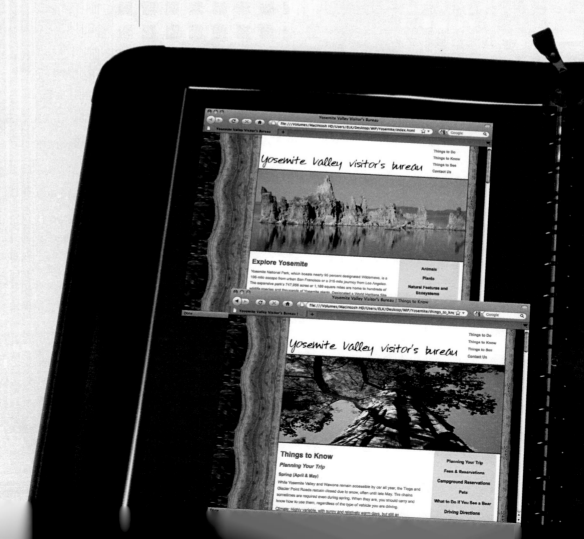

client comments

We've been getting a lot of inquiries now that spring is coming, and we want to create a new Web site to help answer some of the preliminary questions so our administrative time can focus on conservation efforts.

We have a site already but we can't figure out how it was built, so it's extremely difficult to change even a comma. We called the site designer, but he can't work us into his schedule for more than a month — and we don't have the time to wait.

The new site should be very easy to manage and, more importantly, easy to change — whether it's a comma or the entire site layout.

art director comments

I asked the graphic designer to put together the look and feel of the new site. She created a comp image that shows the overall layout, which you should review carefully to see what elements of the new site you need to implement in Dreamweaver.

The client wants to be able to make his own changes to the actual page content, but we don't want him to be able to destroy the integrity of the page layout. Cascading style sheets are the best way to accomplish this goal because the actual HTML pages will be almost entirely text. The layout will be defined in the CSS file, so the client can edit the text all he wants without touching the layout.

CSS separates the page content from the presentational issues like containers and backgrounds, so search engines can more easily scan and rank the actual page content.

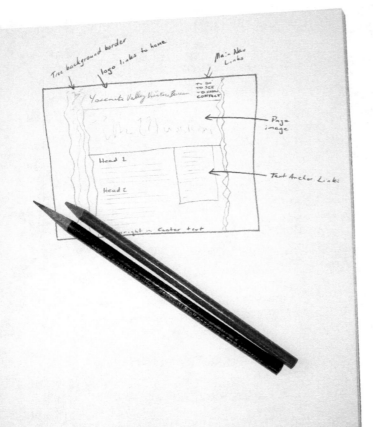

project objectives

To complete this project, you will:

❑ Define a tracing image

❑ Create and link an external CSS file

❑ Create ID selectors

❑ Create a layout with div elements

❑ Edit CSS rules to adjust the layout

❑ Use the float property to control nested divs

❑ Use margins and padding to affect element placement

❑ Define properties for the body tag

❑ Create a template file

❑ Define HTML tag selectors

❑ Create compound tag selectors

❑ Create pseudo-class selectors

Stage 1 Creating Layouts with Style Sheets

A **cascading style sheet** (CSS) is a collection of formatting rules that control the appearance of different elements in a Web page. By attaching a style sheet file to an HTML page and applying the styles to the content of the page, you can control every aspect of the page layout. A CSS file includes formatting instructions in **rules**. A rule consists of two parts: a **selector** (basically, naming the element to be formatted) and **attributes** (such as font, color, width, height, etc.) that will be applied to the selected element.

A style sheet offers a great deal of flexibility in applying styles. Different types of styles can automatically target HTML tags, target HTML tags only in certain places in a page, control specific elements, control multiple elements at once, and control links.

When using a style sheet, you are separating the formatting of a page (CSS) from the structure and content (HTML). To make changes with the CSS formatting, you are usually just editing the style sheet itself rather than the HTML in individual pages. If all pages in a site use the same style sheet, the task of providing control and consistency will be far easier.

DEFINE A TRACING IMAGE

Before creating CSS rules, you should have a clear idea about how the page or site should look. Understanding the appearance (and other requirements) of a site helps you determine what rules you need to create.

In many workflows, the look of a site is designed in a graphics application such as Adobe Photoshop, Fireworks, or Illustrator. In this case, you can import the final image file of the design into Dreamweaver and use it as a map when defining CSS rules to replicate the image as an HTML page. Using the Tracing Image feature, the image you select appears in the background in Design view; you can change the opacity and position of the image as necessary. When you have finished the layout design, you can hide or remove the tracing image.

Note:

A tracing image can be a JPEG, GIF, BMP, or PNG file.

Note:

A tracing image is a Dreamweaver Design view-only feature, it will not appear in Live view or in a Web browser.

1. **Download DW6_RF_Project4.zip from the Student Files Web page.**

2. **Expand the ZIP archive in your WIP folder (Macintosh) or copy the archive contents into your WIP folder (Windows).**

   This results in a folder named **Yosemite**, which contains the files you need for this project.

3. **Create a new site named Yosemite, using the WIP>Yosemite folder as the site root folder.**

   If necessary, refer to the first exercises in Project 1: Bistro Site Organization for more detailed instructions.

4. **With the Yosemite site open in the Files panel, choose New in the File menu. Using the New Document dialog box, create a new, blank HTML page using the XHTML 1.0 Transitional DocType.**

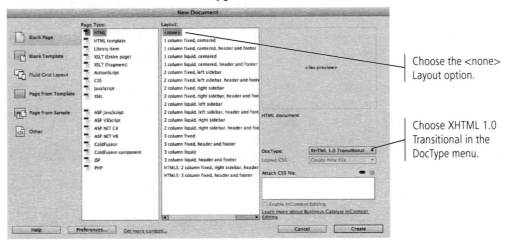

Choose the <none> Layout option.

Choose XHTML 1.0 Transitional in the DocType menu.

5. **Choose File>Save. Save the new page as an HTML file named design.html in the root folder of the Yosemite site.**

Note:

You can also create a new blank HTML page by Control/right-clicking the site name in the Files panel and choosing New File in the contextual menu. The resulting file is automatically placed in the site root folder.

6. **With design.html open in Design view, Click the Page Properties button in the Properties panel.**

7. **Click Tracing Image in the left side of the dialog box to display those options, then click the Browse button to the right of the Tracing Image field.**

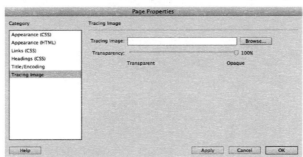

8. **In the Select Image Source dialog box, navigate to the file tracing.jpg in the site root folder (WIP>Yosemite) and click Open/OK.**

When you load a tracing image, the Page Properties dialog box automatically appears. You can use the Tracing Image options to change the transparency of the tracing image, as well as browse to select a different image.

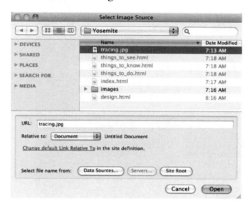

Note:

To show or hide the tracing image, use the Show/Hide toggle control in the View>Tracing Image menu.

Note:

If you hide the tracing image, then close the HTML file and reopen it, the tracing image will again be visible; you can rehide it as necessary.

9. **Click OK to close the resulting Page Properties dialog box.**

You can use this dialog box to define a different tracing image (with the Browse button), or reduce the opacity of the image in the file.

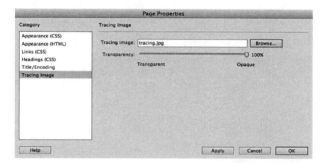

Note:

The other options in the Page Properties dialog box create CSS properties as internal or embedded styles, which means they cannot be reused in other files. It is better to set those properties in an external CSS file, which can be attached to multiple HTML files.

The tracing image appears in design.html. If you have a small screen, you might not be able to see the entire image at 100% magnification.

The tracing image is aligned by default at the insertion point, which is slightly inset from the document edges.

You can't scroll to see the rest of the tracing image.

10. Choose View>Tracing Image>Reset Position.

This command moves the tracing image to the actual document edges.

11. Change your view percentage as necessary to see the entire tracing image.

12. Analyze the image to determine what you need to do to create this site layout.

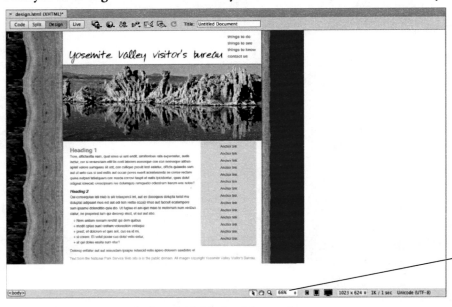

- The layout is attached to the left side of the window.
- The background image should repeat over the entire height of the window.
- The left border area is 200 pixels wide.
- The white space in between the borders is 700 pixels wide.
- The right border area is 50 pixels wide.
- The layout is broken into four rows: header, image, page content, and footer.
- The first and third rows each have two separate areas of content.

Note:

When rulers are visible (View>Rulers>Show), guides can be dragged out from them to mark specific places on the page. This can make it easier to measure elements in a tracing image.

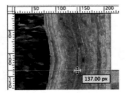

When rulers are visible, you can press Command/ Control to show measurements between guides, as well as between guides and page edges.

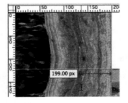

To remove individual guides, click a guide and drag it back to the ruler. To remove all guides, choose View> Guides>Clear Guides.

Use this menu to change the view percentage in the Design view.

Note:

You can also change the viewing percentage in the View>Magnification menu.

13. **Take note of the following information, which was provided by the designer who developed the look of the site:**

- The site should have a green background color that fills in the browser window space behind the background image.

- Each page will have the same layout; only the image in the second row and the text in the third row will differ from page to page.

- The images for the second row are all the same size: 700 px × 280 px.

- A sans-serif font should be applied to all text in the site. The client wants to use gray text instead of plain black text.

- First-level headings and the navigation links in the header should be a dark orange color from the bark in the border image.

- Second-level headings should be a bit smaller than first-level headings, italicized, and use the same color as the main text.

- Link text should not be underlined. In the header navigation area and the main body text, link text should be a dark orange color from the background image. In the sidebar navigation (at the right of the third row), link text should use a green color from the background.

- Links in the two navigation areas should be bold. Links in the side navigation area should be centered within the sidebar space.

- Link text should switch to a lighter color when the mouse rolls over the links.

14. **Reset the view percentage to 100%, save the file, and continue to the next exercise.**

CREATE AN EXTERNAL CSS FILE

There are three types of style sheets: external, embedded (also known as internal), and inline. To make the best use of styles, you should have a clear understanding of these different types — including when each is best suited to a specific goal.

An **external style sheet** is saved as a separate CSS file (with the extension ".css"), which is uploaded to the Web server along with the Web site pages. This file can be attached to multiple HTML pages at one time, applying the same rules to similar elements in the different pages. When a user calls a specific URL, the Web browser reads the HTML, finds the directions to the attached CSS file, and reads the rules in the CSS file to present the HTML content exactly as intended.

An **embedded or internal style sheet** is added directly in an HTML page, within style tags; this type of style affects only the particular HTML page in which it is placed. The following code for an embedded style sheet includes a style that defines the formatting of all H1 elements:

```
<style type="text/css"
<!--
h1 {
    font-size: 24px;
}
-->
</style>
```

An **inline style** applies directly and instantly to an individual element within a tag, affecting only that single element of the HTML page. For example, if you apply a font size and color to a paragraph, the inline style looks like this:

```
<p style="font-size: 10px; color: blue">Paragraph content goes here.</p>
```

Note:

All three types of style sheets can be applied to the same HTML page at the same time.

Note:

The set of <!-- and --> tags prevents a few older browsers from displaying the style rules.

Note:

Because inline styles are not reusable even within the same page and don't appear in Dreamweaver's CSS Styles panel, it is better to use external or internal style sheets.

1. **With `design.html` open, choose File>New.**

2. **In the New Document dialog box, choose Blank Page in the left column. Choose CSS from the Page Type list and click Create.**

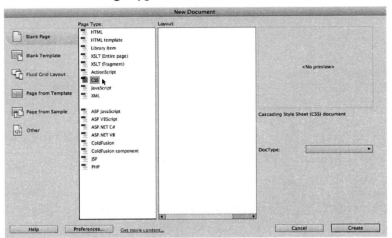

3. **Choose File>Save. Name the file `master.css`, and then click Save to save the file in the site root folder.**

   This file will contain all the selectors you define to format the Yosemite Valley Web site.

4. **Click the design.html tab to make that file active, then choose Window> CSS Styles to show the CSS Styles panel.**

   master.css is open in a separate file.
   It is not yet related to design.html.

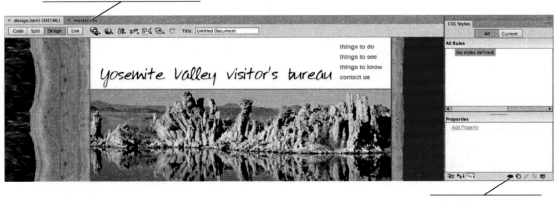

   Attach Style Sheet button

5. **Click the Attach Style Sheet button at the bottom of the CSS Styles panel.**

   The resulting dialog box allows you to select an external style sheet for the active HTML file.

6. **In the resulting Attach External Style Sheet dialog box, select the Link option in the Add As area.**

Using the Link option, the style sheet file is connected to the HTML page using the **<link>** tag in the HTML page's header information. When a user opens the HTML page, the browser merges the instructions in the linked CSS file with the information in the HTML file to present the final page design.

The CSS Styles Panel in Depth

The CSS Styles panel has two modes, which are accessed using the buttons at the top of the panel.

All mode displays style rules from external and embedded style sheets, but does not display inline styles defined within the HTML content. The top half of the panel shows a list of existing selectors. The lower half shows the properties associated with the active selector.

Current mode displays all styles that relate to the current selection in the document window.

This pane shows all properties that apply to the tag that is selected in the document window.

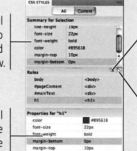

Click to show information about the property that is selected in the top pane.

Click to show all rules that affect the tag that is selected in the document window.

This pane shows all properties of the rule that is selected in the middle pane.

- The Summary for Selection pane shows all properties (and values) that apply to the active selection in the document window.

- The Rules pane shows either the rules that apply to the selection, or information about the property that is selected in the Summary for Selection pane.

- The Properties pane shows the properties of the rule that is selected in the Rules pane; the appearance of properties depends on the active option in the bottom-left corner of the panel. You can use the Properties pane to add new properties or modify the values of existing properties. If a property shows a black line through it, that property has been applied by an enclosing tag rather than by the active selection.

You can view the properties and values in the Properties pane in Show Category view, Show List view, or Show Only Set Properties (the default).

- **Show Category view** categorizes properties in the same groups that are available in the CSS Rule Definition dialog box. Every available property is listed; properties with defined values appear in blue. You can add new properties by clicking the white space to the right of a property and typing a new value or choosing from a menu.

- **Show List view** lists all CSS properties in alphabetical order; the groups from Category view are not included.

- **Show Only Set Properties** shows only the properties that have defined values in the lower half of the panel. You can add new properties by clicking the Add Property link at the bottom of the list.

Show Only Set Properties

Show List View

Show Category View

Attach Style Sheet

New CSS Rule

Edit Rule

Disable/Enable CSS Property

Delete CSS Rule

Five buttons in the bottom-right corner of the CSS Styles panel provide additional functionality. From left to right:

- The **Attach Style Sheet** button attaches an external style sheet to the active HTML page. You can browse to locate an existing file, and attach the saved style sheet to the HTML page by using the import or link method.

- The **New CSS Rule** button creates a new rule for ID selectors, tag selectors, compound selectors, and class selectors.

- The **Edit Rule** button opens the CSS Rule Definition dialog box for the selected style (in the list at the top of the panel).

- The **Disable/Enable CSS Property** button turns a selected property on and off by temporarily commenting out the property in the CSS code, so you can view the effects of specific properties in the open file.

- The **Delete CSS Rule** (or Property) button deletes the selected style (selected in the top half of the panel) or property (selected in the bottom half of the panel).

7. **Click the Browse button to the right of the File/URL field. Navigate to the master.css file that you saved in Step 3 and click Choose/OK.**

8. **When you return to the Attach External Style Sheet dialog box, click OK to attach the style sheet file to design.html.**

9. **Click the All button at the top of the CSS Styles panel.**

master.css is now related to design.html.

10. **Save the file and continue to the next exercise.**

CREATE ID SELECTORS

Using the tracing image and the information you received from the graphic designer, you can now begin to build the overall site layout.

To build a layout with CSS, you need to apply the HTML div element. As you learned in Project 2: Digital Book Chapter and Project 3: Photographer's Web Site, a **<div>** tag marks a division (or section) of a page. A style sheet can define a large number of properties for each div, including height, width, background color, margins, and more.

Each div on a page can have a different identity (defined using the ID attribute), which allows you to define different properties for different areas, as shown here:

```
#header {
    background-color: #999;
}
#footer {
    background-color: #00CCCC;
}
```

Using the code shown above, the header div will have a gray background, and the footer div will have a light aqua background.

You define ID selectors in a style sheet to control the appearance of unique, named HTML div elements. When you insert a div element into a page, you choose a defined ID for that div element; the properties defined in the ID selector (in the style sheet) are then used to format the div in the page.

Note:

If you completed Project 2: Digital Book Chapter and Project 3: Photographer's Web Site, you already know a bit about <div> tags. This project looks more deeply into <div> tags, showing you how to create and control your own divs.

1. **With design.html open, click the New CSS Rule button at the bottom of the CSS Styles panel.**

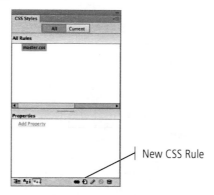

New CSS Rule

2. **Choose ID in the Selector Type menu.**

   In the New CSS Rule dialog box, you can define the type and name of a selector, as well as where to create the rule (in the attached external CSS file or embedded in the active HTML file).

   As the parenthetical notation suggests, an ID selector can apply to only one element on the page; this type of selector identifies specific sections or divisions of a page, each of which must be unique.

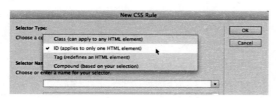

3. **In the Selector Name field, type #header.**

   This ID will be the container for the client's logo and the site's top navigation. The area is 700 pixels wide, so you need the container to be the same width. You also need to move it 200 pixels away from the left edge.

4. **Make sure master.css is selected in the Rule Definition menu (at the bottom of the dialog box).**

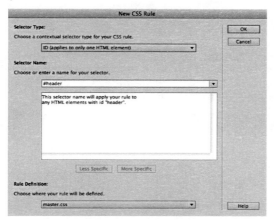

5. **Click OK to open the CSS Rule Definition dialog box.**

   This dialog box includes eight categories of options. All properties that can be saved in a CSS rule are available in the various panes of this dialog box.

Note:

If you have not already created an external CSS file, you can choose New Style Sheet File in the Rule Definition menu. When you click OK, you first name the new style sheet file (which is saved in the active site root folder) before you define the rule properties. The new style sheet file is automatically linked to the active HTML page.

Note:

All ID selector names must begin with the "#" character. If you forget to include the character, Dreamweaver will add it for you.

Note:

ID selector names are case-sensitive. However the rule is named must be exactly how it is used when applied to the appropriate div element.

6. **Click Box in the Category list. Type 700 in the Width field, and make sure px (pixels) is selected in the related menu.**

7. **In the Margin area, uncheck the Same for All check box. Type 200 in the Left field, and make sure px is selected in the related menu.**

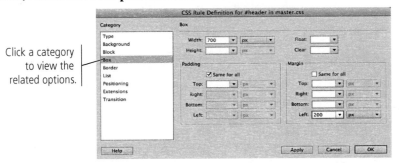

Click a category to view the related options.

Note:

The header of the dialog box includes the name of the selector being edited. For the sake of brevity, we exclude this distinction when we refer to the dialog box.

8. **Click OK to add the rule to the master.css file.**

9. **In the CSS Styles panel, click the arrow/plus sign to expand the master.css item, and then select the #header item in the list.**

   In the Design pane, the design.html file is not affected because the #header div has not yet been placed in the file. The new rule appears only in the CSS Styles panel; specific properties of the rule are listed in the lower half of the panel.

This area shows the two properties you defined for this ID selector.

If you see more than these two properties, click the Show Only Set Properties button.

10. **Click the master.css tab at the top of the document window.**

    You can now see the code for the new rule you defined. Properties and values for the selector are contained within curly brackets; each property is separated by a semicolon.

The asterisk tells you the file has been modified since it was last saved.

11. **Choose File>Save to save the master.css file, then click the Close button on the file's tab to close only that file.**

12. Click the **New CSS Rule** button in the CSS Styles panel.

13. In the resulting dialog box, choose **ID** in the Selector Type menu and type **#image** in the Selector Name field. Make sure **master.css** is selected in the Rule Definition menu and click **OK**.

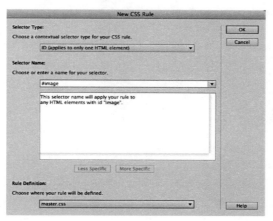

14. In the Box category of options, define a width of **700** pixels, height of **280** pixels, and left margin of **200** pixels.

All of the images for this Web site are 700 pixels wide by 280 pixels high; you're creating the div to fit those images. (We are telling you the correct dimensions to use in this example. In a professional environment, you would have to determine the correct size for this div by evaluating the supplied images.)

Note:

Unless you define a specific width and/ or height, elements fill the containing element horizontally, and their height expands automatically as content is added.

15. In the Border category, uncheck all three Same for All check boxes. Open the menu next to the Top Style field and choose **Solid**.

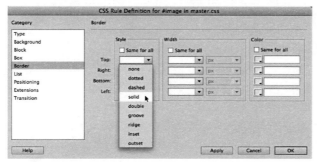

16. Type **3** in the Top Width field and make sure **px** is selected in the related menu.

17. **Click the color swatch for the Top Color field. Move the cursor over the green color on the right side of the tracing image and click to select that color.**

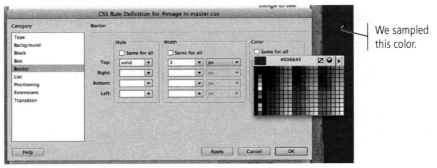

We sampled this color.

18. **Apply the same settings to the Bottom fields, then click OK.**

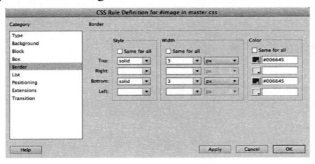

19. **In the Related Files bar above the document window, click the master.css item to show that code in the Code pane.**

Although you intentionally closed the master.css file, it is still open through its relationship to the open HTML file. In the Related Files bar, an asterisk next to the CSS file name shows that the code has been modified since it was last saved. Clicking the CSS file name button automatically switches the document window to Split mode; the CSS file code is displayed in the Code pane.

Clicking master.css in the Related Files bar shows the related code in the Code pane.

20. **Choose File>Save to save your changes to the master.css file.**

DREAMWEAVER FOUNDATIONS

The CSS Rule Definition dialog box is the primary tool for defining CSS rules. When you create a new selector, the CSS Rule Definition dialog box for that selector opens so you can set the selector's properties and values. You can access different categories of options by clicking in the list on the left side of the dialog box.

It should be noted that the dialog box capitalizes the first word of each property name. In CSS code, the property names are entirely lowercase, using a hyphen to separate words.

Type options control the appearance of the text.

- font-family defines the font sequence for the text (e.g., Arial, Helvetica, sans-serif); you can also edit the available list.

- font-size sets the size of the font in a variety of measurement units (using pixels for font-size measurements can prevent text distortion).

- font-weight affects the apparent boldness of the text (normal, bold, bolder, lighter, or specific values).

- font-style specifies the font style (normal, italic, or oblique).

- font-variant sets the text as normal or small-caps.

- line-height determines the height of the line (similar to leading, if you are familiar with print design).

- text-transform controls the capitalization of the text. Capitalize changes the first letter of each word, uppercase shows all letters as capitals, and lowercase shows all letters as lowercase.

- text-decoration sets a predefined text style (underline, overline, line-through, blink, or none). This option is particularly useful for removing the default underline of hyperlink text.

- color specifies the font color.

Background options control the background color and images for a specific selector.

- background-color can be set by typing a hexadecimal color code in the field, by clicking the color swatch and choosing a color from the color picker, or by clicking the color swatch and using the eyedropper cursor to sample a color from anywhere on your screen.

- background-image can be set by typing the path or by clicking the Browse button and navigating to the image location.

- background-repeat determines how background images fill the space available in their containers. No-repeat places the image one time, in the top-left corner. Repeat tiles the image horizontally and vertically. Repeat-x tiles the image only horizontally. Repeat-y tiles the image vertically.

- background-attachment controls how a background image moves in relation to the page. Fixed allows the image to stay in place even if the page scrolls. Scroll allows the background image to stay in the same position relative to the page; the background image scrolls along with the page.

- background-position (X) sets the image to the left, center, or right of the page.

- background-position (Y) sets the image to the top, center, or bottom of the page.

If nothing is selected in these menus, background images default to repeat in both directions, scroll with the page, and are positioned at the left and top corners of the element.

Block options define spacing and alignment for content within a container.

- word-spacing controls the spacing between words.

- letter-spacing controls the spacing between individual characters.

- vertical-align aligns the selected element vertically.

- text-align aligns text to the left, right, center, or justified across the full width of the container.

- text-indent specifies where text begins in a line.

- white-space manages extra spaces and tabs. Normal collapses all whitespace (ignoring double spaces and tabs). Pre retains all whitespace. Nowrap prevents lines of text from wrapping, based on the horizontal dimensions of the container (unless a **
** tag is used).

- display controls how an element should be displayed. "None" makes an element not visible; "Block" makes an element behave like a div tag, which can be sized and positioned; and "Inline" makes an element behave like simple text content.

Box options control the dimensions of elements such as divs and paragraphs.

- width and height control the dimensions of the selected element.

- float determines where an element will be placed in relation to its containing element. Other content in the same element will float around the affected element on the opposite side.

- clear allows an element to "reset" the vertical position and appear below a preceding element that is floating.

- padding is the amount of space that separates the element border and the content in the element.

- margin is the amount of space that separates the element border and surrounding elements.

(Background colors and images appear behind padding areas, but not behind margin areas.)

Border options control the style, width, and color of the borders around the selected elements. You can specify values individually (top, right, bottom, left) or select the Same for All check box to apply the same border attributes to all four sides of an element.

List options control the appearance and style of lists.

- list-style-type specifies the type of identifier to use (disc, circle, square, decimal, lower- or upper-roman, and lower- or upper-alpha).

- list-style-image defines a custom image to use as a bullet character. None disables the list appearance; no bullets will appear.

- list-style-position defines the list position as inside or outside (i.e., the list either wraps indented from the bullet character or wraps to the left margin).

Positioning options control the position of the CSS elements.

- position determines the position of the element (absolute, fixed, relative, or static). Absolute enables the element to remain stable on the page, regardless of the position of the other elements. Fixed positions the element according to the window size. Relative positions the element based on the position of other elements on the page. Static, the default method, positions the element as it appears in an HTML page.

- width and height are the same as the same-named options in the Box category; values entered in one category automatically reflect in the other.

- visibility displays the element in three states. If no visibility property is selected, the element inherits its visibility from the containing element (the parent). Visible displays the element. Hidden hides the element.

- z-index shows the depth of an element in the layer stacking order. Elements with higher z-index values appear above elements with lower z-index values. Z-index is a valid property only for absolute, fixed, and relative positioning; normal static positioning cannot use this property.

- overflow determines how the element should appear when the element exceeds the allotted space. Visible enables the block to expand, so you can view the content. Hidden only shows content that fits in the block; the remaining content is clipped and not hidden. Auto inserts a scrollbar (horizontal, vertical, or both).

- placement defines the specific location of an absolute-positioned element.

- clip specifies the visible parts of an element.

Extensions options create page breaks and apply visual effects.

- page-break-before sets a page break for printing, before the element.

- page-break-after sets a page break for printing, after the element.

- cursor specifies the pointer style when you place the mouse cursor over the element.

- filter adds artistic effects to change the appearance of an element.

Transition options allow animation of CSS properties with duration, delay, and timing functions. (You will use these options in Project 7: BLVD Fluid Grid Site.)

21. **Using the same basic process as outlined for the #header and #image selectors, create two additional ID selectors using the following information:**

Selector name	Settings to Apply
#pageContent	Box Width: 700 pixels, Left Margin: 200 pixels
#footer	Box Width: 700 pixels, Left Margin: 200 pixels

22. **With the master.css file visible in the Code pane, choose File>Save.**

Appropriate code for all selectors has been added to the file.

Note:

When the master.css code is showing in the Code pane, the Rule Definition menu in the New CSS Rule dialog box defaults to This Document Only, referring to the active CSS file.

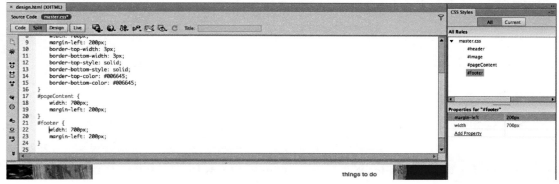

23. **Continue to the next exercise.**

You don't need to save the design.html file, because you haven't actually changed anything in that file throughout this exercise.

CREATE A LAYOUT WITH DIV ELEMENTS

In the previous exercise, as noted, the design.html file was not affected by the new IDs. This is because you must intentionally place div elements associated with those IDs into the HTML file to create the page layout.

1. **With design.html open, click Source Code in the Related Files bar to show the page code in the Code pane.**

2. **Select and delete the code related to the tracing image. Make sure you do not delete the closing > of the body tag.**

You no longer need this image, so it is safe to delete it. If you simply hide it, problems could arise later when you save the file as a template.

Note:

You can also remove a tracing image by clearing the Tracing Image field in the Page Properties dialog box.

Click here to show the page code in the Code pane.

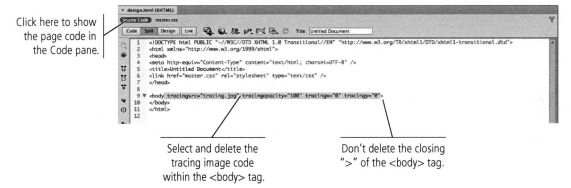

Select and delete the tracing image code within the <body> tag.

Don't delete the closing ">" of the <body> tag.

3. **Click the Refresh button in the Properties panel or the Document toolbar to remove the tracing image.**

4. **Click in the Design pane to place the insertion point in the file, then choose Insert>Layout Objects>Div Tag.**

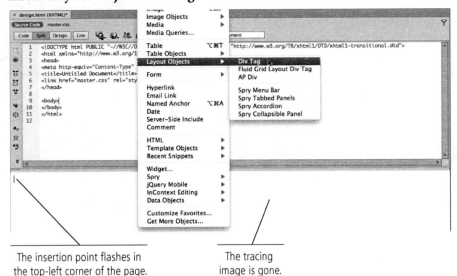

The insertion point flashes in the top-left corner of the page.

The tracing image is gone.

Note:

Other options in the Insert menu will be useful when you start to nest div elements inside each other.

Note:

You can also use the Insert Div Tag button when the Insert bar is in Common or Layout mode.

5. **In the Insert Div Tag dialog box, leave the Insert menu set to At Insertion Point.**

The div you insert will be placed at the current insertion point, which is by default in the top-left corner of the page. The insertion point is slightly indented because Dreamweaver automatically adds several pixels of padding around the content of a new page. (Some browsers do the same, so Dreamweaver tries to accurately show what you will see when you preview the page in a browser.)

6. **Choose header in the ID menu.**

All ID selectors that are defined in the CSS file, but have not yet been used in the active HTML file, are available in this menu.

7. **Click OK to add the <div> tag to the page.**

Because the placeholder text is highlighted in the Design pane, the corresponding text is also highlighted in the Code pane; this allows you to easily identify the code for the placed div element.

In the Design pane, the div element is indented 200 pixels from the left, as defined by the left margin value of the #header ID selector.

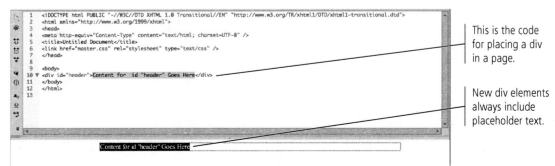

This is the code for placing a div in a page.

New div elements always include placeholder text.

8. In the Design pane, click the edge of the div element to select it.

When a div is selected in the page, you can see various aspects of the CSS Layout Box Model in the design page.

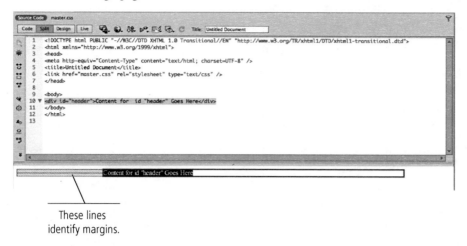

These lines identify margins.

Note:

If you don't see the margin area, make sure CSS Layout Box Model is toggled on in the Visual Aids menu.

9. Choose Insert>Layout Objects>Div Tag again.

10. In the Insert Div Tag dialog box, choose After Tag in the Insert menu. Leave <div id="header"> selected in the secondary menu.

Using the After Tag option, you can place a new div element after any existing div, regardless of the location of the insertion point.

Note:

You can use each ID only once on any given page.

If anything is selected when you insert a div tag, the Insert menu defaults to Wrap Around Selection.

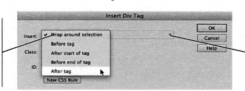

After defining where to add the div tag, choose from the existing named tags in this menu.

Note:

The Wrap Around Selection option is useful if you need to add a new div element around existing content. Because you are creating the layout from scratch, however, this option is not needed at this point.

Understanding the CSS Box Model

DREAMWEAVER FOUNDATIONS

When you design layouts using CSS, think of any block element (such as a div element) as a box made up of four parts: margin, border, padding, and content. The object's overall size — the amount of space it occupies on the page — is the sum of the values for these four properties:

- The **margin** is outside the box edges; it is invisible and has no background color. Margin does not affect content within the element.

- The **border** is the edge of the element, based on the specified dimensions.

- The **padding** lies inside the edge of the element, forming a cushion between the box edge and the box content. (If you are familiar with print-design applications such as Adobe InDesign, think of padding as text inset.)

- The **content** lies inside the padding. When you define the width and height for an element, you are defining the content area.

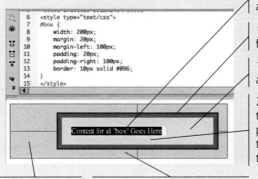

200-pixel width defines the actual content area.

10-pixel border is on all four sides of the box.

100-pixel right padding is added inside the box edge.

20-pixel padding is applied to the other three edges (the padding-right value overrides the padding value for only the right edge).

100-pixel left margin is added outside the box edge.

20-pixel margins are applied to the other three edges (the margin-left value overrides the margin value for only the left edge).

11. Choose image in the ID menu, then click OK to add the div element to the page.

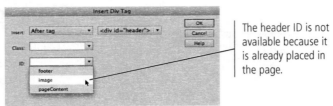

The header ID is not available because it is already placed in the page.

You want to place each row, one right after the other. Since the header div is already in place, you are adding the next **<div>** tag immediately after the existing one.

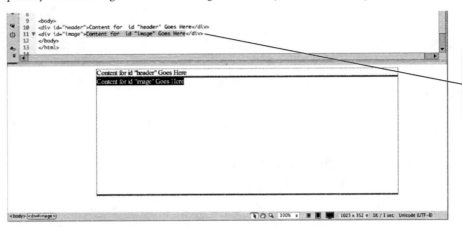

The code shows that the image div is added immediately after the header div (at the same nesting level).

12. Repeat Steps 9–11 to add the pageContent div after the image div, and then add the footer div after the pageContent div.

When you add these divs, make sure you choose the correct div in the secondary Insert menu so that the divs are in the correct order from top to bottom (header, image, pageContent, footer).

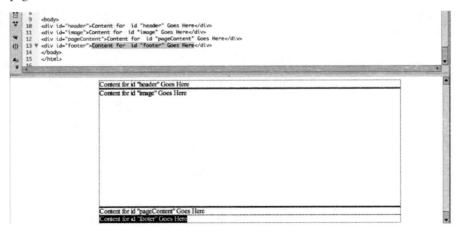

Note:

Adding div elements adds to the page's HTML code. Those elements, however, are very short — they simply identify each div element and add some placeholder content. In the page code, there is no mention of background images, colors, or other attributes that make up the page layout. Those attributes are controlled by editing the ID selectors applied to each div element within the CSS file.

13. Save the design.html file and continue to the next exercise.

USE THE FLOAT PROPERTY TO CONTROL NESTED DIVS

In the previous exercises, you created ID selectors and placed div elements using the selectors you had already defined. If you are experimenting with a layout, or if you want to work within the context of an existing layout, you can also insert div tags and create ID selectors at the same time.

1. **With the design.html page active, select and delete the placeholder content in the pageContent div. Make sure the insertion point remains inside the now empty pageContent div.**

When you remove the div content, the div collapses to the smallest possible height. Because you did not define a specific height in the #pageContent selector rules, the div height will expand as necessary to accommodate whatever you place in the container.

As you saw in the examination of the tracing image, the pageContent needs to be divided into two separate divs — one to hold the main body of text, and another to contain a series of links. This is accomplished by creating **nested divs**, or div elements that exist entirely within other div elements.

2. **Choose Insert>Layout Objects>Div Tag.**

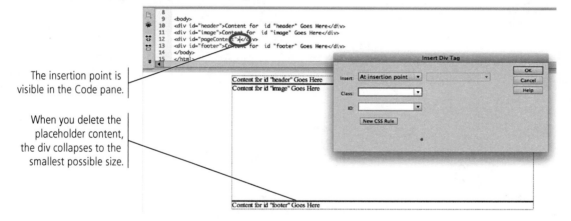

The insertion point is visible in the Code pane.

When you delete the placeholder content, the div collapses to the smallest possible size.

3. **In the Insert Div Tag dialog box, click the New CSS Rule button.**

4. **In the resulting New CSS Rule dialog box, choose ID in the Selector Type menu.**

5. **Type #mainText in the Selector Name field, and make sure master.css is selected in the Rule Definition menu.**

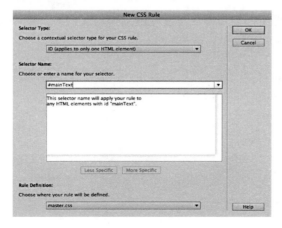

6. **Click OK to define properties for the new selector.**

7. **In the Box options of the CSS Rule Definition dialog box, define the box width as 450 pixels. Choose left in the Float menu.**

   Nested div elements automatically align based on the horizontal alignment properties of the containing element. If no specific alignment is defined, the nested div aligns to the left side of the container. The float property allows you to attach a div to the left or right edge of the containing element, and allows other content to sit beside or wrap around that element. This gives you greater flexibility when creating complex layouts such as the one in this project. In this case, the mainText div will attach to the left edge of the pageContent div.

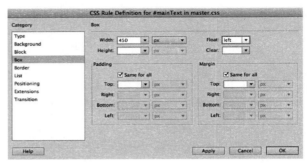

8. **Click OK to return to the Insert Div Tag dialog box, and then click OK again to insert the new div tag into the page at the current insertion point.**

   When you work with nested div elements, unexpected things can sometimes happen in the Design pane. In this case, the left edge of the footer div moves to the middle of the page (to the right of the mainText div) because the mainText div is floating left.

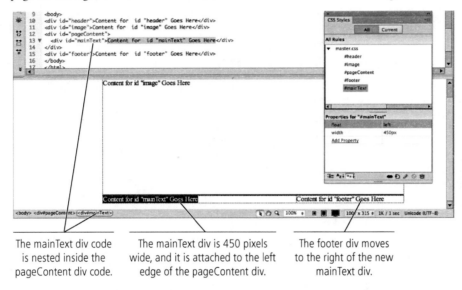

Note:

If you only see "master.css" in the CSS Styles panel, click the arrow/plus sign to expand it and show the selectors in that file.

The mainText div code is nested inside the pageContent div code.

The mainText div is 450 pixels wide, and it is attached to the left edge of the pageContent div.

The footer div moves to the right of the new mainText div.

9. **Select #footer in the CSS Styles panel and click the Edit Rule button at the bottom of the panel.**

10. **In the Box properties, choose left in the Float menu and then click OK.**

    You can edit selectors at any time by selecting one in the panel and clicking the Edit Rule button at the bottom of the panel.

    Adding the float property to the footer div moves the div to attach to the left edge of its container, which is the page body. It no longer appears to the right of the mainText div.

11. **Choose Insert>Layout Objects>Div Tag again.**

12. **Choose After Tag in the Insert menu, choose <div id="mainText"> in the secondary menu, then click New CSS Rule at the bottom of the dialog box.**

    The New CSS Rule button is useful for adding a div that you have not yet created.

13. **In the resulting New CSS Rule dialog box, choose ID in the Selector Type menu. Type #sidebarNav in the Selector Name field, make sure master.css is selected in the Rule Definition menu, and click OK.**

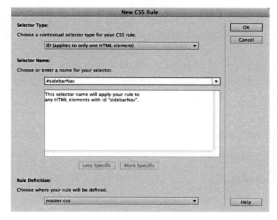

14. **In the Background properties, define the following settings:**

    background-image: back_sidebar.jpg (from the site images folder)

    background-repeat: no-repeat

    background-position (X): center

    background-position (Y): top

15. **In the Box properties, define the following settings:**

    width: 220px

    height: 395px

    float: right

    As with the width of the main content area, you are defining this element to match the size of the provided image. In a professional workflow, you would have to determine the image size yourself so you could create the div element appropriately.

Note:

***Repeat** repeats the image vertically and horizontally.*

***No-repeat** prevents the image from repeating.*

***Repeat-x** repeats the image horizontally.*

***Repeat-y** repeats the image vertically.*

16. **Click OK to return to the Insert Div dialog box, then OK again to return to the document.**

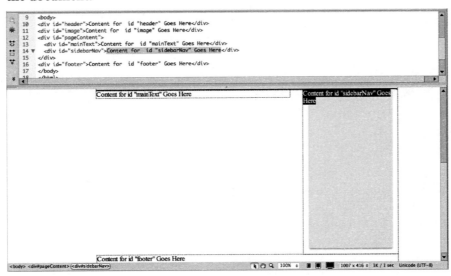

17. **Insert the file yvvb.jpg (from the site images folder) into the header div. Define Yosemite Valley Visitor's Bureau as the alternate text.**

Remember from Project 3: Photographer's Web Site, you can drag an image from the Files panel, use the Common Insert panel, use the Insert>Image command, or use the Assets panel to place an image in a page. Also remember, all images in the foreground require the **alt** attribute.

18. **Delete the placeholder text from the header div.**

If you delete the placeholder text before placing the image, the div collapses to the smallest possible height. It is easier to place the image before you remove the placeholder text.

19. **Place the insertion point before the placed image.**

The insertion point should be in front of the image.

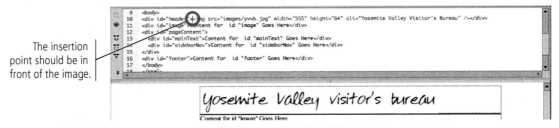

Comparing the <span> and <div> Tags

A **<span>** tag is used for "inline" content (within another piece of text) such as a paragraph. A <span> tag does not create a line break in the text; it applies styles to text (usually a small section) even in the middle of a sentence. For example:

A span tag can <span style="font:14pt verdana">change font</span> in the middle of a sentence.

results in:

A span tag can **change font** in the middle of a sentence.

A **<div>** tag is a "block" element that can be sized and positioned, more commonly used to divide a page into different sections. If you apply a <div> tag in the middle of a sentence, a line break is automatically added before the div. For example:

Using div tags, you can divide a Web page <div style="text-align:center"> into different divisions. </div>

results in:

Using div tags, you can divide a Web page
into different divisions.

20. Using the same process as in Steps 11–16, insert a new ID div at the location of the insertion point. Name the div #topNav, using the following settings:

width: 110px   float: right

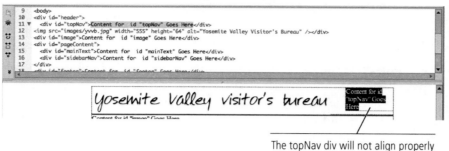

The topNav div will not align properly if you insert it after the image.

Nested divs should appear before other content in the container div. If you place the topNav div after the image, the nested div will not align properly.

21. Save the HTML and CSS files, and then continue to the next exercise.

To save the CSS file, click master.css in the Related Files bar, then choose File>Save. Once the CSS file is saved, click Source Code in the Related Files bar to reshow the actual page code.

 ## DEFINE PROPERTIES FOR THE <BODY> TAG

As you learned in an earlier project, the **<body>** tag surrounds all visible content in a Web page. As with any other HTML tag, you can use a CSS rule to define properties for the **<body>** tag.

1. With design.html open, click the New CSS Rule button at the bottom of the CSS Styles panel.

2. In the New CSS Rule dialog box, choose Tag in the Selector Type menu.

<body> is an HTML tag, so you have to create a tag selector to define properties for the body element.

3. Scroll through the Tag menu (under Selector Name) and click body in the list of options.

This menu lists all HTML tags that can be affected by CSS rules. You can choose from the menu, or simply type a specific tag name in the field if you know the exact tag you want to modify.

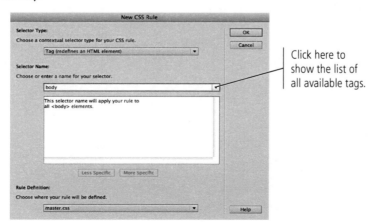

Click here to show the list of all available tags.

Note:

Technically, you do not need to place the insertion point before inserting a div. You could also choose the After Start of Tag option in the Insert menu, then choose <div id="header"> to place the topNav div in the correct location.

Until you are more comfortable creating and placing divs, however, it can be useful to use the insertion point to define exactly where you want a div to be placed.

4. **Make sure master.css is targeted in the Rule Definition menu, and then click OK.**

5. **In the CSS Rule Definition dialog box, change the following settings:**

Type category	font-family: Arial, Helvetica, sans-serif
	font-size: 12px
	line-height: 19px
	color: #666
Background category	background-image: back_yosemite.png
	background-repeat: repeat-y
Box category	padding: 0px (all four edges)
	margin: 0px (all four edges)

6. **Click OK to add the body selector to the master.css file.**

The new body selector is a tag selector, so it does not have the preceding "#" at the beginning of the selector name.

By this point you should understand the concept of nested tags. The <body> tag is the parent of the div tags it contains. Properties of the parent tag are automatically inherited by the child (nested) tags. In this case, the font family, size, line height, and color you defined for the <body> tag are automatically applied to content in the nested divs.

Note:

Web browsers have default values (which can differ) for many elements, including the body element. By specifying padding and margins of 0, you are standardizing these settings and or negating any default values (called "normallizing"), so all browsers will render the body element the same way.

There is no change in the HTML page code.

The 0 margin values remove the white space around the page.

The defined font group and color change the default type appearance for the entire page.

The background image appears behind all placed div elements.

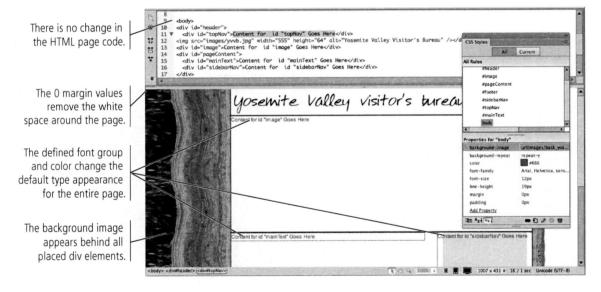

7. **Save the CSS file, and then continue to the next exercise.**

EDIT CSS RULES TO ADJUST THE LAYOUT

Now that the background image is in place, you can see a number of elements that need to be addressed. It's important to realize that layout development is an ongoing evolutionary process; as you continue to work, new issues will pop up. You can always add or remove properties to specific rules, and even add new rules as necessary to meet a project's needs. As long as you work with an external CSS file — as you are in this project — the changes will apply to any HTML file that is linked to the same CSS file.

1. **With design.html open, make sure the body selector is selected in the CSS Styles panel.**

2. **In the lower half of the panel, click the Add Property link at the bottom of the list of current properties.**

3. **Open the resulting menu. Scroll to and select the background-color property.**

   If you know the exact name of the property you want to add, you can also simply type in the resulting field to add that property.

Note:

If you don't see the Add Property link, click the Show Only Set Properties button at the bottom of the panel. The Add Property link is not available when the properties are showing in Category or List view.

Type the exact property name in this field...

...or click here to open a list of all available properties.

4. **To the right of the new background-color property, click the color swatch and then sample a dark green from the existing background image.**

   You couldn't do this when you first created the <body> tag selector because the background image was not yet visible.

We sampled this color.

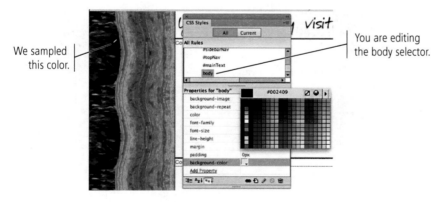

You are editing the body selector.

5. **In the CSS Styles panel, click the #mainText selector.**

   As you can see in the page, the text in this div currently begins at the very edge of the area. You need to move the text away from the edge for better readability.

6. **Click the Edit Rule button to open the CSS Rule Definition dialog box.**

7. In the Box category, deselect the Same For All option in the Margin section. Change the Top and Left margins to 10px.

Unless you're very familiar with CSS property names and coding rules, it is often easier to use the CSS Rule Definition dialog box to make multiple changes like this.

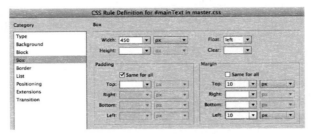

8. Click OK to add the new properties to the #mainText selector.

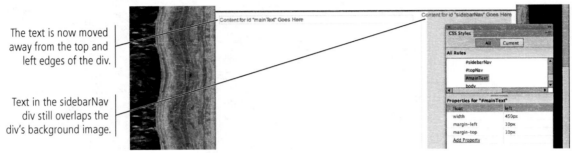

The text is now moved away from the top and left edges of the div.

Text in the sidebarNav div still overlaps the div's background image.

9. In the CSS Styles panel, select the #sidebarNav selector and then click the Add Property link in the lower half of the panel.

10. In the resulting field, type `padding`.

Rather than scroll through the very long menu of properties, you can simply type the propety if you know the exact name. In this case, the "padding" property defines a single padding value for all four edges of the box.

11. In the resulting field to the right of the new padding property, type `15px`. Press Return/Enter to finalize the change.

If you don't type the unit of measurement immediately after the value (with no space character), the property will have no effect.

Note:

In CSS, the unit of measurement must always be specified, unless the value is zero.

Note:

You have to type the "px" in the field when you add the padding property to the selector.

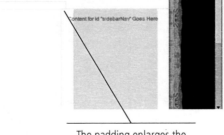
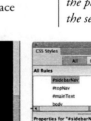

The padding enlarges the overall element area, and moves the div out of position.

It is important to realize that both padding and margins affect the overall size of the element. The sidebarNav div is now 250 pixels wide (220 defined width + 15 left padding + 15 right padding).

When you change the margins and/or padding, you have to make a proportional change to the width/height properties if you want the element to occupy the same overall space.

12. Subtract 30 from both the height and width values of the sidebarNav div.

To change the existing property values, simply click the value to highlight it and then type the new value.

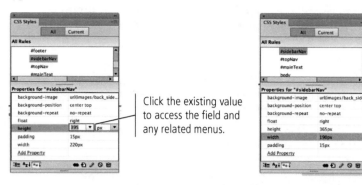

Click the existing value to access the field and any related menus.

Note:

The background image extends into the padding area because the padding is part of the actual element area. Margin values are added outside the element; background images do not extend into the margin area.

After changing the height and width, the sidebarNav div moves back into place.

13. Using the same basic process, edit the #topNav selector to add 10px padding to all four edges.

For this div you are not trying to maintain a certain amount of space, so it is not necessary to remove the extra pixels from the defined width.

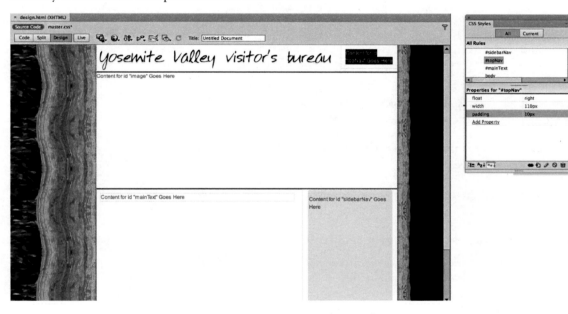

14. Save the CSS file and then continue to the next stage of the project.

Stage 2 Working with a Template

Dreamweaver professionals often use templates (with the ".dwt" extension) to create HTML pages. When you use a template file, you create common page elements only once, rather than recreating them every time you add a new page to a site. A template can contain everything an HTML page requires, including text, graphics, and hyperlinks.

When you create a template, you indicate which elements of a page should remain constant (non-editable; locked) in pages based on that template, and which elements can be changed. While the non-editable regions appear exactly the same from one page to the next, the editable regions enable you to add unique content to each new page.

You can modify a template even after you have created pages based on it. When you modify a template, the locked (non-editable) regions in pages based on the template automatically update to match the changes to the template.

If you open a template file, you can edit everything in it, whether it is marked as editable or locked. If you open a document based on a template file, you can edit only the regions marked as editable. The terms **editable** and **locked** refer to whether a region is editable in a document based on a template, not to whether the region is editable in the template file itself.

CREATE A TEMPLATE

When all pages in a site will have the same basic layout, you can save the common elements as a template, and then apply the template to all pages. This workflow makes it much faster and easier to complete the project.

Following the same logic, keep in mind that the master.css file in this site is attached to the design.html file — which will become the template. Any pages created from the template file will also be attached to the master.css file, so changes made in the master.css file will also affect pages created from the template.

1. **With design.html from the Yosemite site open in Design view, choose File>Save As Template.**

2. **In the Save As Template dialog box, make sure Yosemite is selected in the Site menu.**

3. **In the Description field, type Yosemite Site template.**

   The description is only relevant in Dreamweaver; it will not appear in any page based on the template. You can also modify the template description by choosing Modify>Templates> Description.

4. **Click Save to save the active file as a template.**

   The extension ".dwt" is automatically added on both Macintosh and Windows.

Note:

You can also create a template from the active page by choosing Insert>Template Objects>Make Template.

5. **Click Yes in the resulting dialog box.**

   The template is saved in a Templates folder, which Dreamweaver automatically creates for you when saving the template, in the local root folder of the Yosemite site. To ensure that all images and links function properly, you should allow Dreamweaver to update the link information as necessary.

The template is automatically added to the site in a new Templates folder.

Your template contains the layout structure you created in the first stage of this project. However, after converting the document into a template, all parts of the page become non-editable. Until you define an editable region, you won't be able to add page-specific content to any pages based on this template.

Do not move your templates out of the Templates folder or save any non-template files in the Templates folder. Also, do not move the Templates folder out of your local root folder. Doing so causes errors in paths in the templates.

6. **In the Document toolbar above the design pane, change the Title field to**
   Yosemite Valley Visitor's Bureau.

   When you define a title in a template file, that title is automatically applied to any page attached to the template. You are adding the basic information in the template, so you can then simply add page-specific information in each attached file.

7. **In the Design pane, select the placeholder text in the image div.**

   Make sure you only select the div content, and not the actual div element.

8. **Choose Insert>Template Objects>Editable Region.**

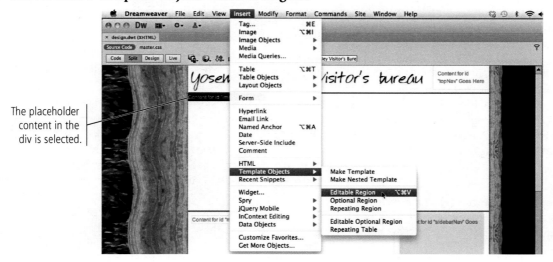

The placeholder content in the div is selected.

9. Type Page Image in the resulting dialog box and then click OK.

When pages are created from this template, the editable regions will be the only areas that can be modified (e.g., adding specific page content).

In the Design view, editable areas are identified with a blue tag and border; these are for design purposes, and will not be visible in the resulting HTML pages. If you don't see a blue tag with the Page Image region name, open the Visual Aids menu (in the Document toolbar) and choose Invisible Elements to toggle on that option.

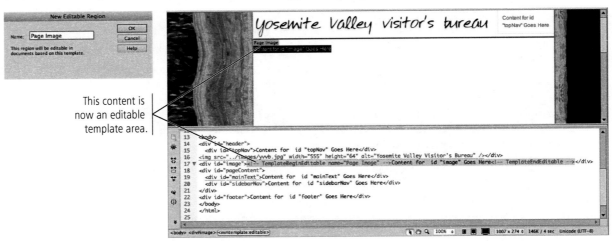

This content is now an editable template area.

10. Click in the placeholder text of the mainText div, then click div#mainText in the Tag Selector to select the entire element.

The Insert>Template Objects Menu in Depth

Template objects consist primarily of different types of regions.

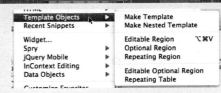

- The **Make Template** option enables you to convert an HTML file into a template. This option automatically prompts you to save the HTML file as a template. If a template is edited, the HTML files created from that template are updated accordingly (and automatically).

- The **Make Nested Template** option enables you to insert a template in a page created from an existing template. The editable region in the nested template displays in green, while the editable region in the original page displays in yellow.

- The **Editable Region** option enables you to create areas of a template that you can modify in pages using the template. You don't add content in the regions in the template itself, but in the pages created from the template. By default, editable regions are highlighted in blue, and locked regions are highlighted in yellow. (You can change these colors in the Highlighting pane of the Preferences dialog box.)

- The **Optional Region** option defines a section of the page that will be shown or hidden, depending on the content being presented. Optional Region is controlled by a conditional "if" statement in Code view — that is, you can show or hide certain areas of the page conditionally.

- The **Repeating Region** option enables you to control the layout of sections of a template that need to be repeated. A repeating region is a section of template content that you can easily duplicate. Although you can apply repeating regions to many elements, they are primarily used in tables and lists.

- The **Editable Optional Region** option combines the Optional Region functionality with the Editable Region functionality. If the Editable Optional Region is shown, the content within the region can be modified.

- **Repeating Table.** Repeating regions are commonly used in tables. Dreamweaver includes a tool that creates both a table and repeating regions simultaneously. Selecting a repeating table object opens the standard table dialog box for defining rows within a repeating region. When inserted, the repeating region contains a separate editable region in each cell.

11. **Choose Insert>Template Objects>Editable Region.**

Place the insertion point in the mainText placeholder content...

...then click the div#mainText tag to select the entire div.

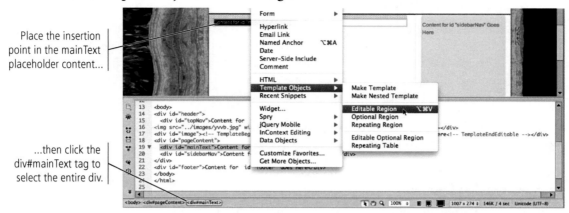

12. **Type** `Page Content` **in the resulting dialog box and then click OK.**

The new editable area is added around the selected div. Because you want the mainText *and* sidebarNav divs inside the editable area, you have to edit the page code.

The editable region code surrounds only the mainText div.

13. **In the page code, move the closing code of the editable region (<!--TemplateEndEditable-->) to be after the closing tag of the sidebarNav div.**

When something is selected in the Code pane, you can click the selected code and drag to move that code to a new position. Alternatively, you can cut (Command/Control-X) the relevant code from its original location, move the insertion point to another position, and then paste (Command/Control-V) the cut code into place.

The editable area now contains the two divs (but not the surrounding pageContent div).

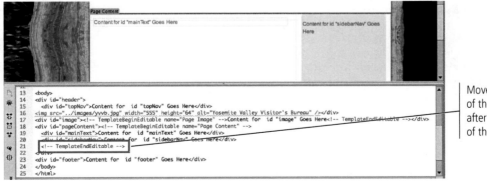

Move the closing code of the editable area after the closing div tag of the sidebarNav div.

14. **Save the file (File>Save) and close it, then continue to the next exercise.**

Unlike other applications, you do not have to use the Save As command to rewrite a Dreamweaver template. You can simply choose File>Save or press Command/Control-S.

APPLY THE TEMPLATE TO EXISTING PAGES

Templates can be applied to existing HTML pages, basically wrapping the template around the existing content. You can simply map existing page content to editable regions in the template, while adding the non-editable regions to the page design. After the template is applied, you can begin to make whatever changes are necessary based on the actual content in the files.

1. **Open the Manage Sites dialog box and select the Yosemite site, then click the Edit button to open the Site Setup dialog box for the selected site.**

2. **Expand the Advanced Settings options and click Templates in the category list to show the related options.**

Select Yosemite in the list of sites.

Click the Edit button to change the site setup.

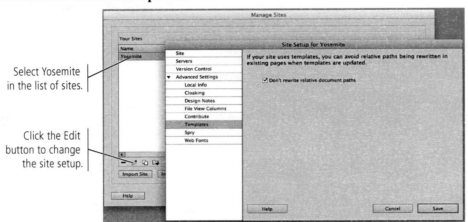

Note:

You can also double-click the Yosemite site name in the Sites menu at the top of the Files panel to open the Site Setup dialog box for a specific site. This method bypasses the Manage Sites dialog box.

3. **Make sure the Don't Rewrite option is checked.**

   When you saved the template file, it was placed in a folder named Templates. Links from this template file to images or other pages must first go up from the Templates folder to the root folder (e.g., **../images/yvvb.jpg**).

   When this template is attached to a page in the root level of the site, the same link would not be accurate. For example, the path from index.html in the root folder to the same image would simply be **images/yvvb.jpg**. If this check box is not active, the links on pages where the template is attached would not work properly.

4. **Click Save to close the Site Setup dialog box, then click Done to close the Manage Sites dialog box.**

5. **Open the file index.html from the root folder of the Yosemite site.**

   Each file in the site contains two areas of content — the primary page content, and a list of links to help users navigate through the long blocks of text. The two sections are already tagged with div ids (#mainText and #sidebarNav) that match the ones you used in the template file. This will direct the appropriate elements of the index page to appear in the defined areas of the template.

6. Choose Modify>Templates>Apply Template to Page.

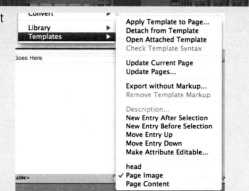

The Modify>Templates Menu in Depth

DREAMWEAVER FOUNDATIONS

The commands on the Modify>Templates menu are useful when you want to make changes to a template or to pages based on a template.

- The **Apply Template to Page** option applies a template to the current HTML page.

- If you don't want a page to be based on a template, **Detach from Template** separates the page from the template. Non-editable regions become editable, but changes in the template do not reflect in the page.

- The **Open Attached Template** option opens the template attached to a page.

- If code is written directly in the code area, there is a chance that the code might contain some errors. The **Check Template Syntax** option enables Dreamweaver to automatically check the code syntax in the template.

- The **Update Current Page** option updates a page if the template on which it is based is modified. Before closing the file, Dreamweaver prompts you to update the page; a dialog box appears, asking if you want to save the changed document.

- If you update only the template and not pages derived from the template, you can use the **Update Pages** option to update all pages based on the template.

- The **Export without Markup** option exports an entire site to a different location by detaching all pages from the templates on which they are based. You can also save the template information in XML by selecting Keep Template Data Files after you choose this command from the menu. If you exported the site earlier, then you can choose to extract only the modified files.

- Use the **Remove Template Markup** option to convert an editable region to a non-editable region.

- The **Description** is simply a textual explanation of the selected file, which does not appear in the body of the page (or any pages created from the template).

- **New Entry After** or **Before Selection.** In template working areas, repeating regions include more than one editable region, which enables you to add repeated page elements such as rows of a table. (Clicking the "+" button of the repeating region's blue tab adds a new entry in the region.)

- Use the **Move Entry Up** or **Down** option to move a repeating element up or down.

- You can use the **Make Attribute Editable** option to make a specific attribute of an HTML tag editable in pages using a template. For example, you can apply Make Attribute Editable to a "class" attribute on a link tag in a navigation bar to have the link appear "on" when you are visiting that page; a CSS class that changes the appearance would be applied to an otherwise locked link tag.

7. **In the Select Template dialog box, make sure Yosemite is selected in the Site menu.**

   Since this is the active site, the menu should default to the correct choice.

8. **Click design in the Templates list to select it, and make sure the Update Page... option is checked at the bottom of the dialog box.**

9. **Click Select to apply the template to the open page.**

   In the Inconsistent Region Names dialog box that appears, you have to determine where to place the named regions of the open file, relative to the editable regions in the template you selected.

10. **In the resulting dialog box, click the Document body (in the Name column) to select it. In the Move Content to New Region menu, choose Page Content.**

    Remember, "Page Content" is the name you assigned to the template's editable region. The page body (named "Document body" by default) will be placed into the "Page Content" editable region when the template is applied to the page.

This refers to content within the <body> section of the HTML page to which you are attaching the template.

Use this menu to map file content to an editable region in the template file.

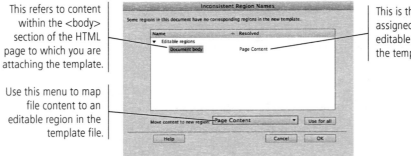

This is the name assigned to the editable region in the template file.

Note:

You can choose Nowhere in the Move Content... menu to exclude specific content in the newly "templated" page.

11. **Click OK to finalize the process.**

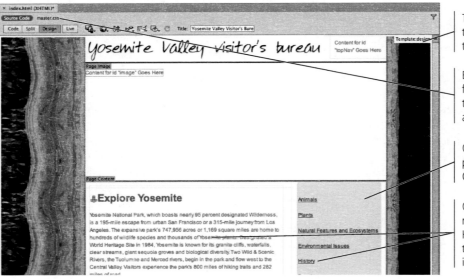

This tag identifies the template that is applied to the HTML file.

Because the master.css file is attached to the template, it is also now attached to this page.

Content in the HTML file is placed into the Page Content region of the page.

Content defined with named divs in the original HTML file is moved into the appropriate location in the template.

12. **Insert the tufas.jpg image (from the site images folder) into the Page Image editable region, and define Tufas at Mono Lake as the alternate text. Delete the placeholder text from the region.**

Because the Page Image area is an editable region, you can place new content (including images) into each page where the template is attached.

Note:

If you move the cursor over areas other than an editable region, an icon indicates that you can't select or modify that area. You can modify only the editable region.

13. **Save the file and close it.**

14. **Repeat this process to attach the design.dwt template to the three remaining pages in the site. Use the following images and alternate text for each page:**

File	Image	Alternate Text
things_to_do.html	flowers.jpg	Wildflowers in bloom
things_to_know.html	trees.jpg	Sequoia grove
things_to_see.html	lake.jpg	Lake overlook

15. **Save and close any open files, and continue to the next exercise.**

Creating a New Page from a Template

DREAMWEAVER FOUNDATIONS

In addition to attaching a template to an existing page, you can also create a new HTML page from an existing template.

You can use the Assets panel (Window>Assets) to show all templates that are available in the current site. Control/right-clicking a specific template file opens a contextual menu, where you can choose New from Template.

This results in a new untitled HTML file containing all the content that is defined in the template, with the template already attached to the HTML page. Any changes in the template file will apply to files created from the template.

Templates

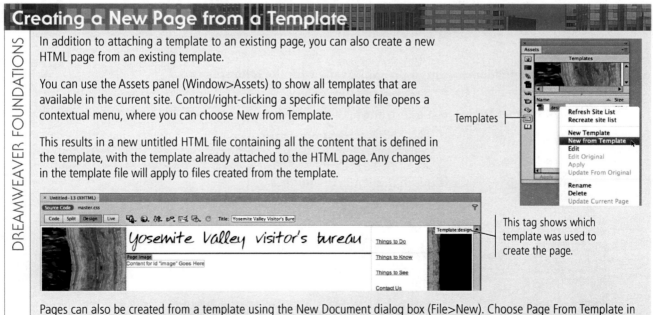

This tag shows which template was used to create the page.

Pages can also be created from a template using the New Document dialog box (File>New). Choose Page From Template in the left column of the New Document dialog box, select your site in the middle column, and then choose the template you want to apply in the right column.

EDIT THE DESIGN TEMPLATE

The header and footer information for this site is common to every page in the site, so you can add the actual content for these areas to the template. When you make changes to the template, those changes automatically apply to any page attached to the template — another advantage of using Dreamweaver template files.

1. **Open design.dwt from the Templates folder.**

2. **Replace the placeholder text in the footer div with the following:**

   Text from the National Park Service Web site is in the public domain. All images copyright Against The Clock, Inc.

3. **In the Properties panel, choose Paragraph in the Format menu.**

4. **Highlight the words "National Park Service Web site". In the Properties panel, type http://www.nps.gov/yose/index.htm in the Link field and choose _blank in the Target menu.**

Note:

Remember, the _blank target causes the link to open in a new browser tab or window.

5. **In the Design pane, highlight the words "Against The Clock, Inc.". In the Properties panel, type http://www.againsttheclock.com in the Link field and choose _blank in the Target menu.**

6. **Select the placed logo in the header and create a link to index.html in the site root folder.**

7. **Replace the placeholder content in the topNav div with the following text, and create links as listed here:**

Things to Do	Link to things-to-do.html
Things to Know	Link to things-to-know.html
Things to See	Link to things-to-see.html
Contact Us	Link to mailto:info@yvvb.atc

   As you can see, the link formatting does not currently fit the space that it should; you will fix that in the next stage of the project.

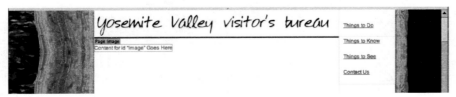

8. **Choose File>Save to save the template file.**

9. **Read the resulting message, then click Update.**

When you save changes to a template file, Dreamweaver recognizes the link from the template to pages where that template is attached. You are automatically asked if you want to update those pages to reflect the new template content.

10. **When the resulting Update Pages dialog box shows "Done", click the Close button.**

This dialog box shows the status of the update process.

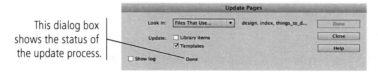

11. **Close the template file, then open things-to-do.html.**

As you can see, the content you added to the template file is automatically added to the page that is attached to the template. This type of workflow makes it much easier to maintain consistency across an entire site — make changes to common content once in the template file, and those changes are automatically applied in any page where the template is attached.

Changes you made in the template appear in all pages where the template is attached.

The image is no longer properly aligned because of the space required by the topNav element.

12. **Using the Title field at the top of the document window, add the text | Things to Do (including a preceding space) to the end of the existing document title.**

13. **Click the Split button to show the page code, and scroll to the top of the code.**

Although you did not specifically define it as an editable area, the <title> tag of each page is always editable, even when attached to a template file.

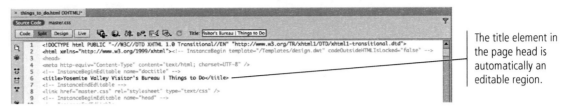

The title element in the page head is automatically an editable region.

14. **Save the file and close it.**

15. **Open things-to-know.html and things-to-see.html, and add appropriate text to each page title.**

16. **Save and close any open files, then continue to the next stage of the project.**

Understanding Named Anchors

Documents with large blocks of copy — like the ones in this site — often benefit from **named anchors**, which mark specific locations on a page that can be linked from other locations within the same page or from other pages. Instead of forcing the reader to search for the information by scrolling or other means, you can create a hyperlink that points to the exact location of the information. Clicking the anchor link moves that anchor to the top-left corner of the frame.

Named anchors can be especially useful on long Web pages. For example, on a page that contains many sections, you can include a table of contents at the top with a link to each section. To help the reader return to the table of contents from any section of the page, it is considered good practice to include a link to the top of the page at the end of each section (such as "Back to Top").

When linking to the named anchor, type the number sign (#) followed by the name of the anchor in the Link field of the dialog box or Properties panel, or choose the appropriate anchor from the Link menu of the Hyperlink dialog box. If you are linking to the anchor from another page, type the name of the file containing the anchor, followed by the number sign and the name of the anchor.

To use named anchors:

1. Place the insertion point where you want to add an anchor, and then click the Named Anchor button in the Common Insert panel (or choose Insert>Named Anchor).

2. Define a name for the anchor; do not use any illegal characters (including spaces).

In Design view, an anchor appears as a small anchor icon.

3. Create a list of links. Select the link text, open the Hyperlink dialog box, and choose one of the named anchors from the Link menu. (You can also choose an existing anchor from the Link menu in the Properties panel.)

The selected text automatically appears in the Text field.

Choose an existing anchor from the Link menu.

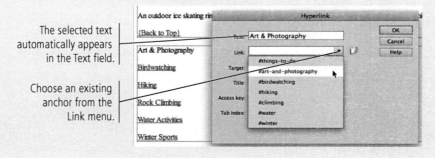

Stage 3   Using CSS to Control Content

The first stage of this project focused on building a layout structure with div tags and ID selectors; in the second stage, you created a template file to more easily apply the defined layout to multiple pages. Although defining structure is a significant part of designing pages, it is only half the story — professional Web design also requires controlling the content in pages.

When you create a complex project such as a complete Web site, it's a good idea to have a solid plan for completing all required work. Consider what you know from the initial project analysis:

- The background image should extend the entire height of the browser window.

- All text in the site should use a sans-serif font.

- Paragraphs of copy in the main text need to be small and dark gray, with large spacing between lines in a single paragraph.

- Heading 1 in the main text area needs to be large, bold, and colored dark orange.

- Heading 2 should be slightly smaller, italic, and should use the same color as main text.

- Text links should appear in orange text in all but the sidebar navigation list. The link text should not be underlined.

- Footer text should be light gray and centered.

- The sidebar links should be centered, and use the same color as the page background.

- Text links should switch to a different color when the mouse rolls over them.

The first three items on this list were accomplished when you defined properties for the **<body>** tag. You now need to complete the remaining items.

 DEFINE HTML TAG SELECTORS

In addition to the **<body>** tag that encloses the page content, properly structured pages use HTML tags to identify different types of content. CSS uses tag selectors to format HTML tags such as paragraphs (**<p>**), headings (**<h1>**, **<h2>**, etc.), unordered lists (**<ul>**), and so on.

1. **Open index.html from the Yosemite site root folder.**

2. **Click the New CSS Rule button at the bottom of the CSS Styles panel.**

3. **Choose Tag in the Selector Type menu, type h1 in the Selector Name field, and make sure master.css is selected in the Rule Definition menu. Click OK to define the new rule.**

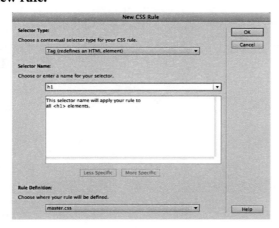

4. **In the Type properties, define the following options:**

   font-size: 22px

   font-weight: bold

   color: sample a dark orange from the bark in the background image

5. **In the Box properties, define the following options:**

   margin-top: 10px

   margin-bottom: 0px

   Content block elements such as headings and paragraphs have default top and bottom margins equivalent to the current text size. When a paragraph is placed below a heading, for example, the larger bottom margin of a heading overrides the smaller top margin of a paragraph. It is common to modify some of these margins with CSS. By defining the bottom margin of 0 for <h1> tags, any subsequent paragraph or heading's top margin will determine the spacing between the elements.

6. **Click OK to return to the document.**

   The first paragraph in the text — which is formatted with the <h1> tag — is affected by the new selector definition.

We sampled this color for the h1 tag selector.

7. **Create another tag selector for the <h2> tag, using the following settings:**

   font-size: 16px

   font-style: italic

   margin: 0px (all four sides)

The margin settings are not yet apparent because the <p> margins are still ambiguous.

8. **Create another tag selector for the <p> tag, using the following settings:**

> margin-top: 5px
>
> margin-bottom: 5px

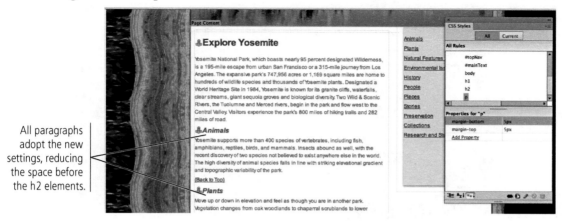

All paragraphs adopt the new settings, reducing the space before the h2 elements.

9. **Edit the h2 selector to add a 10px margin to only the top edge.**

In many cases, editing one tag selector will clarify a need to edit another selector. It is easy to make these adjustments by manipulating the selectors in the attached CSS file.

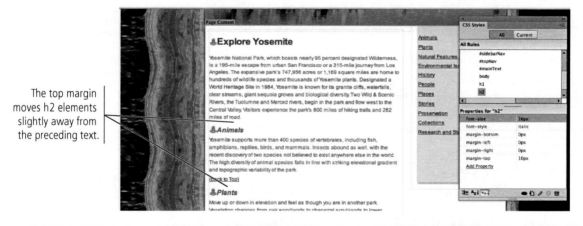

The top margin moves h2 elements slightly away from the preceding text.

CSS Mode of the Properties Panel

You can easily make changes to CSS rules using the options in the CSS mode of the Properties panel:

- Targeted Rule shows the CSS rule applied to the current selection. You can also choose a different target rule in the attached menu, or choose New CSS Rule from the menu to create a new selector.

- Edit Rule opens the CSS Rule Definition dialog box for the targeted rule.

- CSS Panel opens the CSS Styles panel and displays properties for the targeted rule in Current view.

- Font, Size, and Color change the associated options in the targeted rule.

- Bold (B) adds the bold font-weight property to the targeted rule.

- Italic (I) adds the italic font-style property to the targeted rule.

- Align Left, Align Center, Align Right, and Justify change the text-align property of the targeted rule.

10. **Add another tag selector for the <a> tag, using the following settings:**

    color: sample an orange color from the background image

    text-decoration: none

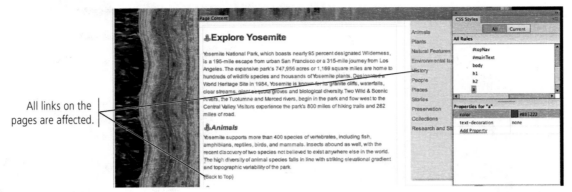

All links on the pages are affected.

11. **Close the HTML file. When asked, click Save to save your changes to the master.css file.**

    You did not change the actual HTML file, so you don't need to save it when you close it. However, you did make changes to the related master.css file. Dreamweaver recognizes the changes in this file even though it isn't technically open, so you are asked to save the CSS file changes before you close the open file.

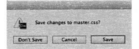

12. **Open things_to_do.html. Scroll and review the document content.**

    This file includes several additional HTML tags that are not included in the index file. You need to define additional selectors for those.

13. **Create new tag selectors as follows:**

h3	font-size: 13px
	font-weight: bold
	margin-top: 10px
	margin-bottom: 0px
ul	margin-top: 5px
	margin-bottom: 5px
li	margin-bottom: 5px

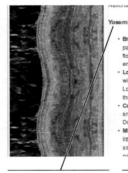

    h3 elements only appear on some pages.   The ul tag formats the overall list.   The li tag formats individual list items.

14. **Close things_to_do.html, saving the changes to master.css when asked.**

15. **Open things_to_know.html and review the page content. Create new tag selectors as follows:**

> **table**   **width: 450px**
>
> **th**   **font-weight: bold**
>
>   **text-align: left**
>
>   **border-bottom-color: orange (from the background image)**
>
>   **border-bottom-style: solid**
>
>   **border-bottom-width: 1px**
>
> **td**   **border-bottom-color: use the same color as the th tag**
>
>   **border-bottom-style: solid**
>
>   **border-bottom-width: 1px**

Note:

The text-align property is in the Block category of the CSS Rule Definition dialog box.

The table tag affects the overall table.   The th tag formats table header cells.   The td tag formats regular table cells.

16. **Close things_to_know.html, saving the changes to master.css when asked.**

17. **Open things_to_see.html and review the page content.**

This file does not include any additional tags that need to be defined. However, it is always a good idea to review each page in a site to see if changes are necessary.

Note:

If you hide visual aids, you will be better able to see the table-cell borders.

18. **Close things_to_see.html, and then continue to the next exercise.**

CREATE DESCENDANT SELECTORS

Three items remain in the list of known formatting requirements:

- Navigation links in the header area should be bold, and should appear entirely above the line that separates the header from the main page image.

- The sidebar links should be centered, and use the same color as the page background.

- Footer text should be light gray and centered.

- All links should switch to a lighter color when the mouse rolls over them.

Each of these items refers to content in a specific area of the page. To meet these requirements without affecting similar tags in other areas, you need to define **descendant selectors**, which are a type of compound selector, to format certain elements only within a specific div tag.

1. **Open design.dwt from the Yosemite site Templates folder.**

Although it isn't necessary to be able to select an object in the layout to define CSS selectors, it can be helpful to be able to select something so you can see what tags affect it. In order to select objects or text in non-editable regions of this site, you need to open the actual template file.

2. **Place the insertion point anywhere in the topNav link text, then click the New CSS Rule button at the bottom of the CSS Styles panel.**

Although you are using this selector to format content in a specific tag (the **\<a\>** or link tag), you also have to identify where the specific links are located on the page. If you don't use a compound selector to format this element, you would change the appearance of every link in the site instead of only the links in the top navigation area.

Note:

You can click the More Specific button to add nested IDs into the current selector name.

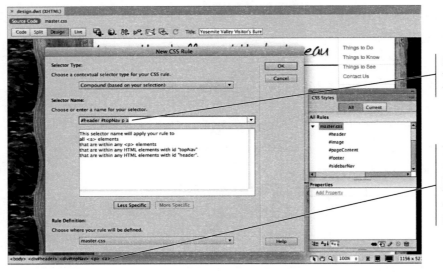

By default, the Selector Name field automatically includes the full path to the active tag.

The insertion point is in the link text \<a\> that is in a paragraph \<p\> that is in the topNav div \<div#topNav\>, which is nested within the header div \<div#header\>.

3. **Click the Less Specific button below the information pane to remove the first part of the selector name.**

This button removes elements from the beginning of the path; each click makes the name less specific. To keep the code short and the selector name easy to read, you are making the descendant selector only as specific as necessary to get the job done.

4. **Delete the p tag from the selector name.**

This tag should format all links in the topNav div, regardless of whether they exist within a paragraph. You can simply remove that character to make the selector less specific.

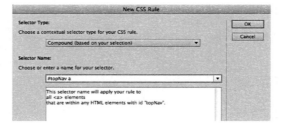

5. **Make sure master.css is selected in the Rule Definition menu, then click OK.**

6. **In the Type category, change the font-weight to bold. Click OK to create the new compound selector.**

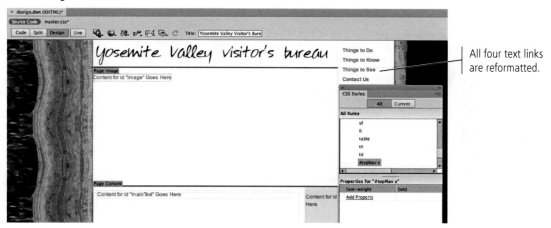

All four text links are reformatted.

7. **Open the index.html file and review the page content.**

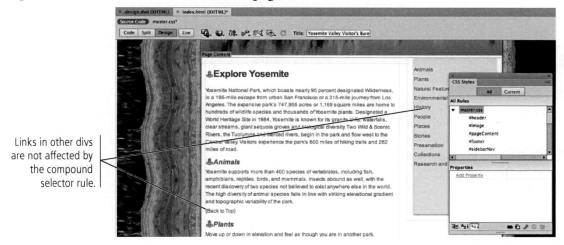

Links in other divs are not affected by the compound selector rule.

8. **With index.html active, click the New CSS Rule button in the CSS Styles panel. In the New CSS Rule dialog box, choose Compound in the Selector Type menu and type #header img in the Selector Name field. Make sure master.css is selected in the Rule Definition menu and click OK.**

If you select an element in the page, the Selector Name field of the New CSS Rule dialog box is already filled with the path to the selected tag. However, it is not necessary to first select the object you want to modify. You can simply type the appropriate compound selector name — in this case, #header img — in the field.

Note:

You are using a descendant selector here because you only want to affect this logo image. Other images in the site, including the main page image, should not have the large top padding applied.

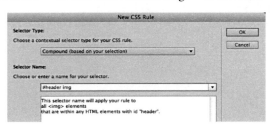

9. Define the following settings for the new selector:

> **border-width: 0px**
>
> **margin-top: 55px**

Note:

The border-width property removes the border that is added to image links by default in some browsers.

Increasing the image padding increases the containing div height.

10. Create another compound selector named **#sidebarNav a** using the following settings:

> **font-size: 13px**
>
> **font-weight: bold**
>
> **color: sample the green color from the page background**

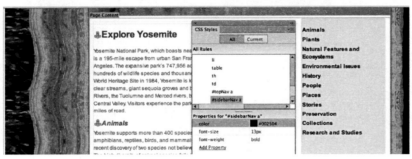

11. Create another compound selector named **#sidebarNav p** using the following settings:

> **margin-bottom: 12px**
>
> **text-align: center**

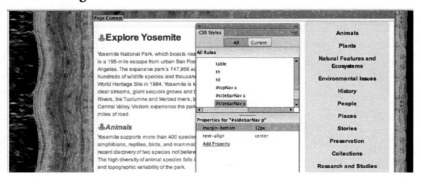

12. Create another compound selector named `#footer p` using the following settings:

> color: #999
>
> text-align: center

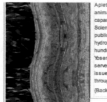 

13. Save all HTML and CSS files, then continue to the next exercise.

CREATE PSEUDO-CLASS SELECTORS

One item remains on your list of things to do:

- Text links should switch to a lighter color when the mouse rolls over the link.

A **class selector** is used when the same style needs to be applied to more than one element in a page. Unlike an ID selector, which is used only once per page, a class selector is used to repeat the same style throughout the page.

As you should remember from the previous exercise, controlling the default appearance of link text is accomplished with the <a> tag selector. To affect the rollover behavior, you have to define **pseudo-classes** (or variants) of the <a> selector. The five pseudo-class selectors relevant to different appearances of links are:

- **a:link** refers to a hyperlink that has not yet been visited.

- **a:visited** refers to a hyperlink that has been visited.

- **a:hover** refers to a hyperlink when the mouse pointer is hovering over the link.

- **a:focus** refers to a hyperlink that has been given "focus," such as when a user presses the Tab key to move through links on a page. This pseudo-class does not appear in Dreamweaver's list, but can be typed in manually.

- **a:active** refers to an active hyperlink (in other words: when the link is clicked before the mouse button is released).

1. With **index.html** open, click the New CSS Rule button in the CSS Styles panel.

2. Choose Compound in the Selector Type menu, then open the Selector Name menu and choose a:hover.

For a compound selector, this menu shows the four pseudo-classes that can be defined for the <a> tag, as well as paths to any selected elements. The hover pseudo-class determines what happens when the cursor moves (hovers) over link text.

Note:

For them to work correctly in all Web browsers, these pseudo-class selectors should be ordered as follows in the CSS file:

> *link*
>
> *visited*
>
> *hover*
>
> *focus*
>
> *active*

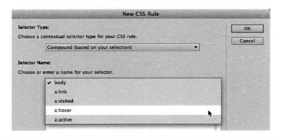

3. **Make sure master.css is selected in the Rule Definition menu and click OK.**

4. **In the Type options, change the color field to a light orange color sampled from the background image.**

5. **Click OK to create the new selector and return to the document.**

6. **With index.html active, switch to Live view, then test the rollover property of the links in the topNav, main, and footer areas.**

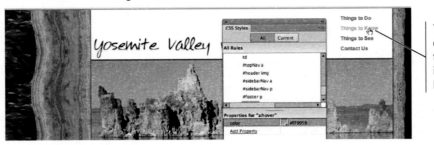

The a:hover selector changes the color of the topNav links, links in the main body, and links in the footer.

7. **Create another new compound selector for the a:hover pseudo-class within the sidebarNav div. Change the type color to a light green sampled from the background image.**

When you choose the a:hover pseudo-class in the menu, the existing selector name is replaced with the pseudo-class name. To change the pseudo-class of links only within a certain div, you have to type the div's ID in front of the pseudo-class name (or type the pseudo-class after an existing compound selector name). The full name of the new selector should be #sidebarNav a:hover.

By adding the ID selector to the pseudo-class, you are defining the behavior for links in the sidebarNav area only. You need to create this selector separately because you have already defined the color of links in this area to be different than the color value defined in the primary **<a>** tag selector.

8. **With Live view active, test the rollover property of the links in the sidebarNav area.**

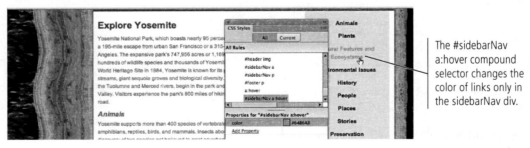

The #sidebarNav a:hover compound selector changes the color of links only in the sidebarNav div.

9. **Save any open files and close them.**

10. **Export a site definition named Yosemite.ste into your WIP>Yosemite folder, and then remove the Yosemite site from Dreamweaver.**

If necessary, refer back to Project 1: Bistro Site Organization for complete instructions on exporting a site definition or removing a site from Dreamweaver.

1. A(n) _____ is a flat image placed in the background of a page, used as a guide for reassembling the component pieces of the page.

2. A(n) _____ is the formal name of a CSS rule.

3. Using the _____ mode of the CSS Styles panel simplifies the panel to show only properties and values related to a selection.

4. Click the _____ button in the CSS Styles panel to define an external CSS file that should be used for the active page.

5. A(n) _____ selector type is used to control unique div elements.

6. A(n) _____ selector type is used to format specific HTML tags.

7. A(n) _____ selector type can be used to format specific tags only within a certain div.

8. The _____ property can be used to attach an object to the right or left side of the containing object.

9. The _____ property exists inside the container; background properties of the container extend into this area.

10. The _____ exists around the container; background properties of the container do not extend into this area.

1. Briefly explain two reasons why CSS is the preferred method for creating a Web page layout.

2. Briefly explain the difference between external, embedded, and inline styles.

3. Briefly explain how padding, margin, and border properties relate to the CSS box model.

Portfolio Builder Project

Use what you learned in this project to complete the following freeform exercise.
Carefully read the art director and client comments, then create your own design to meet the needs of the project.
Use the space below to sketch ideas; when finished, write a brief explanation of your reasoning behind your final design.

art director comments

Al Fresca Café, a French patisserie, has hired you to design a Web site to help promote their new catering services. The café is very popular, but the catering service is new so they want the site to be very accessible and easy to find.

To complete this project, you should:

❏ Create a Web site using the client's text and logo, which are provided in the **DW6_PB_Project4.zip** archive on the Student Files Web site.

❏ Use the client's provided images, or find or create other images as necessary to enhance the different pages of the site.

❏ Use CSS to control the layout and the content formatting.

client comments

Our primary target market is other businesses, although we also hope to capture some of the local social-club functions as well. I don't want the site to be overcrowded with 'stuff' — no glaring colors, or anything flashing or blinking.

Our site needs to have four main buttons: Home, Catering Menu, Testimonials, and The Café.

I sent you the text for the Home and Menu pages, and I sent one quote you can use to experiment with the design for the testimonials page. (There will eventually be lots of quotes, but I have to gather them all together.) The Café link should navigate to the restaurant's site (www.alFrescaMonterey.biz).

I also sent some photos that you can use, but you don't have to. If you have other decorative images, we're open to suggestion — just keep in mind our goal of "simple elegance."

project justification

Cascading style sheets offer tremendous flexibility when you are designing the look and feel of a Web site. By linking multiple HTML files to a single external CSS file — with or without an HTML page template — you can experiment with options by altering the CSS selectors and immediately seeing the effect on all linked pages. In addition to this flexibility, CSS is also compliant with current Web design standards, which means pages designed with CSS are both search-engine and accessibility-software friendly.

By completing this project, you have worked with different types of selectors to control both the layout of an HTML page and the formatting attributes of different elements on different pages in the site. The site structure is entirely controlled by the selectors in the linked CSS file, so you could change the appearance of the entire site without ever touching the individual HTML pages. And the inverse is also true — you can change the content of individual pages without affecting the site structure.

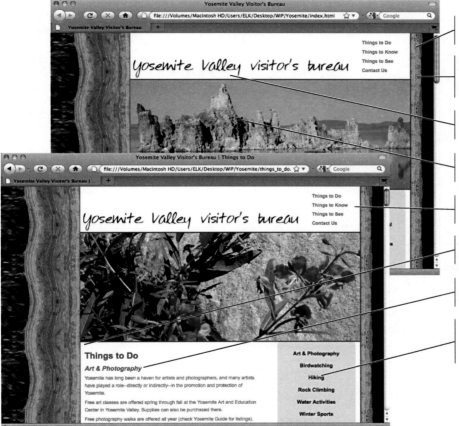

Place a tracing image to review site design requirements

Create an external CSS file to format multiple pages (based on a template file)

Create ID selectors to define layout elements (divs)

Edit CSS rules to adjust layout and content formatting

Use the float property to control nested div positioning

Use margin and padding options to control content positioning

Define tag selectors to control the appearance of specific HTML tags

Define pseudo-class selectors to control the alternate appearance of link text

Cupcake Bakery CSS Site

Your client operates an award-winning gourmet cupcake bakery in Southern California. Your job is to finalize the existing pages in the site and add a form that users can submit to join the client's email list.

This project incorporates the following skills:

❏ Working with CSS classes

❏ Manually editing CSS code

❏ Making an editable attribute in a template

❏ Working with the float and clear properties

❏ Placing a server-side include

❏ Creating a Spry menu bar

❏ Creating, validating, and formatting form fields

Project Meeting

client comments

The working files that we've seen so far are on the right track, but the pages still need some fine-tuning.

We want a different feature image to appear behind the logo on every page in the site.

The images in the different cupcake pages aren't the same size; we'd like them to be consistent so the pages don't look so messy.

Also, we need to be able to update the Weekly Specials page frequently, but we don't want to have to deal with the whole site structure. Can you set it up so we can edit one simple page and have our changes show up on the site?

Finally, we want a form that users can submit to get news of special events, coupons, and things like that. We're offering a free cupcake in the month they were born as incentive for signing up.

art director comments

The basic site design has already been created using a Dreamweaver template and CSS styles. You need to modify the existing template and CSS files where necessary to meet the client's first two goals.

The third objective is fairly easy to accomplish using Dreamweaver's built-in options for creating a server-side include. You will, however, need to apply a couple of simple workarounds when it comes to formatting the elements in the included page.

The final goal is the form. Again, Dreamweaver makes this very easy to accomplish. This doesn't need to be a large form, and you can use built-in tools to create everything you need.

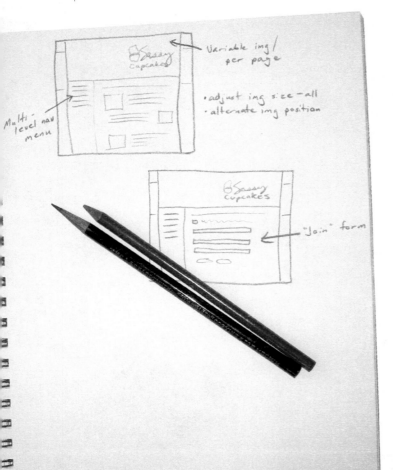

project objectives

To complete this project, you will:

- ❏ Create class selectors to place background images
- ❏ Make an editable attribute in a template
- ❏ Control float and clear properties
- ❏ Search page code to apply classes
- ❏ Apply multiple classes to elements
- ❏ Insert one HTML page into another
- ❏ Create a Spry menu bar
- ❏ Use the Code Navigator to review related styles
- ❏ Use Code Hints to write CSS code
- ❏ Create a form element and form fields
- ❏ Use Spry form-validation widgets
- ❏ Apply CSS to form fields

Stage 1 **Working with Classes**

If you completed Project 4: Yosemite CSS Layout, you worked extensively with CSS to control the appearance of various page elements. To review briefly:

- **Tag selectors** define properties for a specific HTML element; all content on the page with that tag is affected. For example, properties in the **a** tag selector format every instance that is marked with **<a>** tags (all links on the page).

- **ID selectors** define properties for an element that has been named with a specific ID. In the page code, the ID is applied as an attribute of the relevant tag, such as **<div id="header">**.

  It is important to remember that each ID can only be applied once on a particular page, which means each element can be uniquely addressed. ID selector names begin with the # character, such as **#header**.

- **Compound selectors** (also called **descendant selectors**) define properties for a specific HTML element only within a defined path, such as **div#header a** to format all **a** elements (links) only within a div with the ID attribute of "header".

- **Pseudo-classes** define properties for alternate states of an element, such as the **a:hover** pseudo-class, which defines the appearance of a link when the mouse cursor hovers over that link.

You should also understand the nested nature of CSS properties (and HTML in general). Tags in a page contain other tags, creating a nested structure that is a type of **parent-child relationship**. Nested tags (the children) inherit properties from their containing (parent) tags; tags at the same level of nesting are referred to as **siblings**. Consider the following example:

```
<body>
    <div id="header">
    <div id="main">
        <div id="right">
    <div id="footer">
```

Any properties that you define in the **body** tag selector automatically apply to all content on the page, because the **<body>** tag is the parent of all the nested divs. You can override those settings in a specific element by defining different properties for a specific ID.

If you define (for example) a different font size for the **#main** ID selector, the new font size will override the font-size properties in the **body** tag selector for the **<div id="main">** tag. The same font size is also inherited by its child (**<div id="right">**), but not by its siblings (**<div id="header">** and **<div id="footer">**).

REVIEW EXISTING SITE FILES

When you start any new project — especially one where some of the work is already done — you should begin by analyzing the existing files and then determining what work needs to be completed. You will then be better able to create a plan to efficiently accomplish the necessary work.

1. **Download DW6_RF_Project5.zip from the Student Files Web page.**

2. **Expand the ZIP archive in your WIP folder (Macintosh) or copy the archive contents into your WIP folder (Windows).**

   This results in a folder named **Cupcakes**, which contains the files you need for this project.

3. **Create a new site named Cupcakes, using the WIP>Cupcakes folder as the site root folder.**

   If necessary, refer to the first exercises in Project 1: Bistro Site Organization, for more detailed instructions.

4. **In the Files panel, expand the Templates folder and then open the design.dwt file.**

This site includes a number of pages that are based on this template. You should notice that there is only one editable area (named "Page Content"), where all page-specific text and images are placed.

A CSS file (named style.css) is attached to the template, which means it defines properties for all pages that are attached to the template.

To complete this project you need to accomplish a number of tasks:

1. Add a page-specific background image to the header area of the page.
2. Format the content on individual pages to meet aesthetic requirements.
3. Create a navigation menu.
4. Link the "Weekly Update" file to the page that appears in the site.
5. Create a form so users can sign up to receive discounts via email.

5. **Continue to the next exercise.**

Note:

The layout for this project is based on the free "Pinky" template at www.templatemo.com.

Photos were provided courtesy of Samantha Schmitz, Double D Cupcakes, Lancaster, California.

CREATE A CLASS SELECTOR TO PLACE BACKGROUND IMAGES

A **class selector** defines properties for any element that is marked with that class. Classes offer a number of advantages over other kinds of selectors:

- A class can be applied multiple times on a single page, unlike an ID selector which can be applied only once on a page.

- A class can be applied to different HTML tags on the same page, which means you can apply the same class to (for example) an **h2** element and an **img** element.

- A class only applies to specific elements where you attach it, unlike a tag selector that affects all same-tagged elements on the page. For example, an **h2** tag selector affects all **h2** elements on the page; a class selector can be applied to only specific **h2** elements without affecting other **h2** elements on the page.

- You can apply more than one class to a single element, which means you can define classes to perform very specific tasks, and then apply only and exactly what you need to a specific element.

The one primary disadvantage of classes, however, is that they must be intentionally and manually attached to every element where you want those properties to apply. As you will see in the following exercises, this can be time-consuming if you want to apply the same class to a large number of elements on multiple pages.

Note:

Some professional Web designers work almost entirely with classes to create a page design, using classes instead of IDs to define the appearance of various divs and other elements.

1. **With the `design.dwt` template open, click the New CSS Rule button at the bottom of the CSS Styles panel.**

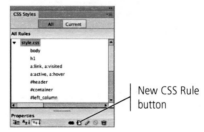

New CSS Rule button

2. **In the resulting dialog box, choose Class in the Selector Type menu.**

3. **In the Selector Name field, type `.bkgHome`.**

    Class selectors always begin with a period. Dreamweaver adds the period for you if you forget, but it's a good idea to get in the habit of typing the period yourself.

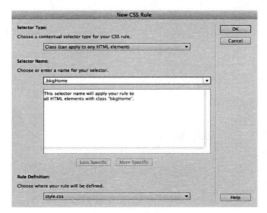

4. **Make sure style.css is selected in the Rule Definition menu, then click OK.**

5. **In the resulting CSS Rule Definition dialog box, show the Background options.**

6. **Click the Browse button for the Background-image property. Navigate to** `back-home.png` **in the images>backgrounds folder, then click Open/OK.**

7. **Choose no-repeat in the Background-repeat menu.**

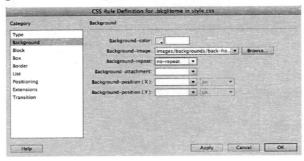

8. **Click OK to create the new class selector.**

   The selector appears in the CSS Styles panel, and the Related Files bar shows that the style.css file has been changed. However, nothing has changed in the open template file. Classes do not affect a page until they are intentionally applied to one or more elements.

Nothing has changed in the page file. The style.css file has changed.

9. **If the new selector does not appear at the bottom of the list in the CSS Styles panel, click the new class selector and drag it to the bottom of the list.**

New classes are automatically added below the previously selected item (yours might have been in a different location than ours). You can reorder them by simply dragging in the panel.

Although this step isn't strictly necessary, it is a good idea to keep your styles organized to make them easier to navigate. We organize the panel in "tag, ID, class" order; as you gain experience, you will determine what method best suits your working habits.

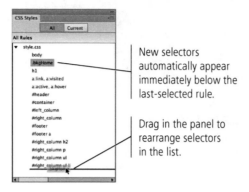

New selectors automatically appear immediately below the last-selected rule.

Drag in the panel to rearrange selectors in the list.

10. **Click to place the insertion point in the header div. In the Tag Selector, click the <div#header> tag to select the entire div.**

11. **In the Properties panel, open the Class menu and choose bkgHome.**

The top section of this menu lists all available classes. Because your CSS file includes only one class, it is the only choice in the list.

The header div is selected.

Use this menu to apply a class to the selection.

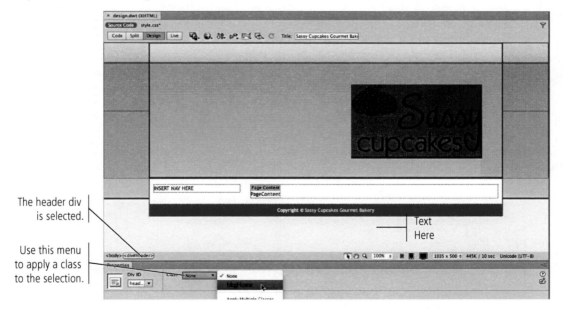

12. Click to place the insertion point back in the div.

This effectively deselects the div and removes the visual aids, so you can better see the results of the applied class — the header div now has a background image.

The applied class is appended to the tag in the Tag Selector.

13. Save the file. When prompted, update all files linked to the template. When the Update Pages dialog box shows the process is done, click the Close button.

14. Click style.css in the Related Files bar to show that file's code, then choose File>Save.

In this exercise, you changed both the page and the attached CSS file, so you need to save both files.

Click style.css to open that file in the Code pane, then save the file.

15. Continue to the next exercise.

MANUALLY EDIT CSS CODE

The class selector you created in the previous exercise defines a background image for the header div. Remember, though, you need to apply different images to the same div on each page. In this exercise, you will define additional classes that you will apply in the next exercise.

1. **With `design.dwt` open, click the Code button in the Document toolbar. If necessary, click `style.css` in the Related Files area to show that file instead of the template page source code.**

2. **Scroll to the bottom of the code and review the class selector that you created in the previous exercise.**

   The selector code appears at the bottom of the file because you dragged it to the bottom of the list in the CSS Styles panel. The order of selector code in the CSS file matches the order you see in the CSS Styles panel.

   CSS code uses the following syntax:

   > **name {**
   >   **property:value;**
   > **}**

```
× design.dwt (XHTML)
Source Code  style.css*
Code  Split  Design  Live              Title: Sassy Cupcakes Gourmet Bake
  95  #right_column ul li {
  96      vertical-align: middle;
  97      display: block;
  98      background-image: url(images/sassy-icon.png);
  99      background-repeat: no-repeat;
 100      padding-left: 25px;
 101      height: 28px;
 102  }
 103  .bkgHome {
 104      background-image: url(images/backgrounds/back-home.png);
 105      background-repeat: no-repeat;
 106  }
 107
```

3. **Click and drag from the line number for line 103 to 106.**

   Clicking a line number selects the entire line of code.

   Click and drag over the line numbers to select entire lines of code.

```
  93      padding-left: 25px;
  94  }
  95  #right_column ul li {
  96      vertical-align: middle;
  97      display: block;
  98      background-image: url(images/sassy-icon.png);
  99      background-repeat: no-repeat;
 100      padding-left: 25px;
 101      height: 28px;
 102  }
 103  .bkgHome {
 104      background-image: url(images/backgrounds/back-home.png);
 105      background-repeat: no-repeat;
 106  }
 107
```

   Rather than using the CSS Styles panel, you are going to simply copy and paste the required code, then make the necessary changes in each version.

4. **Choose Edit>Copy (Command/Control-C) to copy the selected code.**

5. **Click at the beginning of Line 107 to place the insertion point, then choose Edit>Paste (Command/Control-V).**

```
  97      display: block;
  98      background-image: url(images/sassy-icon.png);
  99      background-repeat: no-repeat;
 100      padding-left: 25px;
 101      height: 28px;
 102  }
 103  .bkgHome {
 104      background-image: url(images/backgrounds/back-home.png);
 105      background-repeat: no-repeat;
 106  }
 107  .bkgHome {
 108      background-image: url(images/backgrounds/back-home.png);
 109      background-repeat: no-repeat;
 110  }
 111
```

6. Review the Files panel.

The name of each HTML file gives you an idea of what each page contains. Because you will use a different class to change each page's header background, you should use similarly indicative class names to make your work easier later.

7. In line 107 of the Code pane, change the class name to .bkgEveryday.

Change the class name in the pasted selector code.

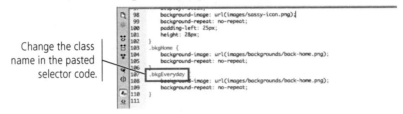

8. In line 108, select and delete the code that defines the image path, including the colon immediately after the property name. Leave the closing semicolon in place.

Select and delete the current value, including the initial colon.

9. Type : to open the Code Hints menu.

When you work directly in the Code pane, Dreamweaver provides code hints related to the current context. Typing a colon after a CSS property name initiates a menu with the possible values for that property.

In this case, the background-image property requires a file path, so the Code Hints menu gives you the option to Browse.

Type a colon to open the Code Hints menu.

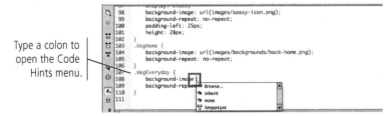

10. Press the Down Arrow key once to highlight the Browse option in the Code Hints menu, then press Return/Enter.

You can also double-click Browse in the menu to open the navigation dialog box.

11. In the resulting navigation dialog box, select back-cupcakes-everyday.png (in the site's images>backgrounds folder) and click Open/OK.

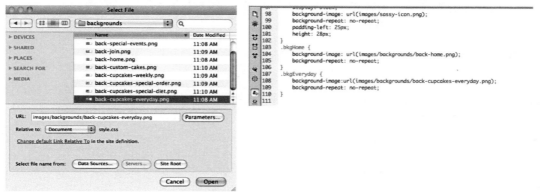

12. Repeat this process to add six more class selectors, using the following information:

Class name	Background Image
bkgSpecialDiets	back-cupcakes-special-diet.png
bkgSpecialOrder	back-cupcakes-special-order.png
bkgWeekly	back-cupcakes-weekly.png
bkgCustomCakes	back-custom-cakes.png
bkgJoinTheClub	back-join.png
bkgSpecialEvents	back-special-events.png

Note:

You can also manually type the required file name in the CSS code. If you choose to use this option, make sure the file names you type match exactly what you see in the Files panel. Capitalization matters!

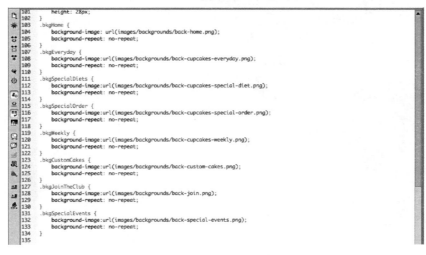

Note:

You don't need a class for weekly-update.html. Later in this project, you are going to place it into cupcakes_weekly.html, which will already have the required div and background image.

13. Save the CSS file and then continue to the next exercise.

MAKE AN EDITABLE ATTRIBUTE IN A TEMPLATE

You need to apply different background images to the header div for each page in this site. However, the header div in the template is not an editable area, which means you can't select it to apply the necessary class.

Rather than creating an editable region, which would leave the placed logo in that div vulnerable on individual pages, you can define an editable attribute in the template, so you can change only that attribute on each page.

1. **With `design.dwt` open, turn on the Split view and show the page source code in the Code pane.**

2. **Place the insertion point in the header div, then click the div name in the Tag Selector to select the entire div.**

   In the Code pane, the code related to the active selection is also highlighted. The first line of the highlighted code shows the opening div tag, along with two attributes — class and id. In the next few steps, you are going to make the class attribute editable in pages that are attached to this template.

3. **Choose Modify>Templates>Make Attribute Editable.**

4. **In the resulting dialog box, make sure CLASS is selected in the Attribute menu, then check the Make Attribute Editable option.**

All attributes of the selected tag are available in this menu (in this case, CLASS and ID).

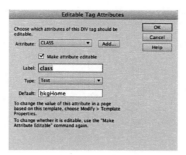

5. **Click OK to apply the change.**

When you make an attribute editable in a template, the previously defined value is removed from the page code. In the Design pane, the background image is no longer visible in the template.

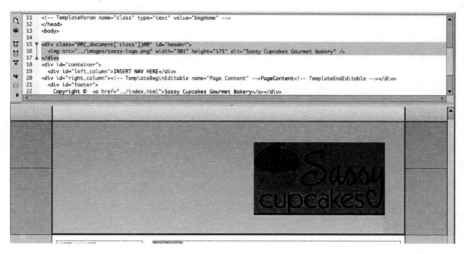

6. **Save the template file, updating linked pages when asked.**

7. **Close the Update Links dialog box, then close the template file.**

8. **Using the Files panel, open the cupcakes-everyday.html file.**

The header div in this page still shows the image from the bkgHome class because that is the default value of the attribute, as defined in the Editable Tag Attributes dialog box (see Step 4).

9. **Scroll the CSS Styles panel so you can see all of the class selector names.**

In the next few steps, you will need to type these exact class names to change the attribute values for individual pages in the site. By displaying the selectors in the CSS Styles panel, you can see exactly what you need to type.

10. **Choose Modify>Template Properties.**

The resulting dialog box shows all editable properties of the applied template. In this case, the class attribute (of the header div, even though this information is not presented in the dialog box).

11. **In the Class field at the bottom of the dialog box, type the name of the class you want to apply (`bkgEveryday`).**

Unfortunately, Dreamweaver does not provide you with a menu of available class names; you have to type the exact class name (without the opening period).

12. **Click OK to apply the change.**

Even though the header div is not selectable or editable on the page, the background image defined in the bkgEveryday class now appears in the header div.

13. **Save the file and close it.**

14. **Repeat the same process to change the class for each page in the site (except weekly-update.html).**

File name	Class
cupcakes-special-diets.html	bkgSpecialDiets
cupcakes-special-order.html	bkgSpecialOrder
cupcakes-weekly.html	bkgWeekly
custom-cakes.html	bkgCustomCakes
join-the-club.html	bkgJoinTheClub
special-events.html	bkgSpecialEvents

Note:

You do not need to modify the index.html file because the default class — bkgHome — is appropriate for that page.

15. **Save and close any open fies, then continue to the next exercise.**

CONTROL FLOAT AND CLEAR PROPERTIES

The Float property of CSS defines how an element attaches to its container, and how other elements appear in relation to the floating element.

- If you define a left float value, the floating element attaches to the left edge of its container; other content wraps around the right edge of the floating element.

- If you define a right float value, the floating element attaches to the right edge of its container; other content wraps around the left edge of the floating element.

- If you define a none float value, the element does not float; other content does not wrap around the non-floating element.

The Clear property defines where other floating content cannot wrap around an element. In other words, if you define a right clear value to an **<img>** tag (for example), no other content can appear on the right side of that image. The clear property can have a value of left, right, both, or none (the default).

1. **Open the file cupcakes-everyday.html. Scroll through the page and review the contents.**

   Each listed cupcake includes a photo and a brief description. If you look closely, however, you will notice that the images are not uniform in size. Rather than manually editing each image, you are going to define a class that controls the size of each image where that class is applied.

   As a general rule, you should avoid scaling images without resampling in Dreamweaver because the Web server still has to transmit all of the file data for the original-size image.

   In this case, the required scaling is very slight, and would not require users to download huge amounts of unnecesary data. As a "best practice", however, it would be better to edit the actual image files in an image-editing application such as Adobe Photoshop.

2. Click the New CSS Rule button at the bottom of the CSS Styles panel.

3. In the resulting dialog box, choose Class in the Selector Type menu and type
   .img150px in the Selector Name field. Make sure style.css is selected in the
   Rule Definition menu and click OK.

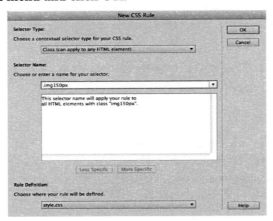

4. Show the Box options in the resulting dialog box, then define the following
   settings:

Width: 150 px	**Margin-right: 5 px**
Height: 150 px	**Margin-bottom: 10 px**
Float: left	**Margin-left: 5 px**

   Note:

   *All of the cupcake images
   in this site are square,
   so you are not changing
   the aspect ratio of these
   images.*

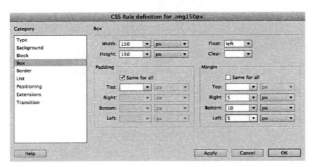

5. Click OK to create the new class.

6. Click the first image in the page content area to select it. In the Properties
   panel, open the Class menu and choose img150px.

   This menu provides the same options as the contextual menu for a specific tag in the
   Tag Selector. You can apply any class that is available in the attached CSS file to the
   selected object.

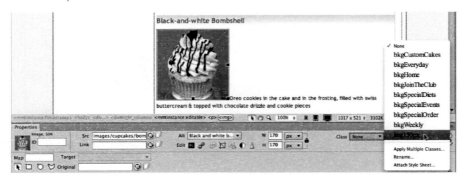

As you can see, the selected image resizes slightly. Because you defined the float:left property, other content is able to wrap around the right edge of the image.

Because the descriptive text for each is short, the next cupcake name is also allowed to wrap to the right of the image. You should correct this problem before continuing.

7. **Place the insertion point in the "Confetti" cupcake name.**

8. **Click the CSS button on the left side of the Properties panel to show those options.**

   When the Properties panel appears in CSS mode, you can easily identify and edit the selector (rule) that affects the active selection.

The Properties panel is in CSS mode.

Click Edit Rule to edit the properties of the selector that defines the selected object.

Note:

Any changes you make in the right side of the panel automatically change the related selector properties.

CSS Mode of the Properties Panel

DREAMWEAVER FOUNDATIONS

You can easily make changes to CSS rules using the options in the CSS mode of the Properties panel:

- Targeted Rule shows the CSS rule applied to the current selection. You can also choose a different target rule in the attached menu, or choose New CSS Rule from the menu to create a new selector.

- Edit Rule opens the CSS Rule Definition dialog box for the targeted rule.

- CSS Panel opens the CSS Styles panel and displays properties for the targeted rule in Current view.

- Font, Size, and Color change the associated options in the targeted rule.

- Bold (B) adds the bold font-weight property to the targeted rule.

- Italic (I) adds the italic font-style property to the targeted rule.

- Align Left, Align Center, Align Right, and Justify change the text-align property of the targeted rule.

9. **Click the Edit Rule button in the left side of the panel.**

   This button opens the CSS Rule Definition dialog box for the selected rule. This is the same as selecting the appropriate rule in the CSS Styles panel and clicking the Edit Rule button. The advantage is that you can very easily target the rule that affects the active selection, without hunting through a long list of styles in the CSS Styles panel.

10. **In the Box option, choose both in the Clear menu, then click OK to change the selector.**

    Because you assigned the clear:both property to the **#right_column h2** selector, the second cupcake name — which is formatted as a level2 heading in the right_column div — is now forced to appear after the image where the float:left property has been applied (by the **img150px** class).

11. **Save the file and continue to the next exercise.**

 ## SEARCH PAGE CODE TO APPLY CLASSES

As we explained previously, classes only work when you intentionally apply them to selected elements. This can be very time consuming when you need to apply the same class to multiple elements on multiple pages in a site.

Whenever you face a repetitive task, it is a good idea to look for a way to automate the process. Although you don't really need an extensive knowledge of HTML or code to successfully create a page or site in Dreamweaver, a foundational understanding does help to find these time-savers.

In this exercise, you are going to use the Find and Replace function to apply the same class to all **img** elements in the entire site.

1. **With cupcakes-everyday.html open, open the other HTML files in the site and review their contents.**

   Three other pages in the site have the same general layout in the page content area as the cupcakes-everyday file:

   cupcakes-special-diets.html

   cupcakes-special-order.html

   weekly-update.html

   The other pages include images, but those images do not suffer from the inconsistent-size problem like the images in the various cupcake lists.

Note:

The cupcakes-weekly.html file is actually a container page, which will be used to present information in the weekly-update.html file. You will complete that process later in this project.

2. **Close all but the four pages that contain lists of cupcakes. If asked, save the style.css file.**

You should have four open files.

3. **Choose Edit>Find and Replace.**

4. **Choose Open Documents in the Find In menu.**

5. **Choose Specific Tag in the Search menu, then type img in the resulting Search field.**

6. **If anything appears immediately below the Search menus, click the Minus button (–) to remove that criteria from the search.**

Click the Minus button to remove any existing options from the Search parameters.

7. **Open the Action menu and choose Set Attribute.**

8. **Type class in the Search field, then choose img150px in the To field menu.**

Dreamweaver is a Web design application, so the Find and Replace dialog box includes options for easily performing exactly the kind of task you need to complete — assigning a single class to multiple elements on multiple pages.

By searching for a specific tag, you can locate all <img> tags at once. Using the Action menu, you can easily apply the selected class (img150px) as an attribute to all <img> tags in all open documents.

Note:

You can also simply type the class name in the To field.

Choose Set Attribute in the Action menu.

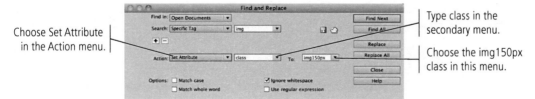

Type class in the secondary menu.

Choose the img150px class in this menu.

9. **Click Replace All, read the resulting message, then click OK.**

Remember, all but one of these files are based on a template. The client's logo, which is placed in the header div, is an image so it uses the <img> tag. However, because the header div is not an editable region, the Find and Replace function is not able to add the attribute for the logo. As we explained earlier, leaving the header div uneditable protects the area from changes, even inadvertent ones that would have been made by this type of Find and Replace.

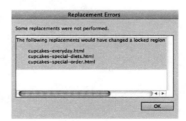

10. **Review the Search panel, then close the tab group.**

When you use the Find and Replace dialog box, the Search panel automatically opens to show the results of the process.

11. **Review the contents of each open file.**

12. **Click one of the images in the weekly-update.html file and review the Tag Selector.**

At this point, the weekly-update.html file does not appear to have the correct formatting, because it is not attached to the style.css file that defines the appearance of various elements.

You can see in the Tag Selector, though, that the required class attribute has been added to the img tag. When you place this file into the cupcakes-weekly.html file, which *is* attached to the style.css file, the various elements will be formatted properly.

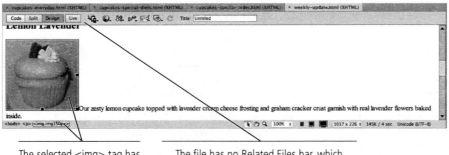

The selected <img> tag has the correct class attribute.

The file has no Related Files bar, which means it does not have an attached CSS file.

13. **Save and close all open files, then continue to the next exercise.**

APPLY MULTIPLE CLASSES TO ELEMENTS

As we explained in the beginning of this project, some professionals define very specific classes to accomplish only a defined goal. This method can make it easier to understand the purpose of various classes, especially after you return to a project you created a long time ago, if you work on files created by another user, or if you hand off your site files to another designer.

Using this technique, however, often requires multiple classes applied to the same element. Fortunately, Dreamweaver makes that process relatively easy. In this exercise, you will create a new class that assigns the float:right property; you will then apply that class to every other image on the cupcake list pages to enhance the visual appeal of those pages.

1. **Open cupcakes-everyday.html and make sure the Design view is active.**

2. **Click the New CSS Rule button at the bottom of the CSS Styles panel.**

3. **In the New CSS Rule dialog box, choose Class in the Selector Type menu, type .imgFloatRight in the Selector Name field, and make sure style.css is selected in the Rule Definition menu. Click OK to create the new selector.**

Note:

The Apply Multiple Classes option is also available in the Class menu of the Properties panel.

4. **In the Box options, choose right in the Float menu, then click OK to create the new class selector.**

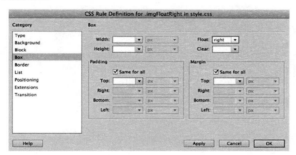

5. **In the Design view, click to select the image under the "Confetti" heading.**

6. **Control/right-click the active <img> tag in the Tag Selector. In the contextual menu, choose Set Class>Apply Multiple Classes.**

The resulting Multiclass Selection dialog box lists all available classes. Because the **img150px** class is already applied to the active tag, that class is already checked.

7. **Check the box for the imgFloatRight class, then click OK.**

8. **Click the Split view to show the Code pane.**

   In the code for the selected **<img>** tag, you can see the two classes are listed inside the quotes for the class attribute.

   If you remember, the **img150px** defined a float:left property. Because the **imgFloatRight** class comes second — it is later in the nesting order — the float:right property overrides the previous float value.

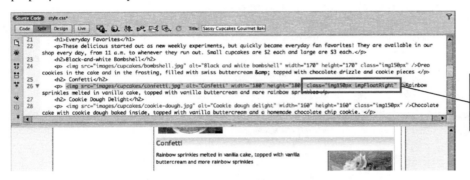

The class attribute for the <img> tag includes two values inside the quotes, separated by a space.

9. **Using the same technique, apply the imgFloatRight class to every other image on the following pages:**

   cupcakes-everyday.html

   cupcakes-special-diets.html

   cupcakes-special-order.html

10. **Open weekly-update.html, then select the image under the "Lemon Lavender" heading.**

11. **Control/right-click the active <img> tag in the Tag Selector and choose Set Class>Apply Multiple Classes.**

    Remember, this file is not attached to the style.css file, so the new **imgFloatRight** class is not available in the list of classes (the class is "not defined" in the file) — either in the menu or in the Multiclass Selection dialog box.

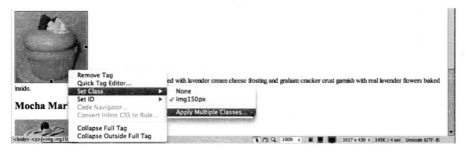

12. **With the insertion point at the end of the existing class name, press the Spacebar, then type** `imgFloatRight`.

Because the class you want doesn't technically exist for this file yet, you have to manually type the class name.

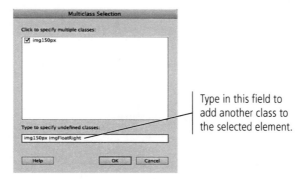

Type in this field to add another class to the selected element.

13. **Click OK to apply the second class to the <img> tag.**

14. **Repeat Steps 11–13 to add the imgFloatRight class to the fourth image on the weekly-update.html page.**

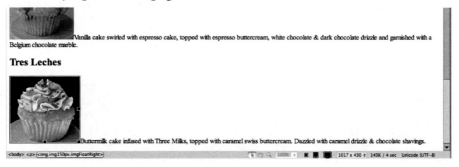

15. **Save and close all open files, then continue to the next exercise.**

 ## INSERT ONE HTML PAGE INTO ANOTHER

As you have seen, the weekly-update.html file does not include any of the same formatting as the other pages in the site. This file is created every week by your client, then emailed to you along with the required image files. (This scenario is not uncommon in professional Web design, whether the included file comes directly from your client or from some other source.)

Rather than copying and pasting the content from one file to another, you can use a **server-side include** (SSI) to place one HTML file into another. When a browser calls the page, the Web server reads the link and delivers ("includes") the linked file as part of the parent page. The styles that apply to the parent page are inherited by the child page, so the content in the SSI file will match the overall site formatting.

1. **Open `cupcakes-weekly.html` and make sure the Design view is active.**

2. **Open the Preferences dialog box and show the Invisible Elements options.**

Remember: Preferences are accessed in the Dreamweaver menu on Macintosh and in the Edit menu on Windows.

3. **Make sure the Show Contents of Included File option is checked, then click OK.**

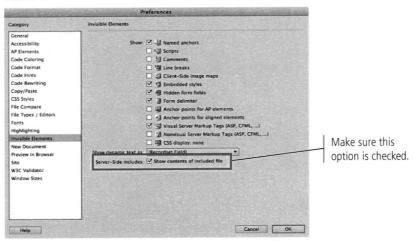

Make sure this option is checked.

4. **Select and delete the placeholder text in the editable area of the open page.**

5. **With the insertion point still in the editable region, choose Insert>Server-Side Include.**

The insertion point should be inside the editable region.

6. **In the resulting dialog box, navigate to weekly-update.html in the site root folder, then click Open/OK.**

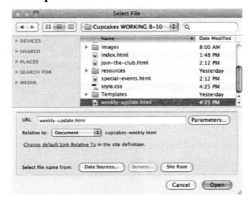

As you can see, the included file appears in the open page, but there are some obvious problems. The included file contains the necessary head code and body tags that define an HTML page. When this file is placed into another HTML page, the duplicated **<html>** and **<body>** tags confuse the server. If you include one HTML file in another, you have to remove the redundant code from the included file.

7. Using the Files panel, open the **weekly-update.html** file, then click the Code button in the Document toolbar.

8. Select and delete all code up to and including the opening <body> tag.

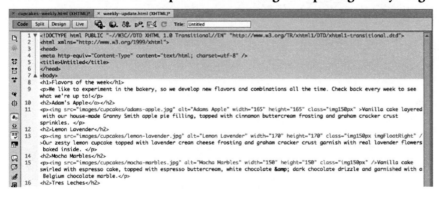

9. Select and delete the closing </body> and </html> tags.

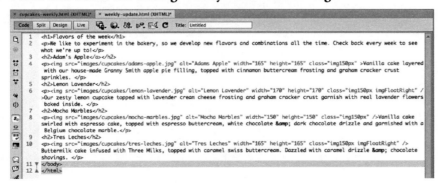

10. Save the file and close it.

When you return to the cupcakes-weekly file, the included page appears correctly in the editable region. Because all elements of the included file were tagged properly, with classes applied where necessary, the included page content seems to flow as a natural part of the parent page.

Note:

Although Dreamweaver accurately shows the result of a server-side include in the Design pane, server-side includes require a server that can correctly process this kind of information.

If the included page is an HTML file, most servers should not have a problem delivering the included content.

If the included page is a different format — PHP, ASP, etc. — you should verify with your host provider that you use the appropriate format for serving the included page.

11. Click the Split button in the document toolbar.

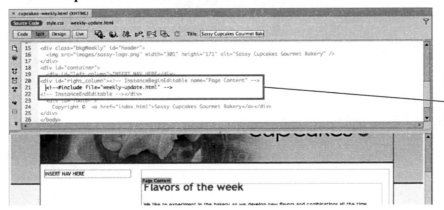

The editable region has only one line, identifying the included file.

12. Save the file and close it, then continue to the next stage of the project.

Stage 2 **Creating a Spry Menu Bar**

A **script** is a set of instructions that performs certain actions in response to an event (generally something the user does, such as clicking an object or typing certain information). JavaScript is one of the most widely used scripting languages because its simple syntax makes it easy to manage — even for non-programmers.

JavaScript scripts can be embedded directly into HTML pages using **<script>** tags. These scripts are interpreted by the Web browser to generate the desired result.

If you want to execute the same JavaScript on several Web pages, you can create the JavaScript in an external JavaScript file and save it with the ".js" extension. You can then attach the external file to an HTML page in the head section of the page code:

<script src="xyz.js"></script>

You don't need to learn to write scripts to use JavaScript in your Web pages. Dreamweaver includes a number of built-in options for creating JavaScript-based page elements without the need to write a single line of code. You can also find a number of free sources for prebuilt JavaScript elements on the Internet.

In this stage of the project, you will use Dreamweaver's built-in options to create a JavaScript-based, multi-level navigation menu.

CREATE A SPRY MENU BAR

The Spry Menu Bar widget can be used to create a navigation bar with up to three levels of links. Second- and third-level links display as fly-out or drop-down menus (for vertical or horizontal menus, respectively).

These types of menus are useful for arranging pages into meaningful categories, as well as for saving space on the page. Users benefit by having direct access to information at deeper levels, instead of having to first navigate to section home pages.

When you insert a Spry menu bar into an HTML page, the required Spry JavaScript and CSS files are included automatically in the Web site's root folder when you save the page.

1. **Open the design.dwt template file (in the Templates folder) from the Cupcakes site.**

2. **Select and delete the words "INSERT NAV HERE" from the left_column div.**

3. **Open the Insert panel and change it to Spry mode.**

4. **With the insertion point still in the left_column div, click the Spry Menu Bar button in the Insert panel.**

> *Note:*
>
> *JavaScript is not the same as Java (the programming language) despite the fact that both share some similar programming structures.*

> *Note:*
>
> *JavaScript works in all major browsers — Firefox, Safari, Chrome, Internet Explorer, Opera, and even Netscape.*

> *Note:*
>
> *If the JavaScript is placed in the page head section, it will run only when an event associated with it is triggered. If the JavaScript is placed in the page body section, the script will execute while the page loads.*

> *Note:*
>
> *You can also use the Insert>Spry menu to add the various Spry objects.*

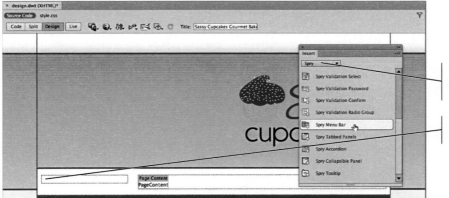

All Spry objects are available in the Spry Insert panel.

The insertion point should be inside this div.

5. In the resulting dialog box, choose the Vertical option and click OK.

The resulting menu bar object is added at the location of the insertion point. The default menu bar has four primary items, which you can edit in the Properties panel or directly in the Design pane.

This is the vertical menu bar.

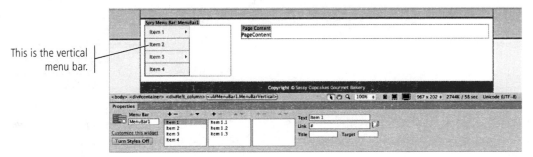

6. In the Design pane, highlight the text of the first menu item and type Cupcakes.

When you interact with menu-bar text in the Design pane, the Properties panel changes to show options related to text, rather than options related to the overall menu object.

7. Select the entire word, then link the selected text to cupcakes-everyday.html in the site root folder.

If you don't see the Link field in the Properties panel, click the HTML button on the left side of the panel to show the panel in HTML mode.

Each item in a Spry menu bar is automatically created as a link, using the # placeholder to add the **<a>** tag to each list item. When you add a Spry menu to a site, you need to define the actual links for each item in the menu.

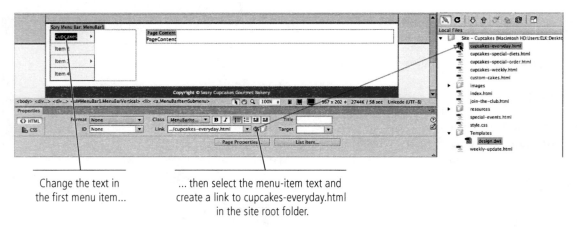

Change the text in the first menu item...

... then select the menu-item text and create a link to cupcakes-everyday.html in the site root folder.

8. Repeat Steps 6–7 to change the text and link of the remaining list items:

Text	Link
Custom Cakes	**custom-cakes.html**
Special Events	**special-events.html**
Join the Club	**join-the-club.html**

9. Click the blue Spry widget tab at the top of the menu object to select the entire Spry object.

When you click the blue tab at the top of a Spry element, properties of the object become available in the Properties panel.

Click the blue bar to select the menu object.

When the menu object is selected, the Properties panel shows options for the overall menu.

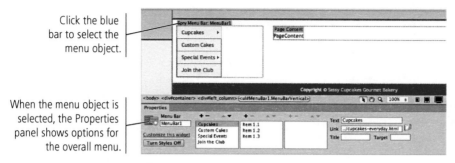

10. In the Properties panel, click the "+" button above the list of menu items.

The navigation bar you are creating needs five links, but the default menu bar contains only four links. You can click the "+" button to add new items to a menu bar, or click the "−" button to remove a selected item from the menu bar.

New items are automatically added below the previously selected list item, so yours might be in a different location than what you see here. It doesn't matter, because you are going to move this new item to the top of the list in the next step.

Note:

The "+" and "−" buttons have the same function for each level of the menu.

Use the arrow buttons to rearrange items in the list.

Use the "+" or "−" button to add or remove items from the list.

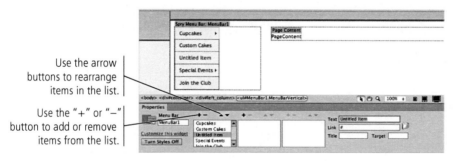

11. With the new list item selected, click the Up Arrow button above the list until the new item appears at the top.

Items in the menu appear in the same order as they appear in the Properties panel list.

12. With the new menu item selected in the list, change the Text field to Home and change the Link field to ../index.html.

Remember, the template file that you are working on is in the Template folder. To access the index file from the template file, the link has to go up one level in the site's folder structure.

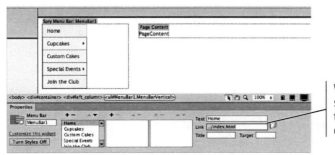

When the menu object is selected, use these fields to change the text and link of the active menu item.

13. **Save the file. Review the information in the resulting message, and then click OK.**

The Spry layout objects include CSS styles that format the various elements. The CSS and JavaScript files required by Spry widgets must be included when you upload files to a Web server. Dreamweaver automatically incorporates the necessary elements into your site folder when you save the HTML file.

14. **When prompted, update all files linked to the template and then close the Update Pages dialog box.**

15. **In the Files panel, expand the SpryAssets folder.**

All files necessary for the menu bar to work properly are added to the site folder.

16. **Continue to the next exercise.**

 MODIFY MENU SUBITEMS

The Spry menu bar object can create up to three levels of navigation, which makes it easy to build a complex nested navigation scheme. Submenus for each primary menu item can be managed easily in the Properties panel. In this exercise, you define a submenu so users can access the different categories of cupcake listings.

1. **With design.dwt open, click the blue Spry widget tab (as on Page 231) to select the entire object.**

2. **In the Properties panel, click Special Events in the first-level list of menu items. In the second-level menu item list, select Item 3.3.**

By default, Dreamweaver includes secondary list items for the original Item 1 (now the "Cupcakes" link) and Item 3 (now the "Special Events" link). You do not need a submenu for the Special Events item, so you need to remove those submenu items.

Note:

In the Design pane, small arrows indicate that submenus exist for those items.

When a submenu item is selected in the Properties panel, the submenu items are visible in the Design pane.

If the selected item has submenu items, they appear in the secondary list.

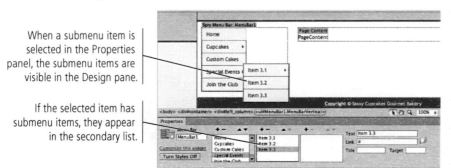

3. **Click the "−" button above the second-level list to remove the selected submenu item from the list.**

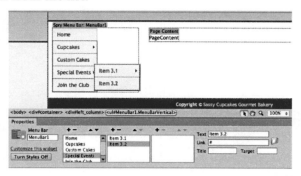

4. **Repeat Step 3 to remove the two remaining second-level items from the Special Events link.**

5. **When you delete the default Item 3.1, read the resulting warning and then click OK.**

The default Item 3.1 actually has a third level of submenu items. When you delete a parent menu item, Dreamweaver warns you that you will also delete all children of that menu item.

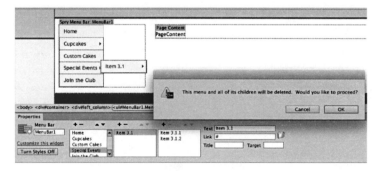

6. **In the bottom-left corner of the Properties panel, click the Turn Styles Off button.**

A Spry menu bar uses JavaScript and CSS code to translate a basic unordered list into a series of interactive menus. In addition to managing menu and submenu items through the Properties panel, you can also disable styles to review and change the unformatted list that makes up the menu.

If you have multiple levels of menu items, each sublevel is indented as a secondary, nested unordered list. You can click the Indent or Outdent buttons in the Properties panel to change the nesting level of a particular list item.

With styles turned off, you can see the basic list-item structure of the menu.

Click this button to toggle between the unformatted list and the interactive menu.

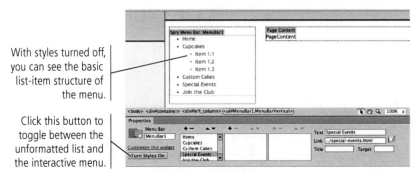

7. **Highlight the Item 1.1 text, then type** Everyday Favorites. **Select the menu item text and create a link to** cupcakes-everyday.html.

8. **Repeat Step 7 to change the other two second-level list items as follows:**

Text	Link
Flavors of the Week	**cupcakes-weekly.html**
Special Dietary Needs	**cupcakes-special-diets.html**

9. **Place the insertion point at the end of the third submenu item, then press Return/Enter to add a new list item.**

    When you use this method to add a new item to a list, the new item is added at the same level as the previous item in the list.

10. **Type** By Special Request, **then highlight the submenu item text and create a link to** cupcakes-special-order.html.

11. **Click the widget tab to select the Spry menu bar object.**

12. **In the Properties panel, click the Turn Styles On button.**

Note:

By definition, a menu bar is a navigational tool, which means items in the menu bar have defined links (using the <a> tag). If you add list items using the Properties panel, all new items automatically have the <a> tag attached. If you manually add to the list while styles are turned off (as you did in this exercise), the new items do not automatically have the <a> tag; make sure you define links for the new items.

If you forget to define a link, the item appears as a <broken item> in the list and the Properties panel shows a warning when that item is selected.

Creating Navigation with a Jump Menu

A **jump menu** is another option for allowing users to navigate around your site. If you choose Insert>Form>Jump Menu (or use the button in the Forms Insert panel), a dialog box opens so you can define the items that will appear in the jump menu.

The Text field defines the text that will appear in the menu for each item; the second field defines the page that will open when a user selects that item. (You can click the + button at the top of the dialog box to add more items to the list, or click the − button to remove an item.)

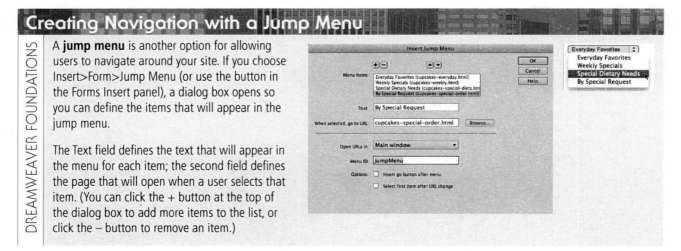

13. In the Properties panel, select the Cupcakes first-level item, then click any of the submenu items to select it.

Remember, when a submenu item is selected in the Properties panel, that submenu becomes visible in the Design pane.

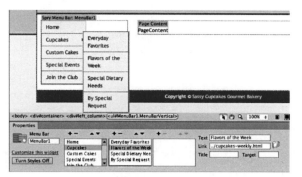

14. In the Properties panel, select the Home link in the first-level list.

Because the Home link has no submenu items, the submenu in the Design pane is now hidden. Although not strictly necessary, hiding the submenus can help avoid distraction as you move forward.

15. Save the file. When prompted, update all files linked to the template and then close the Update Pages dialog box.

This time, you aren't asked to copy dependent files because you have already done so for the menu bar. That process is only required once for each type of Spry layout object.

16. Continue to the next exercise.

USE THE CODE NAVIGATOR TO REVIEW RELATED STYLES

As you learned earlier, when you insert a Spry object into an HTML page, the required Spry JavaScript and CSS files are automatically included in the site folder when you save the page. Spry objects have predefined styles for various elements. You can modify the appearance of the menu bar by editing the selectors that are available in the attached SpryMenuBarVertical.css file.

A Spry menu bar has a simple format by default. To change the appearance of your Spry menu bar, you can simply edit the CSS selectors applied to the various aspects of the menu. Keep in mind the following tags when you review the selectors:

<ul> = unordered list   <li> = list item   <a> = link

1. With design.dwt open, Command-Option-click (Macintosh) or Alt-click (Windows) the Home menu item to show the Code Navigator.

The Code Navigator lists all pieces of code related to the selected item. In this case, you can see the hierarchy of selectors that apply to items in the Spry menu bar.

2. If the Disable check box is not selected in the bottom-right corner of the Code Navigator, click the box to disable the indicator icon.

The Code Navigator icon can be distracting, especially when you work with Spry objects. In this case, we find it easier to manage the various elements in this project when the Code Navigator indicator is disabled.

3. Move your mouse over the first ul.MenuBarVertical link in the Code Navigator.

When you mouse-over an item in the Code Navigator, a pop-up window shows the properties that are defined in that selector.

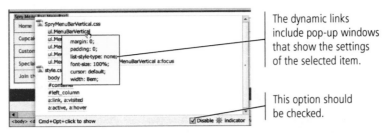

The dynamic links include pop-up windows that show the settings of the selected item.

This option should be checked.

Note:

When the Code Navigator indicator is enabled, an icon appears in the Design pane when you hover your mouse over a specific element. You can click the indicator icon to open the Code Navigator window.

4. Click the second ul.MenuBarVertical link in the Code Navigator.

The Code Navigator does more than simply list the relevant selectors; it also provides a dynamic link to all related code. This is an easy way to find the appropriate code for specific items — especially for files you did not create.

When you use the Code Navigator links, the document window automatically switches to Split view and the appropriate code file displays in the Code pane. The active selector is also selected in the CSS Styles panel. The Related Files bar above the document window shows which code file is active in the Code pane.

Above the selector code, the gray text between /* and */ is a **comment**, which is used to add notes or other helpful information in the code; comments do not affect the functionality of the code.

Note:

As you will see through-out the rest of this project, the selector names used by the various Spry objects can be quite complex. For the sake of clarity, we set these Spry-related selector names in red to distinguish them from surrounding text.

The Related Files bar shows that the CSS file is visible in the Code pane.

Comments give you an idea of the selector's purpose.

The selector you clicked is visible in the Code pane and selected in the CSS Styles panel.

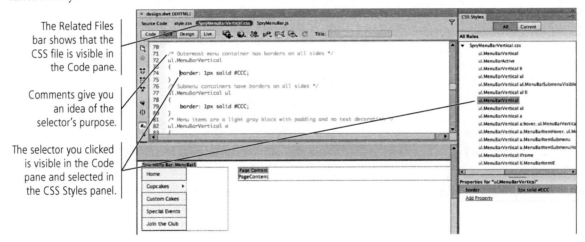

5. Select lines 71–75 in the Code pane and delete them.

This selector adds a border around the entire menu, which you do not want. Since this selector has only one property (defining the border), you can delete the entire selector from the CSS file.

Select and delete all code related to the second ul.MenuBarVertical selector.

Why Multiple Selectors of the Same Name?

When you work with Spry objects, you will occasionally find multiple selectors with the exact same name. This is because the styles for the Spry objects are roughly organized in categories. Unfortunately, there is no way to see this categorization in the CSS Styles panel; if you review the code in the CSS file, however, you can see the categories in the code comments.

Comments in the code show the general categories of the various selectors.

6. **Click the Refresh button in the CSS Styles panel.**

When you manually change the code in a CSS style, you have to refresh to reflect the new style information in the Design pane.

When you make changes in the Code pane, you have to click Refresh to reflect the changes in the Design pane.

At this point, there is no visible difference in the menu's appearance. If you look at the Code pane, you should see that another selector defines a border around unordered lists (ul.MenuBarVertical ul). You need to delete this selector to also remove the border from the unordered list that makes up the menu.

7. **Select and delete lines 71–75 (the ul.MenuBarVertical ul selector) from the Code pane, then refresh the Design pane.**

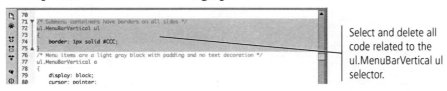

Select and delete all code related to the ul.MenuBarVertical ul selector.

8. Click the Live button in the Document toolbar to toggle on the Live view.

When visual aids are visible in the Design pane, it can be difficult to see the effects of removing the borders. When the Live view is active, you can better see that the border has been removed from the overall menu bar object.

Note:

When you work with Spry layout objects, it's a good idea to toggle the Live view on and off frequently to see exactly how your changes affect the object.

When Live view is active, invisible elements from the regular Design view no longer obscure the menu bar.

```
70
71  /* Menu items are a light gray block with padding and no text decoration */
72  ul.MenuBarVertical a
73  {
74      display: block;
75      cursor: pointer;
76      background-color: #EEE;
77      padding: 0.5em 0.75em;
78      color: #333;
79      text-decoration: none;
80  }
81  /* Menu items that have mouse over or focus have a blue background and white
82  ul.MenuBarVertical a:hover, ul.MenuBarVertical a:focus
83  {
```

PageContent

Home
Cupcakes ▶
Custom Cakes
Special Events
Join the Club

Note:

You don't need to use the Code Navigator links, but they offer an easy way to find code that is related specifically to the item you want to change.

Using Inspect Mode in Live View

In addition to using the Code Navigator, Dreamweaver's Inspect mode makes it easy to find the page code and CSS styles that are associated with specific objects on the page.

When you move the mouse cursor over an object in the Design pane in Live view, different-colored highlights identify the defined padding, border, margin, and content areas of that object (the "box model").

The Code pane also dynamically changes to show code related to the selected object. (Inspect mode works best when Live Code is also enabled, but it isn't necessary.)

If the CSS Styles panel is displayed in Current mode, the panel also changes to show the rules and properties that are related to the object under the mouse cursor.

If you click an element in the Design pane, Dreamweaver automatically exits Inspect mode. Whatever code was highlighted remains selected and visible in the Code pane so you can make changes to the item you were highlighting when Inspect mode was still active.

Inspect mode is active.

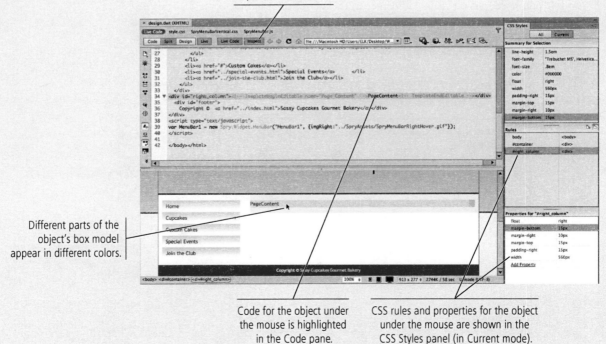

Different parts of the object's box model appear in different colors.

Code for the object under the mouse is highlighted in the Code pane.

CSS rules and properties for the object under the mouse are shown in the CSS Styles panel (in Current mode).

DREAMWEAVER FOUNDATIONS

9. Click the Live button to toggle that option off.

10. Command-Option-click/Alt-click the Home menu item, and then click the **ul.MenuBarVertical li** link in the Code Navigator.

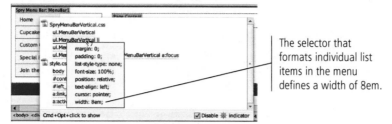

The selector that formats individual list items in the menu defines a width of 8em.

11. In the Properties section of the CSS Styles panel, change the width value to **200**, then choose px in the measurement menu.

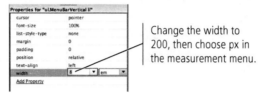

Change the width to 200, then choose px in the measurement menu.

When you make changes in the CSS Styles panel, they are automatically reflected in the Design pane. You should also notice that the selector code (in the Code pane) automatically changes to show the new width value.

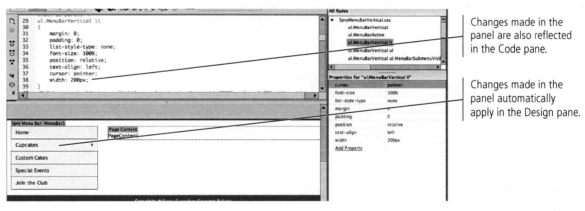

Changes made in the panel are also reflected in the Code pane.

Changes made in the panel automatically apply in the Design pane.

12. Click the Add Property link at the bottom of the list of current properties, then type `background-image` in the resulting field.

13. Click the Browse button to the right of the new property.

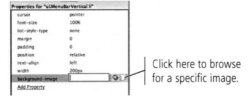

Click here to browse for a specific image.

14. In the resulting dialog box, choose `nav-bkg.gif` (in the site's images>backgrounds folder), then click Open/OK.

This property defines a background image that will appear behind every list item in the menu bar. However, the defined background image is obscured by the background-color property in another selector; you will fix this problem in the next few steps.

Note:

For some reason, the Point To File button in this panel results in a system-specific file path instead of a site-specific path relative to the active site. This type of path will not work properly when the file is moved to the server.

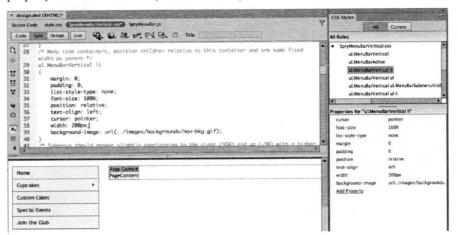

15. Open the Code Navigator for the Home link in the menu bar.

16. Roll your mouse cursor over the last two links in the SpryMenuBarVertical.css section of the list and review the properties in each selector.

Remember, the **<a>** tag defines a link.

ul.MenuBarVertical a refers to links in the menu bar (which means all menu items).

ul.MenuBarVertical a:hover, ul.MenuBarVertical a:focus refers to the rollover (hover) and active (focus) states of links in the menu bar.

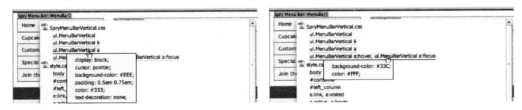

Grouping Selectors

When two or more selectors have the same properties and values, they can be grouped to save time. For example, if you need three element selectors (h1, h2, and h3) with the same margin and padding values, you can write the code as:

```
h1 {
        margin: 0px;
}
h2 {
        margin: 0px;
}
h3 {
        margin: 0px;
}
```

Rather than defining three separate selectors, you can group them by typing all three selector names, separated by commas:

```
h1, h2, h3 {
        margin: 0px;
}
```

17. Click the **ul.MenuBarVertical a** link to show the related code in the Code pane.

18. **In the CSS Styles panel, click to the left of the existing background-color property to disable that property.**

In the Code pane, you can see that the background-color property is commented — it is surrounded by /* and */ characters, and is gray instead of color coded like the active properties.

When the property is disabled, you can see the background image for each list item in the menu.

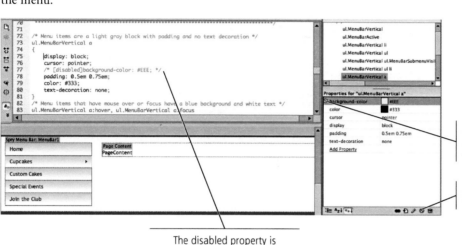

> **Note:**
>
> *When a property is disabled, you can click the disabled icon to toggle the property back on.*

Click to the left of a specific property to disable it.

Disable/Enable CSS Property button

The disabled property is commented out in the Code pane.

19. **With the background-color property selected in the CSS Styles panel, click the Delete button at the bottom of the panel.**

The CSS Styles panel deletes the active selection in the panel. Be very careful using this option; it is easy to forget what you have selected, and delete an entire selector instead of only a single property. If you accidentally delete the wrong thing, you can choose Edit>Undo to restore the deleted code as long as the CSS file is visible in the Code pane.

> **Note:**
>
> *You can also click the Disable/Enable CSS Property button at the bottom of the panel to toggle the selected property on and off.*

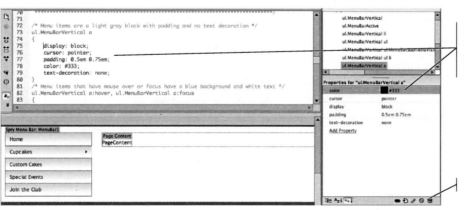

The property is deleted from the CSS Styles panel and from the selector code.

Delete button

20. **Turn on the Live view. Move your mouse cursor over the menu items and review the hover properties.**

Rather than leaving the Dreamweaver interface, you can use Live view to preview dynamic behaviors. This view also allows you to interact with specific dynamic elements, so you can open the Code Navigator for hover behaviors and submenus, and find the styles you need to control the appearance of those elements.

Remember, the a:hover pseudo-class controls the rollover behavior of links. The default blue color is obviously not appropriate for this site.

21. **Save your changes in the SpryMenuBarVertical.css file, and continue to the next exercise.**

 ## Use Code Hints to Write CSS Code

As you know, you can use the CSS Styles panel to edit the rules associated with a specific CSS selector. Once you are comfortable with the basic concepts of CSS, you might find it easier to work directly in the Code pane to make necessary changes.

When you write code, you must follow the proper rules of **syntax** (the formal structure or "grammar" required in code). Dreamweaver Code Hints facilitate writing and changing code; hints make it easier to create the proper syntax and ensure that your code functions as expected.

1. **With design.dwt open, locate the ul.MenuBarVertical a:hover, ul.MenuBarVertical a:focus selector in the Code pane.**

You can click the selector in the CSS Styles panel to show it in the Code pane, or simply scroll the code pane until you find the selector you want.

The background-color property changes the color of the item background.

The color property changes the color of text in the item.

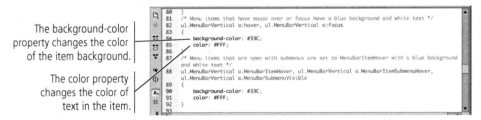

2. **Delete the background-color property for this selector.**

You can use the CSS Styles panel to delete the unwanted property, or select and delete the relevant line from the Code pane.

3. **Place the insertion point after the opening brace of the selector and press Return/Enter.**

Dreamweaver automatically recognizes that you are adding to a CSS selector. Code Hints show all the available properties that can be defined.

All rules for the selector must appear inside the braces.

4. **Type `fo` to scroll the Code Hints menu to the font property, then scroll to (if necessary) and double-click font-weight in the list.**

Code Hints are invaluable for creating the proper code syntax. If you don't know the exact name of a property, you can use the Code Hints menu to find exactly what you need.

After you add a specific property to the selector code, Dreamweaver automatically adds the required colon and shows the default value options in a secondary Code Hints menu.

5. **Choose bold in the resulting Code Hints menu, then type a semicolon at the end of the line.**

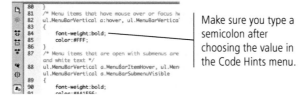

Make sure you type a semicolon after choosing the value in the Code Hints menu.

6. **Macintosh users:**

   - **Delete the existing value of the color property, including the space and colon.**

   - **Type a colon after the "color" property name, then choose Color... from the Code Hints menu.**

   - **When the color palette appears, click with the eyedropper cursor to sample the color in the thick line that separates the header and content divs.**

The color palette that appears is a function of Code Hints. Because the color property needs a color value rather than a keyword or other language element, Code Hints present what you need to enter the appropriate code.

Note:

The color property determines the color of type for that selector.

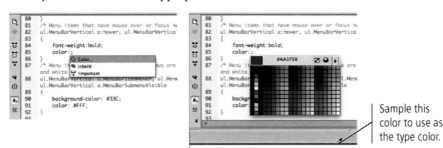

Sample this color to use as the type color.

Windows users:

   - **Delete the existing value of the color property and type `#AA1F56`.**

On Windows, you cannot sample color in the Design pane while you are typing in the Code pane. You can sample a color from the pop-up color palette within the Code pane, or simply type the color value you want to use.

7. Using any method you prefer, apply the same changes to the selector that begins on Line 87 in the Code pane.

This selector — ul.MenuBarVertical a.MenuBarItemHover, ul.MenuBarVertical a.MenuBarItemSubmenuHover, ul.MenuBarVertical a.MenuBarSubmenuVisible — defines a default blue background color and white text for the hover behavior of visible submenu items.

Note:

For some reason, this selector does not appear in the Code Navigator for any of the menu items. The name, however, suggests that it affects the Hover appearance of menu and submenu items.

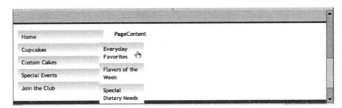

8. With the Live view still active, roll your mouse over the menu items to test the attributes of the edited hover selectors.

The hover behavior now works properly for all menu and submenu items. The only remaining problem is the width of the submenu items, which are long enough to wrap to a second line.

9. Locate the code for the ul.MenuBarVertical ul li selector.

10. Using any method you prefer, change the width value to 160px.

11. In the Design view, roll your mouse over the Cupcakes menu item, then test the hover behavior of the submenu items.

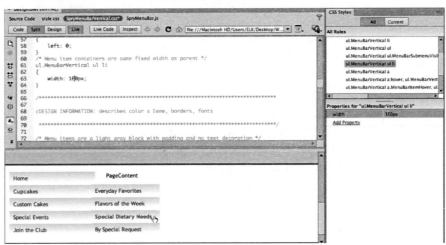

12. Turn off the Live view.

13. Save your changes in the SpryMenuBarVertical.css file.

When this file is visible in the Code pane, you can simply choose File>Save (Command/Control-S) to save the file. If you forget, you will be asked if you want to save it when you close the active HTML file.

14. Close the template file, then continue to the next stage of the project.

Other Spry Layout Objects

Spry Tabbed Panels

Spry tabbed panels (Insert>Layout Objects>Spry Tabbed Panels) are used to present information about multiple categories of information. The tabs appear in a row at the top of the object; content for the active category appears in the lower area.

When you place a tabbed panel group on the page, you can change the active panel by moving the cursor over a tab and clicking the resulting eye icon on the right side of the tab. As long as a tab is active, you can edit the tab text, as well as the content that will appear for that tab.

Like a menu bar, the various aspects of a tabbed panel group are controlled by CSS selectors, which are copied into the site folder for you when you save the file where the tabbed panels are placed.

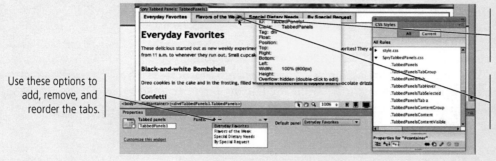

Use these options to add, remove, and reorder the tabs.

Roll your mouse over a specific tab to access that panel's visibility toggle.

Click the visibility toggle to show the associated content for that tab.

Spry Accordions

Like tabbed panels, accordions (Insert>Layout Objects>Spry Accordion) are another option for managing different categories of content within a single HTML page. In this case, the content panel appears directly below only the active tab (unlike tabbed panels, where the content area remains visible regardless of which tab is active).

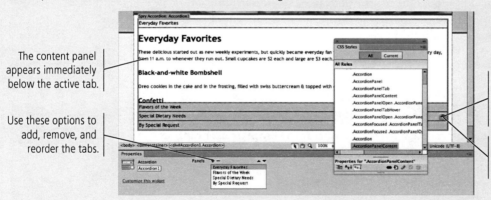

The content panel appears immediately below the active tab.

Use these options to add, remove, and reorder the tabs.

Roll your mouse over the right end of a panel to access the panel's visibility toggle.

Click a panel's visibility toggle to show the associated content.

Spry Collapsible Panels

A collapsible panel (Insert>Layout Objects>Spry Collapsible Panel) is used to contain content that will only be visible when the tab is expanded. This is similar to an accordion, but is typically used for only one category of information. Using the categories in this site as an example, you would create individual collapsible panels for each category (Everyday Favorites, Weekly Specials, etc.).

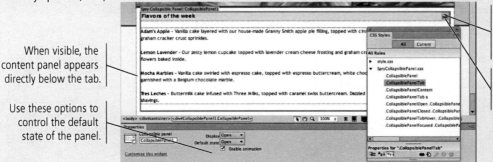

When visible, the content panel appears directly below the tab.

Use these options to control the default state of the panel.

Roll your mouse over the right end of a tab to access the panel's visibility toggle.

Click the visibility toggle to show or hide the associated content.

Stage 3 Creating Online Forms

Online forms are used to collect user information, and then transfer that information to Web servers. Surveys, electronic commerce, guest books, polls, and membership applications all make use of online form technologies. While well-designed forms are easy to use, poorly designed forms prove troublesome for both users (who complete the forms) and Web server managers (who access user data). Fortunately, Dreamweaver makes it easy to create robust yet understandable forms — simplifying and streamlining the interaction between users and Web servers.

Web-based forms are composed of a series of **form objects** (also referred to as **form fields**). Different types of form objects have different purposes, and they gather different types of information. Basically, all form objects allow users to enter data; each object type facilitates a distinct format of data input. You can use Dreamweaver to create a number of different form objects, including text fields, radio buttons, check boxes, menus, and buttons.

It is important to realize that processing a submitted form requires some type of script. These contain instructions to identify the user's data, and then perform tasks based on that data. You can write your own scripts, and many hosting providers offer sample form-processing scripts (as well as instructions on how to implement those scripts when you build a form).

Note:

PHP and CGI scripts are commonly used to process forms. You should consult your hosting provider for specific instructions for serving a form on your Web site.

CREATE A FORM ELEMENT

A **form element** is a distinct element of a Web page; it is the container for all form objects. As a container, the form element ensures that different form objects are related to one another, which makes it possible to combine all of the form information as a single submission. A form's Submit button identifies all related form objects and collects the information they contain in a single string.

1. **Open `join-the-club.html` from the Cupcakes site root folder.**

   This page was created from the defined site template file. You will create the form in the editable region of this page.

2. **In the Design view, place the insertion point in the empty paragraph at the end of the editable region.**

3. **Open the Insert panel and show the Forms options.**

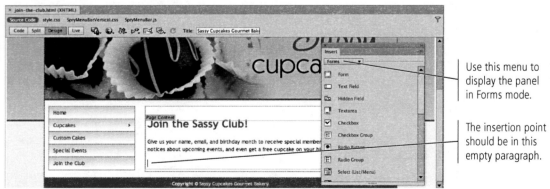

Use this menu to display the panel in Forms mode.

The insertion point should be in this empty paragraph.

4. **Click the Form button in the Insert panel.**

A red outline indicates the boundary of the newly inserted form. (If you don't see this outline, choose View>Visual Aids>Invisible Elements.)

5. **In the Properties panel, type `register` in the Form ID field and type `mailto:info@sassycupcakes.atc` in the Action field. Leave the remaining fields at their default values.**

The form ID creates a unique name for the form you are creating.

The **mailto:** protocol in the Action field is one method of receiving data without using a script. When a user submits the form, the user's default email client opens and creates a message with the form data. This is not a particularly reliable method for receiving form data, but it suits the purpose if you are gathering generic information; however, it is not suitable for gathering sensitive information such as credit card numbers.

The red outline shows the form object boundary.

The form tag now includes the defined name "register", including the "#" sign that indicates an ID.

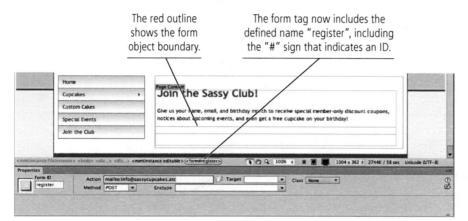

Note:

All form objects can also be created using the Insert>Form menu.

Note:

The form ID will also be useful later when you apply CSS to format the various form elements.

Note:

You use the mailto protocol in this exercise because we cannot be certain that everyone has access to the same script on a specific type of server.

6. **Save the file and continue to the next exercise.**

The Form Properties Panel in Depth

The Form Properties panel allows you to control the options related to a specific form area.

- **Form ID** is a unique name that identifies the form for scripting or CSS formatting.

- **Action** specifies the page or script that will process the form data, essentially determining what should be done with the form content.

- **Target** defines the window or frame in which the server displays the action page's response (data) to the form.

- **Class** allows you to apply a class selector (from a CSS style sheet) to the form.

- **Enctype** (short for "encoding type") specifies the format in which the data will be sent to the server so the server software can interpret the input correctly. The default is **application/x-www-form-urlencoded**. The **text/plain** enctype is used for email replies. If a file is being uploaded with the form, **multipart/form-data** must be used.

- **Method** determines how the browser and Web server present the form data to the application that processes the form (the action page):

  - **Default** uses the browser's default settings to send the form data to the server. According to W3C specifications, the default method for forms is GET.

  - **GET** attaches form data to the URL of the action page that processes the form data. This method limits the amount and format of data that can be passed to the action page.

  - **POST** sends the form data as a standard input to the action page. This method does not impose any limits on the passed data. The POST method is preferred for processing confidential data such as user names, passwords, and credit card numbers, but the data needs to be encrypted to ensure the highest possible security.

CREATE TEXT FIELDS

Text fields are the fundamental building blocks of almost all online forms. Text fields accept alphanumeric characters — that is, letters and numbers. They can be set as single-line, multi-line, or password fields. You can also alter the settings of single-line text fields and password fields to prevent users from entering more than a specified number of characters (such as no more than 16 characters for a credit card number).

Note:

A text area is similar to a standard text field, but intended for larger amounts of text, such as multiple sentences or paragraphs.

1. **With join-the-club.html open in Design view, click to place the insertion point in the form object.**

2. **In the Forms Insert panel, click the Text Field button.**

The insertion point should be inside the form object.

3. **Define the following settings in the Input Tag Accessibility Attributes dialog box:**

If this dialog box does not appear, open the Accessibility pane of the Preferences dialog box and check the Form Objects option.

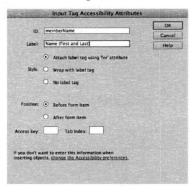

ID:	memberName
Label:	Name (First and Last)
Style:	**Attach Label Tag Using 'for' Attribute**
Position:	**Before Form Item**
Access Key:	**Leave blank**
Tab Index:	**Leave blank**

The Input Tag Accessibility Attributes Dialog Box in Depth

The Input Tag Accessibility Attributes dialog box allows you to set up accessibility aids for form objects so they are more usable to site visitors with disabilities. (Some form objects — such as radio groups, hidden fields, jump menus, labels, and fieldsets — do not need accessibility information, so the dialog box does not appear for those objects.)

The **ID** is the distinct name of the form object.

The **Label** text identifies the form object on the page.

The **Style** area determines how the <label> tag will be attached to the field:

- **Wrap with Label Tag.** As the name suggests, the <label> </label> tag entirely wraps/encloses the code of the form object.

- **Attach Label Tag Using for Attribute.** This creates the <label> tag using the **for** attribute to identify the related form object.

- **No Label Tag.** Using this option, a <label> tag is not attached to the form object.

The **Position** area determines the positioning of label text in relation to the form object:

- **Before Form Item.** The label text is placed before the form object.

- **After Form Item.** The label text is placed after the form object.

Access Key allows you to define a letter that, when typed with the Control (Macintosh) or Alt (Windows) key, brings the selected form object into focus.

Tab Index defines the order in which form objects are selected by pressing the Tab key. By defining specific Tab Index values for different fields, you can control the user's movement through the fields in the form.

DREAMWEAVER FOUNDATIONS

4. **Click OK to create the text field.**

The memberName text field appears in the form object with the text label "Name (First and Last)" before the field (as you defined).

5. **Click the Split button in the Document toolbar to open the Code pane.**

In the Code pane, the **<input>** tags define the text field and **<label>** tags define the text field's label. The field name that you defined is used as both the **name** and the **id** attribute of the **<input>** tag. In the code for the **<label>** tag, the name of the text field is assigned to the **for** attribute — basically defining which text field this is the label *for*.

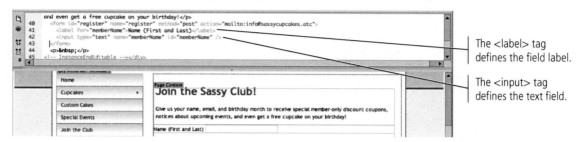

The <label> tag defines the field label.

The <input> tag defines the text field.

6. **In the Design pane, place the insertion point after the existing text field to deselect the existing field and label.**

7. **Press Return/Enter to create a new paragraph.**

When you press Return/Enter, the line with the first text field (and its label) is automatically tagged as a paragraph; the **<label>** and **<input>** tags are now surrounded by opening and closing **<p> </p>** tags.

The <label> and <input> tags are now surrounded by opening and closing paragraph tags.

The Text Field Properties Panel in Depth

The Properties panel for a text field provides access to the attributes of a text field form object.

TextField is the name (ID) of the text field.

Char Width defines the maximum number of characters that can display in the text field (basically, the width of the field). This is better set using CSS.

Max Chars defines the maximum number of characters that can be entered in a single-line text field. If a user tries to input more characters than the defined value, the form produces an alert sound.

Init Val (initial value) defines text that displays in the field when the form loads in the Web page (before a user enters data). This is generally used to include examples or notes.

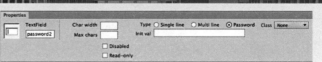

Type defines a text field as a single-line, multiple-line, or password field.

- **Single-line** creates a field that is a single line.

- **Multi-line** creates a field with multiple lines (also called a **text area** field). You can also define the number of lines that will be visible in the field (**Num Lines**).

- **Password** creates a password field. Text entered in a password field appears as asterisks or bullets (dots) to prevent others from observing the text being typed.

8. **Repeat Steps 2–7 to insert four more text fields in the form. For each text field, use the Attach Label Tag Using 'for' Attribute style option and the Before Form Item position option. Leave the Access Key and Tab Index fields empty.**

Field ID	Label
email	**Email Address**
company	**Company Name (Required if you want to enter the monthly drawing for free office cupcakes)**
password1	**Create a Password**
password2	**Retype your Password**

Note:

Later in this project you will use CSS to format the various fields and labels in this form.

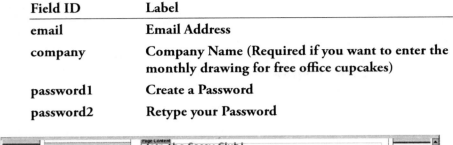

9. **Click the password1 text field to select it. In the Properties panel, click the Password radio button in the Type area.**

   When a text field is designated as a password field, the user-entered text appears as asterisks or dots.

The type attribute of the <input> tag shows that this is now a password field.

10. **Repeat Step 9 to apply the Password type to the password2 field.**

11. **Save the file and continue to the next exercise.**

CREATE A MENU FIELD

Menus and lists display a set of options from which users can select one or more responses. These two types of form fields have the same basic underlying structure, but with different appearances and purposes.

A basic menu shows a single option; when a user clicks the menu, the menu opens (drops down) and more options appear. With a standard menu field, users can choose only a single response from the available options. The menu closes when the user chooses a response, displaying only the selected option.

1. With **join-the-club.html** open, create a new empty paragraph in the form, after the company field.

2. In the Forms Insert panel, click the Select (List/Menu) button.

Create a new empty paragraph here for the menu field.

3. In the Input Tag Accessibility Attributes dialog box, do the following:

   - Type **birthday** in the ID field.

   - Type **When were you born?** in the Label field.

   - Select the Attach Label Tag Using 'for' Attribute style option.

   - Select the Before position option.

4. Click OK to create the menu field.

   A menu or list object is created using the **<select>** tag.

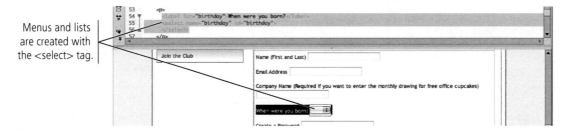

Menus and lists are created with the <select> tag.

5. **Click the new menu object in the Design pane to select it. Make sure the Menu option is selected in the Type area of the Properties panel.**

The field will function as a drop-down menu. The Height and Selections options in the Properties panel are disabled; these properties do not apply to drop-down menus.

Click the actual menu object to select it.

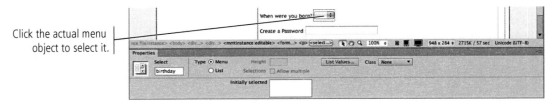

6. **Click the List Values button in the Properties panel to define the selections that will appear in the menu.**

The cursor automatically appears in the first Item Label field in the List Values dialog box.

7. **Type January as the first item label. Press Tab to move to the Value column and type jan.**

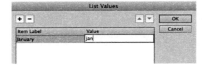

8. **Press Tab again to move to the second line of the Item Label field.**

Each line in the dialog box represents a new list/menu option. When the insertion point is within the last item value, pressing Tab adds a new list item. Alternatively, you can simply click the "+" button above the Item Label column to add a new list item (or click the "−" button to remove the currently selected list item).

The List/Menu Properties Panel in Depth

The Properties panel for a list/menu field provides access to the attributes of a list/menu form object.

Select is the name (ID) of the list/menu.

Type determines whether the selected form object will function as a scrolling list or a drop-down menu. (The number of characters in the longest label determines the width of scrolling lists and drop-down menus.)

Height, which is only available for list type fields, defines the number of options that will be visible in the list. The default/minimum height of a list is 1; a scrolling list appears as a drop-down menu if its height is set to 1 (although users can choose multiple options from the list).

Allow Multiple Selections is also restricted to list objects. When this option is checked, users can choose more than one option in the list.

Clicking the **List Values** button opens the List Values dialog box, where you create and edit the labels and values of items for a specific form list/menu. The order of list/menu items in the form is the same as that in the List Values dialog box. The first item created in the list is the default selection; you can use the Up and Down Arrow buttons to rearrange list items.

Initially Selected determines which item appears by default in a menu object, or which item(s) are already selected in a list object.

---

9. Type **February** as the item label, press Tab, and type **feb** as the item value.

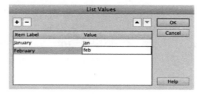

10. **Repeat Steps 8–9 to add ten more list items:**

Item Label	Value
March	mar
April	apr
May	may
June	jun
July	jul
August	aug
September	sep
October	oct
November	nov
December	dec

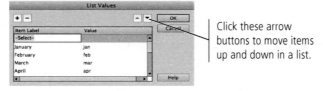

11. **After typing the December value, press Tab to add a final list item.**

12. **Type -Select- in the Item Label field and leave the Value field blank.**

13. **Click the Up Arrow button (above the Value column) until the -Select- option appears at the top of the list.**

Click these arrow buttons to move items up and down in a list.

14. **Click OK to add the list values to the menu field in the form.**

15. **In the Properties panel, choose -Select- in the Initially Selected list.**

    In the Design pane, the width of the placed menu expands to accommodate the longest option in the list.

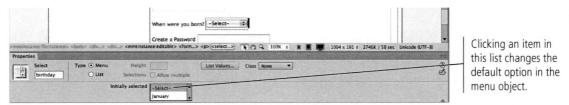

Clicking an item in this list changes the default option in the menu object.

16. **Save the file and continue to the next exercise.**

CREATE A CHECKBOX

Individual **checkboxes**, which have an on or off state, are commonly used to indicate agreement. A **checkbox group** is simply a group of checkboxes with the same name; when the user submits a form, the value of each selected box is sent as the value for that field name.

1. **With `join-the-club.html` open, create a new empty paragraph before the label of the first text field (within the form object).**

   You can place the insertion point before the label, then press Return/Enter to add the new paragraph within the form object.

2. **With the insertion point in the new paragraph, click the Checkbox button in the Forms Insert panel.**

The insertion point should be in this empty paragraph.

3. **In the Input Tag Accessibility Attributes dialog box, define the following options:**

   - **Type `agree` in the ID field.**
   - **Type `Yes! I want to join the Sassy Club!` in the Label field.**
   - **Select the Attach Label Tag Using 'for' Attribute style option.**
   - **Select the After position option.**

4. **Click OK to create the checkbox.**

   In the Properties panel, you can use the **Initial State** options to determine whether a checkbox object is already selected when the form first displays. By default, the checkbox is not selected.

   The **Checked Value** option defines the value that will be sent to the server when the form is submitted. For example, you can define a checked value of "A" for a form object named "Checkbox1"; if the user checks that box, information will be sent to the server as Checkbox1=A. If you do not define a checked value, information will be sent to the server as Checkbox1=ON when the box is checked.

5. **Save the file and continue to the next exercise.**

More about Dreamweaver's Form Fields

In addition to the ones you created in this project, Dreamweaver includes several other form fields.

A **textarea** is simply a multi-line text field. In the Properties panel, you can define the number of lines that are visible in the area. If a user enters more than the defined number of lines, a scrollbar appears on the right side of the area.

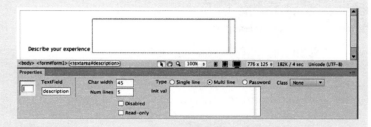

A **file field** is simply a text field with a Browse button. A file field allows users to select a file and upload it to your server. Users can either manually type a file path in the text field, or click the Browse button to search for the file they want to upload. (If you include a file field in your form, the selected file uploads to the server using the POST method; you cannot use the GET method.)

A **checkbox group** is simply a group of checkboxes with the same name. When you create a checkbox group, you first see a dialog box where you define the Label and Value for each item in the group. (To add more than the default two options, you have to use the + button above the Label field.)

Each checkbox has its own label, just like a single checkbox. You can also define a label for the entire group by adding a label in the Code pane, using the for attribute with a value that matches the name of the checkboxes in the group.

(**Fieldsets** can also be used to combine multiple form fields into a group. This method allows you to define a legend for the grouped form objects, as well as to define CSS rules that affect only the objects in a particular fieldset.)

The for="interest" attribute identifies this as the label for the checkbox group.

Each checkbox in the group has the same name attribute.

A **radio button** is a field that has a yes-or-no value, similar to a check box. A **radio group** is a group of radio buttons that have the same name. When you create a radio group, you first define the Label and Value of each radio button, just as you do for a checkbox group.

Unlike a checkbox group, which allows multiple selections, users can select only one option in a radio group.

The for="favorite" attribute identifies this as the label for the radio group.

Each radio button in the group has the same name attribute.

A **select list** is very similar to a select menu, except you can display more than one option in the list at one time. You can also check the Allow Multiple box in the Properties panel so users can choose more than one option in the available list.

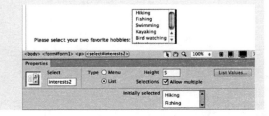

ADD SUBMIT AND RESET BUTTONS

Buttons perform an assigned task when clicked. The **Submit** button is crucial to any form, ensuring that the data is not sent to the server until the user chooses. The **Reset** button clears all entries in form objects and restores the form to its original (empty) state.

By default, buttons in Dreamweaver are set to Submit, although you can easily alter the settings to make them function as Reset buttons. You can even use JavaScript or other programming languages to customize a button to perform a specific task (these customized buttons are called Command buttons in HTML).

1. **With `join-the-club.html` open, create a new empty paragraph after the last text field in the form.**

2. **With the insertion point in the empty paragraph, click the Button button in the Forms Insert panel.**

The insertion point should be in this empty paragraph.

3. **In the Input Tag Accessibility Attributes dialog box, do the following:**

   - **Type `submit` in the ID field.**
   - **Select the No Label Tag style option.**

   Because you are not using a label tag, the Position option is not relevant.

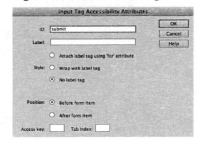

4. **Click OK to create the button.**

5. **In the Properties panel, type `Sign me up!` in the Value field.**

   In the Properties panel, the **Button Name** field shows the ID of the button object. This is just a name used for CSS purposes; it does not control the button's behavior.

   The **Value** field defines the text that appears on the button. The value defaults to "Submit" or "Reset" depending on which action is selected.

The text on a button is defined by the button value, not by the label tag.

6. **Place the insertion point to the right of the existing button.**

7. **Repeat Steps 2–4 to add a second button, using `reset` as the ID.**

    Although you defined "reset" as the button ID, the default value of every new button is "Submit;" the text on the second button defaults to Submit to match the default value.

8. **Select the second button in the Design pane. In the Properties panel, select the Reset Form option.**

    The button **action** defines what happens when the button is clicked:

    - **Submit Form** submits the form data to the server.

    - **Reset Form** clears the entered data.

    - **None** allows a different action to be performed. For example, you can add a JavaScript behavior to open another page when the user clicks the button.

    Because Submit is the default button action in Dreamweaver, every button is initially inserted with the name **"Submit."** After you select the Reset Form option in the Properties panel, the button value and the text on the button automatically change to Reset.

Choosing the Reset Form action changes the button value, which changes the text on the button.

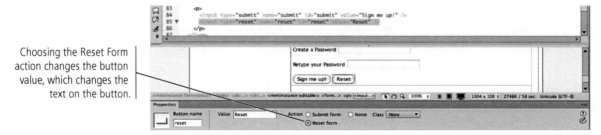

9. **Save the file and continue to the next exercise.**

 ## VALIDATE FORM FIELDS

The information collected through forms plays an important role in corporate marketing efforts. Not only is there a need to collect information, but also to ensure that the information received is correct. To address this business need, forms should include built-in validation that screens user-entered data to ensure that all required information is provided in the correct format.

Validation can be added to a form by designing scripts. This is called **server-side validation** because the form data is submitted to the server, and then a script on the server verifies the data and sends the results to the browser. Some validation must be done by scripts on the server because the server must compare the new form data with the data it already has. For example, a Web site that allows users to create accounts must compare each new ID with IDs already in the database; this validation process ensures that each user ID is unique.

The other type of validation is called **client-side validation**. In this case, scripts are attached to the actual form elements, and the validation is performed before the data reaches the server.

In this exercise, you use Dreamweaver's validation widgets to implement client-side validation of several form fields. These validation widgets were designed using Adobe's Spry framework, which is the same technology that you used to create the menu bar in the second stage of this project.

Note:

Validation widgets can be accessed from the Insert>Form or Insert>Spry menus, the Forms Insert panel, or the Spry Insert panel.

1. **With `join-the-club.html` open, click to select the Name text field.**

2. **In the Forms Insert panel, click the Spry Validation Text Field button.**

   The text field is surrounded by a blue border (or **widget**) that attaches the validation script to the field. To access the validation options, you have to click the widget tab to select the actual Spry object (just as you did when you edited the Spry menu bar in the second stage of this project).

   Note:

   If a field is not currently selected, the widget tab appears only when you move your mouse over that field in the Design view.

3. **In the Properties panel, choose Required in the Preview States menu.**

   When you apply the validation widget to a text field, the Required option is checked by default.

   Validation widgets display error messages to draw attention to improperly structured or omitted information. You can use the Preview States menu in the Properties panel to preview different error messages in the Design view.

The Spry TextField widget is identified with a blue tab.

Validation options for the Spry TextField are available in the Properties panel.

The error message appears based on the choice in the Preview States menu.

4. **In the Design pane, highlight the error message text and then type `Please enter your name.` as the new message.**

   When a specific error message is visible, you can change the message text just as you would change any other text on a page.

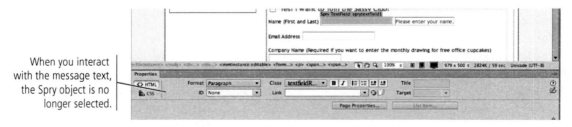

When you interact with the message text, the Spry object is no longer selected.

5. **Click the Spry widget tab to show the widget properties again, then choose Initial in the Preview States menu to hide the message in the Design pane.**

   In the browser window, the appearance of different warning messages is caused by code in the JavaScript file that drives the Spry functionality. The Preview States option in the Dreamweaver interface is simply a way to manage the different messages in the Design view during development.

Choose Initial in this menu to hide all error messages in the Design view.

6. **Select the email text field in the design page, then apply the Spry Validation Text Field option to the field.**

7. **In the Properties panel, choose Email Address in the Type menu.**

A text field requires the user to enter information manually — and that opens the door for users to enter *inappropriate* information in the field. You can also use validation widgets to help make sure users enter the correct type of information in a text field.

This option requires the user to enter text that includes the "at" symbol (@) and a dot.

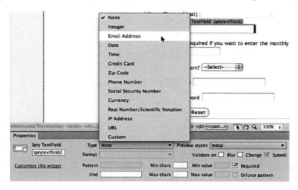

Note:

*In the Properties panel, the **Validate On** group of check boxes determines when validation is performed. If you select Blur, the validation is performed when users click outside the object. If you select Change, the validation is performed only when a user makes a change in the related field. Submit is selected by default, which means the validation is performed when the form is submitted.*

8. **With Invalid Format selected in the Preview States menu, highlight the warning message in the widget and type Please enter a valid email address.**

If you have difficulty changing only the message text, use the Code pane to make sure none of the surrounding code is selected before typing.

9. **Click the widget tab to select it. In the Properties panel, choose Initial in the Preview States menu to hide the error message in the Design view.**

10. **Click the checkbox object at the top of the form, then click the Spry Validation Checkbox button in the Spry Insert panel.**

The Validation Checkbox widget provides two types of validation. The first is when a checkbox needs to be selected by a user, so the checkbox is marked as required. This type of validation is usually applied when a user needs to agree to something (as is the case in this form).

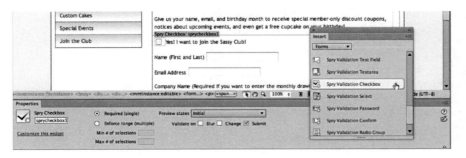

Note:

The second type of validation ensures that users select a minimum number of checkboxes. In this case, you need to first insert the Spry Validation Checkbox widget, and then insert the checkboxes within the widget. In the Properties panel, you can then select the Enforce Range (Multiple) option and type the minimum or maximum number of selections that can be made from the available choices.

11. **In the Properties panel, make sure the Required (Single) option is selected.**

12. **Choose Required in the Preview States menu, and change the warning message to** `You must check this box!`

13. **Click the widget tab to select the Spry object, and then change the Preview States menu to Initial.**

14. **Select the password2 text field, then click the Spry Validation Confirm button in the Spry Insert panel.**

    The Spry Validation Confirm widget displays error messages when the user values in related form fields do not match. For example, you can add a Validation Confirm widget to a password text field that shows an error message such as "Passwords do not match"; in this example, the widget forces users to retype the same password that they specified in the previous field.

Note:

The Spry Validation Password widget restricts the content and format of user-defined passwords, and provides warning messages if the user's input does not meet the defined requirements.

15. **In the Properties panel, make sure the Required check box is selected.**

16. **In the Validate Against menu, choose "password1" in form "register".**

    The Validate Against menu displays a list of all text fields in the form. The menu should default to password1 because that is the only other password field in this form.

17. **Choose Invalid in the Preview States menu of the Properties panel. In the Design pane, change the error message text to** `Passwords do not match.`

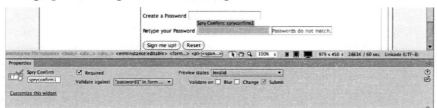

18. **Click the widget tab to select the Spry object, and then choose Initial in the Preview States menu.**

The Properties panel controls the various attributes of Spry validation widgets. Different options are available depending on the type of the selected widget.

DREAMWEAVER FOUNDATIONS

Text Field Validation Properties

- The **Type** menu determines the format visitors must use when they enter data in the text field. If you select None, users can type any character that's supported by the page's encoding type. Dreamweaver provides validation for 12 formats. For some types (e.g., Date, Credit Card, Zip Code, Phone Number), you can choose from a set of standard formats available in the Format menu.

- The **Format** menu is enabled when Date, Time, Credit Card, Zip Code, Phone Number, Currency, or IP address is selected in the Type menu. It contains a list of standard formats for the selected type, which forces users to enter the selected type of information.

- The **Pattern** menu is enabled when Custom is selected in the Type menu, enabling you to define your own format pattern for entering data.

- What you type in the **Hint** field (if anything) displays in the text field when the page loads in the browser. When users click in the text field, the hint disappears.

- The **Min Chars** field requires a minimum number of characters in the field, such as a minimum of 10 characters for a phone number.

- The **Max Chars** field limits the number of characters that users can type in the field, such as no more than 16 characters for a credit card number.

- The **Min Value** and **Max Value** fields are enabled when you select Integer in the Type menu. You can specify these values to ensure that users do not type a number that is less than or greater than certain values.

- When **Required** is checked, users receive an error if they fail to enter a value in the associated field.

- If you specified a custom pattern for the text field entry, checking the **Enforce Pattern** box requires users to enter information according to your defined pattern.

Text Area Validation Properties

- When **Required** is checked, users receive an error if they do not enter a value in the associated field.

- The **Min Chars** field requires a certain minimum number of characters in the field.

- The **Max Chars** field limits the number of characters that users can type in the field.

- The **Counter** options enable you to add a character counter to the associated field. Using the Chars Count option, the counter displays the number of characters typed. If you specify a number in the Max Chars field, the Chars Remaining counter can be enabled to show how many characters remain in the allowed amount.

- The **Block Extra Characters** option, enabled if you specify a number in the Max Chars field, prevents users from typing more than the allowed number of characters. If this option is not selected, users can type more than the allowed number, but they receive an error message when the form is submitted.

- What you type in the **Hint** field (if anything) displays in the text field when the page loads in the browser. When users click in the text field, the hint disappears.

Select Validation Properties

- If you have a list label with no associated value, selecting the **Do Not Allow Blank Value** option prevents the user from submitting the form with the no-value label selected. This option is helpful when there is more than one label in the list that you do not want users to select.

- To prevent users from selecting a certain label in the list, you can check the **Invalid Value** box and then type the specific value for the unacceptable label in the field.

Checkbox Validation Properties

- When **Required** is selected, users receive an error message if they fail to make a required selection.

- When **Enforce range** is selected, users must make a minimum or maximum number of selections (which you can define in the **Min # of Selections** and **Max # of Selections** fields).

19. **Save the file. When you see the Copy Dependent Files message, click OK.**

As with the menu bar you created earlier in this project, each type of Spry object requires a different set of JavaScript and CSS files.

20. **Review the CSS Styles panel and the Files panel.**

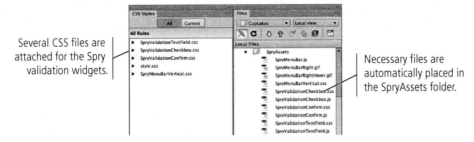

Several CSS files are attached for the Spry validation widgets.

Necessary files are automatically placed in the SpryAssets folder.

21. **Continue to the next exercise.**

Spry Validation Widget Properties (continued)

Password Validation Properties

- When **Required** is checked, users receive an error if they do not enter a value in the associated field.

- The **Min Chars** field requires a certain minimum number of characters in the field.

- The **Max Chars** field limits the number of characters that users can type in the field.

- You can use the **Min/Max Letters**, **Min/Max Numbers**, **Min/Max Uppercase**, and **Min/Max Special Chars** fields to force users to create complex passwords that are considered to be more secure.

Confirm Validation Properties

- When **Required** is checked, users receive an error message if the values they enter in the associated field do not match the values in a similar field.

- You can use the **Validate Against** menu to select the text field that contains the value you want to compare. All text fields with unique IDs appear in the menu.

Radio Group Validation Properties

- When **Required** is checked, users receive an error message if they do not make a selection in the group.

- You can use the **Empty Value** and **Invalid Value** fields to define specific values that will result in errors when a user submits the form. For example, defining a value of "−1" for the "-Select-" menu option allows you to force users to select a different option in the menu.

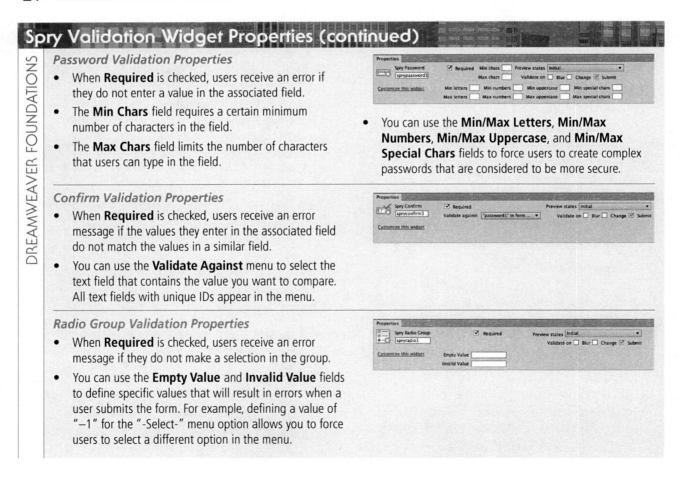

APPLY CSS TO THE FORM

To effectively format forms using CSS, you should remember that several HTML tags are used for most objects in the form:

- The **<form>** tag encloses the entire form.

- The **<input>** tag identifies each form object that allows user input. Different types of form objects are identified with the type attribute, such as:

    <input name="last" type="text" id="last" />
    <input type="reset" name="reset" id="reset" value="Reset" />

- The **<select>** tag creates drop-down menus and selection lists.

- The **<label>** tag creates the text that identifies form fields (including the text of checkboxes).

1. **With `join-the-club.html` open, place the insertion point at the end of the label for the checkbox field.**

    The editable region — which includes the form object — is inside the right_column div. Each line in this form is also tagged as a paragraph (using the **<p>** tag). So, the **#right_column p** selector controls the default appearance of form labels.

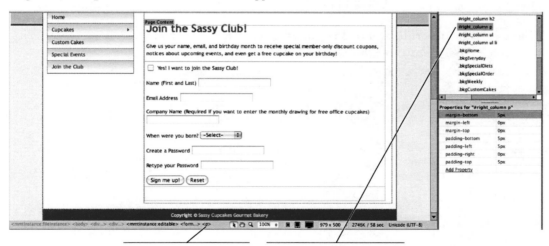

Every line in the form, which is in the right_column div, is marked with the <p> tag.

The #right_column p selector defines the current appearance of each paragraph in the form.

2. **Click the `<p>` tag in the Tag Selector to select the entire paragraph, then choose Heading 2 in the Format menu of the Properties panel.**

Click to select the entire paragraph...

...then apply the Heading 2 format.

After applying the Heading 2, the first line is now tagged with the **`<h2>`** tag instead of the **`<p>`** tag; the applied formatting is now defined by the **#right_column h2** selector.

CSS rules apply to content within a form object just as they do to content in a regular page area. The only difference is that you now have additional tags that can be defined to format specific form objects.

3. **Click the New CSS Rule button at the bottom of the CSS Styles panel.**

4. **Choose Tag in the Selector Type menu, type `input` in the Selector Name field, and make sure style.css is selected in the Rule Definition menu.**

5. **Click OK to create the new rule. In the Box options, define a width of `98%`, choose `left` in the Float menu, and choose `both` in the Clear menu.**

Note:

Remember the principles of parent/child relationships: if you want to affect all text within a form (for example), you can define specific font properties for the `<form>` tag. Those properties would then be inherited by all objects in the form.

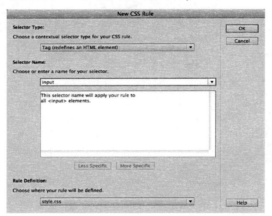

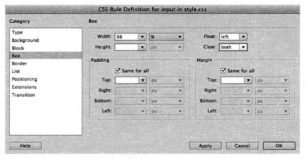

6. **Click OK to create the new selector.**

The input objects are now attached to the left edge of the containing area. The Clear property should force the labels onto their own lines; the Clear property only applies to other floating objects, but the labels have not yet been specifically defined as floating.

7. **Click the New CSS Rule button in the CSS Styles panel.**

8. **Create a new tag selector for the `label` tag in the style.css file. In the Box options, define a width of `100%`, apply the `left` float value, and choose `both` in the Clear menu.**

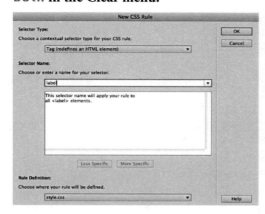 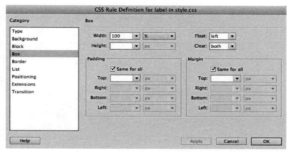

9. **Click OK to create the new selector.**

Note:

You might need to toggle on the Live view to see the true results of the selectors for the various form fields.

These two selectors did most of the formatting work for you. You should notice a few issues that need to be addressed:

- The settings in the **input** tag selector also affected the actual checkbox object and both buttons.

- The settings in the **label** tag selector also affected the label of the checkbox.

To override these selector properties in only certain input and label tags, you will create a class selector.

10. **Click the New CSS Rule button again. Create a new class selector named `.noClear` in the style.css file. In the Box options, choose `auto` in the Width menu and choose `none` in the Clear menu. Click OK to create the new selector.**

The auto value allows the object to occupy only what space is necessary (rather than the defined percentages in the **input** and **label** tag selectors).

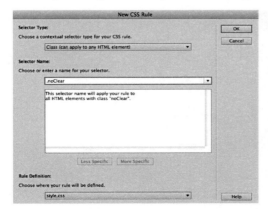 

11. **In the Design pane, click to select the checkbox object at the top of the form. In the Properties panel, open the Class menu and choose noClear.**

There is not much apparent difference yet, because you also need to apply the class to the checkbox label.

12. **Place the insertion point in the label text. Control/right-click the <label> tag in the Tag Selector and choose Set Class>noClear.**

In this case, do not use the Class field in the Properties panel; that would apply the class to the entire Heading 2 (**<h2>** tag) rather than to the specific label tag.

After applying the class to the **<label>** tag, the label appears correctly on one line.

However, removing the **clear:both** property allows the name label to move into the space to the right of the checkbox label; some property in the Spry validation CSS file for the label is overriding the clear property of the label. This type of situation is not uncommon, especially when using selectors that you did not create (such as the ones that are applied by the validation widgets). You will create another selector shortly to work around this issue.

13. **Using any method you prefer, apply the noClear class to both buttons at the bottom of the form.**

Because the noClear class allows objects' width to automatically size, the two buttons no longer fill the width of the containing area; they again appear on a single line.

14. **Click to place the insertion point in any label in the form, then click the New CSS Rule button in the CSS Styles panel.**

The New CSS Rule dialog box defaults to create a compound (descendant) selector based on the insertion point. You want the new selector to apply to paragraphs only in the form, so the compound selector type is appropriate. Because you placed the insertion point in a label, though, the default name includes the label tag at the end of the name.

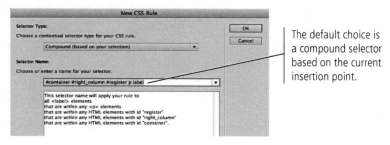

The default choice is a compound selector based on the current insertion point.

15. **Delete the word "label" from the end of the default selector name.**

You want this selector to apply to any paragraph tag in the form, so you have to remove the "label" element of the default name.

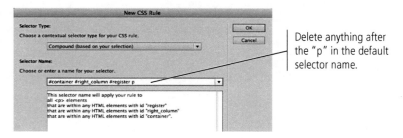

Delete anything after the "p" in the default selector name.

16. **Click OK to create the selector. In the Box options, define a 15px top margin and a 5px bottom margin.**

17. **Click OK to return to the document.**

18. **Save the open HTML file and the style.css file, then close the HTML file.**

19. **Export a site definition named Cupcakes.ste into your WIP>Cupcakes folder, and then remove the site from Dreamweaver.**

1. A(n) _____ can be used to change the appearance of multiple elements on a single page, including elements of different types, once it is applied to those elements.

2. You can make a(n) _____ editable in a template to protect the container's contents in pages where that template is applied.

3. The _____ property can be used to prevent other floating objects from appearing on the same line as an element.

4. A(n) _____ is based on an unordered list with up to three levels of linked list items.

5. _____ in the Code pane identifies a comment.

6. The _____ can be used to find CSS selectors that are related to a specific object.

7. A(n) _____ field presents options from a defined list, where users can choose only one option.

8. The _____ tag creates menus and selection lists.

9. The _____ tag identifies form objects such as text fields, where users can enter text.

10. The _____ determines the text that appears on a Submit or Reset button.

1. Briefly explain the concept of a class in CSS.

2. Briefly explain the function of the Preview States menu in the Properties panel when a Spry validation widget is selected.

3. Briefly explain the significance of the Copy Dependent Files dialog box.

Portfolio Builder Project

Use what you learned in this project to complete the following freeform exercise.
Carefully read the art director and client comments, then create your own design to meet the needs of the project.
Use the space below to sketch ideas; when finished, write a brief explanation of your reasoning behind your final design.

art director comments

Your client, AppleOne, wants to be able to gather exhibitor and attendee input at their upcoming conference. They have hired you to build two form pages for this purpose.

To complete this project, you should:

❏ Use client-supplied documents to build forms that will gather the desired information. The necessary files are provided in the **DW6_PB_Project5.zip** archive on the Student Files Web site

   – Use the AppleOne.dwt template file to create the required pages.

   – Use the text files in the Resources folder to find the questions.

❏ Use different form fields as appropriate to make the form very easy for users to fill out.

❏ Build each form on a separate page, maintaining the same look and feel of the overall site in each new form page.

client comments

Exhibitors and attendees will each receive a card with their registration packet inviting them to fill out the appropriate form, beginning the day after the show concludes.

We have sent you files with the questions we want to include in each survey. Most of the questions will have 1-to-10 radio button options. Several questions will need fields where users can enter their own information. There are also a few questions that will have a 'choose one' set of options.

We've already printed the cards for the registration packets, so make sure you use the correct file names and method:

– The attendee survey page should be appleone.com/at_survey.html

– The exhibitor survey page should be appleone.com/ex_survey.html

– Form submissions should be emailed to thanks@appleone.com

project justification

In this project, you learned more about CSS selectors — specifically, using class selectors to control specific elements in a page. Because of the versatility of using classes, some professional Web designers use only classes to define an entire site layout. You also learned several different techniques for editing CSS selectors, both in the CSS Styles panel and in the Code pane. Once you are familar with all of the options, you can better determine which method suits your working style.

This project also expanded on your knowledge of Dreamweaver templates. You learned how to make only a specific attribute editable, allowing different options on individual pages while protecting placed content.

Using built-in Spry options, you created a multi-level navigation menu and several different form fields, and applied validation options to several form fields. The code for these elements is complex and — in the case of the menu and form validation objects — requires knowledge of JavaScript. By now you should realize that Dreamweaver provides a number of advantages over simply writing page code, especially for beginners or non-programmers.

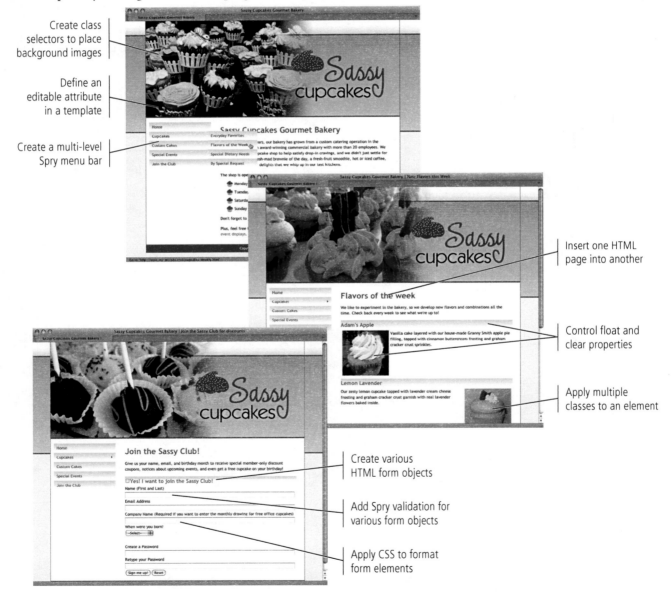

Create class selectors to place background images

Define an editable attribute in a template

Create a multi-level Spry menu bar

Insert one HTML page into another

Control float and clear properties

Apply multiple classes to an element

Create various HTML form objects

Add Spry validation for various form objects

Apply CSS to format form elements

Kayaking HTML5 Site

Your client, Clearwater Kayaking Outfitters, has hired you to create a new site that functions properly in all current browsers. They want to include two different articles on the site home page, as well as video and images from past trips.

This project incorporates the following skills:

❏ Using HTML5 tags to structure page content

❏ Using CSS3 selectors to add aesthetic appeal to page content

❏ Understanding and managing different browser requirements for HTML5/CSS3 options

❏ Adding Web fonts to display page content with specific fonts

❏ Placing video into the page without the need for a browser plug-in

❏ Using prebuilt widgets to create complex JavaScript objects

client comments

Our site doesn't need to be complex, but it does require a few specific elements:

- A basic introduction and list of frequently asked questions
- A video from one of our recent trips
- A photo gallery to show a series of images from past trips and tours

We want to make it very easy for people to find the information they want. If possible, all of the important text — intro and FAQs — should appear directly on the home page.

The old site had embedded Flash files for video and slideshow, but too many people were complaining about not being able to see the content. We get a lot of traffic from people who are traveling, so we want our site to work on mobile devices.

art director comments

HTML5 is the perfect solution to the client's problem of files not working on mobile devices. Even though the standard hasn't been officially adopted yet, a lot of people are using this technology to make sites that work properly in all current browsers — including on tablets and smartphones.

Unfortunately, Dreamweaver hasn't completely incorporated HTML5 and CSS3 options into the user interface. You'll have to work a lot in the page code to make this site work.

Fortunately, everything you already know about HTML and CSS code will make it easier to accomplish your goals. Tags are still tags and CSS selectors still function in the same general way. The difference is the new tags that have been added to HTML5 and the new properties that are available in CSS3.

project objectives

To complete this project, you will:

- ❑ Create a new HTML5 page
- ❑ Add HTML5 tags
- ❑ Attach a CSS style sheet
- ❑ Add rounded corners to an element
- ❑ Define transparency for a background color
- ❑ Create multiple columns of text
- ❑ Download a Web font package
- ❑ Define Web fonts in Dreamweaver
- ❑ Apply Web fonts to page elements
- ❑ Place a video in an HTML5 page
- ❑ Define video tag attributes
- ❑ Use the Adobe Widget Browser
- ❑ Add a widget to an HTML5 page
- ❑ Customize widget content

Stage 1 Working with HTML5 Tags

HTML5 is the next generation of the HTML code language. Although it will not be officially adopted as a standard until 2014, it is already being used in many Web sites. HTML5 incorporates new elements and attributes that are intended to make Web pages function better, both structurally and syntactically. HTML5 also removed (deprecated) elements from previous versions of the language that were obsolete or unnecessary based on the way people currently use the Web.

In this stage of the project, you will create a new HTML5 page and use HTML5 tags to mark up the client's supplied content. Unfortunately, most of the HTML5 elements are not available in the Properties panel menus or the Insert panel buttons. To mark up content with HTML5 tags, you will be spending a lot of time working directly in the Dreamweaver code pane.

CREATE A NEW HTML5 PAGE

Because HTML5 is a revision of an existing language, you will see very little difference in the basic file that you create in Dreamweaver. The only notable difference between an HTML 4/XHTML page and an HTML5 page is the doctype statement at the beginning of the page code.

1. Download **DW6_RF_Project6.zip** from the Student Files Web page.

2. **Expand the ZIP archive in your WIP folder (Macintosh) or copy the archive contents into your WIP folder (Windows).**

   This results in a folder named **Kayaking**, which contains the files you need for this project.

3. **Create a new site named Kayaking, using the WIP>Kayaking folder as the site root folder.**

   If necessary, refer to the first exercises in Project 1: Bistro Site Organization, for more detailed instructions.

4. **Choose File>New. In the New Document dialog box, choose HTML in the Page Type window and choose <none> in the Layout window. On the right side of the dialog box, choose HTML 5 in the DocType menu.**

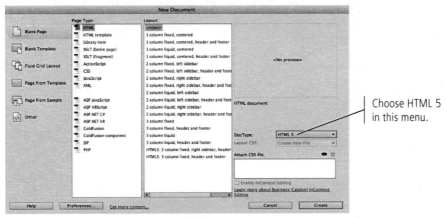

Choose HTML 5 in this menu.

5. **Click Create to create the new file. With the new file open in the Code view, review the existing code.**

   When you create an HTML5 page, the doctype statement at the beginning of the code simply shows "html" rather than a specific version. HTML5-compliant browsers automatically interpret this to mean HTML5.

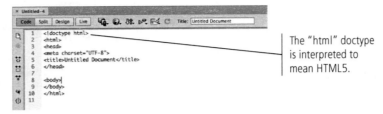

The "html" doctype is interpreted to mean HTML5.

6. **Change the page title (between the opening and closing <title> tags) to** Clearwater Kayak Outfitters.

7. **Click the Refresh button in the Properties panel to reflect the new title in the Document toolbar.**

8. **Save the file as** index.html **in the WIP>Kayaking folder. If the new file does not appear in the Files panel, refresh the panel view.**

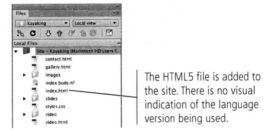

The HTML5 file is added to the site. There is no visual indication of the language version being used.

9. **Double-click the** index body.rtf **file in the Files panel.**

   The file opens in the default text-editor application on your computer.

10. **Select all the content in the file and copy it (Edit>Copy or Command/Control-C).**

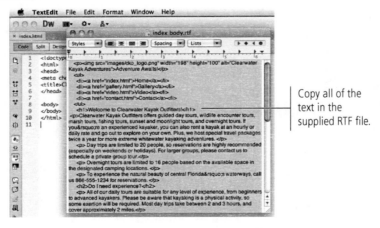

Copy all of the text in the supplied RTF file.

11. **Close the text file and return to Dreamweaver.**

12. **Place the insertion point after the opening `<body>` tag in the code (Line 8) and press Return/Enter to start a new line.**

Add a new line inside the opening and closing `<body>` tags.

13. **With the insertion point on Line 9, paste (Edit>Paste or Command/Control-V) the content you copied in Step 10.**

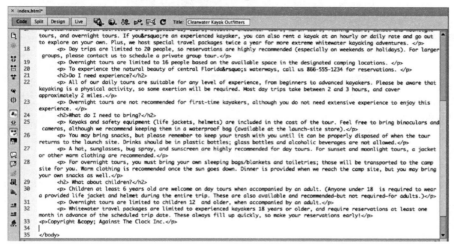

14. **Switch to the Design view and review the page content.**

We already defined the basic content for this page, including a number of headings, a placed image, and a bulleted list. At this point, only default formatting options appear because you have not yet defined the CSS that should apply to the page.

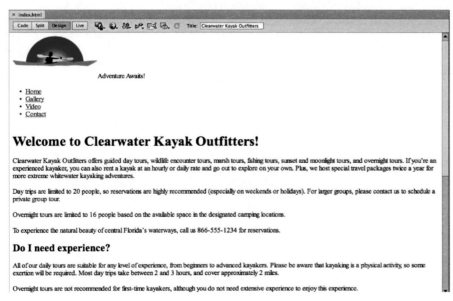

15. **Save the file and continue to the next exercise.**

Learning about HTML5 Tags

A complete list of HTML5 tags is available at www.w3schools.com/html5/html5_reference.asp.

You can click any tag in the list to find out more about its use, as well as important information about browser support for each tag.

Click any tag in the list to learn more about its use.

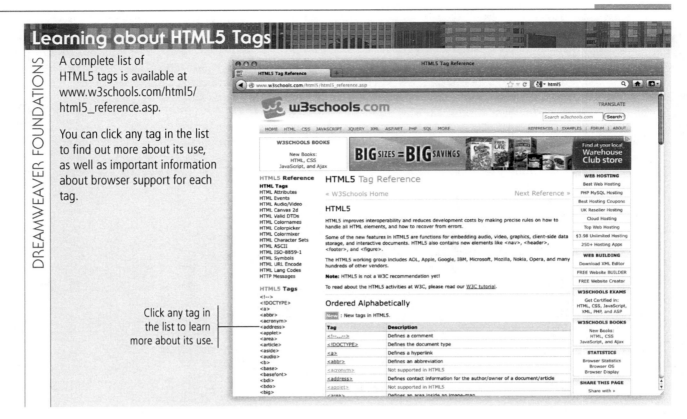

ADD HTML5 TAGS

In the general sense, working with HTML5 is no different than working with the HTML 4 files you have used in previous projects. Adding content to a page, and formatting elements with CSS selectors, are core skills for either version of HTML.

One difference with HTML5 is the addition of new tags that reflect conventions that Web designers have been using for years.

As you completed the previous projects in this book, you might have noticed a number of common div ids being used in various site designs — for example, div#header, div#nav, and div#footer. HTML5 includes new header, nav, and footer elements that allow the same kind of page structure without the need to define and identify multiple divs on a page.

Other elements have been added to HTML5 — such as the section and article elements — to make it easier to define specific content on a page without multiple levels of nested divs.

In this exercise, you will use HTML5 tags to identify various pieces of content as specific areas of the page.

1. **With index.html open, click the Split button in the Document toolbar.**

   It can be very helpful — especially until you are more familiar working with HTML code — to keep the Design and Code panes visible so you can see the effects of your changes in the Code pane.

2. **Place the insertion point anywhere in the first paragraph in the Design view.**

3. **In the Tag Selector, click the <p> tag to select the entire element.**

4. **In the Design pane, Control/right-click anywhere in the active selection and choose Wrap Tag from the contextual menu.**

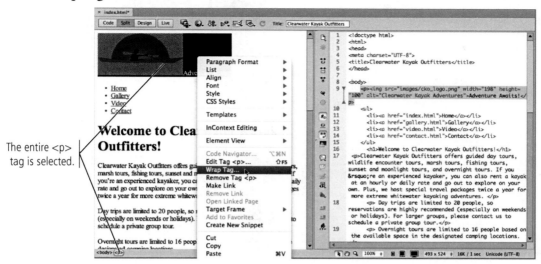

The entire <p> tag is selected.

5. **In the pop-up code editor, type header.**

The header element identifies the header section of the page.

The Code Hint menu automatically scrolls to the option you typed.

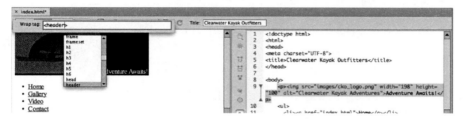

6. **Press Return/Enter to close the Code Hint menu, then press Return/Enter again to apply the tag around the active selection.**

Although Dreamweaver's interface doesn't include buttons for applying HTML5 elements, those elements are included in the Code Hint menu.

Opening and closing <header> tags wrap around the selected paragraph element.

Unlike divs, which can be seen in the Design pane when visual aids are active, the Design pane shows no visual indication that the **<header>** tag has been applied. At this point, there is no visual difference between the original content and the content with a defined header element.

7. **Repeat Steps 2–6 to wrap the <nav> tag around the unordered list near the top of the page.**

   Make sure you select the entire unordered list (with the <ul> tag) and not one of the individual list items (with the <li> tags).

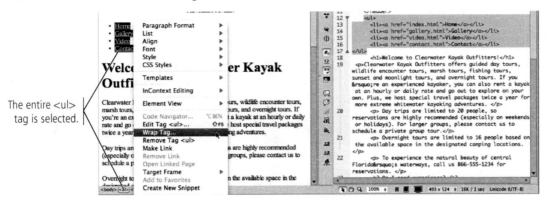

The entire <ul> tag is selected.

The nav element identifies a section that includes navigation links.

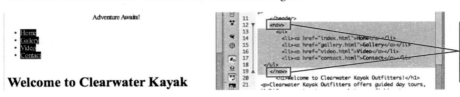

Opening and closing <nav> tags wrap around the selected unordered list element.

8. **Repeat Steps 2–6 to wrap the <footer> tag around the last paragraph on the page.**

   The footer element identifies the footer section of the page.

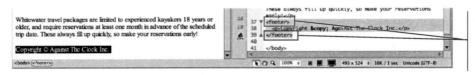

Opening and closing <footer> tags wrap around the selected paragraph element.

9. **In the Code pane, place the insertion point at the end of the closing </nav> tag and press Return/Enter.**

10. **On the new line, type `<section id="content">`.**

    The section element identifies (as you might imagine) a section of the page. By adding an id attribute, you are uniquely identfying this section as distinct from other sections.

    You can place more than one section element on a page to define multiple sections. If you define different id attributes for each section, you could then use CSS ID selectors to apply different formatting to each section.

Note:

Feel free to use the Code Hint menus to add the required code.

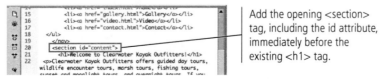

Add the opening <section> tag, including the id attribute, immediately before the existing <h1> tag.

11. Move the insertion point to the end of the last line before the opening footer tag. Press Return/Enter to create a new line, then type `</`.

As with HTML 4 tags, Dreamweaver automatically closes the last opened tag for you. Since the <section> tag is the only unclosed opening tag in the file, the application recognizes that you want to close the <section> tag.

Add the closing </section> tag immediately before the opening <footer> tag.

Because you are wrapping the <section> tags around multiple other tags, you can't use the Wrap Tag option that you used in the first steps of this exercise. To enclose multiple elements in one tag, you have to simply type the new opening and closing tags in the Code pane.

12. In the Code pane, place the insertion point at the end of the closing <h1> tag near the top of the page.

13. Press Return/Enter to start a new line, then type `<article id="intro">`.

The article element identifies individual articles within a page, just as you might find in a printed magazine.

Add the opening <article> tag, including the id attribute, immediately after the existing <h1> tag.

14. Place the insertion point at the end of the last paragraph before the first <h2> tag, then type `</`.

Again, Dreamweaver closes the last unclosed opening tag for you — in this case, the article tag.

Add the closing </article> tag before the first <h2> tag.

15. Repeat this process to define a second article element that begins before the first <h2> tag and ends immediately before the closing </section> tag. Assign the id of `faqs` to the second article tag.

As with the section element, you can place multiple articles in a single page. Using different ids for each article element, you will be able to apply different formatting options to each unique article.

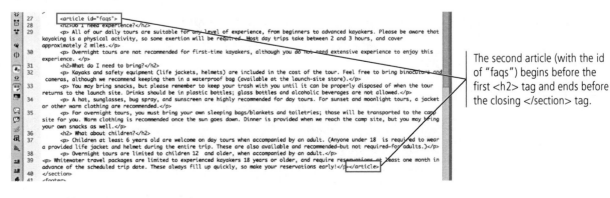

The second article (with the id of "faqs") begins before the first <h2> tag and ends before the closing </section> tag.

16. Save the file and continue to the next exercise.

ATTACH A CSS STYLE SHEET

If you completed the first five projects in this book, you have already learned how to control content and structure with cascading style sheets. Using CSS, you can control the appearance of specific HTML tags (using tag selectors), elements named with a specific id attribute (using ID selectors), tags only within certain elements (using descendant selectors), and specific elements on the page (using class selectors).

In this exercise, you will attach an existing CSS file to the index.html page. Once the CSS has been applied, you will be able to see the effect of using HTML5 tags to format a page.

1. **With `index.html` open, click the Design button in the Document toolbar.**

   At this point, you see only the default formatting of headings, unordered lists, links, and paragraphs.

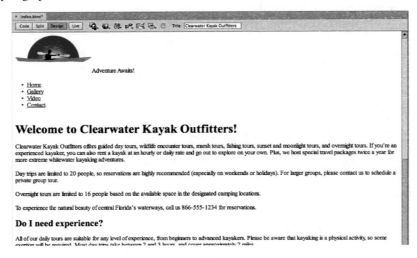

2. **Open the CSS Styles panel and click the Attach Style Sheet button.**

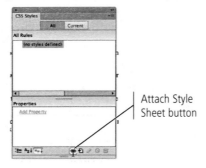

   Attach Style Sheet button

3. **In the Attach External Style Sheet dialog box, click the Browse button.**

4. **Navigate to and select styles.css (in the WIP>Kayaking folder), then click Open.**

5. **Make sure the Link option is selected, then click OK.**

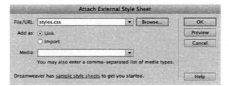

The index file content is now formatted based on the selectors that exist in the CSS file. Although you did not use a single div tag, the various elements — header, navigation links, main page content, and footer — are positioned in a familiar Web page arrangement.

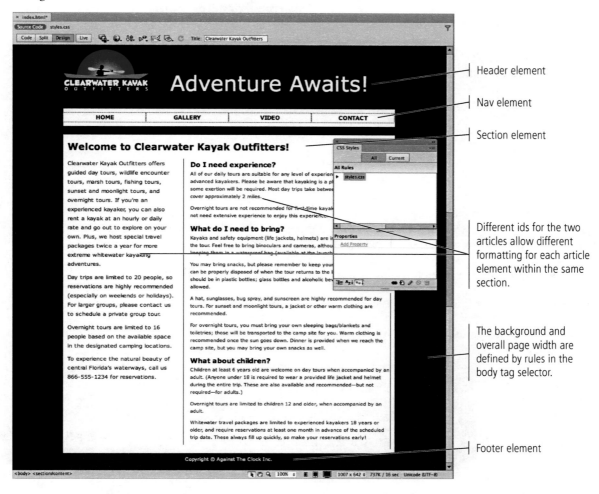

Header element

Nav element

Section element

Different ids for the two articles allow different formatting for each article element within the same section.

The background and overall page width are defined by rules in the body tag selector.

Footer element

6. **In the CSS Styles panel, expand styles.css and review the existing selectors.**

The CSS file for this project has a number of tag, id, and descendant selectors that match the tags you defined in the previous exercise.

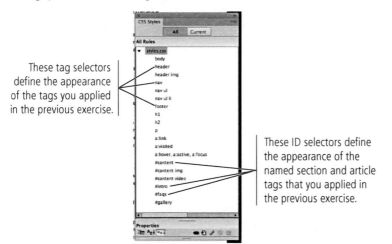

These tag selectors define the appearance of the tags you applied in the previous exercise.

These ID selectors define the appearance of the named section and article tags that you applied in the previous exercise.

Note:

You already learned how to create tag and ID selectors in previous projects. If you need a refresher, refer back to Project 4: Yosemite CSS Layout.

7. **Save the file and continue to the next stage of the project.**

Stage 2 Working with CSS3 Selectors

CSS3 is the next generation of cascading style sheets. The newest edition of the standard adds a number of properties that give you considerably more creative control over the appearance of Web pages. In this stage of the project, you will use several new CSS3 properties to add visual appeal to the index.html page. (Because all files in the site are attached to the same CSS file, your changes in the CSS file will affect the appearance of all four pages in the site.)

Although you can use the CSS Styles panel to add specific properties to a selector, many of the new CSS3 properties are not available in the CSS Rule Definition dialog box. Most of your work in this stage of the project will be done directly in the Code pane.

ADD ROUNDED CORNERS TO AN ELEMENT

Prior to CSS3, adding rounded corners to an HTML element required a series of convoluted and complex image slices, cut apart in an image-editing application such as Adobe Photoshop and then reassembled in the Web page — usually as the background images for a series of divs or (before CSS became the standard) table cells. Using CSS3, rounded corners are very easy to define for any element.

1. **With index.html open, click the Split button in the Document toolbar.**

2. **In the Related Files bar, click styles.css to show that file in the Code pane.**

3. **In the CSS Styles panel, click the nav tag selector to show that selector in the Code pane.**

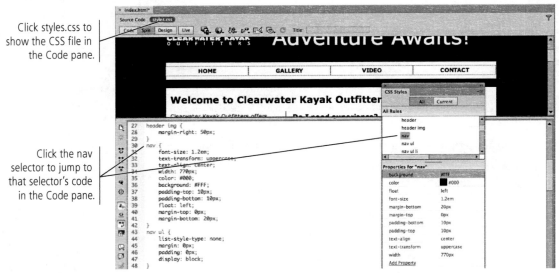

Click styles.css to show the CSS file in the Code pane.

Click the nav selector to jump to that selector's code in the Code pane.

4. **In the Code pane, place the insertion point at the end of the last property in the nav selector.**

5. **Press Return/Enter to add a new property to the selector.**

6. **Type** `border-r`, **then press Return/Enter to accept the border-radius property from the Code Hint menu.**

   As you type, the Code Hint menu scrolls to the available properties that match the characters you type. After you type border-r, the first option — border-radius — is automatically selected. Pressing Return/Enter adds that item to your code, including the required colon after the property name.

   The **border-radius** property defines the same corner radius for all corners of an element.

Note:

You can define a different radius for each corner using the following properties:

border-bottom-left-radius

border-bottom-right-radius

border-top-left-radius

border-top-right-radius

7. **Press the spacebar, and type** `10px;`.

   This is the amount of rounding (the radius) that will be applied to all four corners of the nav element. To understand the concept of corner radius, think of a rectangle with an imaginary circle on top of the corner; the point at which the sides of the rectangle meet the sides of the circle is the **corner radius**.

   This imaginary circle has a 10-px radius.

8. **Click Refresh in the CSS Styles panel to update the Design view.**

   As you can see, the new selector rule has no effect on the nav element in the Design pane. Dreamweaver's Design view does not accurately reflect many CSS3 properties unless the Live view is turned on.

Note:

Moving forward, we will not include the complete instructions for using code hints to add specific CSS properties. You can use the menu to add the necessary code, or simply type the properties and values that you want to add.

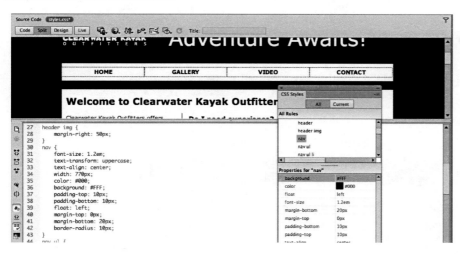

9. **Click the Live button in the Document toolbar.**

   When the Live view is active, you can now see the rounded corners on the nav element.

   In the Live view, you can see the rounded corners that you defined for the nav element.

10. **Turn off the Live view.**

11. **Save the styles.css file and then continue to the next exercise.**

DEFINE TRANSPARENCY FOR A BACKGROUND COLOR

Using CSS3, you can define colors in a number of ways:

- Using a hexadecimal color value, such as #FF0066. Each couplet in the color value defines the red, green, and blue components of that color.

- Using a color name, such as "aqua" or "green." There are 147 defined color names in the HTML and CSS color specification.

- Using specific RGB values, in the following format:

  rgb(255, 0, 100)

  Each number in the parentheses defines the amount of red, green, and blue (respectively) — from 0 (none of a color) to 255 (all of a color) — that makes up the overall color. By combining various percentages of each color component, this method theoretically allows you to define any of the 16.7 million colors in the visible spectrum.

  This flexibility gives you considerably more color options than the basic Web-safe color list that was the standard in earlier generations of Web design. Keep in mind, however, that colors still vary from one display to another. Although you can now define a much wider range of colors, you still can't guarantee that the color you want is the color users will see.

- Using RGBA color values, which adds the alpha property to standard RGB color values in the following format:

  rgba(255, 0, 100, 0.5)

  The fourth parameter in the parentheses is the alpha value, which defines the color's transparency from 0.0 (fully transparent) to 1.0 (fully opaque).

Note:

Refer to http://www. w3schools.com/cssref/ css_colornames.asp for a complete list of supported color names.

Note:

RGBA color values are supported in Internet Explorer 9+, Firefox 3+, Chrome, Safari, and Opera 10+.

1. With index.html open, keep the Split view active and make sure the styles.css file is visible in the Code pane.

2. In the code for the nav selector, delete the existing value for the background property.

Leave the colon and space after the property name.

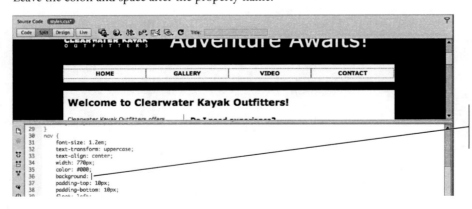

Delete the existing value (#FFF) for the background property.

3. **Type `rgba(255, 255, 255, 0.6);` as the new property value, then refresh the Design view.**

   As with the rounded corners you applied in the previous exercise, the Design view does not accurately render the RGBA color value when the Live view is not active.

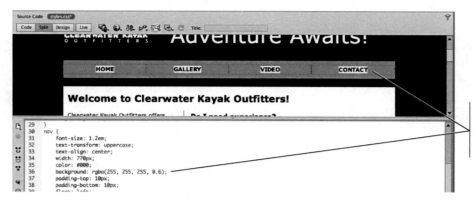

When the Live view is not active, the semi-transparent background color is not rendered accurately.

4. **Turn on the Live view and review the nav element in the Design view.**

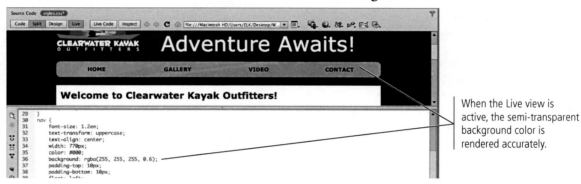

When the Live view is active, the semi-transparent background color is rendered accurately.

5. **Repeat this process to change the background-color property of the #content selector to `rgba(255, 255, 255, 0.8)`.**

   The nav and section#content elements have the same basic background color, but different alpha values. The background image and color are visible behind both elements, but the higher alpha value in the content element allows the text to be more legible.

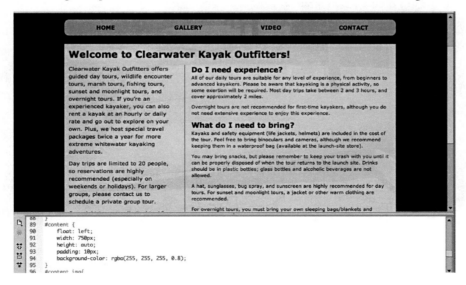

6. **Save the styles.css file and continue to the next exercise.**

CREATE MULTIPLE COLUMNS OF TEXT

As you have already seen, you can use different elements to create the appearance of multiple columns. In the index file you are currently building, the two article tags have unique id attributes; the selectors for those ids define width and float properties that make it seem like the page is laid out with two columns.

Using CSS3, you can also use the **column-count** property to define a number of columns within a single element. In this exercise, you will add this property to the #faqs ID selector to change the text layout only within the article element that is identified as the faqs article.

It is important to note that some CSS3 properties — including the column-count property that you use in this exercise — are not supported by all browsers. In these cases, you can sometimes use a workaround to define options that will work in various browsers.

Note:

You can check whether a property is supported by different browsers at www.w3schools.com/cssref/css3_browsersupport.asp.

1. **With index.html open, keep the Split view active and make sure the styles.css file is visible in the Code pane.**

2. **In the CSS Styles panel, click the #faqs selector to show the relevant code in the Code pane.**

3. **Place the insertion point at the end of the last property in the #faqs selector code and press Return/Enter to add a new line.**

4. **Type -moz-column-count: 2; then press Return/Enter.**

   The "-moz-" prefix at the beginning of the property name identifies that property for the Mozilla Firefox browser.

5. **On the next line, type -webkit-column-count: 2; then press Return/ Enter.**

   The "-webkit-" prefix at the beginning of the property name identifies that property for the Safari and Google Chrome browsers — and for the Dreamweaver CS6 Live view.

6. **On the next line, type column-count: 2;.**

   Without a vendor-specific prefix, this property is only supported by the Opera browser.

   When you add multiple properties in this manner, a browser will continue down the list until it finds one it understands; non-supported properties are ignored.

   Internet Explorer does not support the column-count property even with a prefix, so the page in IE will only show one column in the article#faqs element.

The -moz- prefix is for the Firefox browser.

The -webkit- prefix is for the Safari and Chrome browsers.

The property with no prefix is for the Opera browser.

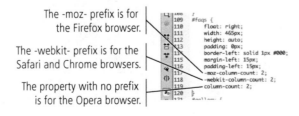

7. **Refresh the Design view and review the page.**

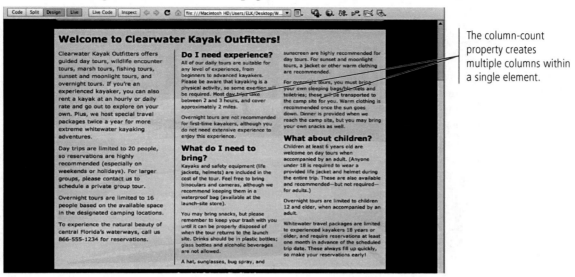

The column-count property creates multiple columns within a single element.

8. **Save the styles.css file, close the active HTML file, and then continue to the next stage of the project.**

Learning More about CSS3 Properties

In this project, we focused on three different properties that highlight various issues you will encounter using CSS3 in Dreamweaver CS6:

- Manually typing code into the CSS file to define CSS3 properties
- Using the Live view to preview CSS3 in Dreamweaver
- Using multiple vendor prefixes to define properties for different browsers

The three properties you used here are hardly exhaustive. In fact, it would be virtually impossible to create a project that included every available CSS3 property.

To learn more about specific CSS properties, including all of the properties that were added in CSS3, visit www.w3schools.com/cssref/default.asp. You can click any property in the list on the left to learn more, including examples and browser support information.

Click any property in this list to find more information.

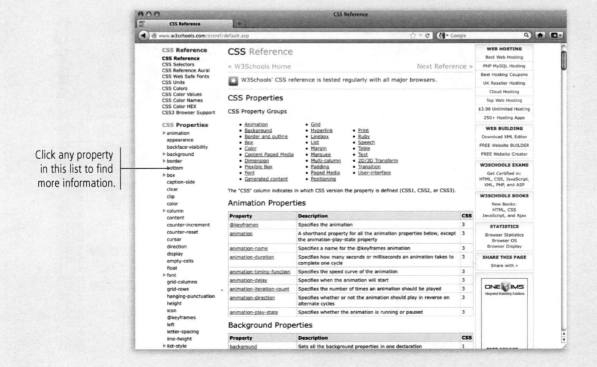

Stage 3 Working with Web Fonts

Prior to CSS3, Web sites were limited to the fonts that were installed on a user's computer. When we design pages, we use font families to define a sequence of possible fonts to use, usually ending with a generic type of font like serif or sans-serif. Even those options weren't guaranteed, because an individual user can customize a browser to display all type in (for example) Comic Sans regardless of the type of font a design defined.

The addition of Web fonts in CSS3 now means that you can embed specific fonts into a Web page; when a user opens your page, the exact fonts you define will be used in the browser.

You do, however, have to find or buy the fonts that you want to use, including all of the formats that are required by different browsers. Firefox, Chrome, Safari, and Opera support TrueType (.ttf) and OpenType (.otf) fonts. Internet Explorer 9+ requires Embedded OpenType (.eot) fonts.

Unlike the elements and properties that you defined in the first two stages of this project, Dreamweaver CS6 does support the use of Web fonts in dialog boxes and various menus; you don't need to manually write the required code.

DOWNLOAD A WEB FONT PACKAGE

Many sources of Web fonts are available on the Internet; some sources are free, some are free only for non-commercial use, and some require a fee just like high-quality fonts for print applications.

In this exercise, you are going to download a Web font package that you can apply to various elements in the kayaking Web site.

1. **Using any browser, navigate to www.fontsquirrel.com.**

   This site is only one of many that offer free Web font packages that you can download and use in your Web sites.

2. **Click the @font-face Kits link in the navigation bar.**

   The font-face kits on this site include all of the font formats that are required by different browsers.

Click the link for @font-face Kits.

3. **Scroll down the page to find the Bubblegum Sans font (in the Display category) and click the Get Kit link.**

Click the Get Kit link for Bubblegum Sans.

4. **Macintosh users: Choose the Save File option, then click OK.**

The file is automatically saved to the Downloads folder on your computer.

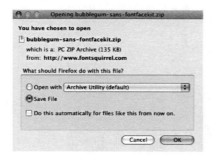

Windows users: Click Save when asked what you want to do with the file. If you are asked, choose your WIP folder (not the WIP>Kayaking folder) as the target location, then click Save.

On some Windows systems, you are asked where you want to save the file you are downloading.

5. **Using the same process that you use for the student files for each project in this book, open the downloaded ZIP archive file and copy its contents into your primary WIP folder (not the WIP>Kayaking folder).**

At this point you are simply downloading the font-face kit and making the files available on your computer. When you add the Web font in Dreamweaver and use it in your site, the necessary files will automatically be placed in the site root folder for you.

6. **Continue to the next exercise.**

DEFINE WEB FONTS IN DREAMWEAVER

After you have downloaded Web fonts, the next step is to add those fonts to Dreamweaver. Web fonts are not specific to a file or site; instead, they are available in Dreamweaver as long as the physical files remain in the same location as they are when you define them in Dreamweaver.

1. **In Dreamweaver, choose Modify>Web Fonts.**

2. **In the Web Fonts Manager dialog box, click the Add Font button.**

Click here to add Web fonts to Dreamweaver.

3. **In the Add Web Font dialog box, click the folder icon to the right of the EOT Font field.**

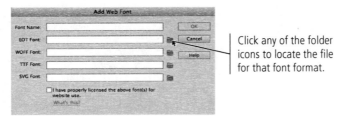

Click any of the folder icons to locate the file for that font format.

4. **In the resulting dialog box, navigate to the WIP>bubblegum-sans-fontfacekit folder. Choose the .eot file in the list and click Open.**

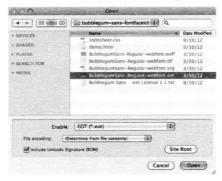

After you select one of the fonts in the kit, Dreamweaver automatically recognizes the other font formats in the same folder.

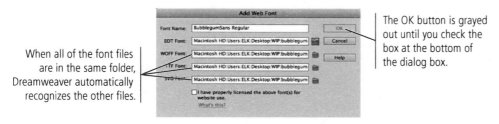

When all of the font files are in the same folder, Dreamweaver automatically recognizes the other files.

The OK button is grayed out until you check the box at the bottom of the dialog box.

5. **At the bottom of the dialog box, check the box to agree that you have properly licensed the font you are adding.**

   The fonts at fontsquirrel.com are — as the site's header says — 100% free for commercial use. Be sure that you check the font license before you use a Web font.

6. **Click OK to return to the Web Fonts Manager, then click Done.**

7. **Choose Modify>Font Families.**

   A **font family** is a sequence of fonts that can be used to display content. When a browser opens a page, it goes through various fonts in the list until it finds one that can be used on the active device.

   Using Web fonts, the page should theoretically only display content in the font you define. However, older browsers do not support Web fonts, so you should still create a font family to at least define the basic category to use if the Web font is not available.

8. **In the Edit Font List dialog box, scroll to the bottom of the Available Fonts window.**

   Installed Web fonts appear at the end of the Available Fonts list, after the font categories.

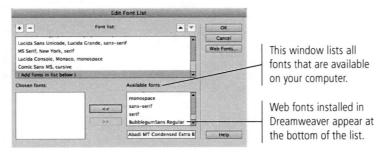

This window lists all fonts that are available on your computer.

Web fonts installed in Dreamweaver appear at the bottom of the list.

9. **Select BubblegumSans Regular in the list and then click the << button.**

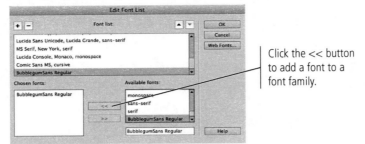

Click the << button
to add a font to a
font family.

10. **Select sans-serif in the Available Fonts list and then click the << button.**

This font family tells the browser:

Use BubblegumSans Regular. If that font cannot be used,
use the default sans-serif font that is defined by the user's browser.

11. **Click OK to close the Edit Font List dialog box.**

12. **Continue to the next exercise.**

 ## APPLY WEB FONTS TO PAGE ELEMENTS

After Web fonts are installed in Dreamweaver and defined in font families, you can apply those Web fonts to page elements just as you would apply the built-in font families. In this exercise, you are going to define the BubblegumSans Regular font for the header element, and for h1 and h2 tags in the kayaking site.

1. **With the Kayaking site open in the Files panel, double-click styles.css to open it.**

   To access the available styles in the CSS Styles panel, you have to open a file that uses the CSS file where you want to edit the styles. You are opening the actual CSS file in this case so you can see the code that is added.

2. **In the CSS Styles panel, select the header selector.**

3. **Click the Add Property link at the bottom of the Properties list. In the resulting field, type font-family.**

   If you don't see the Add Property link, make sure the Show Only Set Properties option is active at the bottom of the panel.

4. Open the resulting menu in the right column and choose BubblegumSans Regular, sans-serif.

It is not necessary to add Web fonts to a font family. As you can see, installed Web fonts are available at the bottom of the list of font families. As we explained in the previous exercise, however, it is a good idea to at least define the generic type of font you want in case a browser can't use the Web font.

After you add a Web font (or family that includes a Web font), an import statement is automatically added to the top of the CSS file. This statement points to a secondary CSS file that defines the location of Web font files. The CSS file is created for you and placed in a "webfonts" folder, which is automatically added to your site root folder.

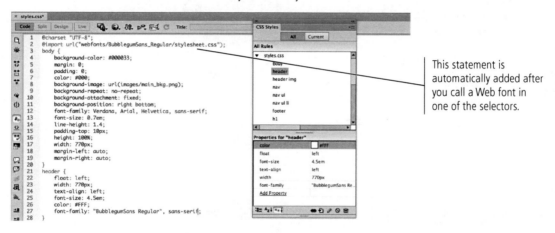

This statement is automatically added after you call a Web font in one of the selectors.

5. In the Files panel, expand the webfonts folder.

The webfonts folder contains the necessary font files for the defined Web font, as well as the stylesheet.css file that is referenced in the CSS file where you added the Web font.

6. Repeat Steps 2–4 to define the same font family for the h1 and h2 tag selectors.

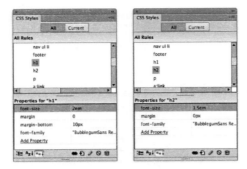

7. Save the CSS file and close it.

8. Double-click index.html in the Files panel to open it.

9. Click the Design button in the Document toolbar to show only the Design view.

10. Click the Live button to turn on the Live view.

As with many other CSS3 properties and features, the Design view does not accurately preview Web fonts unless the Live view is active.

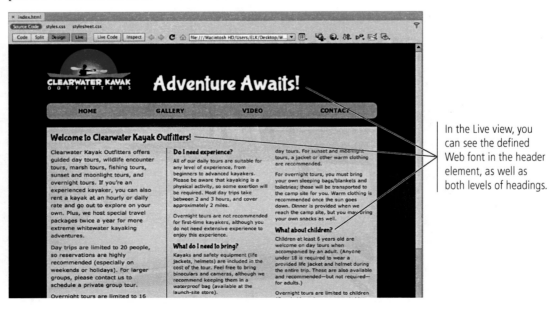

In the Live view, you can see the defined Web font in the header element, as well as both levels of headings.

11. Close the index.html file and then continue to the next stage of the project.

Stage 4 Adding Video in HTML5

One of the advantages of HTML5 is the ability to present multimedia files without the need for a plug-in. Using the new <video> tag, you can define a source for video that will play directly in the page. Because HTML5 is not yet an adopted standard, different browsers require different formats for video placed into an HTML5 page.

- Internet Explorer 9+ supports MPEG 4 (.mp4) files.

- Safari supports MPEG 4 files.

- Firefox supports WebM and Ogg (.ogv) files

- Opera supports WebM and Ogg files

- Google Chrome supports MPEG 4, WebM, and Ogg files.

A number of free video converters are available on the Internet. To create the required files for this project, we used the Freemake Video Converter for Windows (www.freemake.com).

As you saw when you added Web fonts in the last stage of this project, you can work around issues of non-standardization by defining multiple files to use in a given situation. In this stage of the project, you will create a video tag and define multiple sources to meet different browser requirements.

PLACE A VIDEO IN AN HTML5 PAGE

In this exercise, you are going to write the necessary code to place a video file into an HTML page. Keep in mind that the **<video>** tag is new in HTML5; if you open the page in an older browser that does not support HTML5, the video will not be visible.

1. **With the Kayaking site open in the Files panel, double-click the video.html file to open it.**

2. **In the Files panel, expand the video folder.**

   This folder includes three versions of the same video, saved in various formats to be compatible with different browsers.

3. **Click the Split button in the Document toolbar to show both the Code and Design panes.**

Note:

The video you are using in this project, by Scott Dunsmuir, is in the public domain with no rights reserved. It was downloaded from The Internet Archive (www. archive.org), which is an excellent source of free imagery and video. However, be aware that individual files on this site have different use permissions and restrictions, determined by the creator; please respect the ownership and rights of the media you want to use in your work. We removed the audio from the original video to avoid violating the copyright of the artists who created the music.

4. **In the Code pane, place the insertion point after the closing </h1> tag, then press Return/Enter to add a new line in the code.**

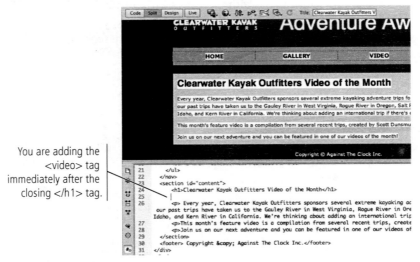

You are adding the <video> tag immediately after the closing </h1> tag.

5. **Type ‹video›, then press Return/Enter.**

The <video> tag specifies a video that is placed directly on the page.

6. **On the next line, type**

   `<source src="video/dunsmuir.mp4" type="video/mp4" />`

   The HTML5 **<source>** tag is used to specify multiple media resources for the <video> tag. When a browser opens the page, it moves through the different <source> tags until it finds one it can use.

   The **src** attribute defines the location of the video file you are using.

   The **type** attribute defines the MIME type of the selected file. This information allows an individual browser to identify a file that it can use.

Note:

You can use the Code Hint menu options to create this line, but it is often just as easy to type the code you want to use.

7. **Press Return/Enter to add another line to the code.**

8. **Create two more lines in the code, defining the src and type attributes for each of the remaining video files:**

   `<source src="video/dunsmuir.ogv" type="video/ogg" />`

   `<source src="video/dunsmuir.webm" type="video/webm" />`

Note:

"OGV" is the correct extension for an OGG video file.

9. **Press Return/Enter after the last statement, then type </.**

   Dreamweaver automatically closes the last open tag — in this case, the <video> tag.

10. **Press Return/Enter after the last <source> statment, then type:**

    Your browser does not support the HTML5 video tag. Please update to a current browser.

    If a user's browser doesn't support HTML5, this statement will appear in place of the video.

```
23   <section id= content >
24        <h1>Clearwater Kayak Outfitters Video of the Month</h1>
25        <video>
26        <source src="video/dunsmuir.mp4" type="video/mp4" />
27        <source src="video/dunsmuir.ogv" type="video/ogg" />
28        <source src="video/dunsmuir.webm" type="video/webm" />
29        Your browser does not support the HTML5 video tag. Please update to a current browser.
30        </video>
31        <p> Fuery year Clearwater Kayak Outfitters sponsors several extreme kayaking adventure
```

11. **Save the file and continue to the next exercise.**

DEFINE VIDEO TAG ATTRIBUTES

The <video> tag supports a nuber of attributes, which control the way the video object appears in the page.

- **autoplay** causes the video to start playing as soon as it is ready.

- **controls** adds video controls to the video object on the page.

- **height** defines the height of the video player (in pixels).

- **loop** specifies that the video will start over again, every time it is finished.

- **muted** specifies that audio output of the video should be muted.

- **poster** defines an image to be shown while the video is downloading, or until the user hits the play button.

- **preload** determines when the video file should be downloaded.

- **src** defines the URL of the video file.

- **width** defines the width of the video player (in pixels).

Some of these attributes support values, added in quotes as you do for other attribute values. The autoplay, controls, loop, and muted attributes do not require specific values; simply adding the attribute to the opening video tag is sufficient.

1. **With video.html open, review the Design pane.**

    The video object is simply a small square. It is aligned to the right side of the containing element because the video tag selector defines the right float property.

2. **Turn on the Live view, then move the mouse over the video object.**

   When the Live view is active, you can see the first frame of the placed video. When you move the mouse over the video, you should notice that there are currently no controls to make the video play.

3. **Turn off the Live view.**

4. **In the Code pane, place the insertion point before the closing > of the opening video tag. Press the spacebar, then type:**

   `width="320" height="240"`

5. **Refresh the Design view.**

   By defining specific height and width attributes, the video object will always appear at the correct size, even before the video has finished downloading.

Note:

We are telling you what dimensions to use for this video. In a professional project, you would have to determine the correct width and height for a specific video file.

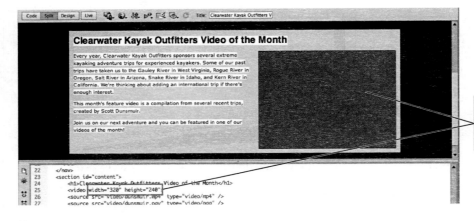

The width and height attributes define a specific size for the video object.

6. **With the insertion point at the end of the height attribute, press the spacebar, then type `preload="auto"`.**

   The **preload** attribute determines when the video file is downloaded. Using the auto value, the video downloads as soon as the page opens. You can use the none value to prevent the video from loading until a user plays the video.

```
24    <h1>Clearwater Kayak Outfitters Video of the Month</h1>
25    <video width="320" height="240" preload="auto">
26    <source src="video/dunsmuir.mp4" type="video/mp4" />
27    <source src="video/dunsmuir.ogv" type="video/ogg" />
```

7. **With the insertion point after the preload attribute, press the spacebar and then type `controls`.**

   This attribute does not need a specific value. When it is included in the video tag, video controls will appear on top of the video object.

```
24    <h1>Clearwater Kayak Outfitters Video of the Month</h1>
25    <video width="320" height="240" preload="auto" controls>
26    <source src="video/dunsmuir.mp4" type="video/mp4" />
27    <source src="video/dunsmuir.ogv" type="video/ogg" />
28    <source src="video/dunsmuir.webm" type="video/webm" />
29    Your browser does not support the HTML5 video tag. Please update to a current browser.
30    </video>
31    <p> Every year, Clearwater Kayak Outfitters sponsors several extreme kayaking adventure
```

8. **Turn on the Live view. Use the video controls to play the video.**

   If you move the mouse away from the video object, the controls disappear; they reappear when the mouse enters back into the video object area.

9. **Turn off the Live view, then save and close the active file.**

10. **Continue to the next stage of the project.**

Stage 5 Working with Widgets

In Project 3: Photographer's Web Site, you created a slideshow using a SWF file that was created in Adobe Flash. As you might know, however, Flash animations are not supported on all devices — specifically, mobile devices that use the iOS operating systems (iPhones and iPads). Adobe also recently stopped supporting the Flash Player plug-in for all mobile devices, which means Flash-based animations will likely fall out of common use in favor of a more universally supported method of delivering animation and interactivity. JavaScript is the most common solution to the problem.

   In Project 5: Cupcake Bakery CSS Site, you used Dreamweaver's built-in options to create a Spry Menu Bar. The menu functionality revolves around JavaScript code, which is automatically copied or created for you when you insert the Spry object.

   In this stage of the project, you are going to create an interactive slideshow that requires a complex block of JavaScript code to function properly. However, this is not a book about JavaScript; we focus instead on how to use Dreamweaver functionality to incorporate JavaScript elements without writing a single line of JavaScript code.

USE THE ADOBE WIDGET BROWSER

The Adobe Widget Browser provides access to a number of prebuilt widgets, which you can use to add complex interactive objects such as slideshows to an HTML5 page. These widgets do not rely on browser plug-ins or SWF files that are not supported on mobile devices. Because they are prebuilt, you can add these elements with little or no interaction with the underlying widget code.

1. **In Dreamweaver, click the Extend Dreamweaver button in the Application/ Menu bar. Choose Widget Browser in the pop-up menu.**

2. **Click the Sign In link in the top-right corner of the Adobe Widget Browser application.**

3. **When the Sign In screen appears, enter your Adobe ID email and password in the appropriate fields, then click the Sign In button.**

   If you do not already have an Adobe ID, click the Create Account button and follow the directions to create your own Adobe ID. There is no cost for this service.

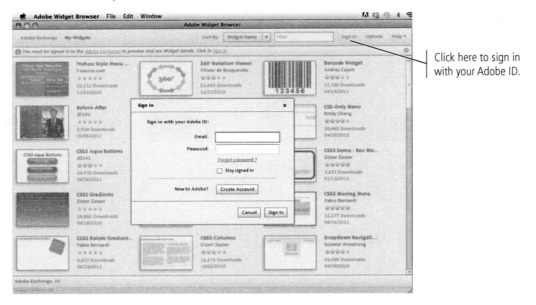

Click here to sign in with your Adobe ID.

4. **Scroll through the Adobe Widget Browser window to find the FlexSlider widget.**

The Adobe Widget Browser defaults to show a number of widgets that are available in the Adobe Exchange.

5. **Double-click the FlexSlider widget.**

   Double-clicking a specific widget shows more basic information about that widget.

6. **Click the Preview button in the top-right corner of the screen.**

The Preview option shows how the selected widget will appear in your page, using default preview images that are built into the widget code.

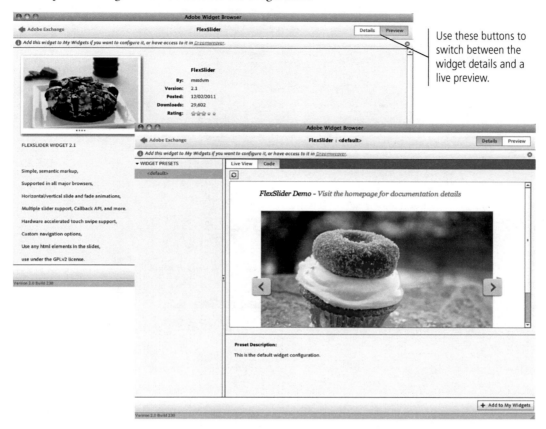

Use these buttons to switch between the widget details and a live preview.

7. **Click the Add to My Widgets button in the bottom-right corner of the window.**

If you want to customize the widget, or be able to access it in Dreamweaver, you have to add that widget to the My Widgets screen.

8. **Read the resulting licensing message and click Accept.**

Whenever you use elements that you did not personally create, make sure you understand and respect any licensing restrictions for those elements.

9. **Read the resulting message and click Go to My Widgets.**

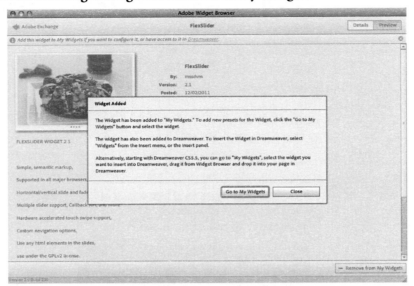

Unless you have added other widgets at another time, the FlexSlider is the only widget in the screen.

10. **Double-click the FlexSlider widget to show the details of the widget.**

After you have added a widget to My Widgets, you can customize the settings for the widget before adding it to a Web page.

After adding a widget to My Widgets, you can click the Configure button to customize a widget before placing it in Dreamweaver.

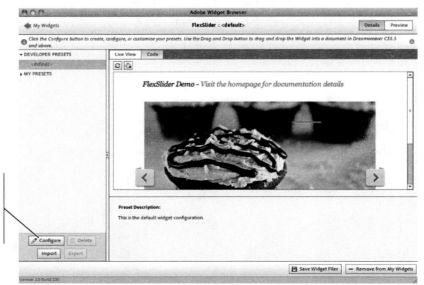

11. **Click the Configure button in the bottom-left corner of the screen.**

All of the behaviors you see in the preview are controlled by some rather complex JavaScript code.

Different widgets have different options; you can use this screen to change the settings without having to manually change the related code. The plain-English labels for each field clearly explain the various options for this widget.

If you change any of the settings for a widget, you can click the Save Preset button to save your choices as a preset version of the widget.

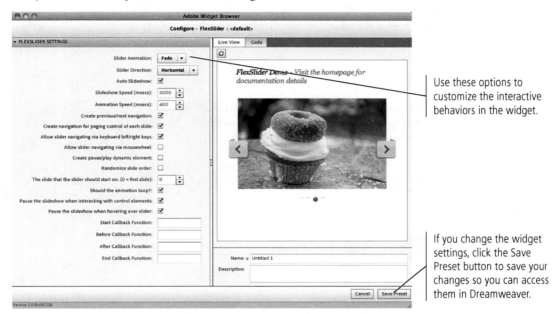

Use these options to customize the interactive behaviors in the widget.

If you change the widget settings, click the Save Preset button to save your changes so you can access them in Dreamweaver.

12. **Click Cancel, then close the Adobe Widget Browser window.**

Closing the window automatically quits the Adobe Widget Browser application and returns you to Dreamweaver.

13. **Continue to the next exercise.**

 ADD A WIDGET TO AN HTML5 PAGE

After a widget is added to the My Widgets screen, you can drag it from the Adobe Widget Browser screen into a Dreamweaver page. You can also use the Insert>Widget command to place a widget at the location of the insertion point, which we find to be a slightly more reliable method of placing a widget.

1. **With the Kayaking site open in the Dreamweaver Files panel, double-click the gallery.html file to open it in the Design view.**

2. **Select and delete the words "INSERT GALLERY HERE" from the main content area. Leave the insertion point in place of the placeholder text.**

Select and delete this placeholder text.

3. **Choose Insert>Widget. In the resulting dialog box, make sure FlexSlider 2.1 is seleted in the Widget menu, and make sure <default> is selected in the Preset menu.**

Note:

If you do not have any other widgets in your My Widgets screen, and did not customize the settings of the widget in the Adobe Widget Browser interface, these menus default to the correct options.

4. **Click OK to insert the widget at the location of the current insertion point.**

5. **Save the open file (gallery.html).**

6. **Review the Copy Dependent Files dialog box, then click OK.**

   JQuery widgets require a variety of files, including scripts and external CSS files. For your page to function properly, Dreamweaver automatically copies the required files into your site root folder when you save the file where the widget is placed.

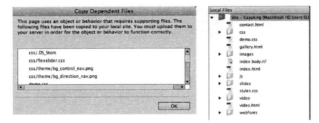

   As you can see, inserting the widget in the gallery page caused a problem; the page elements are no longer aligned properly.

   The Related Files bar at the top of the document window shows that two new CSS files are now related to the page.

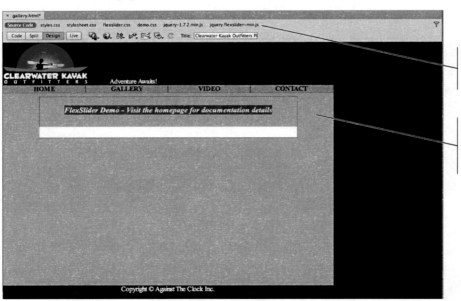

Several more files are now associated with the gallery.html file.

HTML elements no longer appear as you defined in your CSS selectors for this site.

7. **Open the CSS Styles panel. Expand flexslider.css in the panel and review the contents.**

   This file includes a number of selectors that relate specifically to various elements of the FlexSlider widget.

8. **Expand demo.css in the panel and review the contents.**

   This file contains a number of selectors that define options for a variety of HTML tags — including those you had already defined for your site pages.

Selectors in the flexsider.css file control the appearance of objects within the widget.

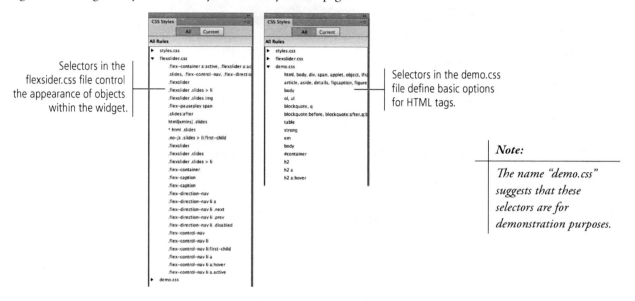

Selectors in the demo.css file define basic options for HTML tags.

Note:

The name "demo.css" suggests that these selectors are for demonstration purposes.

9. **With gallery.html open in Split view, scroll to the top of the Code pane.**

10. **Find and delete the statement that links the demo.css file to the page. Refresh the Design view.**

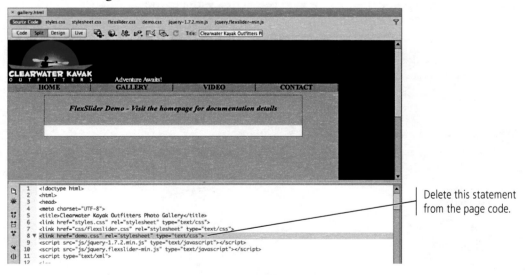

Delete this statement from the page code.

11. **In the Files panel, select and delete the demo.css file. Click Yes when asked if you want to confirm the deletion.**

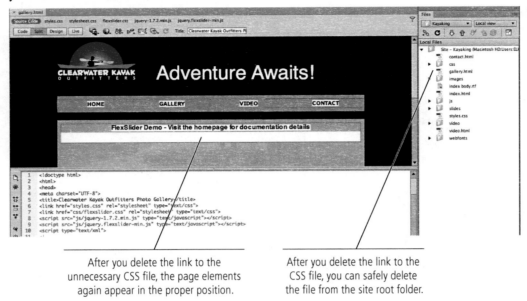

After you delete the link to the unnecessary CSS file, the page elements again appear in the proper position.

After you delete the link to the CSS file, you can safely delete the file from the site root folder.

12. **Save the file and continue to the next exercise.**

 CUSTOMIZE THE WIDGET CONTENT

As we said previously, the prebuilt widgets work with very little (if any) interaction with underlying JavaScript code. Of course, many of the widgets use placeholder content as an example — which you need to replace with the specific content you want to show in your page.

1. **With gallery.html open, activate the Live view. If you can't see the entire slideshow widget, click the Design button in the Document toolbar to close the Code pane.**

This widget uses photos of cupcakes as examples. You need to show a series of kayaking images, which means you need to change the content in the widget code.

Note:

There is no relation between the cupcakes in this example slideshow and the cupcake site you created in Project 5: Cupcake Bakery CSS Site.

2. **Turn off the Live view and make sure the Code pane is visible.**

3. **In the Design pane, place the insertion point in the first line of text in the content area ("FlexSlider Demo..."). Click the <h2> tag in the Tag Selector to select the entire element.**

   In the Code pane, you can see the highlighted code that is related to the active selection. Because this heading was placed when you inserted the widget, you know the highlighted code is part of the widget code; this method gives you a good idea of where the remaining code related to the widget content is located.

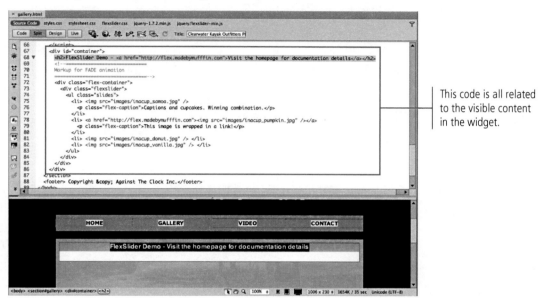

This code is all related to the visible content in the widget.

4. **Delete the highlighted h2 element and then refresh the Design pane.**

5. **Review the remaining code.**

   The opening <ul> tag has a class of "slides", which suggests the following list items are the individual slides in the slideshow.

   Each following <li> tag includes an <img> tag, confirming this statement.

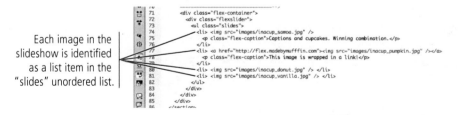

Each image in the slideshow is identified as a list item in the "slides" unordered list.

6. **Select and delete all but the last <li> tag in the widget content code.**

Note:

The first and second <li> tags in the sample code include a <p> tag with a class of "flex-caption"; if you want to include captions for your own photos, you should add the same code to each of your list items (and, of course, change the caption text to the appropriate content).

7. **In the Files panel, expand the slides folder.**

   This folder contains the image files that should appear in your gallery.

Note:

The images for this photo gallery are in the public domain. They were downloaded from www.PublicDomainPictures.net and www.public-domain-image.com.

8. **In the remaining <li> tag, change the src attribute to `slides/canoe-tour.jpg`.**

   Change the src attribute to the actual file for your slideshow.

9. **In the Code pane, add new <li> tags for each item in the slides folder.**

10. **Turn on the Live view and review the slideshow.**

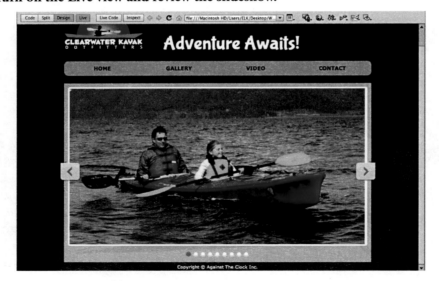

11. **Turn off the Live view. Save the file and close it.**

12. **Export a site definition named `Kayaking.ste` into your WIP>Kayaking folder, and then remove the site from Dreamweaver.**

1. The _____ HTML5 tag identifies information commonly found at the top of a page, such as a company logo and tag line.

2. The _____ HTML5 tag identifies a set of navigation links.

3. The _____ HTML5 tag identifies the information commonly found at the bottom of a page, such as the copyright owner.

4. The _____ property format can be used to define transparency for a color in a CSS3 selector.

5. The _____ CSS3 property can be used to create rounded corners on all four corners of an element.

6. The _____ CSS3 property can be used to create multiple columns of text within a single element.

7. True or false: A Web font is specific to the file that is open when it is installed in Dreamweaver. _____

8. The _____ in Dreamweaver must be used to preview the effects of applying a Web font to a page element.

9. The _____ attribute of the video tag allows a video file to download as soon as the page containing the tag is opened.

10. The _____ can be used to access prebuilt widgets for JavaScript objects such as slideshows.

1. Briefly explain the difference between structuring page content in HTML5 versus HTML 4/XHTML.

2. Briefly explain how to define a CSS3 property for multiple browsers.

3. Briefly explain how to define a <video> tag, including multiple formats for different browsers.

Portfolio Builder Project

Use what you learned in this project to complete the following freeform exercise.
Carefully read the art director and client comments, then create your own design to meet the needs of the project.
Use the space below to sketch ideas; when finished, write a brief explanation of your reasoning behind your final design.

art director comments

The local Athletic Boosters Association has hired you to create a Web site for the various sports teams that compete in the region. Before you complete the entire site, you should design an easy-to-navigate site prototype that features at least two different teams. This will allow you to present your ideas for highlighting individual sports, as well as overall site navgation.

To complete this project, you should:

❏ Identify two local sports teams that you will include in the site prototype.

❏ Take or find photos to use on the site.

❏ If possible, incorporate video into the site.

❏ Find or write any necessary copy to introduce the teams you are featuring.

client comments

Our local sports teams — high school, intramural, and even semi-professional — have been very successful in the past few years. We have had several state championships in the area, and the future looks bright. We're hoping to raise more money to help the youth league teams in the area to continue the tradition.

We would like to design a new Web site that highlights the different local teams and their achievements. We think photos and videos tell the best story, although each team should certainly be identified and introduced.

project justification

_____
_____
_____
_____
_____
_____
_____
_____
_____
_____
_____
_____
_____
_____

HTML5 is the next generation of Web design, intended to adapt the underlying page code to better serve both the way designers work and the way users browse the Internet. This project introduced you to the new HTML5 tags that you can use to structure your pages without requiring a complicated series of nested divs. Coupled with new CSS3 selectors and embedded Web fonts, you now have far greater creative control over the structure and appearance of Web page content.

This project also highlighted a number of issues you should understand when you work with HTML5. First, Dreamweaver is not yet optimized to apply many of the HTML5/CSS3 features through user interface components like the Properties panel or Insert bar; to successfully use HTML5 features in Dreamweaver, you will be required to work directly in the page code.

Second, HTML5 is not yet an official standard and different browsers require different code to function properly; you should remember to verify your code and include the required variations so that your pages will work in as many current browsers as possible. Also, keep in mind that older browsers do not support HTML5/CSS3; over time we can expect older, non-HTML5 browsers to fall out of use but until then, some users will not be able to see the content as you intend it to be displayed.

Use HTML5 tags to define various page sections

Define multiple articles within a single section

Use CSS3 properties to define rounded corners, color transparency, and multiple columns

Use Web fonts to control the appearance of type

Add a widget to create a JavaScript slideshow

Place video directly into an HTML5 page

BLVD Fluid Grid Site

You have been hired by the Chamber of Commerce to create a new Web page for the city of Lancaster, California. You are going to create a single page that adapts to multiple display sizes so that the page looks good on both desktop and mobile devices.

This project incorporates the following skills:

❑ Create a fluid grid page

❑ Work with fluid grid layout divs

❑ Work with fluid grid layout div content

❑ Use CSS to control fluid grid content

❑ Restrict element height and overflow

❑ Use the CSS Transitions panel

❑ Define transition properties for a selector

client comments

In the past two years, millions of dollars have been spent to revitalize the downtown area. Dozens of new businesses have opened, including a number of specialty shops and restaurants.

Our area is visited by a large number of travellers, whether they are here for work or for one of the various national sports tournaments we host. We're also in the immediate path for people heading to the mountains from Los Angeles.

We want you to design a new Web page that will help introduce The BLVD to the digital community.

art director comments

Designing responsive Web pages can be complicated, but Dreamweaver CS6 makes it a bit easier than most other methods — and it's certainly better than designing multiple versions of the same page.

Your existing knowledge of CSS and HTML are going to be extremely important to understanding how Dreamweaver's fluid grid technology works. It can seem a bit confusing at first, but once you've created a couple of fluid grid pages it becomes easier to understand.

After you finish the fluid grid layout, you should add some interactivity to the page. Again, Dreamweaver makes it fairly easy to create this interactivity directly in the page as long as you understand CSS.

project objectives

To complete this project, you will:

- ❏ Create a fluid grid page
- ❏ Work with fluid grid layout divs
- ❏ Work with fluid grid layout div content
- ❏ Use CSS to control fluid grid content
- ❏ Restrict element height and overflow
- ❏ Use the CSS Transitions panel
- ❏ Define transition properties for a selector

Stage 1 Working with Fluid Grids

Web designers have always had to deal with different display sizes when creating pages. For example, different users might have a 30″ desktop monitor or an 11″ laptop; a good Web page should work effectively on both size displays, as well as anything in between. The explosive growth of digital tablets and handheld mobile devices (smartphones) further compounds the problem of designing for multiple display sizes, especially given the much smaller display sizes and multiple orientations of these devices.

With HTML5 and CSS3, Web designers now have the opportunity (and, many argue, the responsibility) to create pages that are optimized for viewing on whatever device a user chooses. Rather than creating multiple versions of a Web site for specific types of devices, fluid grids provide a solution to the need for **responsive design** — individual pages that adapt to suit the medium that is used to display them.

The fluid grid capabilities introduced in Dreamweaver CS6 make it relatively easy to create responsive Web pages. However, working with fluid grids is not a task for beginners. Although the technology built into Dreamweaver CS6 makes responsive design far easier than ever before, you still need a solid foundational knowledge of CSS before you can efficiently and effectively take advantage of the available tools. You should understand how div tags work, and how to create the various types of CSS selectors to control the appearance of different page elements. You should also have a good working knowledge of basic Dreamweaver tasks, such as accessing the page code of various files (including the page source code and the code in related files).

 ## CREATE A FLUID GRID PAGE

To function properly regardless of the display size, elements in a responsive Web page need to be defined based on percentages rather than using specific fixed sizes. When the display size changes, elements that are defined by percentages can dynamically resize as necessary based on the active display size.

A fluid grid page in Dreamweaver uses percentages to build a page grid:

- The overall page width is defined as a percentage of the available display space.

- A fluid grid has a defined number of columns, which have a width defined as a percentage of the page width.

- The space between columns is defined as a percentage of column width.

1. **Download DW6_RF_Project7.zip from the Student Files Web page.**

2. **Expand the ZIP archive in your WIP folder (Macintosh) or copy the archive contents into your WIP folder (Windows).**

   This results in a folder named **BLVD**, which contains the files you need for this project.

3. **In Dreamweaver, create a new site named BLVD, using your WIP>BLVD folder as the site root folder.**

   If necessary, refer to the first exercises in Project 1: Bistro Site Organization, for more detailed instructions.

4. Choose File>New Fluid Grid Layout.

You can also choose File>New, then choose Fluid Grid Layout in the left column of the New Document dialog box.

When you create a fluid grid layout, you can define the number of columns that represent the layout in each of three basic sizes — Mobile, Tablet, and Desktop. Because each basic size can have a different number of columns, you can more easily create layouts that best suit the display sizes of the various devices.

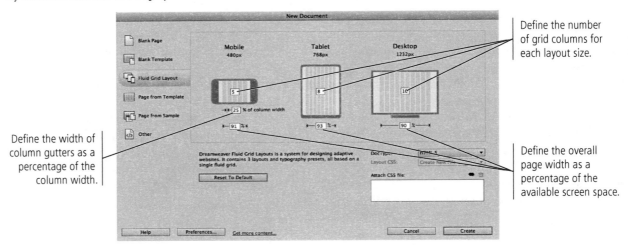

Define the number of grid columns for each layout size.

Define the width of column gutters as a percentage of the column width.

Define the overall page width as a percentage of the available screen space.

5. In the Mobile icon, change the number of columns to 3.

The percentage fields below each icon define the amount of the screen size that the columns will occupy. Using the default amounts, for example, the 3 columns you defined for the Mobile device size will occupy 91% of the available display width.

6. In the Tablet icon, change the number of columns to 6.

7. In the Desktop icon, change the number of columns to 8.

8. Below the Mobile icon, change the Column Gutter field to 10%.

The column gutters, or the spaces between each column, are defined as a percentage of the column width. In other words, you are creating a page with gutters that are 10% of the actual column size.

If you change the size of a browser window on a desktop computer, the column widths adapt to whatever size is necessary based on the available space in the browser window; the gutter widths also adapt based on the current column width.

It is important to understand that the three available sizes in the dialog box are *maximum* widths. If you make a browser window smaller than the stated width of a tablet device (768 px), elements in the browser window will adapt to show the layout that you define for tablet devices.

Note:

You should carefully plan your layout designs before you design a fluid grid layout in Dreamweaver. At the time of this writing, there is no easy way to change the number of columns in a layout after it is created. If you find that the columns you first define do not meet your needs, it is actually easier to start over with a new fluid grid page than it is to modify the number of columns in an existing layout.

9. **Leave the overall width fields at their default values, then click Create.**

The DocType menu defaults to HTML5, which is required for fluid-grid technology to work properly.

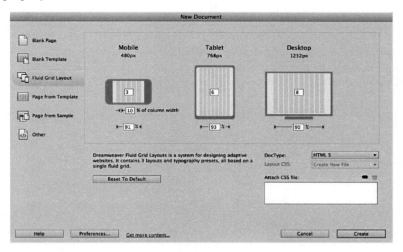

10. **In the resulting dialog box, change the file name to `layout.css`. Navigate to your WIP>BLVD>css folder as the target location, then click Save.**

Fluid grids are built using the capabilities of CSS3. When you create a new fluid grid page, a new CSS file is automatically created to contain the layout settings you just defined. In this step you are simply assigning the new file a name and telling Dreamweaver where you want it to be stored.

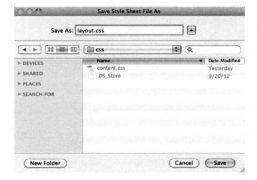

11. **Choose File>Save. In the resulting dialog box, change the file name to `index.html`. Navigate to WIP>BLVD as the target location for the file, then click Save.**

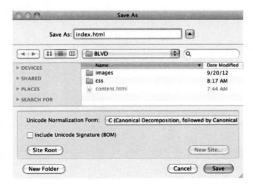

12. Review the Copy Dependent Files information, then click Copy.

The two files listed in this dialog box are required to make your fluid grid layout function properly. When you save the fluid grid layout page, Dreamweaver automatically copies them into your site root folder.

The boilerplate.css file includes a number of selectors that normalize the various HTML tags, which helps to make sure the pages work consistently across various browsers and media types. The respond.min.js file is a JavaScript file that helps provide some of the responsive design functionality in older browsers that do not support HTML5.

13. Review the new file in the Design pane.

When you create a new fluid grid layout page, the Design view default to show the Mobile size layout.

The pink columns represent the columns you defined when you created the page. Each fluid grid layout div has a semi-transparent green background.

These overlays are not visible in the final file; you can hide them by toggling off Fluid Grid Layout Guides in the Visual Aids menu.

Two divs are created on the new page, the second (nested) div includes important information as the placeholder content:

> Use Insert Panel for additional Fluid Grid Layout Div tags. Note: All Layout Div tags must be inserted directly inside the "gridContainer" div tag. Nested layout divs are not currently supported.

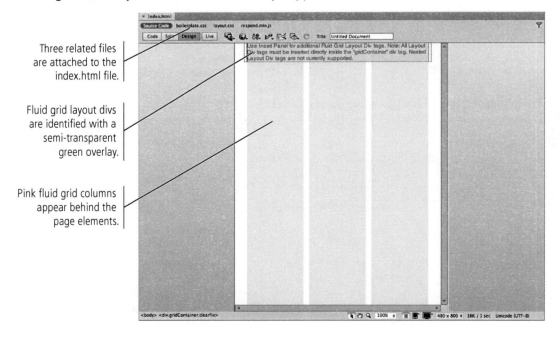

Three related files are attached to the index.html file.

Fluid grid layout divs are identified with a semi-transparent green overlay.

Pink fluid grid columns appear behind the page elements.

14. **Click the Code button in the Document toolbar to show the page code for this file.**

The opening and closing <body> tags include two divs. The outer div (div class="gridContainer clearfix") is the one referred to in the placeholder text of the second, nested div (div id="LayoutDiv1").

The outer div contains all fluid grid layout divs that you add to the page.

The inner div is the first fluid grid layout div, which was added by default when you created the page.

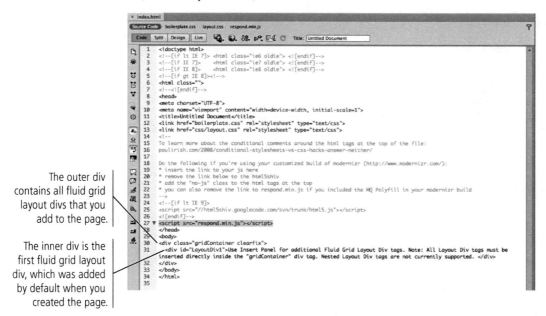

15. **Click the Design button to return to the Design view.**

16. **At the bottom of the document window, click the Tablet Size icon.**

The three buttons represent the three different layouts you defined in the New Document dialog box. You can use these buttons to navigate from one layout to another in the Design pane.

In the Tablet layout, you can see the six columns that you defined for this size display. The visible div on the page includes the same placeholder content that you saw in the Mobile view.

Note:

An asterisk in one of the button icons means that you have not yet looked at that layout.

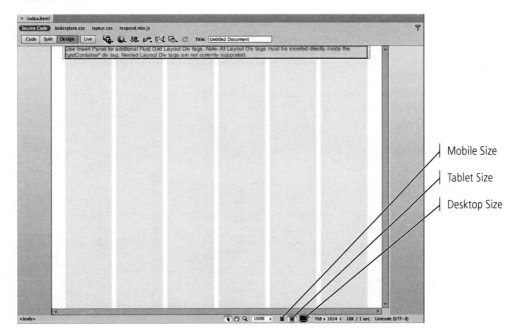

Mobile Size

Tablet Size

Desktop Size

17. **Click the Split button to show the page code in addition to the Design view.**

This step illustrates an important point about working with fluid grids. The HTML page code is exactly the same for all three variations of the layout — which means the *content* in various layout divs will be the same regardless of which layout is being displayed. The position and appearance of that content is controlled entirely through CSS.

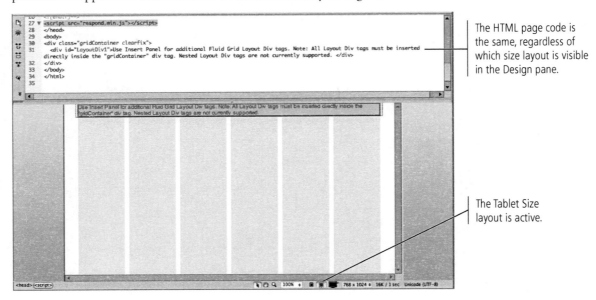

The HTML page code is the same, regardless of which size layout is visible in the Design pane.

The Tablet Size layout is active.

18. **Return the page to the Design view, then continue to the next exercise.**

 WORK WITH FLUID GRID LAYOUT DIVS

Fluid grid layout divs are similar to regular divs, but the process for creating them is slightly different. Fluid grid layout divs are inserted sequentially inside the outermost container div (gridContainer) that is created when you first create the page. You can then use the underlying page grid to change the width of each layout div. Layout divs can be forced to begin a new row, or allowed to occupy the same row as preceding divs if enough space exists in that row.

1. **With index.html open, click the Desktop button at the bottom of the document window.**

2. **Open the CSS Styles panel and expand the layout.css file.**

This file contains the selectors that control the position of default divs in the various layouts. As you can see, there are several selectors of the same name.

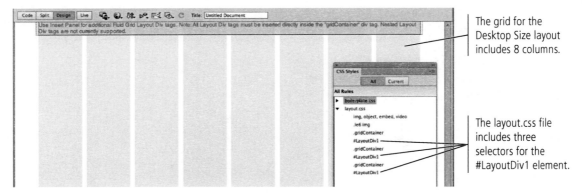

The grid for the Desktop Size layout includes 8 columns.

The layout.css file includes three selectors for the #LayoutDiv1 element.

3. Click layout.css in the Related Files bar to show the CSS code in the Code pane.

Line 29 of the CSS file includes a comment, which indicates that the following styles are for the Mobile Layout. Two selectors (.gridContainer and #LayoutDiv1) appear after the comment.

The .gridContainer selector defines the page width as a percentage of the available screen space (which you specified in the New Document dialog box when you defined the fluid grid options for each layout size).

The #LayoutDiv1 selector defines the default div element that is automatically added when you create a fluid grid page.

On Line 46, another comment indicates that the following selectors relate to the Tablet Layout. The statement on Line 48, called a **media query**, restricts these selectors to screens with a minimum width of 481 pixels.

You should notice that the selectors in both sections have the exact same names. The information defined in the second set of selectors will override the previously defined information when the media screen size is 481 pixels or wider.

On Line 63, another comment shows that the next selectors apply to the Desktop Layout. The media query on Line 65 restricts the following selectors to displays that are 769 px or wider.

Again, the selectors in this section have the exact same names as the selectors in the two previous sections. They will override the previous selectors when the media query requirement (min-width: 769px) is met.

Note:

The first group of selectors does not require a media query statement because they will apply until the first media query statement is triggered.

The gray lines are comments, telling you what each section of the code is for.

These selectors define the default properties for the .gridContainer and #LayoutDiv1 elements.

Media queries specify when the following selectors will apply.

Selectors within a media query are surrounded by curly braces.

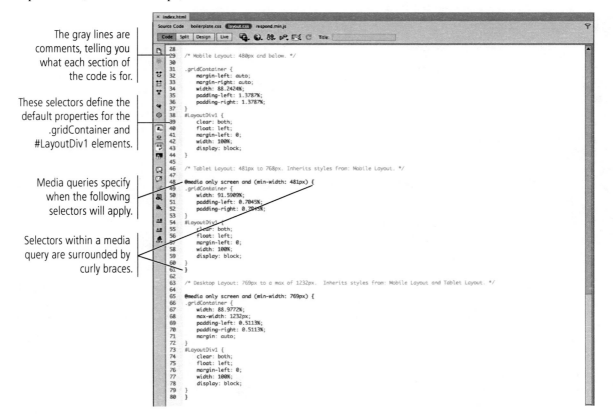

4. **In the Code pane, change the names of all three #LayoutDiv1 selectors to #header.**

This step is not necessary for the page to function properly, but it is a good idea to use indicative names rather than the generic default names. When you do this, however, it is important to change the name of all three selectors, and to use the exact same name in all three sections.

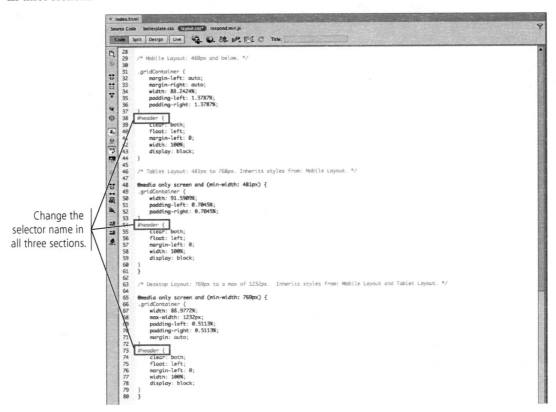

Change the selector name in all three sections.

5. **In the Related Files bar, click the Source Code button to show the page's HTML code.**

6. **Near the bottom of the page code, change the ID attribute of the LayoutDiv1 element to header.**

When you change the name of an ID selector that has already been applied to an element in the HTML page, you also have to remember to change the ID attribute of the element in the page code.

Change the div id attribute in the page source code.

Although fluid grids are based on the capabilities of HTML5, you can't use HTML5 tags such as <header> to define the various sections of a page. You must use fluid grid layout divs, and use ids to identify the different divs.

7. **Activate the Split view. In the Code pane, place the insertion point after the closing </div> tag of the header div.**

As the placeholder text in the div tells you, new layout divs must be added inside the gridContainer div. Using the Code pane to place the insertion point is the easiest way to make sure that the new divs will be added in the correct location.

8. **Open the Insert panel in Layout mode, then click the Insert Fluid Grid Layout Div Tag button.**

You can also choose Insert>Layout Objects>Fluid Grid Layout Div Tag.

The insertion point is here.

Fluid grid layout divs must be inside the closing tag of the gridContainer div.

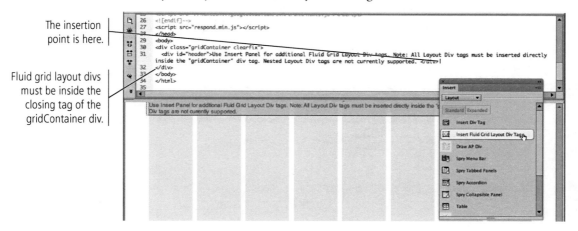

9. **In the resulting dialog box, type `intro` in the ID field. Leave the Start New Row option checked, then click OK.**

If the Start New Row option is not checked, the div can occupy the same row as the previous divs if those take up less than the full page width. (This will make more sense shortly.)

This option is checked by default for every new fluid grid layout div.

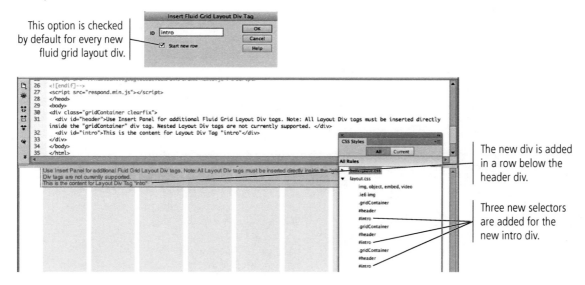

The new div is added in a row below the header div.

Three new selectors are added for the new intro div.

10. **Repeat Steps 8–9 to add four more fluid grid layout div tags to the page:**

ID	Start New Row
shopping	Checked
entertainment	Not checked
events	Not checked
footer	Checked

In the Design pane, you can see the six divs you created. By default, each occupies the full page width. Two divs — entertainment and events — are slightly indented from the left edge of the page; this identifies divs that are allowed to move up to share a row with preceding divs.

The CSS Styles panel shows three selectors for each of your new divs. As with the default divs, the selectors are created for each possible layout size.

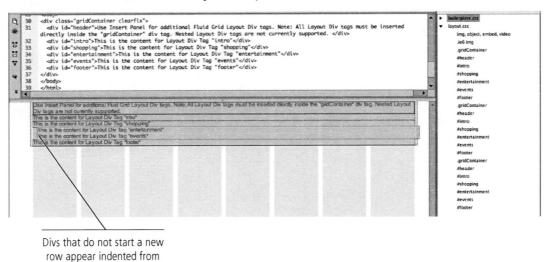

Divs that do not start a new row appear indented from the edge of the grid.

11. **In the Design pane, click to select the header div.**

When a fluid grid layout div is selected, handles on the left side of the div can be used to shift the div right on the page (by increasing the margin-left property for that div).

The handles on the right side of the div can be used to change the div width.

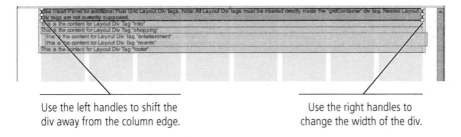

Use the left handles to shift the div away from the column edge.

Use the right handles to change the width of the div.

12. **Click any of the right handles and drag left until the cursor feedback shows that the div will occupy two columns.**

You do not need to be precise when you drag the handles; the width percentage (and number of columns) snaps to the nearest column edge as you drag the handle.

After you resize the div width, its height automatically changes as necessary based on the content that exists inside the div.

13. **Click the intro div to select it. Click any of the Resize Div handles on the right side of the intro div and drag until the div occupies only 6 columns.**

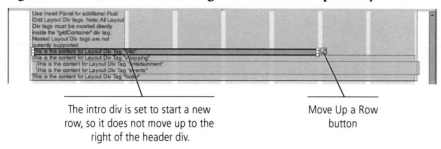

The intro div is set to start a new row, so it does not move up to the right of the header div.

Move Up a Row button

14. **On the right side of the intro div, click the Move Up a Row button.**

When you created this div, you defined it to start a new row. You can always use the Move Up a Row button to allow a div to occupy the same row as the preceding div if enough space is available.

When a div is already allowed to exist in the same row as another div, the Move Up a Row button is replaced by the Starts New Row button. Clicking this button forces the selected div into a new row.

Note:

Allowing multiple divs in the same row or forcing them into separate rows is accomplished by changing the clear property of the divs.

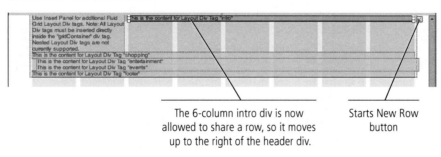

The 6-column intro div is now allowed to share a row, so it moves up to the right of the header div.

Starts New Row button

15. **Click the shopping div to select it, then use the Resize Div handles to change it to two columns.**

16. **Repeat Step 15 for the entertainment and events divs.**

The shopping div is set to start a new row, but the entertainment and events divs are allowed to share the row with the shopping div based on your selections when you created the divs.

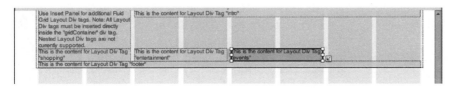

17. Select the shopping div, then click the Move Up a Row button.

The underlying fluid grid columns determine where the various divs *can* go. This layout has eight columns, and the header div is only two columns wide. The intro div occupies six columns, so the two-column shopping div will not fit into the same row as the intro div. But by allowing the shopping div to occupy the same row as preceding divs, the row beginning with the shopping div moves up to the right of the header div.

Note:

Keep in mind that, by changing the div widths and positions, you are changing the layout.css file and not the HTML page code. If you want to use the Undo function, make sure the CSS file is visible in the Code pane, and the Code pane — not the Design pane — is in focus.

18. Click the Tablet Size button at the bottom of the document window.

In the previous steps, you changed the size and position of the layout divs in the Desktop Size layout.

Remember, the layout.css file includes different selectors for each div *in each layout*. The changes you made in the previous steps only affected the divs in the Desktop layout. Dreamweaver's fluid grid layout technology allows you to create separate layouts for each layout size.

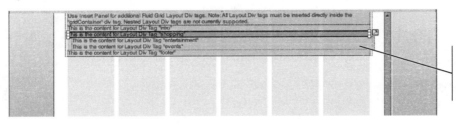

Changes to the Desktop Size layout did not affect the divs in the Tablet Size layout.

19. With the Tablet Size layout visible in the Design pane, make the following changes to the existing layout divs:

header	**Change the width to 1 columns**
intro	**Change the width to 5 columns** **Click the Move Up a Row button**
shopping	**Change the width to 2 columns**
entertainment	**Change the width to 2 columns**
events	**Change the width to 2 columns**

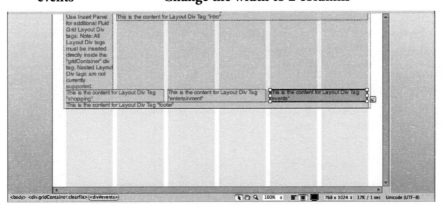

20. **Click the Mobile Size button at the bottom of the document window, then make the following changes to the existing layout divs:**

header	**Change the width to 1 column**
intro	**Change the width to 2 columns**
	Click the Move Up a Row button
entertainment	**Click the Click to Align DIV with Grid button**
events	**Click the Click to Align DIV with Grid button**

If a div is allowed to exist in the same row as another but appears below that row, the Click to Align DIV with Grid button appears on the left side of the div. Clicking this button forces the div to start a new row.

Click to Align
DIV with Grid
button

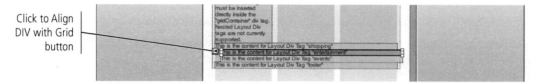

By aligning the entertainment and events divs to the grid, each of these divs now begins a new row.

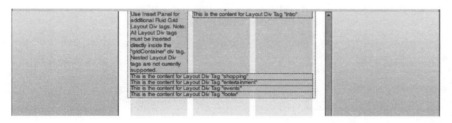

21. **Choose File>Save All.**

When you work with fluid grid layouts, you are dealing with a number of different files — the HTML page, at least two CSS files, and a JavaScript file. The Save All command makes sure that all involved files are saved in a single command; you do not need to activate each related file and save it separately.

22. **Continue to the next exercise.**

 ## WORK WITH FLUID GRID LAYOUT DIV CONTENT

As we explained previously, the HTML page code is exactly the same for all three variations of a fluid grid layout; the content in various layout divs will be the same regardless of which layout is being displayed. The position and appearance of that content is controlled entirely through CSS.

1. **With index.html open, make the Desktop Size layout visible in the Design pane.**

2. **Select and delete the placeholder text in the header div.**

No height property is defined for the layout divs, so the header div collapses to the smallest possible size based on its content (nothing, at this point). The shopping div moves beneath the header div because the current height of the header div does not allow a second row to its right.

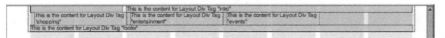

3. **Expand the images folder in the Files panel. Click the `blvd-logo90.png` file and drag it into the header div. When prompted, define `The BLVD` as alternate text for the image.**

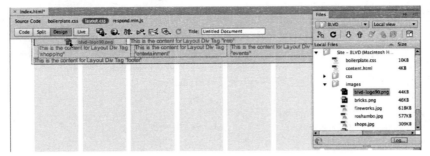

4. **Switch the document window to Split view and review the page source code.**

   When you place an image into a fluid grid div, Dreamweaver does not automatically add height and width attributes. This is important because the image needs to be able to scale to fit the div element based on the screen size.

   If you resize a browser window on a desktop computer, the various layout divs will scale based on the percentages that you allow them to occupy. In the layout.css file, the **img, object, embed, video** selector defines the **max-width** property of 100%, which means those elements (images, etc.) will occupy 100% of the width of the containing element.

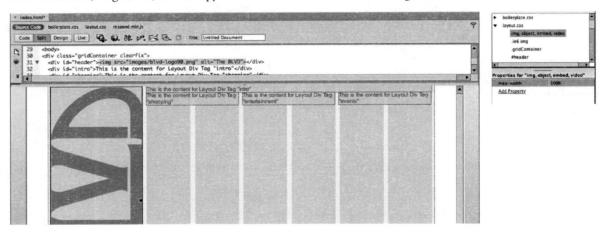

5. **Choose File>Save All, then preview the file in the browser of your choice.**

6. **Click and drag the bottom-right corner of the browser window to resize the window.**

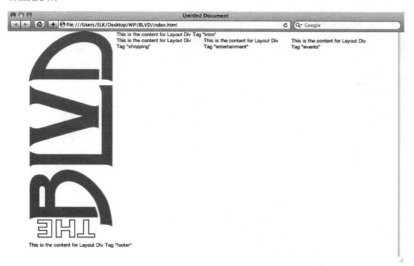

As you make the window smaller, you can see the placed image get smaller — as we explained, it occupies 100% of the defined column width in the containing div.

When the browser window is less than 769 pixels wide, the layout changes to show the structure that you defined for a Tablet Size.

When the browser window is less than 481 pixels wide, the layout again changes to show the structure that you defined for the Mobile Size.

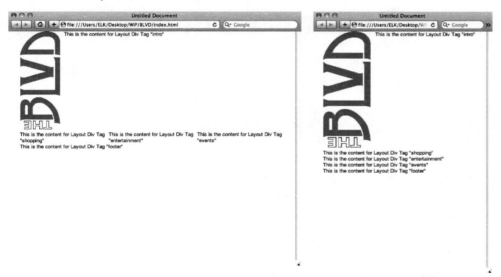

Although you only placed the logo in the Desktop Size layout, it appears in all three variations. Remember, the fluid grid layouts adjust the *appearance* of content and not the content itself. Anything you place in a div in one layout will appear in the same div in all three variations.

7. **Close the browser window and return to Dreamweaver.**

8. Using the Files panel, open the file `content.html`.

This file includes the content that you need to place into the various divs in the page. Basic tags such as headings and paragraphs have already been applied.

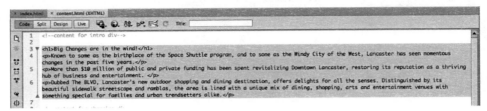

9. Using the Code pane, select and copy the content on Lines 3–6.

You can work in Code view or Split view to complete these steps.

10. Make the index.html page active in the document window. In the Code pane, select and delete the placeholder text for the intro div.

If you paste the copied code into the Design pane, the existing tags do not function properly. Make sure you paste the content into the Code pane.

11. With the insertion point still in the intro div (in the Code pane), paste the content you copied in Step 9.

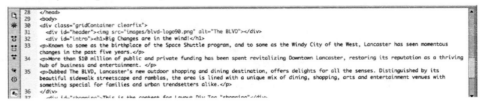

12. Repeat Steps 9–11 to copy the various sections of content from the content.html file and paste them into the appropriate divs in the index.html file.

Each section in the content.html file is identified by comments in the page code.

13. Close the content.html file.

After you paste all of the required content, you could delete the content.html file, or move it into a cloaked folder to prevent it from being uploaded as part of the final site.

14. Refresh the Design pane and review the page.

15. **In the Document toolbar, open the Visual Aids menu and choose Hide All Visual Aids.**

You can also uncheck the Fluid Grid Layout Guides option to turn off only the pink columns, green div overlays, and fluid grid div handles.

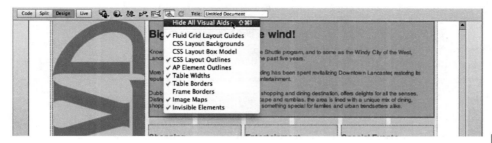

When the visual aids are hidden, you can better see the page content.

Note:

Unlike other layout guides, Fluid Grid Layout Guides can be visible even when the Live view is active in the Design pane.

16. **Using the buttons at the bottom of the document window, review the two other layout variations.**

Once actual content is placed into the various divs, it becomes easier to see the effects of the different layout arrangements.

17. **Choose File>Save All, then continue to the next exercise.**

USE CSS TO CONTROL FLUID GRID CONTENT

As you saw in the previous exercise, elements in the page content use default formatting that is defined in the boilerplate.css and layout.css files.

You do not want to modify the boilerplate.css selectors. Put simply, you should just leave this file alone.

You could simply define new selectors in layout.css file. However, you should already understand the importance of separating and simplifying your code as much as possible. If you add new selectors to the layout.css file, it is very easy to become confused about exactly what goes where.

Instead, you can attach another CSS file to store selectors for the appearance of various elements. This keeps content-related selectors separate from layout-related selectors, which will make it easier to find and modify exactly what you need if you (or someone else) want to make changes later.

Note:

The boilerplate.css file is added to the site when you save the fluid grid layout page. Leave this file alone.

1. **With index.html open, make the Desktop Size layout visible in the Design pane.**

2. **Click the Attach Style Sheet button at the bottom of the CSS Styles panel.**

3. **Navigate to the file content.css in your WIP>BLVD>css folder, then click Open. Make sure the file will be added as a Link, then click OK.**

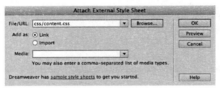

In the Related Files bar, you can see that the new CSS file is now included as related to the index.html file. It is third in the list, which means any selector properties in this file will override the properties of same-named selectors in the first two CSS files.

This file includes a number of selectors that define the appearance of your page's content.

4. **Place the insertion point in the "Shopping" heading.**

5. **In the Tag Selector, Control/right-click the `<div#shopping>` tag and choose Set Class>container.**

   The tag and compound selectors in the content.css file are automatically applied to the appropriate page elements. Class selectors only apply to elements where they are intentionally added, so you have to add this class to each of the three content divs.

   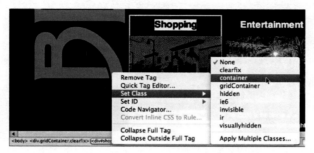

6. **Repeat Step 5 to apply the .container class to the div#entertainment and div#events elements.**

   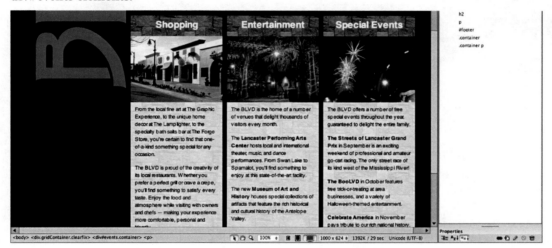

7. **With the Design pane active, click the Multiscreen button in the Document toolbar and choose Multiscreen Preview in the menu.**

   This option allows you to review all three layouts at once.

   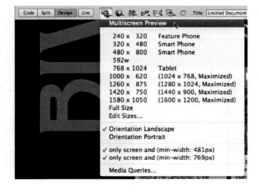

The point of using fluid grid layout is to create files that adapt to the size of the media being used. By previewing the page at different sizes, you can see that some settings — specifically, font sizes — do not ideally suit all three layout sizes.

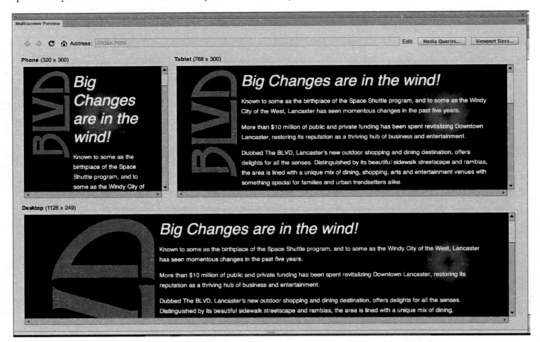

You saw earlier that the layout.css file used media query statements to define different div settings for different layouts. You can use the same technique to define different appearances for content depending on the layout size being viewed.

8. **Close the Multiscreen Preview window.**

If you have a large enough monitor, or if you have two tiled monitors connected to your computer, you can leave the Multiscreen Preview open while you work, then click the Refresh button to immediately preview the results of your changes in all three layout sizes.

9. **Click content.css in the Related Files bar to show that file in the Code pane.**

Before you add media queries to a CSS file, you should remember that selectors apply until they are overridden by a later selector. You should then think about what you need to accomplish.

A media query statement uses the min-width statement to say:

> "The previous properties apply until the media width is X pixels or larger. Then use these properties."

So, the first selectors in the file should define the options for the smallest screen size (the Mobile Layout) and then define different selectors for each successive layout size.

Note:

As a rule of thumb, start small and work your way larger when you define different selectors for different media.

10. **Locate the h1 selector, and change the font-size property value to 20px.**

11. **Locate the p selector, and change the font-size property value to 10px.**

12. Locate the **.container p** selector, and change the font-size property value to **10px**.

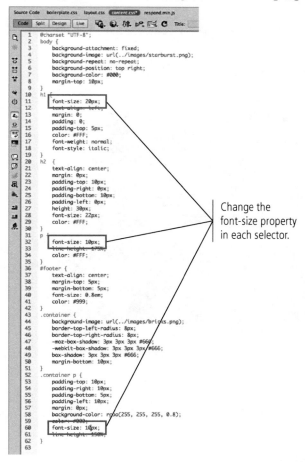

Change the font-size property in each selector.

13. Place the insertion point at the end of the existing selectors and press Return/Enter to add a new line to the code. Type:

```
@media only screen and (min-width: 481px) {
    h1 {
        font-size: 36px;
    }
    p {
        font-size: 14px;
    }
    .container p {
        font-size: 12px;
    }
}
```

The original selectors defined a number of properties for these selectors. You only want to change the font size based on the media size, so you do not need to include all of the properties that were included in the original selectors.

Note:

In this project you are allowing all layouts larger than the Mobile Layout to use the same property values. If you want to define different properties for elements in the Desktop Layout, you would need to add another media query statement and additional selectors.

14. **Click in the Design pane to make it active, then open the Multiscreen Preview again and review the results.**

   If you left the Multiscreen Preview open, click the Refresh button to see the effects of your new styles.

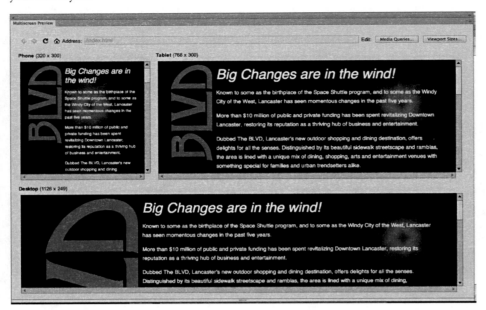

15. **Close the Multiscreen Preview.**

16. **Choose File>Save All, then preview the page in a browser. Resize the browser window and preview the three different layouts.**

17. **Close the browser window and return to Dreamweaver.**

18. **Continue to the next stage of the project.**

Stage 2 Creating CSS3 Transitions

Before HTML5 and CSS3, animating something in a Web page required an external file created in a separate application (such as Adobe Flash), or a script that would manage the change (such as the JavaScript that drives Spry objects like menu bars).

New features in HTML5 and CSS3 allow you to create animations directly in the HTML page without the need for Flash or JavaScript. This has several advantages. First, no plug-ins are required to support the animation because all of the changes (called transitions) are driven by CSS. Second, CSS3 transitions are fairly easy to create if you have a basic understanding of CSS selectors and properties.

Dreamweaver CS6 makes it very easy to define CSS3 transitions based on the selectors in a file. In this stage of the project, you will use two different methods to animate specific elements and properties.

RESTRICT ELEMENT HEIGHT AND OVERFLOW

CSS selectors give you extensive control over the elements on a page. In this exercise, you are going to force the three .container elements to be a specific height, showing only the headings until a user rolls the mouse over those elements. In the next exercise, you will add the transition that makes the overflow content visible when a mouse hovers over the element.

1. **With index.html open, turn on the Live view.**

2. **In the Code pane, locate the code for the .container class selector (in the content.css file).**

3. **Place the insertion point at the end of the last property value, then press Return/Enter to add a new line to the selector code.**

4. **Add two new properties to the selector:**

   ```
   max-height: 50px;
   overflow: hidden;
   ```

   The **max-height** property allows an object to extend *up to* the defined height. This is different than the **height** property, which defines a specific, fixed height for the element.

   However, by default, an element will occupy as much space as necessary to display all of its content. To hide the overflow content (called clipping the content), you also have to add the overflow property.

   The **overflow** property determines what happens when an element contains more content than will fit into the defined space. Possible values for the overflow property include:
   - **auto** adds scrollbars to the element only if some content is clipped.
   - **hidden** clips the overflow content; only content that fits into the defined space will be visible.
   - **inherit** applies the overflow value of the parent element.
   - **scroll** adds scrollbars to the element even if there is no clipped content.
   - **visible** causes all content to be visible, even if it appears outside the element boundaries.

Note:

The max-height property is not available in the CSS Rule Definition dialog box, so you have to type this code manually.

Note:

If you turn off the Live view, the Design pane does not reflect the overflow property, which allows you to select the overflow content in the Design pane as long as the Live view is not active.

5. **Refresh the Design view and review the results of the new properties.**

It doesn't matter which size layout you are viewing; the height of the .container objects changes in all three versions.

You are editing the code in the content.css file.

Live view is active.

Add these two properties to the .container selector.

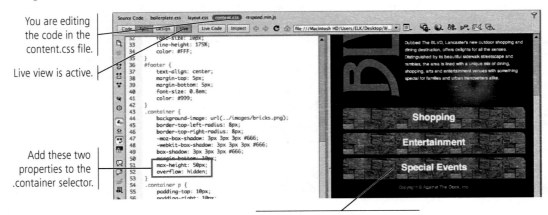

The two new selectors combine to restrict the three .container elements to show only the headings.

6. **Save all files, then continue to the next exercise.**

 ## USE THE CSS TRANSITIONS PANEL

In this exercise, you will use the CSS Transitions panel to show the overflow content of the .container elements when a user's mouse hovers over them. Dreamweaver's CSS Transitions panel makes this process fairly easy; the required CSS code is created for you.

1. **With index.html open, click the Design button in the document toolbar to show only the Design pane.**

2. **Make the Desktop Size layout visible in the Design pane.**

3. **Open the CSS Transitions panel (Window>CSS Transitions).**

4. **Click the Create New Transition button (the + icon) at the top of the panel.**

5. In the resulting dialog box, open the Target Rule menu and choose .container.

Every selector related to the active file (including those in all three linked CSS files) appears in this menu in alphabetical order.

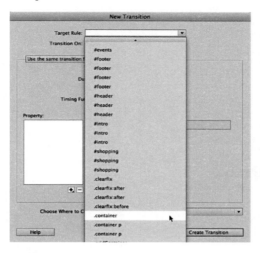

6. In the Transition On menu, choose Hover.

This menu determines what event will trigger the transition. In this case, the transition will occur when a user hovers the mouse over an element where the .container class has been applied.

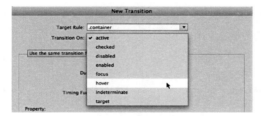

7. Type 0.5 in the Duration field.

The duration is the time it takes for a transition to occur. Dreamweaver uses seconds (s) as the default time increment, but you can also choose milliseconds (ms) in the menu.

8. Type 0 in the Delay field.

The delay is a brief interval between the time the trigger event occurs and the time the transition begins.

9. In the Timing Function menu, choose Linear.

The timing function allows you to control the transition speed over the duration of the transition. In essence, you can make a transition speed up or slow down over time (called **easing**).

Note:

Easing in causes the transition to start slower and speed up over time. Easing out causes the transition to start faster and slow down over time.

10. **On the left side of the dialog box, click the + button below the Property window, and choose max-height from the menu.**

11. **In the End Value field, type 999 and make sure px is selected in the secondary menu.**

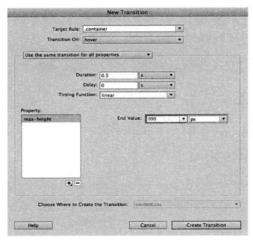

Note:

The menu at the bottom of the dialog box defaults to the file where the selected Target Rule is located.

12. **Click Create Transition to return to the document window.**

The CSS Transitions panel shows the new transition, as well as the instances where that transition occurs. There are three elements with the .container class applied in this file, so the panel shows three instances of the defined transition.

13. **Activate the Live view if it is not still active. If necessary, hide all visual aids (including Fluid Grid Layout Guides).**

Like many of the CSS3 properties, Dreamweaver's Design view does not accurately preview CSS3 transitions unless the Live view is active.

14. Move your mouse over any of the .container elements to test the transition.

15. Click **content.css** in the Related Files bar to review the code for the **.container** selector.

Code for the defined transition requires several versions for the various browsers. Remember, CSS3 is still in development and has not been universally adopted by all browsers. The transition property is not technically supported by any browser, so browser prefixes are required.

Each property line combines the various values into a single line (from left to right):

- The property that is affected by the transition. When this is "all," the same transition settings will apply to all properties that are being animated.
- The duration of the transition
- The timing function of the transition
- The delay of the transition

Transition properties (including the necessary browser prefixes) are added to the .container selector.

A new selector is added to define properties for .container elements when the hover pseudo-class is triggered.

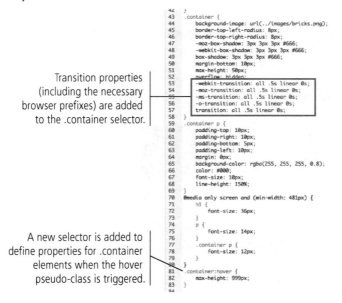

```
42    }
43    .container {
44        background-image: url(../images/bricks.png);
45        border-top-left-radius: 8px;
46        border-top-right-radius: 8px;
47        -moz-box-shadow: 3px 3px 3px #666;
48        -webkit-box-shadow: 3px 3px 3px #666;
49        box-shadow: 3px 3px 3px #666;
50        margin-bottom: 10px;
51        max-height: 50px;
52        overflow: hidden;
53        -webkit-transition: all .5s linear 0s;
54        -moz-transition: all .5s linear 0s;
55        -ms-transition: all .5s linear 0s;
56        -o-transition: all .5s linear 0s;
57        transition: all .5s linear 0s;
58    }
59    .container p {
60        padding-top: 10px;
61        padding-right: 10px;
62        padding-bottom: 5px;
63        padding-left: 10px;
64        margin: 0px;
65        background-color: rgba(255, 255, 255, 0.8);
66        color: #000;
67        font-size: 10px;
68        line-height: 150%;
69    }
70    @media only screen and (min-width: 481px) {
71        h1 {
72            font-size: 36px;
73        }
74        p {
75            font-size: 14px;
76        }
77        .container p {
78            font-size: 12px;
79        }
80    }
81    .container:hover {
82        max-height: 999px;
83    }
84
```

Note:

If you define different transitions for different properties, each would be listed separately on the same line:

transition: property1settings, property2settings;

16. Save the file and continue to the next exercise.

DEFINE TRANSITION PROPERTIES FOR A SELECTOR

You can also use the CSS Rule Definition dialog box to define transitions for a specific selector. This method is just as easy to use as the CSS Transitions panel. The only disadvantage to using this method is that many CSS3 properties are not available in the CSS Rule Definition dialog box. If you want to add CSS3 properties to the selector, you have to do so manually in the Code pane.

1. **With index.html open, click the Design button in the Document toolbar and turn off the Live view.**

   In a few steps, you need to be able to see the paragraphs in the .container elements. Turning off the Live view disables the overflow property so you can see all of the content in those elements.

2. **Click the New CSS Rule button at the bottom of the CSS Styles panel.**

3. **Choose Compound in the Selector Type menu. In the Selector Name field, type h2:hover.**

   Using the :hover pseudo-class, you are defining a selector that changes the h2 elements when the user's cursor moves over those elements.

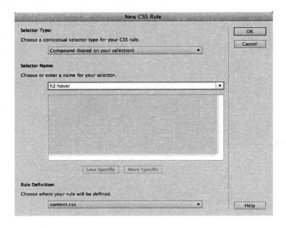

4. **Choose content.css in the Rule Definition menu, then click OK to define the new selector properties.**

5. **In the Type options, click the Color swatch. Move the eyedropper cursor over the background of any paragraph in one of the .container elements and click to select a light brown color.**

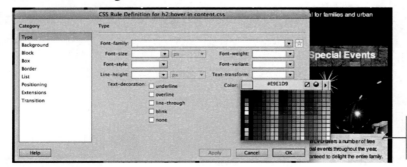

Sample one of the light colors from this area as the new type color.

By itself, this selector is enough to change the color of the h2 text when the mouse cursor hovers over one of those elements; the change occurs immediately as soon as the hover event occurs. To make the color change gradually over time, you are going to add the transition property to the selector.

6. **Select Transition in the list of categories.**

7. **Leave the All Animatable Properties option checked.**

   If you uncheck this option, you can define a transition for only certain properties in the selector.

8. **Type 1 in the Duration field, type 0 in the Delay field, and choose Linear in the Timing Function menu.**

   When this option is checked, the same transition settings will apply to all animatable properties in the selector.

   When All Animatable Properties is unchecked, you can use this button to define different transitions for specific properties.

9. **Click OK to create the new selector.**

10. **Turn on the Live view, then move your mouse over one of the h2 elements on the page.**

    Because you defined a transition property for the h2:hover selector, the type color changes from white to light brown over 1 second (the duration you defined for the transition).

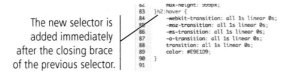

11. **Change to the Split view and show the content.css file in the Code pane.**

12. **Locate the code for the h2:hover selector.**

    There is a slight flaw in the way Dreamweaver adds this selector; instead of placing it on its own line, it might be added immediately after the closing brace of the last selector.

    Although this does not prevent the selector from working properly, it is simply good housekeeping to correct the problem.

    The new selector is added immediately after the closing brace of the previous selector.

13. **Place the insertion point before the h2:hover name and press Return/Enter to move it to its own line in the Code pane.**

14. **Place the insertion point at the end of the last line in the h2:hover selector, then press Return/Enter to add a new line to the selector. Type:**

    ```
    text-shadow: 3px 3px #000;
    ```

    The **text-shadow** property, new in CSS3, can't be added in the CSS Rule Definition dialog box. You have to manually type the code in the selector.

    This property adds a drop shadow behind the text in an element. The values for the property are (in order) the X offset, the Y offset, and the color of the shadow.

    ```
    83    }
    84    h2:hover {
    85        -webkit-transition: all 1s linear 0s;
    86        -moz-transition: all 1s linear 0s;
    87        -ms-transition: all 1s linear 0s;
    88        -o-transition: all 1s linear 0s;
    89        transition: all 1s linear 0s;
    90        color: #E9E1D9;
    91        text-shadow: 3px 3px #000;
    92    }
    93
    ```

Note:

*The **box-shadow** property adds a drop shadow behind the entire element.*

15. **Refresh the Design pane, then move your mouse over one of the h2 elements in the Design pane.**

    When you defined the transition property for the h2:hover selector, you left the All Animatable Properties option checked. When the mouse cursor triggers the h2:hover selector, both the color and the text-shadow property change gradually based on the defined transition property.

16. **Save all files and close them.**

17. **Export a site definition named BLUD.ste into your WIP>BLVD folder, and then remove the site from Dreamweaver.**

Project Review

fill in the blank

1. In a fluid grid layout, the _____ is defined as a percentage of the column width.

2. In a fluid grid layout, the defined number of columns are created as a _____ of the overall page width.

3. In a fluid grid layout, all fluid grid layout divs must be placed inside the _____ div.

4. When you create a fluid grid layout div, the _____ option forces a div to align to the left edge of the grid, regardless of available space in preceding rows.

5. True or false: You can place different content in the same div for each layout size in a fluid grid layout. _____

6. The _____ can be used to simultaneously view all three layouts in a fluid grid page.

7. A(n) _____ can be used to define different CSS properties based on the size of the display being used to view a page.

8. The _____ command saves all files related to the active page in a single command.

9. Animations in an HTML5 page are created by defining _____ properties for a specific CSS selector.

10. The _____ property places a drop shadow behind the text inside an element.

short answer

1. Briefly explain the concept of responsive design.

2. Briefly explain how the concept of rows affects a fluid grid layout div's position on the page.

3. Briefly explain one method of creating a CSS3 transition.

Portfolio Builder Project

Use what you learned in this project to complete the following freeform exercise.
Carefully read the art director and client comments, then create your own design to meet the needs of the project.
Use the space below to sketch ideas; when finished, write a brief explanation of your reasoning behind your final design.

art director comments

The Lancaster city planners were very happy with your work on their rebranding project. Your local city government representatives saw the Web page at a recent convention, and they would like to create a similar site to help promote local tourism.

To complete this project, you should:

❑ Find images (or create your own) that highlight different events and attractions in the local area.

❑ Write compelling copy to promote the area to visitors. Look at the local chamber of commerce and city government Web sites for ideas, or for detailed information about specific events.

❑ Design a Web page to highlight at least three areas of special interest in your community.

client comments

We've been trying to reach out to a larger audience to promote the local attractions and events that make our city special.

We want the new site to be visually appealing, easy to navigate, and equally functional on both desktops and mobile devices.

We don't have any specific text or images in mind, so we're hoping you can find or create whatever you need to make the project successful.

project justification

As digital tablets and smartphones continue to gain in popularity, the way people browse the Internet will continue to adapt to the capabilities of new technology. At least in part to meet the new needs of the mobile community, HTML5 and CSS3 are being developed to allow Web designers more flexibility and functionality to create responsive Web pages that work properly regardless of the medium being used to display the page.

It is important to realize that mobile technology is still in its relative infancy, and its evolution is faster than anything seen before in the communications industry. New devices are being introduced constantly, each with new capabilities and (in some cases) limitations. For the foreseeable future, we can continue to expect frequent and significant changes in both the actual devices and the tools we use to design for them.

This project introduced the concept of responsive design, focusing on the methods that Dreamweaver CS6 includes for building pages that adapt to different display media. Combined with a good understanding of HTML tags and CSS selectors, the skills you learned in this project will be a strong foundation that will allow you to better manage the changing face of Web design.

The second part of this project introduced CSS3 transitions, including the tools Dreamweaver CS6 provides for creating those transitions. Keep in mind that mobile devices do not have a pointing device, so they do not support the hover behavior; we created these exercises to teach you the basic process for creating transitions in Dreamweaver, and we used the hover behavior because its familiarity can help to make it easier to relate what you are doing in this project to other projects. When you design responsive sites, you should carefully consider your options, and design to meet the needs of your audience.

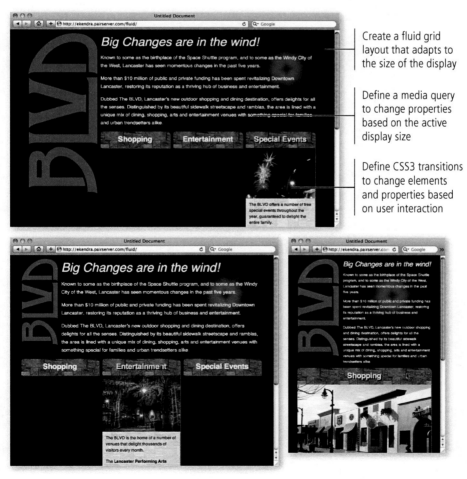

Create a fluid grid layout that adapts to the size of the display

Define a media query to change properties based on the active display size

Define CSS3 transitions to change elements and properties based on user interaction

Just Posters Dynamic Site

Just Posters, Inc. produces posters for professional office environments. It has a nationwide niche market, and it is backed by a strong distribution network. The company does not yet want to bypass its distribution network with a direct online store, but the owner does want an online presence to inform distributors about the company's products.

For the first part of that online presence, the company wants a site that showcases its latest poster collection. To make maintenance easy, the company hired you to build a database-driven site that can be maintained by anyone, without having to learn database technology.

This project incorporates the following skills:

- ❏ Setting up a MySQL database and importing client data
- ❏ Connecting to a database from Dreamweaver
- ❏ Defining a site for server-side processing
- ❏ Working with dynamic text and image placeholders
- ❏ Adding recordset display filters and navigation controls
- ❏ Creating a dynamic page link using a URL parameter filter
- ❏ Displaying data based on dynamic form field values
- ❏ Showing and hiding page regions based on recordset contents
- ❏ Synchronizing local and remote site files

Project Meeting

client comments

I started this company as a one-man operation in my garage. Over the past five years, the company has grown into a national supplier of quality artwork for office and business environments. We've got a strong network of national distributors for the business and office markets, and we're now thinking about moving into the general retail market as well.

Because our operations have been fairly contained until now, we have always used print catalogs for product marketing. But if we move into retail, we need a Web presence that will show what we offer and, eventually, process online orders.

Until we move beyond our distributor supply chain, we want to maintain personal contact with buyers, so we aren't going to offer online ordering yet. For now, we just want a site that lets users review the posters that are available.

I exported our poster database, with all the information we need to display on the site. The file is in SQL format, and it follows the standards we received from your IT director, so hopefully everything will go smoothly.

art director comments

I asked one of the designers to build the pages for the site. The site is template- and CSS-based, so overall changes can be made easily as we move forward. When the designer built the site pages, she defined areas that will hold the various items. You will see the placeholders in the pages when you open them.

I need you, as our resident Web programmer, to take the prepared pages and build in the dynamic catalog functionality. Unfortunately, we're in the middle of upgrading our own server network. We won't have everything up and running for more than a week, so you will have to use a remote server while you develop and test the dynamic elements.

project objectives

To complete this project, you will:

- ❏ Set up a MySQL database and import the client's data
- ❏ Create the site definition for server-side processing
- ❏ Add data placeholders in a PHP page
- ❏ Use a binding to dynamically define alt text
- ❏ Repeat a recordset
- ❏ Add recordset navigation to the gallery
- ❏ Create a dynamic page link
- ❏ Troubleshoot dynamic pages for testing
- ❏ Add a search feature
- ❏ Show and hide regions based on recordset contents
- ❏ Display records with advanced filter criteria
- ❏ Synchronize the local and remote sites

Stage 1 Preparing to Use PHP and MySQL

In the first seven projects, you worked with Dreamweaver to create **static Web pages**, which display the same information to all users. In this project, you learn to create **dynamic Web pages**, where content (text, images, etc.) can change. Dynamic pages enable an interactive experience because users choose what they want to see.

Static Web sites require numerous pages and significant storage space on a Web server; dynamic sites often use only a few structural pages that show different data depending on a user's request. A smaller number of pages also means site maintenance is easier; it's much faster to update pages and links with new information — as well as remove pages and links for items that no longer exist — when you use dynamic content rather than static.

Databases

Databases provide an efficient framework for storing data in a predefined structure. This structure forces you to organize content in a standard format, and it divides your content into smaller units.

Many database platforms are available today. MySQL and Microsoft Access are among the most familiar database platforms. Each database platform has its own set of procedures for retrieving and displaying records from the database on a Web page. In addition, each platform stores information slightly differently.

MySQL is the most popular database platform because it is available free of charge and has proven to be stable. MySQL works on a relational database model, which designates the actual entries (records) as rows and the pieces of information for each entry (fields) as columns in a table.

Database table   Fields for each record

Poster ID	Name	Price	Image Path	Alt Text
JP101	Education	19.99	posters/education1.jpg	Image for Education
JP102	Anticipation	19.99	posters/anticipation1.jpg	Image for Anticipation
JP103	Preparation	19.99	posters/preparation1.jpg	Image for Preparation

Individual records

MySQL uses queries to retrieve information from a database. It can also operate using a graphical user interface (GUI) application such as phpMyAdmin, through which databases can be maintained without having to learn the queries.

Server-Side Technologies

Browsers use HTML code to display the contents of a Web page; the HTML code is sent as-is to the browser. When you view the source code of an HTML page, the code you see is the code used to create the page. This technique leaves little flexibility for dynamic content.

A **server-side language** differs from HTML because the server-side code does not display in the page that appears in the browser. A server-side language such as PHP (Hypertext Preprocessor) generates a Web page according to the arguments contained within the PHP code. To display a record from a database, for example, the code does not contain any actual record details. Instead, the code contains a reference, which is used to fetch a matching record from the database. Server-side technologies are not substitutes for HTML, but rather complement HTML. The page that displays in the browser still contains only HTML code.

Note:

Entire books have been written about building dynamic Web sites with server-side programming. We created this project to give you an idea of what you can do with Dreamweaver to build dynamic pages. If you want to continue your education beyond this project, we encourage you to read an advanced book on this subject.

Note:

PHP is just one of the server-side technologies that Dreamweaver supports, in addition to Active Server Pages (ASP), Java Server Pages (JSP), and ColdFusion.

Setting up and Connecting to a MySQL Database

Unlike the Web sites you developed in the previous projects of this book, a database-driven Web site cannot be created on a computer with a typical configuration. You need to have access to a computer with the languages and environment necessary to support databases. This means that either your computer or another computer on your network must have a Web server, a database application, and the coding language components installed.

If you are using a local server (a server on the same local network as your workstation), ask your network administrator what settings you should use to access and communicate with the local server. To illustrate this project, we are using our free Web server account at Pair Networks to explain the process of creating a dynamic PHP site. If you did not complete Project 1: Bistro Site Organization, refer to Page 52 for information about setting up your own server account.

SET UP A MYSQL DATABASE

Dreamweaver provides a rich set of functionality for creating Web sites that connect to MySQL databases. The one feature Dreamweaver does not provide, however, is actually creating a database or the tables it contains; you first need to use some other mechanism for creating the database tables, and then make the tables available on your server for Dreamweaver to access. (You can, however, use Dreamweaver to create an interface for adding data to the database on your server.)

1. **Download DW6_RF_Project8.zip from the Student Files Web page.**

2. **Expand the ZIP archive in your WIP folder (Macintosh) or copy the archive contents into your WIP folder (Windows).**

   This results in a folder named **Posters**, which contains the files you need for this project.

3. **Open a browser window and log in to your Account Control Center.**

   As we explained, we are using our hosting account at Pair Networks to explain the concepts in this project. If you use a different server or hosting company, the specific details might be slightly different, but the concepts are still the same.

4. **Click the Create a New Database link in the Database Management section.**

5. **In the MySQL Databases screen, type jpdata in the New Database field, and then click Add Database.**

6. When the browser shows that the database has been added, note the Database Name, Database Server, and Full-Access Username and Password.

You will need this information later when you conect to the database in Dreamweaver.

Most hosts append the user or domain name to the database name that you define. In our example, the resulting database name is "ekendra_jpdata".

7. Below the database details, click the "Click Here for Detailed View" button.

8. In the resulting screen, click the Manage Using phpMyAdmin button.

Once you have created a database on your server, you can use the phpMyAdmin utility to manage the tables in the database, including adding new information manually or importing data from an existing SQL file.

We will continue to use our hosting account as an example. If you are using a different hosting company (remote or local), follow the instructions provided by your service provider or network administrator.

9. Enter your full-access database password in the resulting screen, then click Login to phpMyAdmin.

This is the password that was provided in the screen after you created the database.

10. **Click the Import link at the top of the resulting screen.**

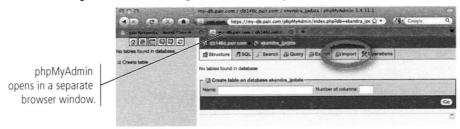

phpMyAdmin opens in a separate browser window.

11. **In the resulting screen, click the Browse button in the File to Import area.**

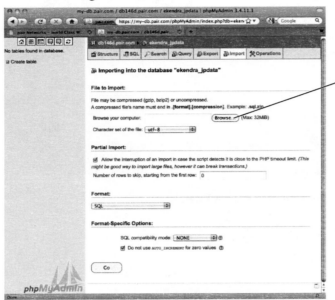

Click Browse to open a navigation dialog box, where you can select the database file to import.

12. **In the resulting dialog box, navigate to the file justposters.sql in the WIP>Posters>SQL Files folder and click Open/Choose.**

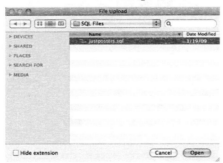

13. **When you return to the phpMyAdmin window, click the Go button at the bottom of the screen.**

Two tables (adminusers and posters) are added to the database.

After the import is complete, two tables have been added to the database on your server.

Note:

The phpMyAdmin screen might look slightly different from one hosting company to another. The functionality, however, should be the same.

Note:

The phpMyAdmin utility is an easy-to-use visual interface provided by many hosting companies to manage SQL database files. You can use phpMyAdmin to create database tables from scratch, manage existing databases, and even export databases for use in another application. In this project, however, you must import the SQL database file that was provided by your client before you can build dynamic data into a Web page.

Note:

The adminusers table has three fields and one record. Each entry contains a name, user ID, and password. This table will be used to check the user ID and password of anyone trying to access the administrative pages you create in this project.

14. On the left side of the screen, click posters. Click the Browse tab at the top of the screen to review the structure of the posters table.

The posters table has ten fields and eleven records. Field names appear in the first row of the table. Individual records appear in the rows below the field names.

Click a table name to review the table structure.

This area shows there are 11 records in the database table.

Each item here is a field in the table.

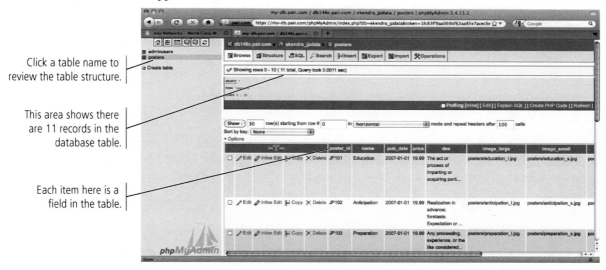

15. Continue to the next exercise.

PREPARE THE SITE STRUCTURE

Most hosting providers require you to place public files inside a specific folder, such as public_html or htdocs. When users navigate to your URL, they see the index page located in the designated folder.

Using our example hosting account, the hosting company requires public files to be placed inside the public_html folder. If a user types "ekendra.pairserver.com" in a browser window, the server returns the index page located at ekendra.pairserver.com/public_html/ (if an index.html file exists in that folder). The public_html folder name is not included in the site URL, but is required when you build, test, and upload files for viewing over the Internet.

Because we are using our own domain name (and not the client's company name) for development, it's a good idea to use a subfolder rather than placing the Just Posters site in the main ekendra.pairserver.com site.

1. If necessary, log in to your Web-hosting Account Control Center. (Make sure you are in the main screen of the Control panel, not the phpMyAdmin screen.)

2. Click the Web option in the Go To a Directory section.

The Web link opens the public_html folder, which is where you place publicly viewable files for your server account, in the Account Control Center.

Click the Web link to show the public_html folder in the browser.

Note:

We recommend that you start building a dynamic Web site locally — that is, either on a computer with the necessary configuration or with access to a local server. Doing so provides much faster response times when you test your Web site. When you work on an online server, every change must be updated over an Internet connection, which invariably takes longer than when you work locally. However, because we can't be sure everyone has the proper configuration locally, we complete this entire project using a remote online server.

3. Click the Create New Directory button near the top of the page.

The public_html folder is active.

Click the Create New Directory button.

4. Type `posters-site` in the New Subdirectory field, then click the Make Directory button. In the Permissions area, leave the world-readable option selected.

This folder will contain the live site, which you will upload once development is complete.

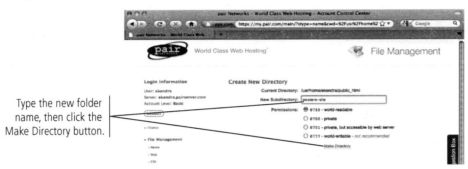

Type the new folder name, then click the Make Directory button.

Note:

The folder creation process might be slightly different for each hosting company. Follow the instructions provided by your hosting service to create the new posters-site folder in the folder that contains pages that will be visible to site users (e.g., public_html).

In a professional workflow, you will commonly develop a new site in a location other than the client's actual domain name. This prevents users from accessing pages that are incorrect or incomplete during the development stage, which could reflect poorly on your client's business.

In the case of this project, you are using a dedicated folder on your own Web server — a common workflow solution. You can provide your client with a link to this folder for review and approval before the site goes "live" on the client's domain. When the site is finished, you can upload the database and then upload the page files to the correct location on the client's Web server.

Note:

Although this might seem like a lot of set-up work, it's quite common for Web developers to build sites using their own servers before uploading the files to the client's actual domain.

The new folder appears in the list of files in the public_html folder.

5. Close the browser, and then continue to the next stage of the project.

This set-up process is required so you can use Dreamweaver to successfully build and manage a dynamic, data-driven Web site. The rest of this project focuses on Dreamweaver's functionality.

Stage 2 Defining a PHP Site Definition

PHP is a server-side scripting language. In other words, a PHP page includes code that is read and executed by the server before the page is delivered to the requesting browser. Using PHP, you can create dynamic pages that are assembled "on the fly," based on code in the pages as well as user-supplied information (such as a search query).

CREATE THE SITE DEFINITION

Creating a site definition for a dynamic site is a little more complex than for a static site, especially if you are hosting the site on a remote server. You need to configure the site definition in such a way that it contains all the requisite details for connecting to the database, using the correct programming language and including the correct authentication details.

1. **In Dreamweaver, open the Manage Sites dialog box using the Directory menu in the Files panel.**

2. **Click New Site in the Manage Sites dialog box.**

3. **In the Site pane of the Site Setup dialog box, type** Posters **in the Site Name field. Navigate to and choose your WIP>Posters>Site Content folder as the local site folder.**

    Make sure you use the Site Content folder as the root, and not the primary Posters folder.

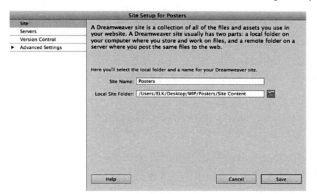

4. **Click Servers in the list of categories, then click the + button near the bottom of the dialog box.**

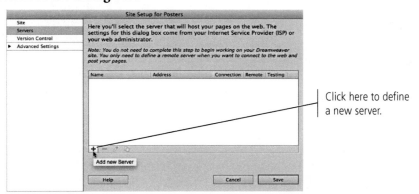

Click here to define a new server.

Note:

You can define a separate server to use as the testing server, or simply create a secondary test folder on your existing server.

5. **In the Basic options, type a name for the server you are using.**

   In our example, we are using the Web server at our hosting company, Pair Networks.

6. **Assuming you are working with a remote server, choose FTP in the Connect Using menu.**

   If you are using a local server, consult your network administrator for the settings to use.

7. **In the FTP Address field, type the hostname for your server.**

   In our example, the FTP host is ekendra.pairserver.com. Check your hosting account documentation for your FTP hostname and account information.

8. **Type your FTP login (username) and password in the related fields.**

   These are the username and password for your actual hosting account, not the database you created earlier. (Again, consult your server documentation for the correct information to use; this information was probably sent to you via email when you first set up the hosting account.)

9. **In the Root Directory field, type the location of the folder where you want the files to be placed.**

   This is the location where Dreamweaver's FTP functionality places and synchronizes publicly visible files. In our example, the host directory is public_html/posters-site/. (Remember, you create the posters-site folder in the previous exercise.)

10. **In the Web URL field, type the URL at which users will access the site.**

    Dreamweaver automatically defines this URL based on your other choices in this dialog box; the default value will be "http://" plus the FTP Address plus the Root Directory. In our example, the default was http://ekendra.pairserver.com/public_html/posters-site/

    You need to change the URL to the path a user would type in a browser to access your site. In our example, the address is http://ekendra.pairserver.com/posters-site/. (Note that we did not include the public_html folder.) Make sure you enter the correct information for your domain name.

Note:

Consult your hosting company's documentation for specific information about the directory to use for pages that will be viewable on the Web.

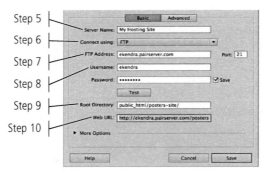

11. **Make sure the Save check box (next to the Password field) is checked, and then click Test.**

    You must receive a message stating that Dreamweaver successfully connected to the Web server. If a connection with the Web server cannot be established, check your entries to make sure your Internet connection is active, and then try again.

    (If you are working on a shared computer, you might want to uncheck the Save option. However, you will have to retype your username and password every time you upload files to your hosting account.)

12. Click the Advanced button to show those options.

13. In the Testing Server Server Model menu, choose PHP MySQL.

This option defines what type of database and processing instructions (software) you are using so you can preview dynamic Web pages in Dreamweaver during development.

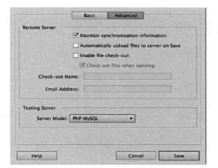

14. Click Save to return to the Site Setup dialog box.

15. In the list of available servers, check the Testing box for the server you defined.

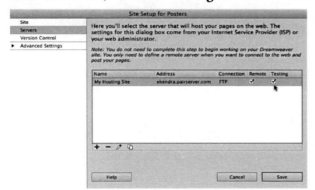

Note:

You can use the Remote and Testing check boxes to define multiple servers, so that you can use a testing server separate from your actual "live" Web server.

16. Expand the Advanced Settings options and select the Local Info category.

17. Check the Case-Sensitive Links Checking option.

Many Web servers run on the UNIX operating system, which follows strict case-sensitivity rules. This option ensures that Dreamweaver looks for proper case in the links of the site.

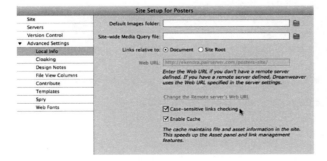

18. Click Save to return to the Manage Sites dialog box.

19. In the Manage Sites dialog box, make sure the Posters site appears in the list of sites, and then click Done.

20. Continue to the next exercise.

UPLOAD FILES TO A REMOTE SITE

If you are working on a remote server, you can use the hosting provider's file management utility to upload the site files. However, Dreamweaver's FTP functionality makes it easy to put files into the remote site folder (defined in the Servers pane of the Site Setup dialog box). You can even synchronize all files on the remote and local sites — which is useful when you are ready to publish the site for public Internet access.

1. **With the Posters site open in the Files panel, click the Expand button in the Files panel to show both the local and remote sites.**

Click here to expand the Files panel.

Note:

If the Files panel is docked when you click the Expand button, the expanded Files panel fills the entire document window.

2. **Above the Remote Server pane, click the Connection button to link to and show the remote site.**

Click here to connect to the remote site.

After the connection has been made, the remote site appears in the left pane.

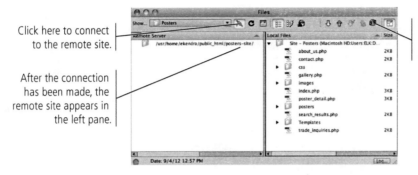

Click this button to synchronize the remote and local site folders.

3. **Click the Synchronize button at the top of the expanded Files panel.**

The full name of the Synchronize button includes the server name that you defined in the Site Setup dialog box. We simply refer to it as "Synchronize" because yours might be different, depending on what server company you use.

4. **In the Synchronize Files dialog box, choose Entire 'Posters' Site in the Synchronize menu, and choose Put Newer Files to Remote in the Direction menu.**

This utility enables you to synchronize an entire site or only selected files. You can also determine which version (local or remote) to synchronize from. For example, if you accidentally delete files from your local site folder, you can choose to synchronize files from remote to local to restore the missing files.

5. **Click the Preview button.**

After a few seconds, the Synchronize dialog box shows a list of all files that will be affected by the process. In this case, this is the first time you are uploading to the remote site, so all site files need to be put onto the remote site.

Click these buttons to change the options for selected files in the list.

6. **Click OK to put the files onto the remote site.**

When you upload files to the remote server, Dreamweaver keeps a log of affected files. The Background File Activity dialog box shows a list of each file, including any potential problems encountered during the transfer process.

7. **In the Background File Activity dialog box, click the arrow button to the left of the word "Details."**

Clicking this button expands the dialog box and shows the progress of the synchronization. After the synchronization is complete, the files appear in both the remote site and the local site pane of the Files panel.

Click here to show or hide the synchronization details.

All files should show "Put operation successful".

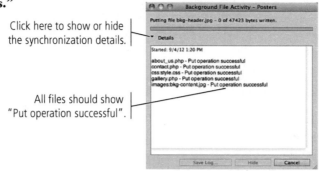

Note:

Dreamweaver will warn you if a file uploads incorrectly or does not upload at all.

Note:

The upload process might take a while, depending on your connection speed and how many files are being uploaded.

Note:

When you upload files to the remote server, Dreamweaver keeps a log of the files that are affected. You can access this log in the FTP Log tab of the Results panel (Window>Results).

8. **Open a browser window. In the navigation bar, type the URL of the Just Posters site.**

Type the same URL you defined in the Servers pane of the Site Setup dialog box. In our example, the URL is http://ekendra.pairserver.com/posters-site/.

You don't need to type "index.php." This page is recognized as the default file for the defined path.

9. **Close the browser and return to Dreamweaver.**

10. **Continue to the next stage of the project.**

Stage 3 Creating Data-Driven Pages

Every page that needs to interact with a database needs access information for that database: the location of the database, its name, and the required user ID and password.

The PHP code required to access the database is generated automatically when you define the connection details. Since this code must be available in every page that accesses the database, Dreamweaver creates a separate page with this code, and places the page in a folder named Connections in your local site root folder. A reference to this page is automatically added to every page that needs access to the database using the **require** function, which refers to other files that *must be* available for a page to work properly. The require function uses the following format:

```
<?php require-once('Connections/jpdata.php'); ?>
```

The PHP **include** command allows you to place a reference to one page inside another page. If changes are required in the included content, you need to change only the included page. The code format of the include function is as follows:

```
<?php include('filename.php'); ?>
```

Note:

*The **require-once** function is a variation of the require function. This function ensures the file's details are copied to the page only once, to avoid duplication that can interfere with the structure of the page.*

CREATE THE MYSQL CONNECTION

The Databases panel is the primary interface for connecting to and interacting with a database. Once the connection is created, the information is stored in a file in the site's Connections folder.

1. **With the Posters site open in the Files panel, collapse the Files panel to Standard view and make sure the local site is showing.**

2. **Double-click gallery.php to open it in Design view.**

3. **Open the Databases panel (Window>Databases).**

   Before you can create a database connection, a file must be open.

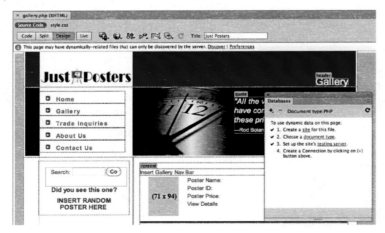

Note:

You can edit or delete connection information from the included file by right-clicking a connection in the Databases panel and choosing from the contextual menu.

4. **Click the "+" button in the Databases panel, and then choose MySQL Connection from the menu.**

5. **In the Connection Name field, type `posterdata`.**

   This name is applied to the file in the Connections folder; all database references in the other page files will refer to the file with this name.

6. **In the MySQL Server field, type the location of the database.**

   When we created the database on our hosting server, the database server was provided in the New Database Details screen (see Page 353, Step 6). That is the information you need to enter in this field.

7. **Type the username and password for the database in the related fields.**

   Use the name and password you defined when you created the database; it is not the username and password for your primary hosting account.

8. **Click the Select button next to the Database field.**

   You could simply type the name of the database you created, but clicking the Select button allows Dreamweaver to test the connection to your MySQL server using the details you provided in the previous steps.

   The resulting Select Database dialog box shows the names of databases to which you have access.

9. **In the Select Database dialog box, select the database you created for the Just Posters site, and then click OK.**

   After clicking OK in the Select Database dialog box, the database you selected appears here.

10. **Click OK to close the MySQL Connection dialog box.**

    The posterdata connection is added to the Databases panel, and a Connections folder is added to the local site files.

11. **In the Databases panel, expand the posterdata connection and expand the list of tables in the connection.**

    These are the two tables in the database file (as you saw when you imported the client's data).

12. **In the Files panel, expand the Connections folder. If you don't see the posterdata.php file, refresh the Files panel.**

    Dreamweaver uses this file to tell each page how to connect to the selected database.

13. **Continue to the next exercise.**

Note:

Many remote servers run on the UNIX operating system, which converts the case of file and folder names to lowercase, and then enforces case-matching when looking for files. The references to the Connections folder in your site, however, will still contain the uppercase folder name. To avoid this problem, you can change the name of the folder in the Files panel to start with the lower-case c; when asked, make sure you update links to the changed folder name.

DISPLAY RECORDS FROM THE DATABASE

Now that you have established a connection to the database, you are ready to add the data-driven elements to the site pages. The first page you need to build is a gallery of the client's products. Each item in the gallery will link to a separate page that shows the details of a specific poster.

Working with a database to design pages is basically a matter of specifying which content (data) to display in the page. By designing pages around the database, you don't need to spend hours or days creating a large number of static pages for every conceivable need. This type of dynamic site also makes it easy to change the data in the database — for example, adding new products without manually generating new static pages.

1. **With gallery.php open in Design view, open the Server Behaviors panel.**

    By default, the Server Behaviors panel is grouped with the Databases panel. If the panel is not visible, choose Window>Server Behaviors.

2. **Click the "+" button on the Server Behaviors panel and choose Recordset from the menu.**

    Recordsets are instructions for retrieving records from a table in a database. The resulting dialog box lets you specify the parameters for which records will be retrieved.

    Unlike the connection details, which are stored in a separate file, recordset instructions are stored in the <head> area of the page you are working on. A separate recordset is required to get records from different tables, and individual recordsets can include parameters for retrieving only those records that match certain criteria.

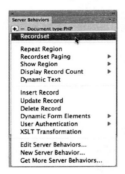 

3. **Make sure you are working in Simple mode.**

    Check the buttons on the right side of the dialog box. If the button above Help says "Advanced," you are working in Simple mode.

4. **Change the Name field to `getPosterList`.**

    The recordset will be referred to as getPosterList in the page code.

5. **In the Connection menu, choose posterdata (if it is not already selected).**

    The connection tells the recordset the location and authentication details of the database from which records must be retrieved.

6. **In the Table menu, choose posters.**

    This is the table in the database that contains all poster details. Each recordset can retrieve details from a single table.

    You need to create a different recordset for each table from which you want to retrieve records.

Note:

You can use only numbers, letters, and the underscore symbol (_) in recordset names. You cannot use spaces.

7. Click the Selected radio button above the Columns window.

When you define a recordset, you can specify the table columns (data fields) from which data must be retrieved. You don't necessarily need to display every field for a record on a given page. If you select All when all fields are not actually needed, the result could be an unnecessary delay in displaying the page because the page is forced to download more data than it needs.

8. Press Command/Control and click the following columns to select them:

- poster_id
- name
- price
- image_medium
- alt_text

These fields will display for each poster in the gallery.php page.

9. Make sure None is selected in the Filter menu.

As long as a recordset is not filtered, all records in the database will display — which is what you want in this case. (Later, you will add a behavior to limit the displayed records to five at a time.)

10. Click Test.

The resulting Test SQL Statement dialog box must display all 11 posters, with the details from the selected columns.

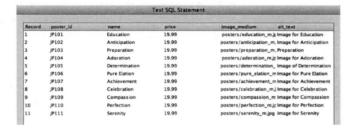

11. Click OK to close the Test SQL Statement dialog box, and then click OK to close the Recordset dialog box.

The getPosterList recordset is added to the Server Behaviors panel. You will use this recordset to display all posters from the database in the gallery.php page.

12. Save the file and continue to the next exercise.

Available behaviors can be accessed by clicking the "+" button on the Server Behaviors panel toolbar. (Delete an existing behavior by selecting it in the panel and clicking the "−" button.)

- **Recordset.** A recordset is a query that contains the criteria for retrieving records from a database table.

- **Repeat Region.** This causes a selected region to repeat until all records retrieved by the recordset are displayed.

- **Recordset Paging.** This set of behaviors adds links that can be used to navigate through groups of records in the same set. Specific options in this menu are:

Move To First Page	Move To Next Page
Move To Previous Page	Move To Last Page

- **Show Region.** These behaviors can be used to either hide or display a region under certain conditions. Options in this menu are:

Show If Recordset Is Empty	
Show If Recordset Is Not Empty	
Show If First Page	Show If Not First Page
Show If Last Page	Show If Not Last Page

- **Display Record Count.** This set of behaviors displays the first, last, and total number of records displayed on the page. Options in this menu are:

  Display Starting Record Number
  Display Ending Record Number
  Display Total Records

- **Dynamic Text.** This behavior is used to show the contents of a specific database table field.

- **Insert Record.** This is used for adding a record to a database table by collecting values from a form.

- **Update Record.** This is used for updating a record in a database table by collecting values from a form.

- **Delete Record.** This is used for deleting a record from the database.

- **Dynamic Form Elements.** Sometimes a form needs to have default values; using this set of behaviors, you can populate these default values from the database. You can create lists, check boxes, and radio button groups with dynamic values. Options are:

Dynamic Text Field	Dynamic CheckBox
Dynamic Radio Group	Dynamic List/Menu

- **User Authentication.** This set of behaviors is used to restrict areas of your site to only those users who have permission. (Account details are saved in a database, and these behaviors compare the user ID and password provided by users to the records in the database table.) Options in this menu are:

Log In User	Restrict Access To Page
Log Out User	Check New Username

- **XSLT Transformation.** This feature is useful for collecting content received in XML files and displaying that content as an ordinary Web page. Content from RSS (Rich Site Summary) feeds is in the XML format.

- **Edit Server Behavior** and **New Server Behavior** are used for modifying and creating custom behaviors.

- **Get More Server Behaviors** directs you to a page that lists some free and for-sale Dreamweaver behaviors that are not available in the application as it is shipped.

Using the Data Insert Panel

All behaviors listed in the Server Behaviors panel can also be accessed from the Data Insert panel. A few other options also appear in the Data Insert panel.

- The Spry buttons are used to create dynamic areas with underlying Spry technology.

- The Dynamic Data button menu includes options for adding dynamic text, as well as the dynamic form fields.

- The Recordset Paging button menu includes an option to create a Recordset Navigation Bar (which you will use later in this project). The menu in the Server Behaviors panel only offers the individual navigation options.

- The Display Record Count button menu includes a Recordset Navigation Status option.

- The Insert Record button menu includes an option to open the Record Insertion Form Wizard.

- The Update Record button menu includes an option to open the Record Update Form Wizard.

ADD DATA PLACEHOLDERS IN A PHP PAGE

The gallery.php page has an empty table in the editable PageContent area. You will use this table to hold the information for each poster in the catalog, based on the data in the getPosterList recordset.

1. **With gallery.php open in Design view, click to place the insertion point after the words "Poster Name:"**

   The labels for the dynamic content can be static text.

2. **In the Server Behaviors panel, click the "+" button and choose Dynamic Text.**

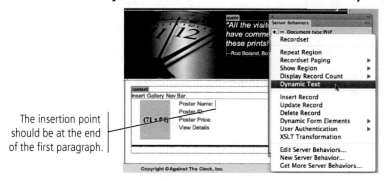

The insertion point should be at the end of the first paragraph.

The resulting Dynamic Text dialog box lists the available recordsets, which you can expand to show the table fields that can be inserted in the page.

3. **If the getPosterList recordset is not expanded in the Dynamic Text dialog box, expand the recordset now. Click name in the list to select that table field.**

   The Code field at the bottom of the dialog box displays the code that will be inserted into the page to display the data. You don't need to modify this code.

4. **Click OK to close the Dynamic Text dialog box.**

   A dynamic text placeholder is added to the page, showing the recordset and specific database field that will display when a user views the page in a browser. The dynamic text definition is also added to the Server Behaviors panel.

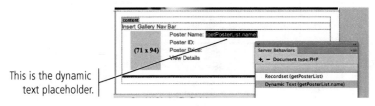

This is the dynamic text placeholder.

5. **Repeat this process to add dynamic text placeholders for the Poster ID and Price (as shown in the following image).**

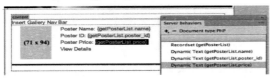

6. **Select and delete the image placeholder to the left of the existing text.**

7. **With the insertion point in the same position as the deleted image placeholder, choose Insert>Image.**

8. **In the Select Image Source dialog box, click the Data Sources button.**

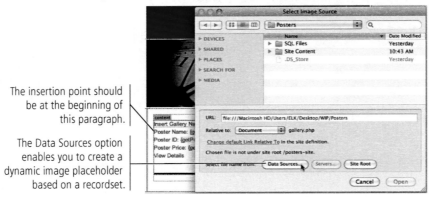

The insertion point should be at the beginning of this paragraph.

The Data Sources option enables you to create a dynamic image placeholder based on a recordset.

Note:

On Windows, the Data Sources option is a radio button instead of an actual button.

9. **Expand the getPosterList recordset (if necessary). Select image_medium and click OK.**

A list of the available recordsets displays in the Field pane of the Dynamic Data dialog box. So far, you have created only one recordset, so only one is available.

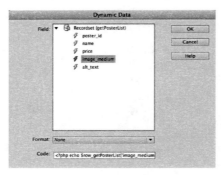

Note:

Although you can upload images to a database, it is widely considered bad practice because it bloats the size of the database.

10. **In the resulting Image Tag Accessibility Attributes dialog box, choose <empty> in the Alternate Text menu, and then click OK.**

The database for this project does not contain actual images; instead, the records contain paths to image files of various sizes (small, medium, and large). When you insert the contents of a field that contains an image path, Dreamweaver creates an image placeholder. The definition in the Server Behaviors panel appears as a dynamic attribute.

This is the dynamic image placeholder.

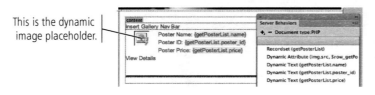

Note:

The Dynamic Attribute option might not appear in the panel until you close and reopen the gallery.php file. This is a bug in the software. As long as you see the placeholder object on the page, the dynamic image should be placed properly.

11. **Save the file and continue to the next exercise.**

Database fields of the BLOB type can be used to upload image files to a database table. While some designers find it useful to store a few images that are not too large, most caution against using this feature. Images have the potential to bloat the database and reduce its speed. The alternative to storing images in the database is to store the image name or file path. (This is what has been provided to you as part of the database file in this project.)

An important warning about this method: since the pages that use images might be at different locations in the site structure, the file path in the database might not be correct. For example:

    image/pic1.jpg

refers to an image folder at the same level as the page calling the pic1.jpg file. If the calling page is in a subfolder, the path "image/pic1.jpg" will not find the correct image.

To avoid this problem, you can store only the image name in the database. When selecting the data source, the URL field displays the reference to the image field that will be added to the page. At the beginning of this reference, you can add the correct folder path of the image. For example, if the code reference is:

    <?php echo $row_getRecords['pic1.jpg'];?>,

and the file named in the database is located in the graphics folder, then modify the reference to:

    graphics/<?php echo $row_getRecords['pic1.jpg'];?>,

USE A BINDING TO DYNAMICALLY DEFINE ALT TEXT

In the previous exercise, you added an image placeholder to the page. Because this placeholder will be an image in the actual served page, you need to include alternate text. By selecting the <empty> option in the Image Tag Accessibility Attributes dialog box, the appropriate code was added to the page. The next step is to add the alternate text dynamically.

1. **With gallery.php open, make sure the image placeholder on the page is selected.**

2. **Display the Bindings panel (Window>Bindings, or grouped by default with the Databases and Server Behaviors panels).**

3. **Expand the getPosterList recordset and click alt_text in the list.**

4. **In the Bind To menu at the bottom of the panel, select img.alt.**

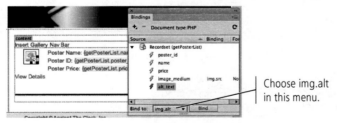

Choose img.alt in this menu.

5. **Click Bind.**

    This command associates (binds) the contents of the alt_text column to the alt attribute of the image tag. (As soon as you click the Bind button, the alt_text item is no longer selected in the panel.)

You are associating the selected field (alt_text)…

…to the alt attribute of the image tag.

6. **Save the page, then click the Live button in the document toolbar.**

   Because this file relies on data that resides on the server, the Live view displays the pages from the remote server. Before that can occur, however, you have to update the remote files you changed locally.

7. **Click Yes when asked if you want to update the file on the testing server.**

8. **Click Yes again when asked if you want to upload (put) dependent files.**

   To preview a file properly, the page's dependent files (images, CSS files, etc.) must also be added to the testing server. Knowing this, Dreamweaver asks if you want to put (upload) the dependent files as well.

   The Background File Activity dialog box shows the progress of the upload, including a list of the dependent files that were uploaded to the testing server.

   When the necessary files have been uploaded, the page displays in the browser. As you can see, however, only one record appears in the page. You need the entire catalog to appear; you will correct this problem in the next exercise.

   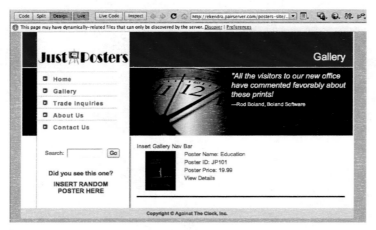

9. **Turn off the Live view, then continue to the next exercise.**

Note:

Dreamweaver provides both of these warning messages every time you preview a file (unless you check the "Don't show me this message again" option).

If you don't see the Update Copy on Testing Server or Dependent Files messages, open the Preferences dialog box and display the Site category. Make sure the Prompt On Put/Check In option is checked and click OK.

REPEAT A RECORDSET

For the page to show the entire catalog, you must repeat the table for each record in the database. However, manually adding dynamic placeholders for each record would defeat the purpose of creating a dynamic page. Fortunately, Dreamweaver includes the ability to dynamically repeat a region to show more than one record in the recordset without the need to create additional data placeholders.

1. **With gallery.php open, place the insertion point anywhere in the existing content. Using the Tag Selector, click to select the entire <div#gallery> object.**

2. **In the Server Behaviors panel, click the "+" button, and then click Repeat Region.**

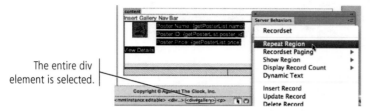

The entire div element is selected.

3. **In the resulting Repeat Region dialog box, select the first Show option, type 5 in the associated field, and then click OK.**

The getPosterList recordset is selected by default because it is the only available recordset.

This server behavior causes the div element to repeat to show more than one record in a database. In this case, you are also limiting the repeat to show only 5 records at a time.

It is important to understand that the Repeat Region behavior doesn't necessarily show all records in a database. Instead, the number of records displayed is limited by the number of records you allowed when you created the recordset. In this case, the getPosterList recordset has no limiting filter criteria, so the page displays all records.

4. **Save the file, and then turn on the Live view. When asked, update the file on the testing server, and upload any dependent files.**

Previewing a PHP file in Dreamweaver's Live view follows the same underlying process as previewing in a browser. You are asked to update files on the testing server before they can be displayed properly.

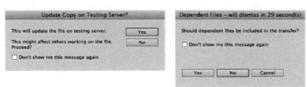

The first five posters in the database display on the page. However, as you learned in previous projects, Dreamweaver does not always perfectly render CSS formatting, which has been used to format the various elements on these pages.

5. **Preview the file in a browser. When asked if you want to update the file on the server, click No.**

You just updated the files when you activated the Live view; it isn't necessary to do so again since you have done nothing since updating the server files.

6. **Close the browser, return to Dreamweaver, and turn off the Live view.**

7. **Continue to the next exercise.**

ADD RECORDSET NAVIGATION TO THE GALLERY

To prevent a page from becoming too long, many Web developers limit the number of records that can display on the page at one time; this is why you limited the Repeat Region behavior to show only five records. As the page is currently designed, however, users have no way to access the remaining records in the set.

Dreamweaver's Recordset Navigation Bar behavior allows you to create the navigation links that enable users to move between sets of records. The behavior does not create new pages, but simply retrieves the next or previous set of records, and then displays those records on the same page.

1. **With gallery.php open, select and delete the words "Insert Gallery Nav Bar" from the top of the content area.**

2. **Leave the insertion point in the same place as the deleted text.**

3. **In the Data Insert panel, click the arrow of the Recordset Paging button and choose Recordset Navigation Bar from the menu.**

The insertion point is in front of the <div#gallery> object.

4. **In the resulting Recordset Navigation Bar dialog box, make sure getPosterList is selected in the Recordset menu, select Text in the Display Using options, and then click OK.**

Four links are added to the page (First, Previous, Next, and Last).

You should notice a series of gray tabs above each link, identifying the server behaviors that are applied to a specific object. Another tab also identifies the Repeating Region that you defined previously (until now, this tab was obscured by the "content" tab that identifies the editable template region).

The gray tabs identify server behaviors.

5. **Save the file and preview it in your browser. Update the file on the testing server and upload any dependent files.**

You are using the browser in this case because you can more easily test the navigation bar above the repeating recordset.

Note:

If you select Images in the Recordset Navigation Bar dialog box, Dreamweaver inserts images as the navigational elements. These images have the same functionality as text navigational elements, enabling users to move through the records. If you prefer, you can replace the default images with customized image files.

Note:

If you do not see the server behavior tabs, toggle on the Invisible Elements option in the Visual Aids menu of the Document toolbar.

6. **Test the recordset navigation links above the repeating table.**

If the records need to display in more than two sets, the first page displays only the Next and Last links. The second page displays all four links. The last page displays only the First and Previous links.

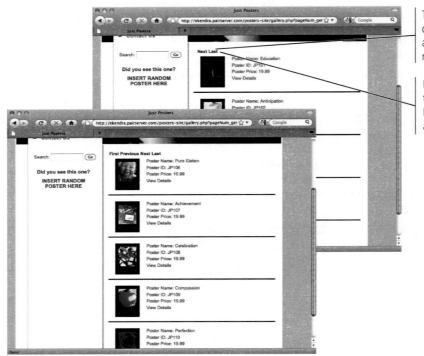

The Recordset Navigation Bar displays only the links that are necessary, based on the number of records to display.

For example, the first page in the set does not display the First link because you are already on the first page.

Note:

Depending on the length of your page, you might also consider adding navigation links at the bottom of the page, as well as at the top.

7. **Close the browser and return to Dreamweaver.**

8. **Continue to the next exercise.**

 ## CREATE A DYNAMIC PAGE LINK

The final piece of necessary information in the gallery page is a link to the full details of the selected poster. Because each link needs to open the poster_detail page with the information for a specific record in the database, you need to pass the correct information — in the form of the poster ID — to the poster_detail page.

1. **With gallery.php open in Design view, select the words "View Details" in the fourth paragraph. In the Properties panel, click the Browse for File button next to the Link field.**

Browse for File button

2. **In the Select File dialog box, single-click `poster_detail.php` (in the Site Content folder) to select it.**

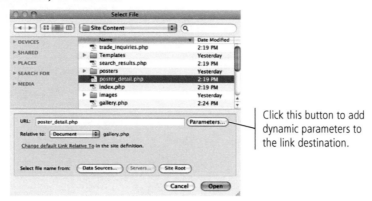

Click this button to add dynamic parameters to the link destination.

3. **Click the Parameters button next to the URL field.**

4. **In the resulting Parameters dialog box, click the Name column and type `poster_id`.**

   Poster_id is the name of the parameter that will be added to the link's destination URL.

5. **Click in the Value column, and then click the lightning bolt icon that displays beside it.**

6. **In the resulting Dynamic Data dialog box, expand the getPosterList recordset and click poster_id.**

7. **Click OK to return to the Parameters dialog box.**

8. **Click OK to return to the Select File dialog box.**

The URL field now shows that the link destination will open the poster_detail.php page, using the poster_id of the selected record to display the details for the correct link.

9. **Click Open/OK to create the link and return to the gallery.php page.**

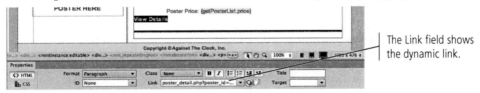

The Link field shows the dynamic link.

10. **Save the file and continue to the next exercise.**

 CREATE THE POSTER DETAILS

Clicking a View Details link in the gallery page needs to open the poster_detail page, showing the detailed information for the selected poster. In the previous exercise, you created a link that passes the poster ID of the selected record to the poster_detail page. Because recordsets are page-specific, however, you now need to create the necessary recordset and dynamic placeholders so the poster_detail page shows the correct information.

1. **In the Files panel, double-click `poster_detail.php` to open that file.**

2. **In the Server Behaviors panel, click the "+" button and choose Recordset from the menu.**

   Each page that needs to connect to a table in a database must have its own defined recordset.

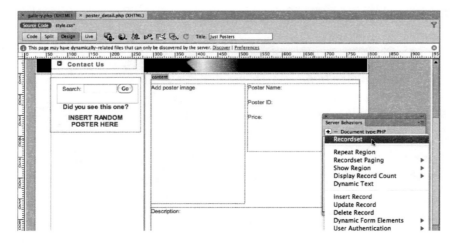

3. **Change the Name field to `getPosterDetail`. Select posterdata in the Connection menu, and select posters in the Table menu. Click Selected in the Columns options, and then select the following column names:**

   - poster_id
   - name
   - price
   - des
   - image_large
   - alt_text

4. **In the first Filter menu, choose poster_id.**

This is the database field you want to search, so you are defining a filter based on that field.

The second filter menu defaults to the "=" sign. This menu determines the operator for the filter.

The third filter menu (on the second line) defaults to URL Parameter.

The fourth filter field defaults to poster_id because it is the only parameter you defined for a URL (poster_id is the name you assigned to the parameter in the link to this page from gallery.php).

In plain English, this filter statement tells the page:

> Look for the record where the poster_id field is the same as the value of the poster_id URL parameter.

To access the poster_detail page, a user has to click a link in the gallery page. When a user clicks a specific link, the value of the poster_id field for that record passes to the URL as a parameter named poster_id.

In the poster_detail page, then, the value stored in that parameter filters the recordset and finds the correct record in the database table.

5. **Click OK to create the recordset.**

   The getPosterDetail recordset is added to the Server Behaviors panel. Next, you add the dynamic content placeholders, using the same technique as in the gallery.php page.

Note:

Because the ID of a single record is sent to this page, the page displays a single record. There is no need to sort the displayed records.

6. Place the insertion point after the words "Poster Name:" in the top right div, then press the spacebar to add a space after the colon.

7. In the Server Behaviors panel, click the "+" button and choose Dynamic Text from the menu.

8. In the Dynamic Text dialog box, expand the getPosterDetail recordset, select name, and click OK.

A placeholder for the poster name is added in the div, and the dynamic text definition is added to the Server Behaviors panel.

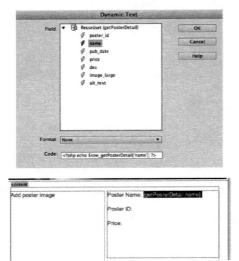

9. Repeat the same procedure to add dynamic text placeholders for the Poster ID and Price lines.

10. Click to place the insertion point in the empty paragraph after the Description: heading (in the <div#description> object). Add a dynamic text placeholder in the paragraph, using the des column from the recordset.

11. Select and delete the "Add poster image" static text in the top-left div. With the insertion point in the now-empty div, choose Insert>Image.

12. In the Select Image Source dialog box, click the Data Sources button. Select image_large and then click OK.

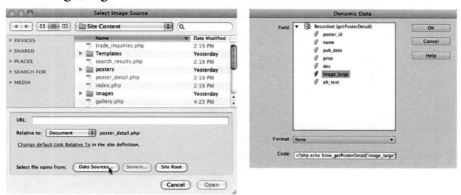

13. In the Image Tag Accessibility Attributes dialog box, choose <empty> from the Alternate Text menu, and then click OK.

You have successfully added placeholders for all details that need to display on the poster_detail page.

14. With the image placeholder selected, use the Bindings panel to bind the alt_text database field to img.alt.

15. Save the file and continue to the next exercise.

Previewing/testing dynamic pages is vitally important, but it can also be troublesome. One problem with this type of testing is that dynamically linked pages are not considered "dependent," so they are not uploaded when you test a page that contains the dynamic link. The only way to solve this problem is to manually upload the files to the testing server.

1. **Make gallery.php the active page in Dreamweaver. Preview that page in your browser (upload dependent files as necessary).**

2. **Click the View Details link of any record on the page.**

   The resulting page should display the details of the record for the link you clicked. At this point, however, the page simply shows the original static-text placeholders that were in the original file. Because linked pages are not considered dependent files, the edited poster_detail page was not uploaded when you tested the gallery page.

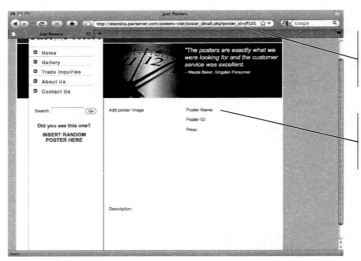

This is the URL parameter, which includes the value of the poster_id field for the link you clicked.

The dynamic placeholders are not present because you did not yet upload the edited poster_detail file.

3. **Close the browser and return to Dreamweaver.**

4. **Make poster_detail.php the active page, and then click the Live button in the Document toolbar. Update the file on the server when asked, and upload dependent files as necessary.**

The resulting page does not show any poster information because the data for this file is dependent on the link you click (on the gallery page) to get to this page. The important point here is that switching to the Live view updates the poster_detail.php file on the server.

5. **Turn off the Live view, then make gallery.php the active page. Preview the page in your browser (upload dependent files as necessary).**

6. **In the browser window, click the View Details link for any poster in the gallery.**

Because the updated poster_detail page now exists on the testing server, you can see the details for the poster you selected in the gallery page.

7. **Close the browser window and return to Dreamweaver.**

8. **Save and close both open files, and then continue to the next exercise.**

ADD A SEARCH FEATURE

Dreamweaver makes it fairly easy to create a search feature that compares user-supplied keywords to the contents of a specific database column, returning only the relevant results. In the client-supplied database, the posters table has a column called "keywords", which contains certain terms that users might enter when looking for a specific poster. In this exercise, you build the functionality to make the search feature look up the contents of this column and display the appropriate matching records.

1. **In the Files panel, double-click design.dwt.php (in the Templates folder) to open the file.**

   The Search text field has already been placed at the top-right corner of the page. This is where users will enter keywords that they want to search.

2. **Click the Search form field on the left side of the page to select it. In the Properties panel, change the TextField content to userkeys.**

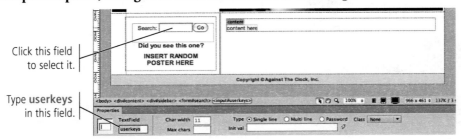

3. **Select the entire form by clicking the <form#search> tag in the Tag Selector.**

4. **In the Properties panel, make sure POST is the selected method. Click the Browse for File button to the right of the Action field. Select search_results.php, then click Open/OK.**

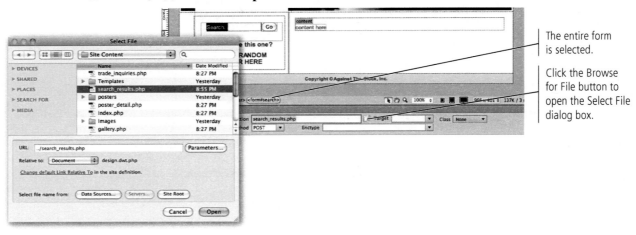

5. **Save the template page and update any files based on the template.**

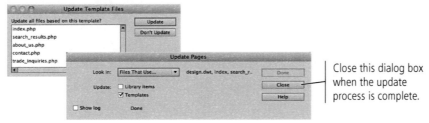

6. **Close the template file.**

7. **In the Files panel, double-click search_results.php to open the file in Design view.**

8. **In the Server Behaviors panel, click the "+" button, and then choose Recordset from the menu.**

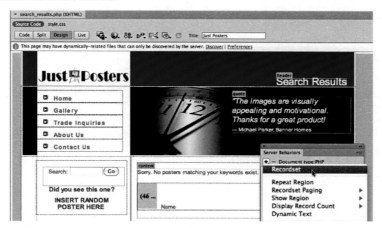

9. **In the Recordset dialog box, change the Name field to getSearchResults. Select the posterdata connection, the posters table, and the following columns:**

- poster_id
- name
- image_small
- alt_text
- keywords

The first column (poster_id) needs to be retrieved so the value can be passed (as a parameter value) to the poster_detail page.

The second and third columns (name and image_small) need to be retrieved so those pieces of information can display in the results page.

The fourth column (alt_text) needs to be retrieved so the appropriate information can be bound to the dynamic thumbnail.

The fifth column (keywords) needs to be retrieved so the server can compare values in the database to user-supplied values passed from the Search form.

10. **Select keywords in the first Filter menu, and then choose contains from the second-level menu.**

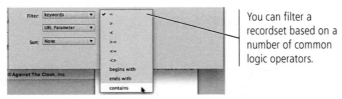

You can filter a recordset based on a number of common logic operators.

Note:

The contains operator ensures the search keywords need not exactly match the contents of the column. As long as the keywords are present anywhere in the column, the record will be retrieved.

11. Select Form Variable from the first menu in the second row.

You are using the Form Variable method because you want to filter this recordset based on what a user types in a form field.

12. Type `userkeys` in the adjacent field, and then click OK.

Remember, the text field ID in the Search form is "userkeys"; by typing that same name here, you are passing the user-entered data from that field to the filter.

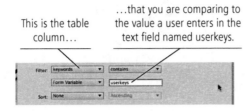

This is the table column…   …that you are comparing to the value a user enters in the text field named userkeys.

Basically, you defined a filter that limits the getSearchResults recordset to only records where the contents of the userkeys field (in the Search form) is contained in the contents of the record's keywords column.

13. In the "content" editable region of the page, select and delete the image placeholder. With the insertion point in the same place, choose Insert>Image.

The insertion point is in front of the "Name" placeholder text.

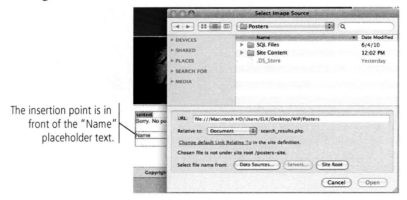

14. In the Select Image Source dialog box, select the Data Sources option. Expand the getSearchResults recordset, and then choose image_small from the list.

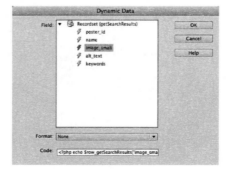

15. **Click OK to insert the dynamic placeholder. When prompted, select \<empty\> for the alternate text and click OK to close the Image Tag Accessibility Attributes dialog box.**

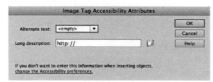

16. **In the Bindings panel, expand the getSearchResults recordset, and then click alt_text in the list. Select img.alt in the Bind To menu, and then click Bind.**

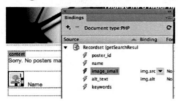

17. **Select and delete the word "Name" to the right of the image placeholder.**

18. **With the insertion point in the same place, click the "+" button in the Server Behaviors panel, and then choose Dynamic Text. In the Dynamic Text dialog box, expand the recordset, select name in the list, and click OK.**

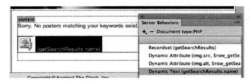

Note:

If there is more than one recordset on the page, you must select the correct recordset.

19. **Save the file and continue to the next exercise.**

SHOW AND HIDE REGIONS BASED ON RECORDSET CONTENTS

You might have noticed that the first row in the search-results table says, "Sorry, No posters matching your keywords exist." Obviously, you don't want this message to display if some posters *do* match the search results. In addition to defining a repeating region, you can also use server behaviors to determine whether a specific area will be visible, based on specific filtering criteria.

1. **With search_results.php open, place the insertion point anywhere in the first paragraph, then click the \<p\> tag in the Tag Selector to select the entire paragraph.**

This paragraph should appear only when no results are found.

2. **In the Server Behaviors panel, click the "+" button, and then choose Show Region>Show If Recordset Is Empty.**

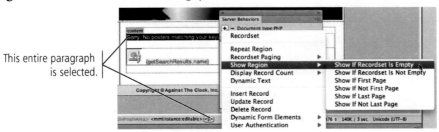

This entire paragraph is selected.

3. **In the resulting dialog box, the only recordset for the page is selected by default. Click OK.**

   This behavior ensures that this paragraph appears only if no matching records are found.

4. **Click to select the dynamic image placeholder, then click the `<div#searchResult>` tag in the Tag Selector to select the entire div object.**

5. **In the Server Behaviors panel, click the "+" button, and then choose Show Region>Show If Recordset Is Not Empty.**

The entire div object is selected.

6. **In the resulting dialog box, the only recordset for the page is selected by default. Click OK.**

   This behavior ensures that the row (and its contents) display only when matching records are found.

7. **With the same div object still selected, click the "+" button in the Server Behaviors panel and choose Repeat Region.**

The entire div is still selected.

8. **In the Repeat Region dialog box, choose the All Records option, and then click OK.**

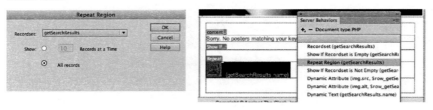

Note:

If you are working with large database tables with numerous records, you might want to limit the number of search results on each page (as you did on the gallery.php page).

9. **Select the name placeholder you inserted in the previous exercise, then click the Browse for File button to the right of the Link field in the Properties panel.**

10. **In the Select File dialog box, choose poster_detail.php from your WIP>Posters>Site Content folder. Click the Parameters button, and then define a parameter named `poster_id` with the value of the poster_id field in the recordset.**

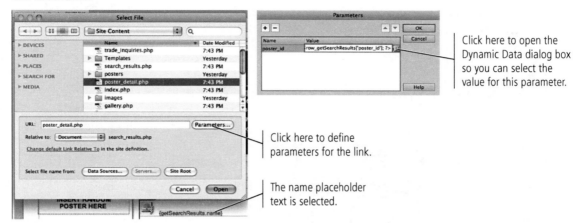

Click here to open the Dynamic Data dialog box so you can select the value for this parameter.

Click here to define parameters for the link.

The name placeholder text is selected.

11. **Click OK to close the Parameters dialog box, and then click Open/OK to close the Select File dialog box.**

12. **Save the file, and then preview the page in your browser (updating the file and uploading dependent files as necessary).**

    Nothing appears in the list because you haven't yet executed a search.

13. **Type `exam` in the Search field, and then click Go.**

    The results page should display the Education and Preparation posters. (If you look at the keywords columns for these posters, they both contain the word "examination.")

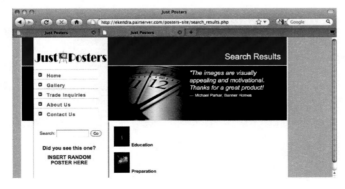

14. **Close the browser and return to Dreamweaver.**

15. **Close all open files and continue to the next exercise.**

DISPLAY RECORDS WITH ADVANCED FILTER CRITERIA

Dreamweaver creates MySQL **queries** — the means for interacting with the database file on the server — based on the options you select when creating a recordset. In this exercise, you modify a MySQL query to display a random set of posters every time the home page reloads.

1. **Double-click design.dwt.php (from the Templates folder) in the Files panel to open the template file in Design view.**

2. **In the Server Behaviors panel, click the "+" button and choose Recordset from the menu.**

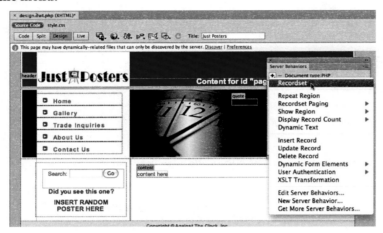

3. **In the Recordset dialog box, change the Name field to getRandomPosters. Select posterdata in the Connection menu, and select posters in the Table menu. Leave the All option selected in the Columns area.**

4. **Click the Advanced button on the right side of the Recordset dialog box.**

   The SQL text area displays the SQL query that is created when you select the table. The asterisk (*) in the first line indicates that the query will retrieve all records from the selected table (listed in the second line).

5. In the SQL text area, click at the end of the second line and press Return/Enter. In the new line, type ORDER BY RAND( ) LIMIT 1 (using all capital letters).

The RAND() command is used to arrange records randomly; the Limit command is used to retrieve only a certain number of records.

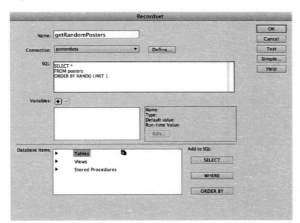

Note:

The Database Items list and the Add to SQL buttons can be used to create complex MySQL queries. Except for Select, which is used to select a table from which records must be retrieved, you can use the buttons only after you select a field.

6. Click OK to add the recordset.

7. On the design.dwt.php page, select and delete the static placeholder text in the left div (under the sentence "Did you see this one?").

8. With the insertion point in the now-empty paragraph, choose Insert>Image.

9. In the Select Image Source dialog box, choose the Data Sources option. Expand the getRandomPosters recordset, select image_small, and click OK to insert the image placeholder. Apply the <empty> alternate text option when prompted.

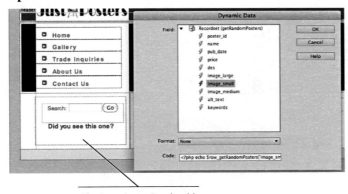

The insertion point should be in this empty paragraph.

10. In the Bindings panel, expand the getRandomPosters recordset and click alt_text in the list. Select img.alt in the Bind To menu, and then click Bind.

11. **Click to place the insertion point after the image placeholder, then press Shift-Return/Enter to add a line break. In the Server Behaviors panel, click the "+" button and choose Dynamic Text from the menu. In the Dynamic Text dialog box, expand the getRandomPosters recordset, select name, and then click OK.**

12. **Using the same technique as in the previous exercise, create a link from the poster name (dynamic text placeholder) to the poster_detail.php file.**

13. **Save the page, updating template files when prompted.**

14. **Open index.php in the Design view. Preview the page in a browser (uploading dependent files as necessary). Refresh the page at least once to see the effect of randomly displaying posters every time the page reloads.**

    When you preview the page in the browser, it displays a thumbnail image and name for one random poster. When you refresh the page, you will see a different poster.

Note:

Although you selected All Records in the Repeat Region dialog box, only one displays because of the limit placed in the MySQL query.

15. Click the text link under the random poster image to test the link.

The specific poster in your browser might be different, but the important issue is that the link opens the poster-details.php page.

You should also notice that the poster_detail page does not include a random poster below the navigation. This is the result of a problem with using dynamic data and Dreamweaver template files, which you will correct in the next exercise.

16. Close the browser and return to Dreamweaver.

17. Continue to the next exercise.

COPY AND PASTE RECORDSETS

As you saw in the previous exercise, the random poster does not currently display on all pages in the site. There seems to be a bug in the software that doesn't properly copy the getRandomPoster recordset from the template file to any file that already has at least one existing recordset. You can fix this by copying and pasting the recordset from one file to another.

1. With the Posters site open in the Files panel, open the design.dwt.php file from the Templates folder.

2. In the Server Behaviors panel, click to select the existing recordset (getRandomPosters).

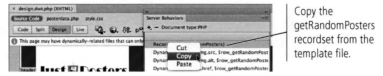

Copy the getRandomPosters recordset from the template file.

3. Control/right-click the selected recordset and choose Copy in the contextual menu.

4. Close the template file.

5. Open gallery.php.

6. **Control/right-click the empty area at the bottom of the Server Behaviors panel and choose Paste in the contextual menu.**

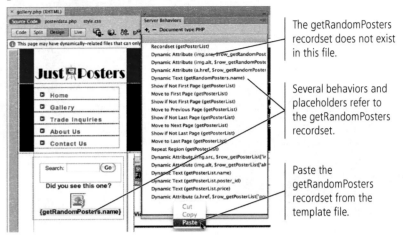

The getRandomPosters recordset does not exist in this file.

Several behaviors and placeholders refer to the getRandomPosters recordset.

Paste the getRandomPosters recordset from the template file.

After you paste the recordset into the file, the getRandomPoster dynamic objects will function properly in this page.

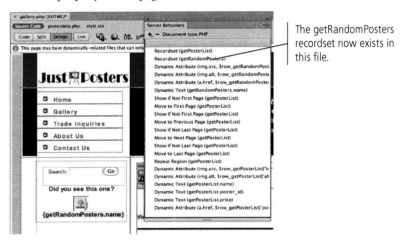

The getRandomPosters recordset now exists in this file.

7. **Save the gallery.php file and close it.**

8. **Repeat Steps 5–7 for the `poster_detail.php` and `search_results.php` files.**

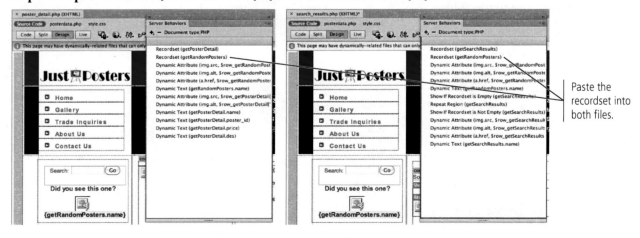

Paste the recordset into both files.

9. **Close any open files and continue to the final exercise.**

SYNCHRONIZE THE LOCAL AND REMOTE SITES

Earlier in this project, you uploaded files to the remote server that you defined in the Site Definition dialog box. Since then, you have made a number of changes to various pages. Now that development is complete, you need to re-upload the site files to the remote server location to make sure all the remote files are the most current versions. Dreamweaver's FTP functionality makes this process easy.

1. **With the Posters site open in the Files panel, click the Expand button in the Files panel to show both the local and remote sites.**

2. **Above the Remote Server pane, click the Connect button to link to and display the remote site.**

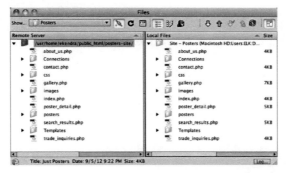

3. **At the top of the Files panel, click the Synchronize button.**

4. **In the resulting dialog box, choose Entire 'Posters' Site in the Synchronize menu. Choose Put Newer Files to Remote in the Direction menu, and then click Preview.**

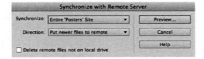

5. **Review the information in the Synchronize dialog box, and then click OK.**

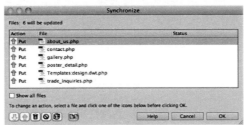

6. **When the Background File Activity dialog box disappears, review the files that were placed on the remote server.**

7. **Open the Manage Sites dialog box from the Directory menu in the Files panel.**

8. **Select Posters in the Manage Sites dialog box, and then click Export.**

9. **When asked, back up all settings, including login and password information. Click OK.**

Dreamweaver includes this step to prevent you from accidentally sending sensitive password information that you do not want to share with other users.

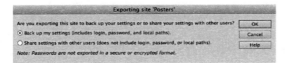

10. **Export the site definition file into your WIP>Posters folder.**

11. **Remove the Posters site from the Manage Sites list, and then quit Dreamweaver.**

1. Each _____ in a MySQL database table represents a record.

2. The _____ utility is an easy-to-use visual interface provided by many hosting companies to manage SQL database files.

3. The _____ options in the Site Setup dialog box define the method and location for uploading files to be visible on the Web.

4. Clicking the _____ button in the Files panel allows you to view both the local and remote sites at one time.

5. Clicking the _____ button in the Files panel provides an easy method for making sure files on the remote site match the files on the local site.

6. The _____ in Dreamweaver is used to define the connection for the remote database information.

7. The PHP _____ command can be used to place a reference to another page that *must be* available for a page to work properly.

8. A(n) _____ is an instruction for retrieving records from a table in a database.

9. You can use the _____ option in the Select Image Source dialog box to place a dynamic image placeholder into a page.

10. You can use the _____ server behavior to display multiple database records in a single layout arrangement.

1. Briefly explain two advantages of dynamic Web pages.

2. Briefly explain what is meant by "server-side processing."

3. Briefly explain the concept of the PHP require function.

Portfolio Builder Project

Use what you learned in this project to complete the following freeform exercise.
Carefully read the art director and client comments, then create your own design to meet the needs of the project.
Use the space below to sketch ideas; when finished, write a brief explanation of your reasoning behind your final design.

art director comments

Every professional Web designer or developer needs a portfolio to display their work to prospective clients. By completing the projects in this book, you have created a number of different examples that showcase your Dreamweaver skills.

The eight projects in this book were specifically designed to include a wide variety of skills and techniques, as well as different types of sites for different types of clients. Your portfolio should follow the same basic principle, offering a variety of samples of both creative and technical skills.

client comments

For this project, you are your own client. Using the following suggestions, gather your work and create your own portfolio.

❏ If possible, set up your own domain name to host your portfolio site. If you can't set up a personal domain name, use a free subdomain name from an established server company.

❏ Include links to sites you have created, whether the pages are kept in folders of your own domain or posted on other public servers.

❏ If you can't include links to certain sites, take screen shots and post those images on your site.

❏ For each sample site you include, add a brief description or explanation of your role in creating the site. (Did you design it? What techniques were used to build the site?)

❏ Be sure to include full contact information in a prominent location on your site.

project justification

_____
_____
_____
_____
_____
_____
_____
_____
_____
_____
_____
_____
_____
_____

Project Summary

To complete this project, you used PHP coding to build a dynamic site that interacts with a MySQL database. You also added an interactive Search feature that allows users to interact with the database to find what they need. By incorporating various server behaviors, you created four Web pages that can dynamically display information for any number of products.

This site incorporated only a small part of what you can achieve with the dynamic-data tools available in Dreamweaver. If you plan to extend your career into Web development, we encourage you to read a book or attend a class devoted specifically to dynamic Web programming.

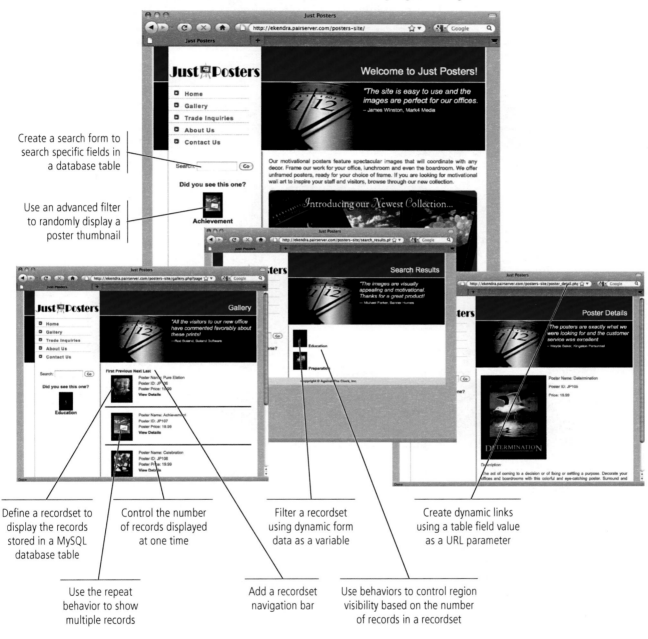

Create a search form to search specific fields in a database table

Use an advanced filter to randomly display a poster thumbnail

Define a recordset to display the records stored in a MySQL database table

Control the number of records displayed at one time

Filter a recordset using dynamic form data as a variable

Create dynamic links using a table field value as a URL parameter

Use the repeat behavior to show multiple records

Add a recordset navigation bar

Use behaviors to control region visibility based on the number of records in a recordset

Index

Index

W

Web fonts 288–294
Web fonts manager 290
Web hosting 52
Web server 47, 48, 352
-webkit 286
WebM video 295
welcome screen 2
white-space property 163
widget browser 299–303

widgets 36, 257, 299–308
width attribute 115
width property 164
Window menu 7
word-spacing property 163
word wrap 80
workspace 1, 8–10
Workspace switcher 1, 8, 10
wrap around selection 167
wrap tag 75, 277, 279

wrap with label tag 248

X

XML 138, 139
XSL transformation 366

Z

z-index 164

Use our portfolio to build yours.

The Against The Clock Professional Portfolio Series walks you step-by-step through the tools and techniques of graphic design professionals.

Order online at www.againsttheclock.com
Use code **PFS712** for a 10% discount

Go to **www.againsttheclock.com** to enter our monthly drawing for a free book of your choice.